ASTRIDE THE MOON
A Theatrical Life

Vincent Dowling

Astride the Moon

A Theatrical Life

WOLFHOUND PRESS

First Published in 2000 by
Wolfhound Press
68 Mountjoy Square
Dublin 1, Ireland
Tel: (353-1) 874 0354
Fax: (353-1) 872 0207

British Library Cataloguing in Publication Data
A catalogue record for this book is available from the British Library

ISBN 0-86327-828-0

10 9 8 7 6 5 4 3 2 1

The publishers have made every reasonable effort to contact the copyright holders of photographs reproduced in this book. If any involuntary infringement of copyright has occurred, sincere apologies are offered and the owners of such copyright are requested to contact the publishers.

Typesetting by Wolfhound Press
Cover design by Wolfhound Press
Printed by MPG Books Ltd., Bodmin, Cornwall

For Olwen, all our children and grandchildren;
my mother, Mai, and hers.

Contents

Overture — Tom Hanks

Work in the Theater is more fun than Fun.

For every moment I have spent as an actor there has never been a saying more true. That neat little quote was first said to me by Vincent Dowling in a rehearsal hall in California in 1977. I didn't realise it, but the only thing I really had to understand about being a professional actor I learned then and there. The secret reason I was in that rehearsal hall in the first place was succinctly explained: To be in the theater is to experience joy.

Vincent Dowling, God bless him, carries the theater with him wherever he is. He is a man of the theater who needs no stage, because to him all the world's a stage. He needs no officially scripted play, for the play's the thing wherein his consciousness resides. His audience is everyone within hearing distance of his voice. The applause he receives is not necessarily the overt clapping of hands, but simply the attention and delight of those who listen to his voice which is so graced with lilt, seasoned with humour, salted with blarney, all springing from the joy of being an actor.

To be directed by Vincent is to be celebrated by him, a great cheerleader out in the house who will preface every note and soften every criticism with the word 'Darlin''. To act with Vincent on the stage is to share the wings with a master who will pause the three beats before his entrance with the panache of Ballanchine and reflect three beats after a show with the self-evaluation of say, Jesse Owens after crossing a finish line. To have a jar with Vincent is to give oneself over to the great brotherhood of Actors — to share the stories and steal the secrets of a fellow player who has countless times gone before an audience and lived to tell the tales.

To have once worked with Vincent is to miss the experience, to hope that all your jobs could be so specially rewarding, that all your roles could have been so lovingly supervised, that all your moments spent in front of an audience could have been as fun as Fun.

Vincent, from this place in a career, which you yourself started, I say congratulations to you on being awarded the Walks of Life Award of the Irish American Archives Society. Imagine my surprise to discover, all these years later, that you were an Irishman....

Safe home,

Tom Hanks
Los Angeles, California, 25 February 2000

Curtain-raiser

'What are you going to be when you grow up? Tinker, tailor, soldier, sailor, rich man, poor man, beggar man, thief?' went the game of chance we played, over and over, to find out what we were fated to be.

I never was a 'tinker' in the sense of an itinerant tinsmith, but an itinerant I always have been, and am. Like Kipling, 'Speaking in general, I tried 'em all, the happy roads that take you o'er the world.'

Tailors and tailoring have held great appeal for me ever since I got my first long trousers made, by a tailor in a tenement in Dublin, when I was twelve — just a pair of brown pinstripe pants, no jacket. I was proud as Punch, or a peacock, parading past my female fancies. Soldier I have been, and sailor; rich man, poor man, beggar — aye, and thief, too. I have stolen hearts, happiness, virtues, money, ideas, from time to time. If I didn't actually steal lives of human beings, I have been a thoughtless accessory. I once killed a bird deliberately. All those roles, plus lover, husband, father, friend, citizen, I play in my ordinary life to this day. They are important.

Perhaps more important is what I call my real life. It is my life in the theatre, as actor, director, playwright. For over fifty years now, I have been learning to play myself — not just my immediate self, but extensions of me. I play them more deeply with each passing play and year, more honestly, I like to think. I play them to expose indecently my inner self — the god and the devil, if you like — to myself and others, in the belief that they make sense of the slings and arrows of outrageous life and inevitable death.

I was born with the ability, or acquired it very young, to present chameleon-like a face to mask my misdeeds, my wicked desires, and above all my fears. I was a fearful child, afraid of being alone in the dark; I wet the bed till I was twelve because I was afraid to go in the night alone to the lavatory down the hall. I was afraid of rats, heights, and being disliked, and lived in continual hidden anxiety that someone in the family would die before me and come back as a ghost to haunt me. My greatest fear was that the woman I loved most — then my mother, later others — would leave me. I feared that the weekly money from my departed father (not dead, just departed) would not arrive. I lived with the fear of not having enough to eat, of losing the house and furniture because the mortgage and instalments hadn't been paid. I dreaded that my friends and schoolmates would discover that my father didn't live with us, and how poor we were. Ingredients for disaster, you might think. At least one sister and brother of mine had painfully unhappy lives.

Did anyone, family or friend, know of my fears? No. Intuitively I presented the mask each person expected to see, supported by the appropriate gesture, voice and attitude. What they came to expect of me was a happy face — not comic in the clownish sense, but comic in the true sense: full of happy life, fun and love. These fronts or faces that I assumed were projections of what I deeply was. Otherwise they would have fooled no one, least of all my mother, sisters and brothers. The masks were more like sieves: they held back from others some of the pains, the wounds, the fear, the darkness, the loneliness and the private longings inside.

I still don't know what I'll be when I grow up. All I do is grow older. However, I did become a professional actor when I was twenty. Chance led me to the spoken word, my eldest brother steered me towards poetry and plays, a girl led me a merry dance to acting school, an unhappy homosexual genius brought me to the art of acting. An ogre led me into the Abbey, the National Theatre of Ireland, one of the great theatres in world drama. My Lady Luck, and a dash of talent, took me to the great theatre capitals of the world. And from birth to more than three score and ten, blessed have I been among friends and some wonderful women.

Stealing from Shakespeare, which I am not ashamed to admit, 'Thereby hangs my tale.' It has been seventy years in the making. I would call it 'comical-tragical-historical-hysterical-sexual-pastoral-romantic-adventuresome'!

1

The Lower Depths – Altar Boys and the IRA

He'll make a lovely priest, won't he?

I was the sixth of seven children. My mother cordially disliked my father. I wonder how many they might have had if she'd liked him? Like everyone else I know, I was born an atheist. I arrived with my mother's lunch on 7 September 1929 — the crash was heard around the world!

My parents were Catholics, my father a very strict believer, my mother a sensible one. After an altercation, I was baptised in the Church of Mary Immaculate, Refuge of Sinners, the blue-domed parish church of Rathmines, Dublin. My eldest brother Jack had been sent with me and the money, but the brazen priest refused to baptise me for the two shillings and sixpence which Mammy had given him.

'It's all she has,' Jack told the cash-conscious cleric. 'If you don't baptise my baby brother, I'll do it myself. The Catechism says that any lay man or woman can do it!'

That shook His Reverence into action, and so I became a bargain-basement Catholic, cleansed of original sin for 'two and a kick', as the Dubliners called the half-crown. Me, accepted unto our Lord, for the same price as a Baby Jameson, and the water of life poured on my head in my first walk-on (or rather, carry-on) part.

The baptism money might have been better spent on whiskey. I lost the faith in my mid-thirties, even though I made my Holy Communion at six (collecting three half-crowns in the process) and was declared a 'strong and perfect Christian' in confirmation by the bishop himself at ten (when the total take was two pounds, more money than I had ever held in one hand).

One of those pounds was given to me by a priest, Father Luke Donnellan, a friend of the family. It was a lot to get from one person, and it was given on two conditions: I was to take the name Bertrand for my confirmation, and I was not to take the pledge, as it was known — no alcoholic liquor till you were 18! Not taking the pledge was easier agreed to than done. The pledge and confirmation were administered by the bishop in the same breath, in the presence of the Christian Brother who had prepared us for this Holy

Sacrament. Of course, it was your choice — as long as you chose to take it. If you chose not to take the pledge, you risked dire repercussions for days and years to come.

When I got home after the ceremony, Father Donnellan, who was staying at our house, asked, 'Are you Vincent Gerard Bertrand Dowling now?'

'Yes, Father,' I said, knowing what was coming next and that a fortune swung in the balance.

'Did you take the pledge?' The question came from under bushy red eyebrows.

'I did not, Father.'

'Capital,' he said with satisfaction. 'Drink that!'

He handed me a glass of claret and a pound note.

'What did you say when the bishop asked you would you take the pledge?' Mammy asked anxiously.

'I said "yes" and crossed my fingers behind my back. That stops it being a lie.'

'Capital,' Father Luke said again, with satisfaction, and touched my wineglass with his.

As I grew up, Church and State were not separated; they were more like Siamese twins. The National Schools were managed by parish priests, though the teachers were Catholic laity. When, at eight, I moved on to the Christian Brothers in Dun Laoghaire, they proved neither Christian nor brotherly. And at thirteen, I transferred to St Mary's College, Rathmines, under the spiritual guidance — if you can call it that — of the Holy Ghost Fathers. Holy some of them most certainly were not, though I am haunted still by some of the things they taught me. The school motto was *Fidelitas in Ardius*, and that was printed on my blue school cap if not on my heart.

Filthy lucre would again sour the relationship between me and these men of God at a turning point in my life. I made my first Sacrament of Marriage up the flight of granite steps of the neoclassical Catholic church on Griffith Avenue in Dublin's north side. The wedding ceremony netted the priest more than I had made from all the other sacraments put together.

Still, for all the money in the world, I would not be without the anguish and joy of my glorious Irish Catholic upbringing. It brought a pleasure to the sin of sex and to the reclamation of the state of grace on Saturdays that has been hard to beat since. Those sexperiences, both the great and the fleeting, have played their parts in the several ages of this man — but first, a diversion to the magic world of a Dublin childhood of the 1930s.

My siblings Jack, Marie, Kitty, Carmel and Paul, in descending order, were separated from each other by about two years. It was while the family was in Australia, in Punch Bowl, Sydney, that I was conceived. Plans were afoot for Mammy to take the children back to Ireland while Daddy would wait until he could work his passage. He had been a Ship's Officer on the merchant ships and they had left Ireland in poverty — brought on, Daddy claimed, by the curse of his 'gammy leg', a legacy from the Great War when a German torpedo had blown him, part of his leg, and all his future as a master of sail and steam out of the waters of the Mediterranean near Oran. I like to think that, since they were to be separated, Mammy lifted the boom she had lowered on sex three and a half years before, when Paul was born. Perhaps she was grateful to be escaping the unfriendly heat and economic destitution they had suffered in Australia, though their prospects in the Irish Free State were even murkier. It had taken her about fourteen years to lower the boom on his 'God-given right to her body whenever it pleased him', which of course was a 'right' exercised without the benefit of any artificial means of birth control, the said benefit being forbidden by the Holy Roman Catholic Church and until quite recently by the laws of the Irish Republic. Woe is me that the laws didn't change even in time for my own adulthood or adultery!

Mammy never seemed to regret the coming of her sixth child. She carried me on the *S.S. Barradine* through seas and oceans fair and stormy, without a husband, and with five young children hanging on her coat-tails for the six-week voyage back to her homeland. I believe that this sea voyage in a hold within a hold had such a soothing effect on me that, for more than thirty years, angst seldom if ever distorted my otherwise angelic visage.

The money for our passage had been raised by the Coldricks, Uncle Paddy and Auntie Cis, who lived in Navan, and my Kelly Uncle Vincent and Auntie Carmel, from their own savings and from donations from other friends and relatives. The Coldricks were a generous, loving couple. As he was a plumbing contractor, he always owned a motor vehicle of some sort, which gave him an unusual cachet for the time. They both had strong Meath accents. Mammy, being originally from Trim, had one too, but it only made itself plain when she spoke on the telephone — or shouted down it, I should say; until the day she died, she believed in phones as miles and miles of long, thin corridors between herself and the person at the other end.

My Uncle Vincent lived at No. 67 Merrion Square , and we were to live 'below stairs' there for the next four years. I have a nigh-perfect recollection of the basement in which we made our home; I can still feel the relief we always felt on going upstairs or outside to the fresh air and daylight. As residents, though poor relations, we had a key to the Square, as we called it — a pleasant retreat of trees, paths, bushes, flowers and grass. Climbing up from our mean abode below the street, we saw government buildings, the National History Museum and the National Gallery. On the northeast corner of the Square was the house where Oscar Wilde had lived, forty years earlier, when not at boarding school. The electric trams ran past the Wilde house, on their way north to Dublin's centre and south to the seaside towns of Blackrock, Dun Laoghaire (which the older people and Protestants still called Kingstown), Dalkey and Killiney. From the south side of the park, if you climbed a tree, you could see the Dublin Mountains.

As I was climbing one of those trees one day, a small branch broke under me. I slithered down the narrow trunk and found the broken piece of stick stuck well into my fleshy calf. Adam Shields, the boy I was playing with, called his mother. She was a beautiful and comforting woman in a camel-hair coat. 'This is what they did in India,' she told me as she held my calf with one hand and pulled out the stick with the other. I thought her the most exotic creature I had ever met, and when she put me onto Adam's red four-wheeled chariot and pulled me along the pathways until the blood dried, I was in heaven. Later she took us both to their upstairs flat, on the same side of the Square as ours. She cleaned us in the bath, bandaged me and gave us milk and biscuits, and told Adam's father, when he came home from work, who I was, and what had happened. I don't remember his being impressed! Then she took me home. I loved her. I liked Adam, too, but maybe not as much as his red wagon. Afterwards I often went to the Square with them. Adam and I sometimes pulled Mrs Shields around in the wagon. I enjoyed that! Adam's father, I wasn't sure about. He seemed gruff. I felt it was my fault, because I had 'disturbed' him. She called him Arthur. He was an actor, she said, at the Abbey Theatre! He was probably doing his lines in his head, or waiting for John Ford to discover him and his brother, Will — a.k.a. Barry Fitzgerald.

One day — I would have been four, Paul eight and Sam two — we were walking together along a path and Paul was boasting about having been in Australia. I asked if I had been there. 'No,' he said scornfully, 'you weren't even born.' Then he added, 'But Sam was. Sam and I were in Australia. You're the only one in the family who wasn't!'

Another time, when I joined in singing with the two of them, Paul said, 'Oh, shut up, you! You can't sing. You're a crow.' I believed him. Accepted it.

Paul was a wonderful brother to me; and yet, every once in a long while, he'd jab the knife in with unerring aim and give it a little twist. Many years later, when Paul died of Alzheimer's, alone in an old people's home in England, I realised that he felt I had taken the place he had held for four years, closest to our mother's heart.

The best thing that happened during those years was a party Uncle Vincent gave in his big, elegant drawing-room. My sister Kitty says it was in 1933. The excitement was palpable. Up the stairs, to bright lights, laughter, clinking glasses, carpets, and people. I remember lemonade, cakes and, most clearly, a curtain in the centre of the room. I was shooed away from it and made to sit in a corner on the floor. Jack's voice warned people not to look till the curtain opened.

And finally it did. Jack was there, a boy king with a paper crown, a towel-cloak and a wooden sword. Marie and Kitty and Carmel looked like grown-ups; I suppose they were wearing Mammy's and Auntie Carmel's clothes. Jack was talking, and saving them, and fighting people and dragons, it seemed to me, and there were poems and songs somewhere during it all, and I have absolutely no memory of what it was about — except that it was the most wonderful thing that had ever happened, and I never wanted it to be over! And, in a very real sense, it never has been.

Then there was the day of the rat! My sister Carmel saw it in the stone passage, under the stairs leading up to Uncle Vincent's. Jack somehow hit it with something. I ran from the living-room to see what the excitement was, but Marie or Kitty held me back from getting close to where it lay. In making me aware of how dangerous rats are, they unintentionally frightened me. Then, as children will, I convinced myself that I had seen it. For some reason my image of it, for a long time — until I really saw a rat — was of a thick, whitish, hard, insole-shaped thing! I'm still afraid of rats, a little less of mice. I'd rather leave a house than share it with either of them. I always feel they know what I'm thinking. They probably do!

Daddy had come home by now, and his presence permeated the house. Small, but very strong, with a limp and a walking-stick, he was often about with his sleeves rolled up, polishing shoes or playing the mandolin, a tattoo on his arm. He had an autocratic nose and a little concave circular wound on his forehead that intrigued me. It was a souvenir of the Great War. Leaving things lying around, touching things he had laid down — however interesting — or using things he might possibly want to use could 'disturb your daddy'. If Daddy was disturbed, he would shout and quite often hit someone, probably Mammy. I don't believe he ever hit me. I was told that Daddy had hit Mammy the night before Sam was born, two years after me. Uncle Vincent took him to task verbally about that. I think Daddy couldn't take it, and it led to his leaving.

Two very different dinners while Daddy was still with the family have stayed with me.

The first: it was Christmas. Daddy was carving the turkey and ham, Mammy and the girls serving, Daddy telling stories, singing and playing his mandolin — all of which he did expertly. The mandolin would have come after the turkey, the stuffing, the roast and mashed potatoes, the raw celery and the traditional Brussels sprouts. It would have been with the champagne from Uncle Vincent. Paper hats on everyone, and us all pulling crackers in the candlelight. A mandolin introduction to the flaming pudding and whipped cream. There were riddles and laughter through it all, and as I laughed, everyone else laughed with me. The worse my giggles got, the sillier everyone else became. It was after midnight when I fell asleep, still laughing. I was of course, fluthered — hilariously drunk on several silver baptismal mugs of not champagne cider but the real thing. I had been drinking from someone else's mug! Daddy, to everyone's relief, enjoyed it all enormously.

The second: the whole family was sitting around the table having dinner. It was probably a Sunday afternoon. It was bright daylight, rare down there in our basement. A row started, probably about table manners, the curse of us Dowling men. Mammy intervened on, probably, Paul's behalf. Daddy started shouting at her. Jack, who was fourteen, launched himself at Daddy and hit him.

Time seemed to stop. No one moved. Then Daddy said, very low, 'Excuse me,' and left the table. Minutes later, with hat, stick and overcoat on, he limped out the front door and up the outside stone stairs. Gone! We, at the table, breathed again. I'm convinced even now that that punch marks the moment when Daddy decided there was no longer room for him within our family.

Daddy made his exit from the bosom of our family while I was in Navan. I have no sense of anyone, especially me, missing him. Maybe I am wrong about that; maybe Carmel did. Later she told me that she did. That could have been to get her own back on Mammy. They spent a lot of their later years 'not speaking' to each other; that meant they spoke too much to each other, in not-very-kind terms! This rift in their relationship probably resulted from the entry, or re-entry, into our lives of Reverend Father Luke Donnellan, curate at Crossmaglen, County Armagh — a small Catholic nationalist enclave near the border. 'From Carrickmacross to Crossmaglen there are more rogues than honest men,' they'll still tell you in those parts!

Father Luke had married my Aunt Cis. Well, married her to her first husband. Father Luke knew the Kellys, in Trim. He was some kind of distant relation by marriage, we always heard. He was a collector of Irish folklore with the Folklore Commission, a Member of the Institute of Advanced Studies, a performed and published composer, a collector of classical music, an inventor who had held a patent for an early form of television, a gourmet cook and a wine connoisseur; he spoke Irish, Greek, and Latin, was well travelled and incredibly well read. Like most people living along the border between 'the North of Ireland' and 'the Free State', he was a brazen smuggler of whatever was cheaper and/or better on the other side. As a priest, he had a pass to drive on 'unapproved roads' — that is, roads without manned customs posts — though they were patrolled by the dreaded B-specials. During the Irish War of Independence he had been a chaplain to the IRA boys; before that he had played rugby for his college. He was disenchanted, by this time, with both sorts of violence!

Father Luke never called my youngest brother, Sam, anything except 'Dam' — 'ever since' — as he loved to tell — 'I was having breakfast in the living-room of that damp, unhealthy basement in Merrion Square, and this manly little mite went out to the door with his mother to greet the milkman delivering the morning milk. He came back in carrying a full bottle of milk and pushed it into my hands, proudly proclaiming, "Dam the milk bottles!"' Then Father Luke would always add, with conviction, 'Dam is the best man!'

It was Father Luke who put down the deposit on a new house for us at 34 Sycamore Road, Mount Merrion, in South County Dublin, still one of the loveliest, most desirable suburbs in the Republic. The total cost of our house was six hundred pounds. We moved to Mount Merrion in September, 1934. This house was a wonderful gift, given to our family in pure generosity. He wanted us out of the damp, unhealthy, airless underground.

But, as Mammy often said, 'There's nothing for nothing this side of Kilcock — and damn little the far side.' Each member of the family would pay a different price, one that is still hard to gauge.

Mount Merrion was part of the Pembroke Estate, which included the Big House, complete with the Ballroom, the Office and the Forge. Everything there, it seemed, had a 'the' and resounded with capital letters. The Avenue, long and straight, ran from the Big Gates on the Bray Road up to the Big House with the Lawn and the Tennis Court. Well-kept grass grew to the edge of the deep and mysterious Woods. South of there was the Orchard, surrounded by high stone walls, with the Swinging Gate and the Mound where we played 'I'm the King of the Castle — get down, you dirty rascal!'

In a huge green field next to the Mound was the Peep-Hole Tree, hollow and dangerous; but if you were prepared to brave fox or, worse still, rat, you could crawl up the trunk, into one of two great branches, and peep out at the world way below. (Well, at least six feet below.) North of the Lawn, with a six-foot bank bordering it, was the Meadow, complete with the Pond which froze over in the winter. The Pond provided us with tadpoles and frogs, wettings and perilous 'ice-skating' without skates. We would run as fast as we could and then slide. More than once we all landed in a heap together in the middle of the pond. If the ice had broken, I dread to think what might have happened. Cows still grazed in the Meadow then, amongst countless cowslips, many of which found their way into tumblers, where they hung their heads dejectedly in front of holy pictures and statues on many Mount Merrion home altars.

Behind Mount Merrion Woods was another field with a tadpole-rich quarry. Stone outcroppings in this field mark the spot where my first attempt at sexual intercourse fizzled out. Since I was not quite seven at the time, it's not surprising, though nonetheless it disappointed me then. In a hollow between those outcroppings, Paul — about eleven at the time — two girls of about eight and I tried to have sex. Paul had invited me on the grounds that there was only one of him and there were two of them. One of the girls had seen her parents doing this thing — 'It's called courting,' he told me, and played it up as a great adventure. Without understanding in the slightest what he was talking about, but fully aware that it was Wrong, I enthusiastically went along. The older of the girls seemed to know exactly what to do. In no uncertain terms she instructed me *where* I should put my *what*. The trouble was, my *what* was a rubbery little worm and wouldn't oblige by going anywhere she thought it should. I couldn't quite see the point of the exercise, although I knew I had somehow failed — the girl's face told me! Whether Paul succeeded any better than me, I couldn't tell.

We all felt the wrongdoing weighing on us, and on the way home, in spite of the fact that one of the girls was a Protestant, we went into the chapel. I said an Act of Contrition because Paul told me to. Years later my 'sin' began to gnaw at my conscience. My religious instructors — first the Christian Brothers, then the Holy Ghost Fathers, then those who gave the Missions, Redemptorists, Franciscans and Passionists — all combined to create and nourish my guilt. That guilt built into such a force that I tried regularly for seven agonising years, using euphemism after euphemism, to articulate in Confession what I had *not* done behind Mount Merrion Woods. I was under no illusion that anything but a clear description of the misdeed would earn me absolution for my mortal sin of the flesh and save me from damnation in the eternal fires of Hell.

Out of Hell there is no redemption
When you get there you get your pension
Tuppence a week for working hard,
Chasing the divil around the yard!

Finally, at the age of fourteen, after days of rehearsal with a more knowledgeable school pal (one Liam Graham), I told the Missioner who was conducting the annual retreat at St Mary's exactly what had happened in that field when I was seven. He laughed so long and so loud that I was ashamed going out into the passage and averted my eyes from the other young sinners who waited their turn to make a clean breast of it. It proved too much for Liam. He was holding his stomach and tears were popping out of his eyes with the fit of giggling he was trying to hold in. I heard him mutter 'Excuse me — short-taken,' as he followed me out to find out what had happened.

Mount Merrion and its environs were my outdoor kindergarten. Paul went that first year to Kilmacud National School in Stillorgan, an old-fashioned village then, a mile south of us on the tarred Bray Road. I was too young to go with him. Sam was too young to be out with me without a grown-up in attendance. There was no question of 'kindergarten' for me, as we couldn't afford it. We were 'nice people' with 'nice manners', but we had no money at all, save the two pounds a week that my father sent — usually without fail, but missed often enough to be a real weekly concern.

I was provided with a rewarding occupation, most of the time Paul was at school, by the new concrete roads and semi-detached houses being built all over Mount Merrion; by the men and materials needed to build them; and by the open fires, with billy-cans of hot tea and bread-and-butter sandwiches, needed to feed those stalwarts. I was what Mammy called 'an Inspector of Public Buildings'! I learned some very profitable lessons in that job: how to make 'tay' (tea to you!) on an open fire without it getting 'smoky', by breaking a tiny piece of wood and floating it on the water when it starts to boil ('bile,' they'd say); never to put the tea leaves into the can until the water is boiling; to wait till you're 'axed' to sit at the fire and have a mug of 'tay' or 'a bit of a sangwidge'; always to offer to help before you're told to do it; that if you say 'thank you' you'll probably be given more; and never to eat with your mouth half-full! Fill it!

At home, when I would use words like 'tay', 'bile', 'ax' and 'sangwidge', Kitty would say triumphantly, 'See! I told you not to let him play with that Dessie Larkin!' Give a dog a bad name and they'll be hanging him yet!

If there was only one word allowed to describe my life in Mount Merrion, it would be 'play'. 'Go out and play', play a tune, play skipping, play ball, rugby, soccer, tennis, marbles, hopscotch, rounders; perform a play; play Tarzan to the sound of Tarzan's 'mating-call' swing from tree to tree.... Okay, so we were only six inches above the ground, but we felt we were Tarzans, Janes, monkeys and whatever!

My most vivid daydream, which I enjoyed well into my teens, was that I had won the Irish Hospital Sweepstakes and spent the money buying, for all my pals and me, horses, saddles, cowboy suits, hats, gunbelts with tied-down holsters and guns with chambers that spun. Do kids now really play-act as much as we did? From Doctors-and-Nurses to Mammies-and-Daddies, from Tip-and-Tig to Conkers with chestnuts on strings, to War, played with popguns, tin helmets and groundsheets. There was the War in Spain ('We're the Catholics'), the Finno-Russian War ('We're the Finns in white sheets skiing down the slopes to ambush the dirty Russians'), and World War II ('We're the Germans fighting the English to free all Ireland'). Then it was kissing games, Spin-the-Bottle and Truth-or-Dare. Kissing games were my favourite, and the local girls voted me the best kisser in Mount Merrion on account of the fact that I didn't keep my lips all tight. They didn't know that I had learned this at home. We were a kissing family; we kissed hello and good night and greeted all the women visitors to our house with a kiss. Our home was always full of women, my sisters' and older brother's friends and my mother's women friends. Little did they know how much Paul and I loved it. With the ones I really liked, I'd pretend I'd made a mistake and kiss them a second time around.

Always there was the Gang. Paul and Joe Shannon were the leaders. When they moved on, the leadership should have devolved to me; but being afraid of heights led me to lose the crucial vote. Robert Taylor — one of the gang and my age — held an election on top of a ruined tower in the Priory. By the time I got the courage to climb carefully and slowly up there, I was voted out.

Like a good Irish Republican, I caused a split, taking my followers — who were mostly girls and infant boys — to build our own hut. We also wrecked the old gang's hut in a surprise and cowardly attack! There we smashed a big mirror into smithereens. I knew at once it was the wrong thing to do and felt ashamed, but I brazened it out with the tenacity of youth: 'Anyway, you started it!' Toy guns gave way to bows and arrows, homemade catapults and, in winter, snowballs — if there were stones inside you were thought despicable. Finally we moved on to the Diana pellet-guns which were our pride and joy.

One Sunday morning I shot dead a sparrow which was sitting on the electric wire that brought power into the side of our house. I was so proud of myself that I brought my sisters to see it. They were shocked and disappointed and made me promise never to do anything like that again. Somehow they handled it just right; after that talking-to, I never felt inclined to repeat the feat. Just as well that Mammy was away.

She would be away a lot — at least twice each year, for three to four weeks — staying with Father Luke up in Crossmaglen. Later, when he was made parish priest in Loughgall, Co. Armagh, she would go there. The feeling of going to bed, waking up, most of all coming home from school, and finding Mammy not there was like what the fallen angels must have felt, or the damned, I used to think when I believed in those things. The same feeling comes back, even now, when the woman I love is not there waiting. Yes, and when some girl I really felt I loved seemed to stop loving me, or went off with someone else.

Life improved when our two gangs reunited to face a foreign foe — to keep the 'gutties' and the 'corner boys' from Booterstown out of our Woods, off our Lawn, away from our Quarry and our Orchard. Ambush them!

Surrender or else! Tie them up and sting them with nettles! Escort the little savages (them, or us?) out of our Estate!

Suddenly we decided to be good, to wage a moral crusade. We were going to the Christian Brothers by this time. We were the S.A.D. boys; our motto was 'stop all dirt'. Especially the dirt between the 'skivvies' (the house-maids) and their messenger-boy or private-soldier boyfriends. On summer evenings the couples would come up from Booterstown and Blackrock, or down from Donnybrook and Stillorgan, to 'coort' on coats or rain-capes laid out on grassy banks in the far fields and in the undergrowth of our woods. It was the only thing they could afford after their twelve-hour days for miserly wages, but what did we know? We were tuppence looking down on a penny ha'penny! They called us the plus-fours with empty bellies. It was class war-fare. We'd leave mysterious warning notes to courting couples in favourite nooks. Better still, we'd stalk them, watch from vantage points; and when they started kissing, rolling over, him on top of her, we'd saunter across casually and say, 'Excuse me, Mister, have you got the time, please?'

Afterward we'd saunter back to our hidden accomplices, whereupon we'd all burst into laughter as we dropped out of their sight — though they hadn't dropped out of ours!

Of course, sometimes you'd meet a pair of lovers who weren't impressed with your accent and clothes, and then it was a race for your life — well, your dignity, anyway. When one of those got you, you were likely to have to explain a thick ear, a bloody nose, or extreme reluctance to sit down when you got home. I'd like to be able to blame our families, school or Church for this sexual vigilante-ism, but I can't. It was something we conjured out of our own overactive bodies and jealous minds.

We joyfully played, practised and dressed for each different role or game, whether it was seasonal, annual or a once-off response to particular world events as reported in the newspapers, newsreels or radio. Our own family didn't own a radio, though we rented one when we had the money, which wasn't often. What fed our imaginations, even the games we played, more than anything else was 'going to the pictures' once or twice a week at the Regent Cinema in Blackrock. I had two lives. In one I lived my family life, went to school and church; virtually everything else, even when I was alone, was living the making of one movie after another, made without camera or script, where even the audience was in my imagination.

A woman in the congregation would sigh audibly, 'He'll make a lovely priest,' as I or some other curly-headed, angelic demon prepared the altar for Mass or Devotions. This would have been while I was likely to be entertaining romantic rather than sexual fantasies. At the same time, I firmly believed that anything I asked God for at the Consecration would be granted. Invariably I was asking for a miracle that would wipe a rival off the face of the Earth and bend a certain girl's affection in my direction. This did not render me unable to give all the rest of my heart and soul to the service of God! In fact, these longings for love made me pray louder, pour the water and wine more liberally, swing the thurible more energetically and genuflect more humbly and reverentially. With any luck, *she* would be watching from a pew in the front row.

Like the 'pros' which we were, we were able, too, to give even a little more than our best for a special audience — such as a visiting priest, who could be counted on for at least thirty pieces of copper, one silver half-crown. More importantly, a foreign priest might, in his confusion with a different language or custom, do something extraordinary like hand you the chalice without any covering on it. Then you could boast, modestly, that you had held the consecrated chalice in your hand, a mortal sin unless you were ordered by a priest to do it — or so we firmly believed. There were other perks, more earthly but no less satisfactory, like getting the only box of liqueur chocolates from the priest at Christmas. I would find later that many actors I met, in Europe and the United States, started out as altar boys.

The first of the Gang to be an altar boy was Joe Shannon. He was an amazing character, the kind that in any American high school would have been voted Boy Most Likely to Succeed. He could do anything. He helped teach me Latin, knew all the words of any new song — 'South of the Border', 'Red River Valley', 'Oh, Johnny', 'I'm leaning on a lamppost' and a dirty version of 'The Camptown Races' ('I gave her a crown and she lay down, doo-dah ...'); he could play the jew's harp and convert an abandoned four-foot builders' tool-box into a rain-resistant, camouflaged gang hut in the bushes that you could crawl past without seeing. Joe wrote plays and directed productions with us acting in them. He also planned the fundraising to stage them. I played the Maggot in *Bugs Serati*, a play he wrote about an American mobster. My role was to carry a brown paper parcel, supposedly with a Tommy gun inside — a cheap way to provide a difficult prop. 'My fish and chips,' the Maggot called it. *Rat-ta-ta-tat* and I'd mow them down!

It was Joe who inspired us to create our own annual Sports Day. At least, it was annual for two years, complete with donated prizes. And Joe was artistic advisor to our film club. We hired films from Kodak's in Grafton Street, Dublin, each week and showed them with our neighbour Mr Goff's projector on Saturday night in the Ballroom. We charged fourpence for children and a sixpenny piece for adults. Charlie Chaplin (I can still see the big bad fellow bending lampposts on Quality Street); Harold Lloyd with his glasses, walking along ledges high above New York; the Three Stooges, banging heads; Charlie Chase ... all honouring us with their talents, week after week. They never had more appreciative audiences; disciples, some of us.

Joe and my brother Paul worked in close partnership in the creation and development of our schemes. I was, you could say, lieutenant to these captains in both the artistic and entrepreneurial activities. They both should have credits on my acting and directing resumés.

About thirty years later, I was an actor and director at the Abbey Theatre and a few of us were being driven to a reception in a US Embassy limousine. It was the kind of automobile that causes the Dublin kids to point at the radiator and jeer, 'Hey, Mister, can you get Radio Luxembourg on that, Mister?' We were late for the event and were motoring along to Ballsbridge at a clipping pace.

'Driver, will you be taking us back to the theatre?' I asked.

'No, Mr Dowling,' he replied.

I knew the voice at once, recognised the hair on the back of his neck, under his chauffeur's cap.

'You're Joe Shannon!'

'Yes, Mr Dowling,' he said again.

'Call me Vincent, for God's sake. We're late for this thing. Give me a ring at the Abbey, will you? We have to get together.'

He didn't, of course, and I did not call him either. It was my loss.

The grown-ups held whist drives in the Ballroom in the early days. One evening, for no reason I can think of, I hid under one of the tables for the whole event, without moving. I don't think I heard or saw anything notable, but when I did reveal myself, I was treated to a scrumptious dinner in the pantry before being taken home to my anxious family. The pantry may well have been my purpose. We were always hungry for sweet things, never for the stewed meat and vegetables which were our staple food at dinner, as we called the midday meal.

Paul hated stew. He would fill his handkerchief with carrots and white greasy fat, then, when we were safely out of sight, sling them into a bush or drain. I tried it once, but my sister Carmel caught me scattering my 'mess of pottage'. From then on, I always pictured that as what Jacob sold his birthright for in the Bible.

'You'll get this for your tea,' she said. (We called our evening meal 'tea', as everyone did except really posh people.) 'And,' she went on, 'if you don't eat it then, you'll get it for your breakfast, dinner and tea tomorrow, until you do eat it.'

It was a fearful threat and I believed her. There was nothing to do but eat up. Did they really believe that fat was good for us? Or was it that they couldn't afford to waste it? A bit of both, I suppose.

We got a serving of delicious fatty food every morning in the form of fry-bread (or fried bread, as we found it was actually called when we got older). It was thick slices fried in bacon fat and we loved it. I still do, especially when it's made from home-made brown bread and fried until it's crispy brown.

Though all the family were good at cards, they seldom, if ever, played at the whist drives. They couldn't afford it, at least until Marie started working in the Civil Service in 1938. Apart from gifts and occasional 'help' from Mammy's side of the family, from her wonderful friends and from Father Luke, our regular income consisted of the two pounds that arrived almost every Saturday in a registered envelope from Daddy. It was known to all of us as the Registered Letter. There was seldom any communication with the two pound notes; simply, in his copperplate handwriting, 'Herewith two pounds, WFD,' from William Francis Dowling.

The anxiety engendered by the idea of waste, and the insecurity about money that attacks me still in the form of irrational explosions of panic, are linked directly to the weekly tension surrounding the arrival, delay of, and/or rare non-appearance of the Registered Letter. When Daddy occasionally had to buy the coat, suit or shoes necessary to maintain his position as Captain of the dredger *The Sandpiper*, a short letter explaining the failure to send the money would occupy the registered letter instead. Not the happiest moment of that week in the life of 34 Sycamore Road. I guess that all of us, without instruction, knew how to swallow the fear, so that it was kept out of sight, if not out of mind. We swallowed not only the fear but everything else, too — except certain parts of the Dowling diet.

Our mother had to feed herself, seven of us, and often a housekeeper. Jack, the eldest, was mostly away by this stage. Every month she had to pay the mortgage on the house, as well as instalments to Cavendish's of Grafton Street, who had supplied most of our furniture on the never-never. Then there were school fees, bus and tram fares to school, and Mammy's insurance, to bury her. She somehow paid it, though often late. I took it over years later and paid until she died at eighty-five. It paid out ten pounds. The company was called the Royal Liver Friendly Society. With friends like that.... I remember her pawning her wedding ring to pay outstanding premiums. She was never able to redeem it. She had at least three different wedding rings during my growing-up. The last one was silver. She gave it to me for Olwen, my second wife. In exchange, I gave her an American Indian ring I had bought in Arizona.

In spite of the cash crunch, the house was always full of people. The girls' boyfriends; Jack's girlfriends (whom he invariably bequeathed to us as he moved on to the next one); Mammy's friends; Auntie Cis and, occasionally, Uncle Vincent used to come too. When Father Luke stayed with us, for three to four weeks twice a year, boyfriends were less in evidence. However, when Mammy was up North, visiting Father Luke, the boys were 'much more welcomer', as the fella said.

Clothes were passed down from one child to the next, and Paul and I were next to the girls, which could cause its own problems.

'I'm not going to wear that!' was my response to a blue beret that my sister Carmel had put on me to go to school one winter's day.

'You look just like a little Frenchman. It's lovely on you,' she said admiringly. 'It's what all the Frenchmen wear.'

'I don't care what they wear. It's a girl's hat and I'm not wearing it.'

Of course, I had to wear it and defend myself against the jeers of my schoolmates and, worse still, the dirty little urchins in the back streets of Dun Laoghaire.

The hand-me-downs were taken in, let out, or repaired by Mammy or our sisters. New clothes came as presents from friends and family. The girls won prizes at tennis and by doing crosswords in the Sunday papers, which gave them a little extra money to spend on clothes. The purchases would be mulled over and decided on only after great consultation between them.

With money so tight, we had no bicycles. Getting a loan of a pal's bike was an unreliable substitute for one of your own. You had to have something he wanted. It wasn't often we had some material thing that a kid with a bike wouldn't have; so we had to know something, or be going somewhere, doing something, that we could 'make him jealous' with. And though I learned these tricks from the genius, Paul, even he failed more often than he succeeded. So you were driven to influence the gang into playing a game in which the limited number of bicycles *had* to be used by *everybody*. This could be difficult to do. There was always some clever bike-owner to persuade the other bike-owners to play an 'owners only' game. Then you had to be even more creative. And we often were. We were constantly inventing games that made the bicyclists so jealous of being excluded that we could negotiate long-term use of their machines as the price for letting them play with us. Poverty is not necessarily ennobling!

Then a new family moved in behind us. We shared a back fence. Their house fronted onto the Bray Road. The father was Headmaster of Booterstown National School, and they spoke Irish as well as English. Their name was O'Farrell. Mr O'Farrell shared the strong republican sentiments of my brother Jack. They had a 'paying guest', a red-headed teacher in the same school who came from Kerry, and he and my sister Máire took a shine to each other.

The O'Farrells had two daughters, and the younger, Maureen, was my age. She had a new blue Fairy bicycle. It was a real bicycle, not a tricycle — a children's bicycle, no less. She became friends with my friends the Devines, who lived opposite her, and I got to know her. She liked me! I was allowed to ride her bicycle. Heaven on earth stretched blissfully and endlessly in front of me.

Then I got it into my head that I would save up and bring her to the Regent Cinema in Blackrock, where we went on Sunday afternoons. We would go to the sixpenny seats, not the fourpenny ones with the poor kids (although our family had no money, we lived in Mount Merrion, so we were 'rich' kids), and I would buy my little girlfriend a packet of Rowntree's Clear Gums to boot. I suppose I got the idea from seeing my sister's boyfriends coming with boxes of chocolates to take them out. Or it could have been from the 'goings-on' of one Mickey Rooney, alias Andy Hardy. He and Judy Garland were almost as popular with us as cowboys were.

In the meantime, daily spins on the bike were the order of the day. One night, a sleep-over was dreamt up in a tent in the Devines' back garden. My friend Gerry Devine and his sister, the two O'Farrell girls, Sam and I — complete with pyjamas, sandwiches, a pillow and a rug each — met in the garden. It was still bright. We ate up everything we'd brought, then played Hide-and-Seek, Tip-and-Tig, Ring-a-Rosy and See-the-Robber-Passing-By, in the gathering dark. The darker it got, the more I thought about robbers and wondered how I could get out of sleeping in the tent without anyone, particularly Maureen, finding out that I was afraid for my life of the whole rotten idea. Not a single saving solution could I conjure up. I could see that Fairy bicycle disappearing down a long dark tunnel, ridden by screaming robbers and red devils, and going out of my life for all eternity.

Then the ungentle Irish rain splashed down on the others' dreams and washed away my nightmare. We rushed to the house for hot cocoa, biscuits and hastily improvised sleeping arrangements. I was louder than anyone in the expression of my deep disappointment at missing the chance of sleeping under the stars. I didn't think of it as acting, or even as lying — just as surviving. As Mammy used to say, 'Needs must when the devil drives.'

Finally, the day arrived to take my Alice-in-Wonderland-like little friend on my first date. I was about eight years old. I had four thruppenny pieces (tiny silver coins) saved, some of it a levy imposed on my unsuspecting mother's grocery-shopping fund. I put the coins in one pocket of my brown woollen cardigan; in the other pocket I put the Clear Gums I had bought at Bull's Newsagents and Tobacconists earlier. As we started the mile-and-a-quarter walk down Mount Merrion Avenue to Blackrock, I gave Maureen the long cylinder of hard many-coloured gums. She thanked me, opened them and offered one each to the two Devines, her sister, Maura, Sam and me, then daintily popped one into her own mouth — sweeter, I thought, than all the sweets I had ever seen.

Squirming with delight and embarrassment in equal amounts, I dug my hands into my little woollen cardigan pockets and urged the littler ones not to lose their money, and to hurry up, because there was always the awful chance that the queue would be so long we wouldn't get into the cinema before the programme started, that we would be too late to get seats together, or that, horror of horrors, we wouldn't get in at all. Well, we arrived, in time, and there was no queue. I reminded Maureen that I had invited her to the pictures and walked, bravely, up to the cashier. I felt around for the four thruppenny bits, first in one pocket, then, with a sinking heart, in the other. I found only a small hole in the corner.

'I've lost the money,' I said. 'It was there when I took out the Clear Gums. I must have dropped it. I'll run back and look for it.'

'No,' Maureen said, calmly. 'You won't get back in time. I have enough money for both of us.'

She didn't wait for an answer, but put a shilling through the opening in the glass partition.

'Two sixpennies, please,' she said. She took the tickets, handed them to me and walked into the packed, pink-lighted, piss-smelling cinema.

I don't remember what films we saw. There were always two features, a short, the Movietone News and the advertisements, the most notable of which was for Locke's Kilbeggan Whiskey. I don't remember where we sat. I do know that we walked back the way we had come, but there was nary a sign of my four thruppenny bits.

My sister Kitty was very understanding. She tried to make me feel that it wouldn't matter to Maureen, which it didn't. I think I may have paid the shilling back, but all I remember is the shame of it. I don't recall ever riding her bike again. As the advertisement for ZAM Buck ointment used to say in the *Dublin Evening Mail* of the time, 'X marks the spot where romance perished!'

Politically, the 30s were a decade that raised high emotion. The Blueshirts had been formed in 1932 and were connected with the new Fine Gael party in 1933. The Irish Republican Army had been declared illegal in 1931, though that didn't do anything to stop republican youths from joining first the Fianna boy scouts and then the IRA. My brother Jack was one such youth. He was the man of the house, though he was mostly away in those years, training with the Fianna in makeshift training camps out in the Wicklow Mountains.

In 1935, republican sentiment ran particularly high when nine people were killed and thousands of Catholics were intimidated out of their homes across Northern Ireland in riots surrounding the Twelfth of July parades. In my mind, Jack was the quintessential Irish hero, the hero who would help to free Ireland at last from the yoke of the English. He was my big brother, my protector, almost my surrogate father, and eventually my mentor. 'You'll be sorry when Jack comes home,' we each said to other members of the family on occasion. Even Mammy would use this threat, especially when she couldn't control Paul. In fact, Jack never actually made anyone 'sorry'; he never chastised or ridiculed us. But I do remember that it was always a happier and more interesting place when he was home.

Jack was the only person who reliably had a bicycle, probably lent to him by the IRA. One fine day the bike came flying over the back fence, followed closely by Jack. Bent double, he ran along the fence between us and the O'Reillys, and slipped into the house through the kitchen door. I was at the French windows; I stood there watching as he came casually into the dining-room and tucked himself down into Mammy's armchair.

'Vin, did anyone follow me?' he said.

'No.'

'If anyone comes in asking questions, tell them I've been here since yesterday. I haven't been out today and I slept here last night. Do you understand that?' He spoke carefully. 'It's very important.'

'All right,' I said.

At that moment Mam came in, her face looking drawn and upset.

'Go up and tidy your room,' she said, 'and don't say anything to anyone outside. Anyone!' She was almost shouting, which was very unusual for her.

I went upstairs as I was told. The boys' room had two single beds, one for Paul and one for Sam and me. The window looked out on our badly kept back garden. No one in the house was interested in gardening. We owned one spade, a rake and a lawnmower that needed heavy pushing. I could barely see the bike for the weeds. I scanned the gardens behind and to the sides of us, beyond the six-foot wooden fences.

'There's no sign of anyone anywhere out back,' I called down.

'I thought I told you to tidy your room,' came my mother's voice.

'I tidied it this morning,' I muttered to myself.

As I was closing the door behind me, I heard Jack say, 'Thanks, Vin. Good man.'

That made me feel better.

Jack — handsome, with wavy hair and strong, white, even teeth — was charming and educated, with a true love of learning. He couldn't stand small talk. He delighted in good conversation and enjoyed tossing what he called 'primary questions' into the domestic chatter of the household. He remained, up to the beginning of the Second World War, an active member of the IRA. He was also, to the end, a Catholic and a Socialist. The IRA of the immediate post-de Valera period had distinctly leftist leanings. Interestingly, if you walked up Sycamore Road to Trees Road, turned left, then turned right onto the Bray Road, you would be at the new home of Eoin O'Duffy, General Eoin O'Duffy, leader of the fascistic Blueshirts.

At this same period in history, while Fascism in Germany, Italy, Spain and England was clothing itself in various colours, Ireland wasn't 'a-wearin of the green'. No, we were advocating blue shirts; and figures no less important than William Butler Yeats — poet, playwright, senator and founder of the Abbey Theatre — and Earnán de Blaghd, Vice President and Minister of Finance of the first Free State Government, were said to be trying on blue shirts to see if they'd fit. Well, we all make mistakes; we all look for simple answers to complex problems.

'What we need is a benevolent dictator,' I heard in Ireland over and over, down through the years.

'Thank God you weren't listening,' says the atheist!

Jack and his IRA comrades, in the meantime, were simply and sincerely concerned about the Blueshirts, who were hoping for a groundswell of support as they proceeded on a well-publicised march on Dublin, bent on a *coup d'état* and the setting-up of a Fascist-style dictatorship! So Jack and his comrades were out training in the Wicklow Hills. They intended to 'shadow' the march, and if the authorities didn't intervene, the IRA would! Of course, I was blissfully unaware of this then, but that's how Jack explained it to me a long time afterwards.

Oddly enough, in later years one of Jack's greatest loves was the poetry of Yeats, and he helped me to know and love it. Earnán de Blaghd, a.k.a. Ernest Blythe — the man who ordered the execution of seventy-seven of his former IRA comrades during the Civil War, and who, as Minister of Finance, gave the Abbey Theatre the first government subsidy ever given to a theatre in the English-speaking world — took me into the Abbey Theatre company, which he contrived to control as a dictator for more than twenty years, till I played a key role in breaking his stranglehold on its artistic life.

But that was later; for now, there was the question of whether Jack's Fianna uniform might be passed on to Paul, who had found it under the stairs. It consisted of a dark-green homespun shirt, long woollen stockings with green tabbed garters, a white lanyard, a heavy leather belt and a yellow kerchief with its own toggle. To cap it all there was a green beret. I kept 'nix' while Paul got it up to our room and put it on.

Jack, who was home at the time, came in and saw Paul in the uniform. 'It's yours if you want to join the Fianna boys. Come on, let's show Mammy Paul in it.'

Innocently we trooped down to the dining-room. Mammy rose slowly from her chair by the fire, with a look on her face that we had not seen before and hoped never to see again.

'Paul, get that off you this minute,' she said, very quietly. 'Then bring it back down here.'

She was as white as a sheet.

'Vincent, Paul, go out and play. I want to talk to Jack.'

It wasn't like her at all. I don't think anyone else said a word. We heard voices as we went up the stairs, but we didn't even try to listen. I don't remember seeing the uniform, or hearing talk of it, ever again. I accepted its disappearance without question or comment.

It is clear to me now that I had, in fact, an accepting nature. I believed in Santa Claus until I was eleven. Or at least, I believed until I was nine, and pretended until I was eleven. One Christmas, when others my age were doubting, I told them straight that there must be a Santa Claus, as my mother wouldn't have the money for the dinner and crackers as well as for presents. I still don't know how, even with the help of friends and of Father Luke, she managed the kind and number of presents we got.

Christmas started for us on 1 December, with helping Mammy to make the Christmas plum pudding. We all had to mix it, then fight over who would lick the wooden spoon. Writing letters to Santa and sending them up the chimney, sending and getting Christmas cards, going to see Santa Clauses in the big stores in Dublin — Clery's, Brown Thomas, Woolworths ... these were all part of that peculiar and delightful season.

It was exciting to shake hands with the Santas — old and young men in beards that wouldn't fool a blind man, and sometimes even a girl. After a 'ride' through snowy mountains in a train or plane or sleigh, which didn't actually go anywhere but seemed as if it did, you would be given a wrapped present — blue for a boy, pink for a girl! Sometimes little children got the wrong one and cried. Sometimes you got a pink one and it was better than a boy's. Tea at Bewleys or Arnotts could follow, or, best of all, cream buns at the DBC in Stephen's Green, with the willow pattern on the walls. Then the bargain-hunting to get presents for Mammy and Marie and Carmel and Kitty and Jack and Paul and Sam, and don't forget Father Luke.... You were lucky if you had half a crown to buy the lot, but it was nearly as much fun as seeing Santy. Then, when it was getting dark, going up Grafton Street, with the carol singers in doorways collecting money, providing endless *Adestes* and 'Silent Night's. 'Please, can I have a penny to give them?' Last of all, Moore Street, with the 'shawlies' and their nasal, high-pitched Dublin accents, crying, 'Apples and oranges a penny each. A penny ha'penny the bananas' or 'Get the last of your dancing monkeys.' Each year there was a different catch-cry. During the year of the UN involvement in Katanga with the Baluba tribe's soldiers, when the Irish lads died in an ambush, it was 'Get the last of your Baluba babies!'

On one particular Christmas, as my mother told it, 'It was coming up to half-five, and Cavendish's closed at half past five sharp. If I didn't pay them, they'd be out here the day after Stephen's Day and take the furniture from under us. Anyway, I made it. I had two English five-pound notes left. I gave the girl in Cavendish's one and put the other in my coat pocket to get the Christmas stockings for the boys, the Christmas crackers, and a few small presents, up the street in Woolworths. I got a receipt and change from the cashier: half a crown and some coppers. *Enough for the bus fare home*, I said to myself. The door was locked behind me and I stood in an empty porch, got my bags and parcels into a more comfortable position, and pushed out into the cold, crowded street. Woolworths was, of course, packed. I got up to the toy counter — at the top end of the shop, needless to say. I was able to get everything I wanted from the one girl, adding the costs together in my head till I was at four pounds seventeen and elevenpence. I'd still have enough for a jar of vanishing cream at the cosmetics counter on the way out! "Four pounds seventeen and elevenpence," said the assistant. I opened my hand-bag, opened my purse — nothing but the coins! Then, remembering — "Oh, I forgot" — I smiled and put my hand in my right pocket. Nothing! Shifted my shopping to the other side, put my other hand into my left pocket ... nothing! Went back into my bag, my purse ... nothing! Piled everything I was carrying in front of me on the counter. "I must have it — I just paid a bill a few minutes ago in Cavendish's!" I took everything slowly out of my handbag. Then my purse. Then my shopping bag. Nothing. Empty!

'"Go back and try Cavendish's," the shop assistant said to me.

'"They're closed," I said. I was numb with despair.

'"Go on," she said. "I'll keep these things here, in case." And she put the things I had bought behind her.

'"Dear God, let it be there," I said over and over, as I crossed the crowded street, through happy shoppers and carollers singing of Jesus and 'Angels we have heard on High', down to the only darkened shopfront — Cavendish's. I walked into the empty porch; there was a dim light showing behind the glass door of the shop, with its CLOSED sign. I looked hopelessly from the sign down to the cream terrazzo floor — and there it lay. I bent down and picked up the white-paper, black-printed English five-pound note!'

We had our own Christmas miracle on Grafton Street! Even the discovery, next morning, that the cat from next door had come in through the 'left-open-to-air-it' kitchen pantry window, and torn shreds out of our Christmas turkey, could not dampen our Christmas spirits! In those days, of course, there were no shops open on Christmas Day. Neither we nor our neighbours had a car or a telephone, but somehow, somewhere, someone got two chick-ens, and Christmas was as magical as ever for the Dowlings.

One Christmas, when I was old enough to be in town with Paul, without any grown-ups, I saw in Elvery's — the Elephant House, then on the corner of Nassau and Dawson Streets — my dream cowboy gun. I went in and asked if I could look at it. It had a cylinder that spun at every pull of the trigger. You could 'break' the gun like they did in the pictures and load it with a single round cap that had six separate explosive points on it. It was all metal, no false stuff on the handle. The barrel was hollow. It really was a near-perfect replica of a .38. It was nearly twice the price of the pearl-handled .45 with the chamber that didn't spin, and it was way beyond possibility for me, ever. I could think and talk of nothing else.

Christmas Eve: after tea and bread, and lighting a candle in the window for the baby Jesus in case He and His Mother came looking for a place to sleep, we were sent to bed, having been reminded again and again by every adult in the house — as if we needed to be — that we must be fast asleep when Santa came, or he would leave us nothing! That always reminded me of a very poor boy named Christy at the national school in Stillorgan. We were asked, after Christmas, to tell in class what we had got from Santa Claus. When Christy was asked, he stood up and said, 'I got nothing because I was awake when Santa Claus came.'

Six o'clock in the dark December morning — with the torch that Paul had secreted under the mattress, the night before, under the bedclothes — Paul, Sam and I, hearts beating with excitement and quiet as mice, took our stockings and parcels from the end of the bed, into the light beneath the clothes. Slowly and methodically, we examined and identified the ownership of every single item, down to the tangerine in the toe of each stocking.

Last of all was the wrapped 'big' present, with 'To Paul [or Vincent, or Sam] from Santa Claus' on it. Mine, that Christmas, was by far the smallest. 'Never mind,' said Paul, 'there's good goods in small parcels.' And, by Santa Claus, he was right. There was the goodest good in my small parcel. There was an all-metal, spin-cylinder .38 revolver, with a box of round six-shot caps!

I lived on Cloud Nine that Christmas Day, St Stephen's Day and every day for days and days. Then on New Year's Day Paul capped it all by giving me a pure leather belt, with two shiny buckles to close it and a holster tied down with two leather thongs, all hand-made for my revolver. Paul had made it himself from an old leather school satchel. It was perfect. It was beautiful. I cannot believe that there was ever a happier boy in the world.

A few weeks later, Paul and I had had a row over something. We weren't speaking to each other. He said he was taking back *his* holster.

'You can't do that,' I said. 'Give a thing and take it back, God will ask you where's that? You say you don't know, God will send you down below!'

Well, he did take it, and search as I did, I couldn't find it anywhere. The gods didn't punish him, either; they got me instead.

I was sleeping with Sam that night, as I still was not speaking to Paul. Suddenly, in the middle of the night, a rough hand was shaking me while a light shone straight into my eyes. There were dark figures round the bed. I heard Mammy's voice: 'It's all right, Vin darling....'

'I'll do the talking,' said a strange loud voice.

'That's enough, Sergeant,' said another strange voice, but a kindlier one. 'You'll only frighten him.'

And a man in a raincoat, carrying a hat, moved in beside me. 'Vincent. Is that your name?'

'Yes,' I said.

'Mine is O'Brien. I'm a detective. You needn't be afraid. I just want to ask you a few simple questions, and I want you to answer them truthfully. Then we'll let you go back to sleep. Now, do you have a brother Jack?'

'I do.'

'Where is he?'

'He's away, I think.'

'Where?'

'I don't know,' I answered truthfully.

He must have believed me, because he went on, 'Where does he sleep when he's here?'

'On the divan bed in the drawing-room. That's his bed.'

'Do you have a toy gun?'

'Yes,' I replied.

'Where did you get it?'

'I got it from Santa for Christmas.'

'Have you a holster for it?'

'Yes.'

'What is it like?'

'Did you find it?' I asked eagerly.

'Never you mind. Just answer the question,' the Sergeant burst out angrily.

'Sh, Sergeant,' said O'Brien. 'You'll frighten the boy. Now, tell me where you got the holster. From your brother Jack, was it?'

'No, from my brother Paul. He made it from a school-bag, and he gave it to me, and he took it back 'cause we had a fight, and ...'

'All right, tell me what it's like.'

And I did. Every detail.

'Is that it?' He held it out to me.

'Yes, thank you,' I said, reaching out for it.

'Good boy,' said the detective. 'I'll hang it over your head, on the bedstead. Go to sleep now, lad.'

He ruffled my hair and they went out. Mammy kissed us and followed them. It was only then that I saw the three girls and Paul were in the room too, and all looking scared. I put my arms around Sam and went straight to sleep.

When I woke up in the morning, the holster was gone. I jumped on top of Paul in the other bed.

'Where's my holster?'

'How do I know?' Paul said. 'I haven't got it, I swear.'

'Mammy took it downstairs,' said Sam.

She wasn't in the kitchen. As I came into the dining-room, she was standing up from the fire.

'Can I have my holster, please?'

'No, you can't, Vincent. I burnt it. There's nothing left of it, and there'll be no more holsters in this house ever again. It's the grace of God it didn't land Jack in gaol. I'm sorry, Vincent, but that's the end of it!'

And she walked past me into the kitchen.

'But he said it was all right. The policeman knew it was mine!' I shouted desperately after her.

She was gone. I ran to the fire, took up the poker and searched frantically through the red coals. I couldn't find a thing — not even the little metal buckles; just black thick ashes that crumbled as I poked them.

'But it's stupid,' I said, 'just stupid. He knew it was mine. What's the use of burning it now?'

A couple of years later — we were still living in Mount Merrion — one of the girls came home with a copy of the *Irish Independent*. 'You'll never believe what happened! Listen: "In a Dublin housing complex yesterday, in a shoot-out between members of the Special Branch and a wanted IRA man, one of the detectives was shot dead." It was Detective O'Brien, Mammy, the one who raided the house.'

'May he rest in peace,' said Mammy, blessing herself. 'He was a very nice man.'

We were all genuinely sad. Jack was, too, when he heard about it, which I thought was strange at the time, since they were on different sides. Naturally we found ourselves cheering for what our brother believed in more often than not — as was to happen at another Christmas, in 1941, when the IRA held up the army guards at the Magazine Fort in Phoenix Park and got away with a load of arms and ammunition. Jack didn't come home that Christmas. Paul and I were disappointed to hear from him, later, that he had had no part in it — though we weren't, and still aren't, quite sure what the truth was.

Always, when Christmastime was over, after Little Christmas which is on 6 January, a dismal prospect stretched ahead: an endless, dark, dull, joyless desert of days, weeks, and months till next Christmas. Always it turned out not to be like that. In no time, we had mouthwatering visions of pancakes on Pancake Tuesday; picnics, parades, old crock races and an interval to the Lenten resolutions on St Patrick's Day; palms on Palm Sunday; the purple in the churches and the mysteries of Holy Week — ashes on Ash Wednesday, visiting the seven churches on Holy Thursday, hot cross buns on Good Friday, and on Saturday the end of Lent and all the sweets you'd saved to eat, and the light, bright feast of Easter eggs, Easter High Mass, Easter dinner, maybe something new to wear. Above all, ten days or more of no school.

No more English! No more French!
No more sitting on a hard board bench!
Kick up tables! Kick up chairs!
Kick Brother Bill down the stairs!
If O'Gorman interferes,
Take him down and box his ears!

2

Initiations and Mount Merrion Woods

We're here for the Communion breakfast, Father.

U ntil I was fifteen I never told anyone, at school or at play, that Daddy didn't live with us. Whether Sam did the same I don't know. Paul and I never decided not to tell, nor did the older ones ever suggest it. We just arrived instinctively at the same decision. When our friends, their families, neighbours or strangers asked us about him, we lied.

'He's at sea,' we'd say.

From time to time, we'd embellish it.

'Daddy was home last night, just for the night. He had to leave first thing this morning, for all over the world!'

To this day, I am not absolutely sure whether he came home one night and stayed when Mammy was away. I don't remember seeing or speaking to him again until I was fourteen — but that's another story. What I do know is that I never regretted having no father at home.

Another of our lies was that Father Luke was a kind of uncle by marriage to Mammy's family in Trim. A couple of times a year he would arrive in his car. A 'Swift' could seat five inside, and two of us little ones in the 'dickie' seat, which was outside the car at the back. Often, Mammy would travel back up North with him for a few weeks. I dreaded that with a dread so deep, so painful, it seemed to collapse my stomach.

'She's going to Crossmaglen for a little holiday, and God knows she needs it,' we were told. 'She has to go and look after Father Luke while the house-keeper gets her holidays.' Later, when Father Luke became a parish priest, it was Loughgall she went to.

The 'little holiday' would almost always be lengthened. If her going away was bad, these extensions were shattering. Marie, Kitty and Carmel, how-ever, looked after us while Mammy was away. Three young mothers took over; they cooked, washed our clothes, got us ready for school, helped us with homework, looked after the money. They put us to bed and saw to it that we said our prayers. If they had visitors in for supper, they brought us up some of whatever was cooking. The smell of frying bacon, when I'm in bed, still makes my mouth water. Every Sunday, they gave us pocket money for 'the pictures' at the Regent Cinema in Blackrock. They were our protectors.

In the meantime, who protected them as they went to school or held down jobs, played tennis at Blackrock Tennis Club, won prizes — sometimes money — went to dances, fell in and out of love and struggled with their own growing into womanhood? Daddy, not at all. Jack — mostly he was not at home, but yes, to a degree. And Mammy, certainly, when she was there. One of the nights when Mammy went away on one of those trips, Marie, the eldest, encouraged me to say a novena when going to bed.

'Say twenty-four Glory Be to the Fathers for twenty-four nights, and well before you're even finished it, she'll be home.'

I started there and then, kept count every night. Twenty-five nights later I started again. I was well into the second novena when she came home. As was always the case, she arrived with much-needed new clothing and footwear, tins of biscuits, wine, a carton of Senior Service cigarettes, and — the greatest treat of all during the war years — loaves of snow-white bread. Happiness had come once more to live at 34 Sycamore.

The *Bugs Serati* piece by Joe Shannon was never fully staged, apart from a performance on the floor of the Ballroom with no set and with Sam Walter and Anita Goff, our next-door friends, as the only audience. That's why I like to say that my first appearance on the stage was at the St Laurence O'Toole Parochial Hall in Stillorgan in 1936. I'm not sure whether it was early or late in that year. If it was early, I was six; if it was after September, I was seven years of age. What's the difference? Well, seven was when you reached the age of reason, as I was taught in my catechism class, and I like to think of my going on the stage as purely intuitive and absolutely unreasonable.

My older brothers and sisters were all going to appear, over a weekend of performances, in a play in Irish called *Iosagán* in which I was given not a 'walk-on' part but a 'sit-on' part. I sat on the floor as the baby Jesus while the others pretended to row an imaginary boat. Where and why they were rowing me while singing '*Óró mo Bháidín*', I have not the faintest idea. Seared in my memory, though, is the fact that, at the beginning of the first variety concert of that weekend, I was going to recite a poem. I had picked the shortest poem in a book I'd found at home, for the good reason that I'd just learned to read. I kept the book hidden behind the sofa in the drawing-room, which was only used for visitors and for Jack to sleep in when he was home. I knew where the key was kept and would lock myself in to learn the poem. In the process, I copied out the big words I could not pronounce, like 'connoisseur', and got different members of the family to say each one for me.

I refused to tell anyone what I was learning. My siblings thought I was too young to appear in their show, but Mammy supported me.

The Big Night came. The hall was packed with parents, children, teachers and, in the front row, priests and nuns. I was put in Carmel's charge and we stood at the side of the stage while someone spoke to the audience. Then, to clapping, I was gently propelled by Carmel towards centre stage into a single spotlight.

I had long curly blond hair and was wearing my First Communion suit of short black velvet trousers, knee-length white stockings, patent leather shoes with silver buckles and a white ballet shirt. There was a hushed silence as I appeared, then the great, breathy, sentimental sigh of 'Aaaaah' that Irish women always gave when they saw a little child on stage or screen.

Then I piped up with, 'I hailed me a woman from the streets'! This is the first line of the shortest poem in Robert Service's book of Gold Rush sagas, *Songs of a Sourdough*. The poem is called 'My Madonna'. It tells the story of an artist who used 'a woman from the streets' as a model. A connoisseur thinks it's the Virgin Mary. The artist paints a halo round her head and sells the painting to a church in France.

In light of that performance, I suppose my subsequent appearance as the Child Jesus in *Iosagán* did not really enhance the pious mood of that delicate little play written by that leader of the 1916 Rising, Patrick Pearse. At any rate, I wasn't asked to do another play in Mount Merrion for a long time!

At my First Confession, I confessed that I had committed two hundred sins since my birth.

'What were your sins?' said the parish priest gently, behind his wire grating.

'Lies and forgetting my prayers,' I replied.

'How many times each?' he prompted.

'A hundred,' I said, without hesitation.

I got three Hail Marys to say for my penance.

Kilmacud National School was spiritually, if not physically, attached to the Catholic Church of St Laurence O'Toole. St Laurence, we knew, was the one-time Archbishop and present patron saint of the Archdiocese of Dublin. The manager of the school was the parish priest, as was the norm. He was Father Blake and we liked him — though he let me down badly when I made my First Communion.

Word had started to whirl around the school that Father Blake would give a Communion breakfast to all the First Communicants after the ceremony. It seems to me that, rather than casting doubt on the story, older students, family and friends kept adding delicious dishes to the feast we could expect.

Certainly I convinced Mammy that I wouldn't need any breakfast when I got home that day. (We had to go to Communion fasting.)

Nothing was said about the breakfast during the ceremony. That was a little puzzling. Then we were marched out of the church, told that we had the day off, and wished 'Happy holy day' by our teacher, Mrs Dowdall.

I was dumbfounded. 'But we were *told*,' I kept saying. 'They're getting it ready. Let's just wait a bit.'

And we did. Time seemed to have stopped still. Eventually — 'I'm going to Father Blake's house, I betcha they have it ready for us!' I said.

Someone came with me. We knocked. Father Blake's housekeeper opened the door. 'Yes?' she asked.

'We're here for the Communion breakfast,' I stammered.

'What are you talking about? There's no breakfast here for you. Your mothers will have it for you at home.' And she closed the door.

So strong was my conviction that Father Blake had committed to this breakfast, I knocked again. The door was pulled open and His Reverence, with fiery glare, stood in front of me. 'What's going on here?' he demanded.

'The Communion breakfast we were promised —' I said.

'What are you talking about?' he said. 'There's no breakfast here. Off home with you, now.' And he mounted his bicycle and rode off towards the village, leaving us gawking where we stood. I am sure Mammy managed to produce a worthy breakfast when I got home, but I have no memory of it.

Other than my First Communion day, my years at Kilmacud all roll, more or less, into one long similar day. We were called at half past seven. 'Wash your face, hands, neck, behind your ears and the backs as well as the fronts of your hands!' one of the girls always reminded us. Breakfast was porridge with milk and sugar, fried bread with salt on it and plenty of hot tea with milk and sugar. A lot of the credit for later ulcers and anginas must be given to this delicious and deadly repast. A sandwich made with two buttered slices of batch loaf, jam, cold meat or some slices of bacon — rashers, as we called them — along with maybe a piece of apple, orange or cake, and cold milk in a clean baby Power's bottle, was packed and taken to school for lunch each day.

Thus washed and fed, Paul and I — or, later, Sam and I — would walk up Sycamore Road, turn left down Trees Road, picking up some pals on the way, cross the Main Bray Road, turn right and go past the Priory Gates and along by a high stone wall to Stillorgan village, half a mile south of us. The road — the main Dublin-to-Bray road, mark you — was so quiet in those days that we would take turns at identifying by the engines, without looking back, the four or five motor cars that would come up behind us. Baby Ford — Vauxhall — Armstrong Siddley — Austin — Dodge.... We were rarely wrong. At

Stillorgan village, we'd cross over to the built-up side after we passed a little row of old one-storied artisan cottages. We were afraid to pass close to these on the footpath in front of them, because there was a witch living in the last one who might run out, as she had done to some boy one time, and attack us with a hatchet! A few yards farther on, there was Laurence O'Toole Church Hall and then two petrol pumps, with their nozzles stuck into their sides just below their glass heads, in which the fuel foamed when operated. These pumps reminded me of the first outer-space joke I ever heard:

Two Martians landed in Stillorgan, walked up to the petrol pumps and demanded to be taken to their leader. There was no reply from the pumps. The Martians repeated the demand, only louder. Still no reply. 'Maybe they can't speak,' said the first Martian. 'Of course they can speak,' said the second. 'They just can't hear with their mickeys in their ears!' (Mickey was our slang for prick or penis — words I never even heard until twenty years later.)

The school itself was pebble-dashed and well kept, with a spacious yard surrounded by iron railings. There were three full-time teachers: Mrs Dowdall, a pleasant matronly woman who taught the two youngest classes; 'Brother Bill', so called because he was the headmaster's brother, a tall, thin, gentle individual who taught the third and fourth classes; and the Head, Mr O'Gorman, a small, bespectacled, nattily dressed man who taught fifth and sixth classes. They all wielded bamboo canes from time to time, but used them very sparingly — most of the time.

We started school at half-nine (our way of saying 9.30). A prayer opened the day, and at eleven we had a *sos* — a ten-minute break. We were lined up, made to mark time in two languages and marched from the yard back into class — 'Left, right, left, right', '*Clé, deas, clé, deas,*' and 'Left, left, left, I had a good job and I left, left, left. I had a good job and I might, might, right, left ...' and so on. Inside we resumed lessons, breaking for the Angelus at noon. The main responses were in English, the Hail Marys in Irish. At one, we wolfed our sandwiches and milk, then ran around in ever-changing formations playing rounders, relievio, and Towns and Counties, interspersed with occasional fisticuffs and accompanied by non-stop shouts and screams. All of this meant endless scraped knees, elbows, and sometimes foreheads and noses, for everyone except me; somehow I was never ruffled.

I learned 'joined-up' writing by copying out a printed line in cursive style which was at the top of each page of a green copybook, published by the Educational Company of Ireland. Each page had several blank lines for us to complete below the text.

Very quickly it was noticed that I was left-handed. I was told to write with my right hand; if I forgot, which happened often, I was reminded with a tap on the knuckles from a ruler or cane. In my next school, this tap could become a painful crack from similar blunt instruments wielded by hairy-handed Christian Brothers and impatient lay teachers. It all had a bad effect on my handwriting. I write equally badly with both hands.

At lunch hour one day, a man with rolled-up sleeves and muscular arms — he somehow reminded me of my father — walked up to Mrs Dowdall, who was overseeing us, and demanded to see 'the man who's teaching my son'. Brother Bill came out and approached the intruder. The man, with raised voice and wild gestures, circled the poor teacher; then, suddenly, amazingly, unbelievably, he punched Brother Bill, knocking him to the hard ground. Then he turned on his heel and left the playground.

Mr O'Gorman was summoned, and he helped his brother into the school. They both reappeared at the end of lunch hour, Brother Bill with a plaster on his nose, and we were marched back to class. By this time we all knew, don't ask me how, that the man was Mr Whelan, father of a boy in fifth class. The boy had gone home the night before and told his father that he had been severely and unjustly caned by his teacher — Mr O'Gorman! We had witnessed the outcome. Brother Bill had felt it.

The Christian Brothers school to which we graduated was St Michael's College, Dun Laoghaire. CBC had a national school, too, where lessons were taught through Irish. At the college, fees were charged: ten shillings per term, with three terms in the year. Over the years we received some reduction because there were two siblings — three when Sam came. Father Luke sponsored this education, and in retrospect we are all grateful to him for it — though the time would come when we dreaded going to school there.

If the Brothers were tough, some of the lay teachers — all men — were even tougher. One gentleman in junior school, who taught us in fourth class, would wield the leg of a wooden kitchen chair as his weapon of choice. He used it on hands, legs, or backsides. If you really annoyed him, which most of us learned not to, he resorted to a wooden ruler applied to the side of the head. I boasted a few bruised hands, but I witnessed some pretty severe wounds on less fortunate classmates. Eventually, I told them at home. Some communication was established with the Head Brother, and the more barbaric practices were discontinued — for a time.

Another teacher, something of a 'Mickey Dazzler' (a dandy), whilst continuing with his teaching, would walk down to a boy who was talking or who was not listening, take the short hairs of the boy's side-locks between his thumb and forefinger, and, twisting firmly, would bring the boy slowly to his knees, then down flat on the floor. Still continuing quietly with the lesson, he'd place his foot gently but firmly on the boy's back and keep him there, often addressing him, pleasantly, until the end of the class. We did not object to this behaviour in any way. It was much less hurtful than the normal punishment by cane or leather strap. It was rumoured that the straps were lined with lead.

One of our favourite teachers — we had him my first year there — was 'Buck' Cunningham. He got that name because of the speed with which he threw back his jacket, drew his leather from his back pocket, delivered three sharp smacks to your outstretched hand, and returned his weapon to his back pocket. He rivalled Buck Jones's fastest draws in the cowboy pictures. Buck was a very fair person, bald, short, and humorous. Besides, he never really tried to hurt anyone. For the record, I moved from first class in Kilmacud to third class at CBC. It says something for the national school teaching.

Dun Laoghaire was about seven or eight miles from Mount Merrion. We travelled by public transport. We could pick up a single-decker bus, the 46A, at 'the shops' at the end of Trees Road; it would take us through Stillorgan, past St John o' God's, a 'rest home' for alcoholics, mostly clerics in those days. (In the 50s and 60s it was more like an actors' home.) A half-mile on came Galloping Green — my favourite name for a village anywhere — with Byrne's Pub, which is almost unchanged on the outside to this day. At Foxrock Church we took a ninety-degree turn towards the sea and Dun Laoghaire. We raised our school caps or made the sign of the cross, 'blessing ourselves,' as we passed. Jesus Christ, we were told, was alive and present in every Catholic church. He could do that because He was God. Nobody told us that Samuel Beckett was alive and present, too, in Foxrock. He was Waiting for Godot to come, though nobody in Dublin much cared for another twenty years or so. As we made the turn downhill, we could see Dalkey and Killiney Hills and catch glimpses of the Irish Sea. At the bottom of the hill was Kill o' the Grange, with its graveyard to the left. There many an actor friend lies buried now. A couple of tree-lined miles along, with a stop at another pub, we entered the built-up area of the Borough of Dun Laoghaire.

The bus, after passing St Michael's Church, passed the Town Hall, though we were always looking longingly at the Pavilion Cinema, on the opposite side, and the railway station. The bus terminated its journey at the edge of the harbour. The morning mailboat to Holyhead, on the Isle of Anglesey, was always steamed up and ready to leave, laden with lonely men and women seeking employment and others returning to the jobs they had found in Britain's factories or armed forces. Even in peace-time, a lot of Ireland's very wealthiest and very poorest served the monarchy. In war-time the flow became a flood.

As we tumbled out of the bus, we checked the clock on the Town Hall to see if there was still time to finish the homework given the day before. Five minutes could make a hell of a difference. The bus fare was tuppence each, and that included entertainment. The bus conductors were often amateur comics. One of them, on the 46A, delighted in telling us, boys and girls, about his 'riding' exploits. In common Dublin parlance, 'to ride' meant — still means — to copulate.

We soon learned to get up a little earlier, walk the mile and a quarter down Mount Merrion Avenue, in all weathers, and take the electric tram from Blackrock Park Gate. This joyride took us through Blackrock, past the Regent Cinema, our romantic glory hole, and past an optician's clock with 'Prescott's' — the owner's name — printed on it, where we checked the time. We were supposed to raise our hats to the Catholic church, a little further up, on the opposite side. When I wasn't thinking, to my embarrassment, I'd often find myself raising my cap or blessing myself as I passed the clock! If I realised it in time, I would try to turn the blessing into a little scratch at my forehead! Then there were the tram sheds, where the trams slept overnight or were hospitalised for repairs. Sometimes, mostly when we were late for school, we would have to change trams there, which made us later. The chance of getting away without paying your fare, in the confusion of the change, was balanced by the certainty of getting slapped for being late. I admit I became so expert at creating imaginative acceptable excuses that I rarely received the pro-scribed latecomers' punishment!

Opposite the tram sheds, in quite a 'posh' flat, lived one of Mammy's most glamorous girlfriends, 'Baby' Finucane. She looked and dressed like a 1930s film star. Mammy would occasionally send me to deliver a message to her. It was as exciting as going to the pictures — especially when Baby was resting and I was greeted with a warm hug and sat beside her bed with milk and biscuits, telling my stories and listening to hers, while marvelling at the intoxicating silks, scents, and glamorous look of her, knowing I would be kissed and hugged again on leaving. It was pure sex. I mean pure. It was perfectly, beautifully innocent, but it was magical because she was woman, and beautiful.

On leaving Blackrock, the tram took us away from the sea for a few hundred yards, then turned onto Monkstown Road, a straight mile of im-posing brick houses in trees and gardens. At the end of the road was a granite church with a granite cross on the top of it. This was not a Catholic church. That was puzzling. Only Catholic churches should have crosses, we thought. The Gothic-style Catholic church was across the road to the right. We believed the granite-crossed church had been taken from the Catholics by the Protestant English. Many were the plans we made to take it back!

As the tram swayed up the hill from Monkstown into Dun Laoghaire proper, we could see, from our seats on the top of the tram, the East Pier, with yachts, fishing trawlers, the yellow-funnelled Irish light-ship, and Howth

Head in the distance, behind and above it all. The main shopping street was called Upper George's Street. Both sides of the street were lined with every conceivable kind of shop, from Woolworths to fish-and-chip shops (our favourite lunch was a chip butty — two slices of bread and butter with fourpence worth of chips sandwiched between them), from a coal yard to the pawnbroker where my mother pawned her wedding ring, from a little home bakery (two square inches of gur cake for a halfpenny — it was so fruity and heavy it could give you lead poisoning) to a bicycle shop.

Of course, there was a pub, and of course the tram stopped outside it. There was a black sign with white writing on it over the entrance of the pub: 'Licensed for the sale of wine, beer and spirits for consumption on the premises.' I swear, for decades I took it for granted that you had to suffer from consumption to drink there! The word 'consumption' was never said out loud in our house. It was whispered, with exaggerated syllables, right into the ears of aunts and female contemporaries.

Just past the Ideal Bakery was a bookshop, where we alighted from the tram while it was still moving, because it was stated in Irish and English, everywhere you looked inside the tram: '*Ná turlaing go stad an tram. Do not alight till the tram stops.*' The tram fare was a penny, which gave us twopence a day, six days every week, to spend — a shilling! That, you might say, was money! Well, it gave us a shilling until the girls found out we were going by tram, and how much it cost. Thereafter, we only got the fourpence for the 46A bus if we were not too well, if we were late through someone else's fault (which allowed for some abuse by us), or if the weather was extremely bad. Even in that extremity, we would walk home, hail, rain, or snow, and pocket a penny a day — 'a tanner', as we'd say, a week. Better than a slap on the belly with a wet herring!

Paul would always be four years older, and, year after year, the emotional and behavioural gap grew wider. In the autumn of my second year at CBC, we had joined a classmate of Paul's near the Blackrock end of Mount Merrion Avenue and, despite running as if our lives depended on it, we missed the tram.

'Unless another tram comes almost immediately, we're late for school,' Paul observed. Now, as I look back, I know of course I was being 'conned'. Paul knew I had a shilling and tenpence, to pay for an English Reader, in my pocket.

'There won't be another one for eight minutes,' his classmate Paddy chipped in.

'Why don't we take the day off and go into Dublin? We'll get biffed [slapped] anyway,' said Paul.

'I'm game,' said his mate.

'What about you, Vinno?' asked Paul innocently.

'How would we get there?' I asked, always the Virgo.

'Haven't you got money for a book?' said Paul.

'I can't spend that!' I said. 'It was supposed to be paid weeks ago. Where would I get the money by tomorrow?'

'Don't worry about that. We'll get it between us. Besides, we won't spend it all. We have our lunches; it's just the difference in the fares,' Paul explained, convincingly. 'Won't we, Paddy?'

'Sure,' said Paddy. 'Anyway, you can tell them you forgot it and say you'll bring it in the next day. I've often done that for months.'

That should have warned me. But I hesitated; and he who hesitates, in the words of a former saint, is — you know what! And I was. I should say the shilling and tenpence was. As good as lost, that is!

We had a great day, walked towards town as far as Booterstown to save a penny each, spent twopence each on bars of Cadbury's chocolate, took the tram to Merrion Gates, crossed over the railway line at the level crossing and walked along Sandymount Strand of James Joyce fame. The tide was out, nearly to Howth, it seemed to us. Dubliners, as usual, were digging for cockles in the wet sand. Drawn to the Martello Tower, not by its architecture or Napoleonic association but by the sweet shop built into its side, we spent the first of my book money on wine gums, a bag between us. Then we walked and talked our way past the great Shakespearean actor Anew McMaster's house, and a little further on past the house of the Bennetts, whose grand-daughter Olwen I would marry, second time around, in a distant, undreamed-of future. Then the tall chimney of the Pigeon House out along the South Wall of the Post of Dublin, coal-fired to give our city electricity, beckoned. Next, the nearby village-in-a-city called Ringsend was enriched to the tune of sixpence in exchange for greasy chips, liberally doused with salt and vinegar, wrapped in newspaper, and eagerly consumed with our packed lunch, washed down with our baby Power's bottles of milk.

The Grand Canal claimed our attention. No wonder the poet Patrick Kavanagh sought this as his memorial: the green banks, the clean water — you could see and almost read a newspaper at the bottom of it — the locks and sluices with their foaming waters, and if you were lucky, and we were, a barge going through to Athlone or Portumna. Moving on towards the city, around the Peppercanister Church, along Upper Mount Street to Merrion Square. The garden was locked, alas, and we now had no key. 'Let's go to Uncle Vincent —' I started to say; then I realised, with Paul, we were on the run, 'mitching' from school, and must draw no attention from adults friendly or unknown.

'We'd better hide our books and Vincent's school-bag,' said Paddy.

Surreptitiously, we dropped them over the two-foot stone wall, through the railings, into thick dark-green bushes. Then we cut past the little Catholic chapel on Fitzwilliam Street, turned right onto Baggot Street, went window shopping along Merrion Row towards the Shelbourne Hotel and St Stephen's Green — all familiar territory to Paul and me. Dodging in and out of the trees in St Stephen's Green, watching the ducks being fed in ponds, and avoiding places like Grafton Street, where people who knew us worked, took afternoon tea and shopped. We exited the Green by a small side gate near the top of Dawson Street. Then we scurried along the rails to Kildare Street, crossed by the side of the Shelbourne Hotel, and ambled down to the National Museum. Paul's idea!

We were lost in the wonder and magic of gold and silver, ornaments, Celtic crosses, prehistoric farm implements, tapestries, and illuminated manuscripts; the hours flew by. It was closing time before we knew it.

'Why aren't you at school?' a uniformed museum attendant boomed at me. My heart stopped. Paul and Paddy were nowhere to be seen.

'We got the day off,' I said, 'because our master was sick. My big brother,' I went on politely, hoping he would picture 'big' like Jack, not Paul, 'took me to see the museum. It's great, isn't it?'

'You'd better find him, unless you want to stay the night. We're closing up,' he said.

Before you could say 'Jack Robinson' I was out on the granite steps of the museum, where Paul and Paddy were lurking behind a granite pillar. They had seen the attendant accost me, and, being the heroes they were, had made a hasty exit, leaving me to my fate. They would probably have put a lot more distance between themselves and me if I had not had the sense to keep custody of the money!

Having recovered their school-books and my school-bag, we took a tram from Merrion Square, without running into anyone from Uncle Vincent's office, or household, who might know us. As we walked up Mount Merrion Avenue we invented and refined our stories to explain coming home so late. This was hungry work for boys. The last of my money was spent at the shop on the corner of Cross Avenue on two tooth-decaying favourites of ours, Crunchies. Only two, as we naturally waited till we dropped Paddy at his house, so as not to involve him in further sinful practice.

I don't remember how our excuses for being late were received; but I remember what torture I endured, alone, with evasions, excuses, promises, for the remainder of that term, for my failure to pay the shilling and tenpence I owed for my English Reader. Of course, neither Paul nor Paddy made the slightest attempt to find the money. Paul forged our excuses in Mammy's handwriting. Eventually, after Christmas, I persuaded my trusting mother that she still owed the school one and ten for my English book from last term! Of course, she believed me.

Whatever else suffered due to my one day of 'mitching' from school, my education didn't. I learned more that day than I ever did in one day at school — and not just about museums. You could sing that if you had an air to it!

I remember clearly the day the war started — 2 September 1939 (this was the day Éamon de Valera announced we would be neutral). It was our first day back at school, a week before my tenth birthday. Some of the older boys were told in class that Germany had invaded Poland and that Britain had declared war.

I see, in my mind's eye, two of my classmates who were brothers. We travelled home on the tram together nearly every day. Their name was O'Broin — Eimear and Colin. Eimear was short and stocky, and his fair hair was cropped close to his head. Colin was tall and thin, with dark hair that fell easily over his brow. Eimear took after his mother, who may have been German. They were both fluent in English and Irish and spoke some German. The O'Broins, like most Irish nationalists, particularly Christian Brothers, regarded England as the ancient enemy. Germany was the friend who would win back Northern Ireland for us! This, in spite of the fact that so many Irish men and women would flock to the British forces. Personally, I thought everything the British press and radio told us was propaganda — until I saw a documentary on Buchenwald and Belsen after the war. Well, when we heard that war had been declared, Eimear let out a yelp of delight. I can see him now as I write, his arms outstretched, zooming in and out between the boys and Brothers in the crowded schoolyard, followed by Colin, imitating — nay, *being* — Messerschmidt fighters, gleefully shooting down one RAF Spitfire and Hurricane after another.

All too soon, we were mourning the loss of one of my sister Kitty's admirers. He was a tall, handsome, curly-haired boy, Donal Morrissey, from the Howth Road, a frequent and popular visitor to Sycamore Road. He was shot down in his Spitfire somewhere over England, by a Messerschmidt.

Officially, we in the Irish Free State, Southern Ireland, did not have a war between 1939 and 1945. We had 'the Emergency'. Most of us were happy about being 'neutral', though some were more neutral towards Germany — the nationalists, like the Brothers and the students at CBC. Some were more neutral towards Britain, like my mother and her friends.

We did not fully escape the inconveniences of war. We had air-raid wardens, gas masks, darkened streets, blackout curtains, a local defence force (poorly armed, but with a couple of rousing marching songs), pretty severe food shortages and rationing. At one period we had an ounce of butter per week per person. And, most mourned of all, there was no white bread. As the popular parody ran:

> Bless 'em all,
> Bless 'em all,
> The long and the short and the tall.
> Bless De Valera and Seán McEntee [the Minister of Supplies],
> For they give us brown bread and a half-ounce of tea.
> So we are saying goodbye to them all
> As back to our rations we crawl;
> You'll get very weak tea
> This side of the sea —
> So cheer up lads, bless them all!

We had a number of air-raids — German planes dropping their bombs on Dublin and Dun Laoghaire, by mistake, it seems. Mistake or not, a number of people were killed and homes were wiped out on Dublin's North Strand. From time to time German — and, less often, RAF — planes crash-landed in Ireland. Their pilots were interned at the Curragh of Kildare. At least, the Germans were. The British ones, we are told, were sent back. The Germans were allowed to visit Dublin; I knew at least one, George Fleishman, who married an Irish girl and settled in Ireland. He earned his living as a documentary film-maker.

The IRA split. The way Jack explained it, some said that they would join with Germany if she landed in Ireland, but would join with the Free State Army if Britain invaded us. The other faction declared that they would join with the Irish Free State Army and repulse any invader. That was Jack's position.

Jack himself left the IRA and joined the Irish Free State Army as a private soldier in the Corps of Engineers. For his ingenuity and bravery in fighting a fire in a woollen mills in Athlone, he earned a commission — well, that was how we characterised it.

I remember him telling us that the Special Branch Police knew every move he ever made in the IRA. He later became ADC to a number of high-ranking officers, eventually to General MacNeill. We were very proud of that. Jack retired after the Emergency as a captain.

He played an important part in organising the great Military Tattoo. It was held in the Royal Dublin Society's grand halls and showgrounds, and featured, amongst other attractions, a re-enactment of the Battle of Benburb, an important battle in Ireland's struggle against England. Jack later produced the first Pageant of St Patrick on the Hills of Tara and Slane, with a cast of thousands, animal, vegetable, mineral and human, starring Anew McMaster.

Mac's favourite moments as St Patrick were off the stage, when the locals would kneel to the actor-costumed-as-bishop and kiss his ring.

I followed the course of the war assiduously. At any given time I could tell you what general in what army was where and doing what to what other general or field-marshal. Prompted by my Christian Brother teachers and teachings, I was quietly but firmly pro-German, especially on the eastern front, where the God-fearing Nazis were fighting the atheistic communists.

They called Paul 'Jelly' Dowling at school, because he had told them that we came from the family of well-known sweet manufacturers famous for their jelly beans, J.W. Dowling. They addressed me as 'Little Jelly'!

'Little Jelly,' said daring Phil Hickey, who would leave Woolworths with several unpaid-for fountain pens clipped into the end of his sleeve, then return later and put them back, just for the thrill of it, 'you are no doubt aware that the good, patriotic Brothers have discontinued rugby in our esteemed institution, deeming it a foreign game?'

'There's no more rugby,' I said.

'Precisely. It's foreign, and forbidden on the hallowed grounds of Sallynoggin playing field.'

'Yes,' I said, flattered to be spoken to by this eminent personage.

'To make a long story even longer,' said he, to the guffaws of his cronies, 'we have arranged a friendly game with a few lads from Christian Brothers Glass-Tool [a not-too-subtle suggestion of a breakable penis; the correct name was Glasthule] next Wednesday after school. Brother Rice likes you, and is really a rugby man at heart. We have elected you, unanimously, to ask him to let us use Sallynoggin playing field. Of course we want you on our team,' he added hurriedly. 'You will, won't you, Little Jelly? He's over there in the corner.'

Before I could answer I was propelled firmly in that direction.

'Don't forget,' he whispered, 'it's only a friendly game.'

Brother Rice was a white-haired, apparently amiable, intelligent man. He listened to my story attentively. He asked me to assure him that we were not playing against the Glasthule school *team*.

'Oh, no,' I said, 'it's only a friendly, with a few lads from Glasthule.'

'Very well,' he said, and wished me luck. He didn't specify *good* luck. And it wasn't, as it turned out!

Wednesday was our half-day; we finished school at 12.30. We made our way about two miles inland to the playing field at Sallynoggin. There are fifteen players in a Rugby Union team. We certainly did not have that many. It was decided that I would play fullback, probably to keep me as far out of the way as possible. Most but not all of us had our old CBC jerseys, there were assorted rugby shorts and stockings, and several of us, including me, had no proper rugby boots!

Glasthule arrived in a bus. They had a Brother in charge of them. They had seventeen immaculately turned-out giants — a full team of fifteen and two linesmen. On a whistle from their Reverend trainer they broke into disciplined runs, passing movements, scrimmages, and line-outs, while one of them sent drop-kicks and place-kicks over the bar, between the goalposts, with frightening regularity. That was the pre-game warm-up.

The game was a rout. The only times we ever kept possession of the ball for any length of time were when we kicked off, to start the game, and after the endless tries, conversions and drop goals they scored against us. The score was about forty-something to nil. We were the nil. Once during the game I made a half-hearted attempt to tackle one of these giants. He 'handed me off' with such force that I did about three somersaults and landed with a thud on the hard dry ground, about ten feet away. I spent the rest of the game using any skill or speed I possessed to get as far away from any man with the ball as I could.

There was no pavilion, shower, running water or toilet. We struggled back into our clothes, dirty, sweaty, bruised and demoralised. When we got to the bus stop, Paul and I found we had no money. He had spent his fare. My money was lost or stolen. Carrying our football togs and school-books, we dragged ourselves the five or six miles home via Foxrock to Mount Merrion, sitting down on the edge of the footpath from time to time to remove pebbles which always worked their way in. Maybe Sam Beckett saw us and got his inspiration for the tramps in *Godot*! Darkness came and joined us about an hour before we reached home. Love, understanding, a bath and tea, which were waiting for us, were only temporary respites in what would become, for me, more than three months of intermittent sadistic cruelty inflicted by an unChristian and decidedly unbrotherly Brother Rice.

On Saturday the *Evening Herald*, on its sports page, carried a brief report of a match between St Michael's Christian Brothers College and the Christian Brothers Glasthule. It gave the score, the names of the scorers, and the referee.

Brother Rice sent for me on the following Monday. I was a liar, a conniver, a hypocrite. I had taken advantage of his trust and betrayed him and it. I was a disgrace to the school, my family, my religion, and my country. He never wanted to see me again, and if he had his way I would be expelled from St Michael's and my name expunged from the rolls and record. I protested in vain that I had only told him what I had been asked to tell him; if he heard, he gave no sign. I was dismissed from his sight as though I were an abomination and unclean. I still relive the terror and contempt in my dreams. Did I say dreams? That's not true. They were nightmares.

It was the overwhelming sense of total injustice that stayed with me. Did he really believe that this eleven-year-old had arranged the game with another school and talked a gang of fifteen-year-olds into making up the team? Even if he did, why didn't they exonerate me? I don't know. Paul is dead, poor fellow, and I never asked him. I've known for a long time, as an actor, that a man, woman, or child whom whiplashes cannot break can succumb to unexpected kindness or to injustice — particularly to injustice. That was something worth learning.

On St Stephen's Day every year we went to see the pantomime — 'panto' for short — at the Gaiety Theatre. For those deprived of this experience, I should note that there was rarely any mime involved in this kind of show. The Principal Boy (be it a prince, or some other hero-type) was always played by a fine-looking girl with obvious bosoms, really good long legs exposed from ankle to thigh, and a good contralto voice. She — or is it he? — played the romantic lead opposite the Principal Girl, usually a smaller, prettier, ingenue soprano. They sang several solos, duets and numbers with the chorus. The audience was encouraged to join in. For a finale, they had an elaborate wedding scene after the hero had rescued his love from the Bad Baron and his comic henchmen. The real star of the show was the heroine's mother, 'the Dame', played robustly by a man in an obvious wig and with ample padding. Jimmy O'Dea, the great clown and character actor, made this part his own while I was growing up.

The Gaiety panto opened the day after Christmas and, if successful, often ran until early March. The script was written around well-loved fairy tales and children's stories such as 'Cinderella', 'Jack and the Beanstalk' and 'Robin Hood', with topical references and political personalities interjected to satirise current events and scandals. The comic characters would sing wicked parodies of well-known songs. Lavish scenery, costumes, sound and special effects, a chorus of beautiful long-legged female dancers, and a 'Speciality Act', all accompanied by a large pit orchestra, were required ingredients of this great music-hall Christmas tradition, which still survives virtually intact. My memories of going into town for this event are bright with the moving lights of the Bovril advertisement at the bottom of Grafton Street as we passed by on the bus on the way home, the excitement of the packed theatre and the slapstick and glitter on the stage that delighted year after year. The night of the panto was a night in Wonderland!

It is not surprising that I first fell in love — really fell in love — watching a young girl on a stage. She wore a long purple Grecian dress, with a thin golden string around her straight shiny hair. She was singing 'Somewhere Over the Rainbow' solo at a Mount Merrion fête on an open-air stage. I was sitting on the grass of the Lawn, and I remained there through the whole show and for a repeat performance an hour later. Hanging around between performances, I bumped into her accidentally, on purpose.

I saw that she had brown eyes and a thin, very white line running from her upper lip towards her nose. She must have had a cut there stitched as a baby. It was the most beautiful adornment to a face that I ever saw. Her name was Noreen Hooper.

I hoped to see her again, but the next day I was diagnosed with pleurisy. The doctor said I had probably got it from sitting on damp grass and ordered me to bed for six weeks. My mother overreacted, for fear of the (whispered only) 'consumption', and kept me out of school for several months. All the time I was confined to the house, I would dream about Noreen and how I was going to see her again. When I was well enough and alone, I sang endlessly, 'When songs of spring are sung, remember that morning in May, remember you loved me when we were young one day....' But as Shakespeare knew, the course of true love never did run smooth.

Lying in bed for six weeks in bed with 'dry' pleurisy, as Dr Wilson described it, gave me ample time for studying my mother's big bed with its green eiderdown. (How do you get down off a donkey? You can't. You can only get down off a duck!) There was a commode in an old-fashioned wooden chair, and it was a special amusement that visitors (after the first two weeks, when they weren't permitted) sat, unknowingly, on my private toilet seat.

The whole six weeks seemed to be sunny outside the bay window that overlooked the concrete Sycamore Road. Through the windowpanes on the right-hand side I could see the green leaves of the huge sycamore tree that stood, surrounded by a low, thick cement parapet, in the middle of the road. There were two such trees on our road but only one on Trees Road. That struck me as odd.

In or about 'our' tree, the evening life of the youngsters in our neighbour-hood took place. I lay in bed evening after evening, instantly recognising every voice and picturing every move and expression, while they played Towns-and-Counties, Tip-and-Tag, Relievio, hopscotch and football, and talked, laughed, argued over goals, fouls, cheating, wins and losses. I saw myself joining them, running, kicking, catching, hopping, brilliantly bringing victory to my team in every game, all reflected in the adoring eyes of Noreen Hooper — and always followed by the hollow realisation that I was lying alone in my sickbed. The long silent hours of the day flowed, oh! so slowly, from insipid soups, semolina, syrups, liquids, and crustless fingers of toast dipped in soft-boiled eggs, to drawn curtains and countless 'naps'. Always somewhere in my consciousness was a longing for the sweet taste of Cadbury's flaky chocolate — forbidden, like everything I liked, until I was better. Eventually I got better, but I was not really free to rejoin the life of my brothers and friends for a year.

September saw everyone else going back to school. I won't lie to you — that caused me as much regret as being told there was no liver or parsnips left for me! Mammy had made up her mind: for one year I was not to go back to school, swim, stay up late, or do anything that would get me hot and sweaty (which pained my sisters, who didn't 'sweat' — they perspired). Oddly enough, she didn't stop smoking around me or keep me from going to the pictures. For that relief, I still give much thanks. Through the good offices of 'Baby' Finucane I went free to the Regent Cinema, seeing both of the weekday changes of programme plus our usual paid Sunday early show (they were all double features). So I saw six-plus films a week for almost fifty weeks. That couldn't have had anything to do with my becoming an actor or going to live in America, could it?

I read a lot, too, I'm glad to say — everything I could lay my hands on round the house. Dickens — *David Copperfield* for sure; several Rafael Sabatinis; *Scaramouche*; a number of Maurice Walsh's novels, starting with *The Small Dark Man*; *The Hunchback of Notre Dame* and *Les Misérables* by Dumas. I suppose it is no coincidence that most of these were also movie titles.

The book that had the most effect on me was called *The Arrant Rover* by one Bruce Arnold. The best that could be said of it was that it had a hard cover. Red. It belonged to one of the girls. It told the story of a handsome, devil-may-care womaniser with wavy hair that he didn't like a woman to ruffle. He drove a sports car — a drop-head coupé, he called it, which I prefer to 'convertible'. He drove it around England from pretty girl to pretty girl, falling in love with one after another, but always moving on when any one of them fell in love with him, which most of them did. I blush to think how young I was when I commenced living that character and how old when I stopped.

As well as bringing us Blanche Brosnan Murphy, a friend of my mother who found the air-raids in London 'got on her nerves', the war in Europe brought three extra children to our road to live: the Thompson girls from Streatham, London.

There was Daisy, the eldest; she was dark, slim, private, almost Romany-looking. She was about Paul's age. Eileen, the youngest, had short, straight hair and a tomboy personality. She seemed to be always doing something. She was Sam's age. And there was Sheila; she had soft, wavy, brown hair, budding breasts beneath cotton shirts, lovely skin, and an open, friendly, good-humoured, attractive face. She was a little older than I. The unspoken opinion from the very first — and, I think, the spoken one as well — was that these girls were made for the three Dowling boys. Well, for a time Daisy was Paul's girl; Eileen was Sam's, young as they were; but, alas, though I had a great crush on Sheila, I never achieved the enviable state of being her boyfriend.

The 'Thompson Three' were a great addition to our gang. They were great players, innovators, sports, and, as John Muir would say, 'as unfussy as the trees'. Of course, they loved the woods and were fearless climbers. There was a great old hemlock or pine tree up the path, immediately south of the Lawn. It had great, thick, spreading limbs, the first of them about ten feet above the ground. This became the favourite gathering place of our gang.

The bravest of the boys and girls would climb up to the tip-top of this thirty- or forty-foot tree and then along the stronger limbs to the very edges. Nearly everyone would climb up to that first big branch, hoosh themselves up to a slightly thinner branch above and parallel to it and seat themselves there, and play out the talk, laughter, hand-holding and kissing games like Truth-or-Dare and Forfeits for hours and hours, day after day. Everyone except me, that is. Much as I longed, much as I was laughed at and teased, much as I was secretly ashamed, I could not climb up there. I'd stand around the base of the trunk with a couldn't-care-less attitude, answering taunts and teasings with whatever wit I could muster but dying inside with the longing and shame. That was the start of my isolation. If Paul didn't actually encourage the rendezvous at the big tree, he certainly did not discourage them. And he certainly knew of my fear of climbing.

Sheila and some of the girls had made a new hideout. It was outside and against the south wall of the Pembroke Estate farm buildings. The high stone wall of an orchard ran about six feet away from the building and parallel to it. The area was protected on the woods side by a high wall with a locked gate in it and no key. We boys, who had gone everywhere in and about Mount Merrion, had rarely, if ever, penetrated this uninviting weed-choked space.

'If you want to help, this could be the gang's secret hideout,' Sheila told us.

Would we help? Would a duck take to water? And the days were filled with tree-cutting, bush-trimming, stone-gathering, path-making, linoleum-, furniture-, picture- and utensil-finding, brushing, mopping, sponging, nailing, hammering and wall-hanging. Vases of flowers appeared, to be accepted or rejected by the Lady Sheila. Soon the little shed and garden was the art, craft, social, and play centre of our lives.

I'm not sure how it started — something about a mysterious love note signed 'The Phantom' which was left in the shed for Sheila, followed by the searches and traps to find the identity of the anonymous writer. The fact that a pal of my age, Jimmy Burke, who lived in the gate lodge on Mount Merrion

Avenue, outside Mount Merrion, had a crush on Eileen like mine for Sheila — not reciprocated — all led to Jimmy and me being frozen out, exiled, or exiling ourselves from this Garden of Eden. We never found out who the snake was. I suspect this particular snake — a poor, hurt snake, really no snake at all — lived and slept very close to my own family bosom! Jimmy and I spent many melodramatic months miserably mooning about the woods together, keening 'He done me wrong' or 'She done me wrong' songs and writing mysterious love notes, signed by our invented mysterious characters, to the girls and threatening ones to the gang, and going to ridiculous lengths to leave them at the hideout without being unmasked. Of course, it was all a melodrama that we wrote, directed, and acted in for ourselves. The audience who we had hoped would be moved by our pitiful plight — Eileen and Sheila Thompson, of course — never gave any sign that they saw it, let alone cared a kern's hoot about it or us.

The period from September to Christmas that year, 1940, was almost perfect in every way, as far as I can remember.

I would do the shopping at Parsons Grocery, Bulls, Roches Chemist, the shoemaker's, and the butcher's shop. We had 'a bill' — a charge account — at Parsons. It was called an account on account of the fact we always owed money on it. I would be sent for 'the messages'. I would memorise a long list, which I was soon able to put prices against, so I could come out with a total by the time Mammy, the girls, or Blanche Brosnan had finished articulating the list. Usually I was given a totally inadequate amount of money. When I protested this truth — which I always did, because the encounters with the kindly Mr Parsons really embarrassed me — the reply would be, 'Pay him the half-crown [or whatever] and ask him to put the rest of it on the bill.' This meant there was nothing in it for me. On the rare occasions when we owed nothing to Mr Parsons, and I was given more than the cost of the items, with a cautionary 'Don't lose the change,' I could, by shrewd shopping, squeeze a penny or two out for myself without it being questioned. I was a pretty savvy shopper, and even in those circumstances I saved the family money. Still, it was stealing — 'fecking,' in our slang.

Now, when Blanche sent me shopping, she paid cash — mostly in crisp new English pounds or ten-shilling notes, sometimes even a larger white English fiver. Her shopping list always included a visit to Roches Chemist for a bottle of 'cocktail' (either Pimm's No. 1 or No. 2), which for some reason Roches stocked in fancy glass bottles, though they had no license to sell liquor for consumption on or off the premises. There was no 'fecking' about with Blanche's money. She always tipped lavishly — a silver thruppenny or sixpenny bit.

Blanche was beautiful. One of three beautiful auburn-haired Brosnan sisters. We adored them all. Blanche was married to an Irish doctor working in England, but she preferred Dublin by far during war-time. Her presence and the visits of her sisters, husband, and friends were invariably full of interest, fun, and festive fare. More than that, what Blanche contributed to the family finances every week was, as Mammy would say repeatedly, 'a very welcome addition'. The father of Geraldine Fitzgerald (the Irish actress and Hollywood film star), a successful stockbroker, used to come some Sundays and take Blanche, Paul, Sam and me for a drive up to the Dublin Mountains in his posh Armstrong Siddley touring car. We loved that, too! He was a dashingly dressed, handsome, older man, with beautiful manners and a whiskey nose.

With the shopping done and everyone else at school, the rest of the day was my own. Alone, but never lonely, I wandered around Mount Merrion. If there was a raffle being held in the locality, at school or for my sister's tennis club, I would go to the friendly houses like Shevlin's, where I was always welcomed and fed, and a book of tickets was bought. Each book of tickets had a free ticket for the seller. I always sold that and took the cash and let the credit go.

Otherwise I worked my way up the Avenue, trying to knock down walnuts, with improvised boomerangs, from the walnut tree near the Rise. Once, and never again, I sickened myself smoking rolled dry beech leaves. Mostly, I was poking about in the bushes around the new school attached to Mount Merrion Church, probably singing 'When It's Springtime in the Rockies', 'Red River Valley' or 'South of the Border'. If the shopping had left room for profit, I would have a roll of Rowntrees Clear Gums in my pocket, and I would add a wild flower or two to the little bunch I had 'fecked' from neighbours' gardens.

The gums, flowers, and songs were all for Noreen Hooper. Fighting my innate cowardice and fear of heights, I had finally conquered the old pine tree that grew thick, tall, and forked opposite the window where Noreen sat in class. There I would sit singing my cowboy love songs, signalling a cool 'Hello' when she looked my way, doing a disappearing act if her teacher approached the window. Eventually a message came to me, via the priest, to play somewhere else as I was distracting the children from their work. I would wait around until their lunch break, sidle up to Noreen in the schoolyard, thrust the flowers and gums into her hand, and flee without saying a word. During all that time I don't think I ever had a conversation with her.

Some months later, when I was back at school myself, I did meet Noreen, face to face, at the fence around the church grounds, on the opposite side of the Avenue from the walnut tree. It was almost dark. Paul was with me. She told us she was leaving Mount Merrion soon, to live in Raglan Road, Ballsbridge. I was devastated. She might as well have said she was going to the moon.

What I said, I don't know, but Paul said, 'Don't mind him. He still wets the bed.'

Then everything goes blank till Paul and I were at home. In bed going to sleep, I said something about it being 'a lousy thing to say'.

'Well, it's true,' he said; and it was.

Somehow, I made a date with Noreen. I have no idea how or when. What I am sure of is that I arrived one dry, sunny day, by car, to collect Noreen at her flat in Raglan Road, down from where the American Embassy is now. Sam, two other boys his age, and their older sister were with me. It was probably one of their parents that drove us. Noreen had a younger sister or cousin with her. Together we all bussed it to the Green Cinema on St Stephen's Green. Whether I sat beside her, held her hand, or put my arm around her, I don't know. That I longed to, I'm sure. But the curtain is down on it all. I don't even remember the name of the movie. I never saw her again; but in some extraordinary way I loved the idea of her, and, though in time it ceased to hurt, it never left me.

'They want you to come back to school, Vincent,' Mammy told me early in 1941. 'Brother Whelan, the Head Brother, was very nice. He wants to have you on the rolls, now that you should be moving into secondary school, and he suggested that you come in for a half-day every day. You wouldn't need to do any homework. Do you think you're able for that?'

What more — or, should I say, what less — could a twelve-year-old ask for! 'Yes,' I answered, 'I'd like that. I'm sure I can keep up.'

'Of course,' she said, as an afterthought, 'not on very wet or very cold days. But never mind that; "Sufficient unto the day is the evil thereof!"'

Since we mostly had winter weather in Ireland, it looked as if I wasn't going to be too taxed — though, as Mammy was wont to say, 'You can't be sure, and if you are, you can't be certain!'

My teacher in first-year Intermediate, as it was officially termed, was the esteemed Brother Rice. The earlier image of a reasonably pleasant-faced, middle-aged man is unwillingly replaced in my mind by a big, fat, evil-intentioned bullfrog sitting on the desk in front of us in the upstairs class-room. Around his neck was the narrow white clerical collar the brothers wore — a little more than sacristans and less than priests!

'Now you, Dowling,' he would croak, as he went round the room from boy to boy with a question or a verse from the homework given the previous day, to be answered or recited promptly, accurately, and 'by heart'.

'I'm excused from homework, Brother, because of my health,' I answered with a smile, the second day I was back at school, and I sat down.

'Stand up when I'm talking to you,' he snapped. 'Or are you too weak to stand?'

'No, sir,' I said quickly, jumping up.

'Go to the Head Brother's office and tell him you did not do your homework.'

Alex Gosse, my classmate, one of the ones I liked best, bravely launched into 'Oft I think of Lucy Grey and when she crossed the wild....' I hesitated at the door, with it half-open.

'Well, what are you waiting for now?' Rice barked, over Alex Gosse's faltering voice intoning the words, '... solitary child.'

'Brother Whelan knows, Brother. It was Brother Whelan told Mammy I didn't have to do any homework,' I said, reasonably.

'Get out of here,' he replied, quietly and menacingly, 'and don't come back until you have spoken to him.'

I closed the door, carefully, and stepped out into the dark hallway. Down some steps, then back along another dark, wood-panelled hall to an opaque-glassed door, with a sign of some sort indicating that this was where the Head Brother had his office. I knocked, timidly; no answer. I waited; knocked again, trying to make it sound apologetic. No answer. Waited. Waited. Knocked a little louder; waited again. Gave a brisk clear knock, waited a moment and entered.

It was empty. Well, Brother Whelan was not there. His desk, the chairs my mother and I had sat on a week before, were there; the glass-fronted bookcase; the window overlooking the street; and Brother Rice — Ignatius Rice, the founder of the Christian Brothers, that is — there on the wall, looking down disapprovingly at miserable me.

'I'd better get back to class,' I thought, 'or I'll get into more trouble.' Wrong thinking, Vincent!

I went back, knocked on the classroom door. 'Come in,' Rice called out. I opened the door and put my head in. 'Well?' he demanded.

'Brother Whelan is not in his office. I ...'

Before I could finish — 'Get out of here and don't come back till you've seen him!' he shouted.

No Shakespearean actor ever exited so quickly, even pursued by a bear! It wasn't funny at that time, or at any of the scores of times that I played out the same scenario.

Brother Whelan was always fair, thoughtful, gentle with me. The first few times he simply sent me back. He would say, regretfully, something like, 'I know, I know. Brother Rice. Ah well, just go back to your class.' After a letter from my mother, I was transferred to another class after the Easter holidays.

These early happenings in Mount Merrion must be what trigger the relief and gratitude I always feel when I meet someone who really wants my approbation and friendship. To this day, except in my theatre work, I always feel, with men, that I am a child being spoken to by the schoolmaster. With girls and young women, who attracted me until I met Olwen, my wife, I was driven to 'win' them, and when I did, to drop them, before they could drop me. If they threw themselves at me, which some did, I was completely turned off. For me, this discovery was quite startling because it was so obvious. Yet it has taken me nearly sixty years to realise it. As the country fellow coming to Dublin used to say, 'I may not be long up, but I'm well up' — now!

3

The Standard Life – VD or Not VD?

What would you say to a good office job?

My friend Dessie Larkin, whose Dublin city accent had so offended my sisters' suburban sensibilities, went to live in the country. His father retired and bought a farmhouse outside Crosspatrick village in County Kilkenny, very near the border with Tipperary in Ireland's central plain. Dessie's mother, hearing of my pleurisy and convalescence, invited to me to visit them for the summer. If it hadn't been for sitting on the damp grass listening to Noreen Hooper, I would have missed the greatest holiday of my childhood!

This area of small farms lies to the east of a range of mountains with a gap in them, clearly visible for as far as the eye can see, which is called the Devil's Bit; the Devil was said to have taken a bite out of the mountains. There were peat (or turf) bogs a-plenty in the region. The small country roads, some tarred, more dirt, were lined with hawthorn hedges – which as kids we called 'bread-and-butter trees' – and an abundance of bushes of small, black, sour sloes. These roads, which we cycled and walked on, with an occasional motor-car ride, joined us to Urlingford and Johnstown, two busy small towns. I never knew exactly how far we were from these places; when I asked the distance to anything in that area, the only answer I ever got was, 'A mile, a bit, and a little bit, and the little bit is longer than the mile and a bit!'

The locals, especially the farming community, had another odd practice – perhaps I should say abstinence – in those days. They steadfastly refused to recognise daylight saving time, which was introduced to Ireland during the Emergency. The country people in Ireland generally, and in Crosspatrick in particular, referred to it contemptuously as 'new time' and kept their clocks and pocket watches at 'old time' – in other words, an hour earlier! It all added to the fun of living in the country, if not to the efficiency. I was constantly adding an hour to the time given me by anyone with a country accent. This led to many mistakes – missed meals, buses, trains, and church services – as government employees and townspeople, who had country accents but didn't practise the gentle craft of farming, would give me 'new time' whilst I assumed they were giving me 'old time'. Of course, I *never* used this as an excuse if I was late coming home for meals or bed, which I mostly was!

The Larkins' farmhouse presented an exterior of weatherbeaten cement; it was two-storied, comfortable and well kept, with an indoor toilet and a pleasant homey feeling. The gable end stood windowless at the roadside. The bedroom that I shared with Des was on the inside of that gable. Nights, lying awake in terror when Des had punished me for some difference during the day by sleeping in another room, the rare motor vehicle that passed by seemed to take a supernatural length of time to fade from my hearing. I've never understood why that was, but it frightened the bejasus out of me.

A hay-barn and a chicken-house faced the house across the yard. To the left a five-barred gate opened into an uncultivated field, surrounded by hedges. In those hedges we boys were encouraged to answer the calls of nature. The hedges were also used by the rogue hens, who went to extraordinary lengths to lay their eggs anywhere but in their nests in the hen-house. I can still see a certain young black hen, little more than a pullet, looking like a male ballet dancer in black tights as she strode cockily into the farmyard from the field, boasting lustily that she had once again outwitted the farmer's wife. The fowl wanderer hadn't counted on the cunning, patient city boy. I became the Hawkeye of hen-watchers, often gathering a dozen eggs in a day from the three or four rogues who would change their secret depositories every time they were discovered.

I spent every daylight hour, Monday through Friday and often Saturday, working at the O'Briens' farm down the road. At first I was helping to feed the chickens; bring galvanized buckets of milk to the hungry, cuddly, bucket-banging, mooing calves; bring in the cows for milking, with Michael, the adult son of the house; separate the milk and make the butter — in short, woman's work!

It didn't take them long to see that they could depend on me and that I loved working on the farm — everywhere on the farm. I think the turning point came when I said I wanted to join them in weeding turnips, and spent the whole day on my knees, from dawn to dusk, in the unusually warm sun, pulling out weeds and thistles — *and* came back day after day till that job was finished! I loved every minute of it; but I loved, too, the tea and lunch breaks — lying in the shade of a crab-apple tree or a hawthorn hedge, with the men and girls drinking fresh milk from a clean, corked lemonade bottle, with thick soda bread and country buttered sandwiches and talk of things local, national, international and supernatural.

From that turnip-weeding time, the windows of opportunity on the life of the O'Briens' farm were wide open to me. 'Flagging' the potato drills was my favourite. I've never come across this farm practice anywhere else; not many people I've met even know what it is! A large granite flagstone wedge, flat on top, its front like the prow of a landing craft, slanted back underneath to a thickness of about two inches at the rear; there was a hole just behind the prow, for a chain that was linked to a simple harness. The great big (to me) farmhorse was yoked into the harness; the driver (soon mostly me) stood on the stone, reins in hand, and drove the horse between the rows of potato stalks, making and/or strengthening the potato 'drills'. No American teenager — not even Andy Hardy — in the latest, largest drop-head coupé ever experienced the thrill or the pride that I did, standing alone on that stone as I careered up the 'drill' in this one-horsepower contraption, making perfect hairpin turns at the top and bottom of every lap, at maybe one mile an hour.

I milked cows, having driven them in from far fields myself. I rode the big workhorse bareback along the road to and from meadows and, later in the summer, cornfields; I drove the horse-drawn grass- and corn-cutting machines; I 'made' the hay, right through from cutting it to building the high hayricks in the farmyard; I 'stooked' the corn in the fields to dry, and brought it by horse and cart to the travelling man with his threshing machine that turned it into bags of grain.

My pay — and I felt well paid — came at one o'clock in the day, when I sat down at a scrubbed deal table, opposite one of the working men, a plate and spoon before me. Mrs O'Brien placed on the table a great dish of colcannon — creamy mashed potatoes mixed with finely chopped raw onions and parsley, a mountain of it — between me and the man across from me. Her daughter made a hole with a wooden spoon in the top of each mountain and dropped into it a huge lump of country butter, which melted on contact, so the mountain became a steaming volcano; Mrs O'Brien came back with a bag full of salt and dumped a fistful beside each potato peak. And sticking my spoon into the bottom of the mountain of food, scooping out a generous spoonful, dunking it in the well of butter and touching the spoon in the salt, I'd open wide my gob and shovel the sinfully succulent mush into my hungry gullet. No caviar in Moscow, sole in London, oyster in Galway, cassoulet in France — no delicacy I have had anywhere — can match the magic and memory of that taste. Try as Mammy and my sisters did to replicate the making of it, theirs never produced the ecstasy of the Crosspatrick colcannon. Of course, they never served one dish between two people, or poured the salt on a scrubbed deal table for me, though it wasn't for want of pleading on my part.

Mrs Larkin, a large, dignified, warm and fair-minded woman, soon discovered my talent for shopping. Urlingford was nearer than Johnstown and had a better butcher; that was all-important in those days. Mrs Larkin impressed on me, every single time there was meat on my shopping list, 'Tell him it's for Mrs Larkin and you want the lamb kidneys in their fat; otherwise they'll peel off all the suet and sell it separately.' I was puzzled by this the first time, but when I saw how she cooked the kidneys I understood why she said that, so well that I still buy kidneys that way when I get them. She grilled the kidneys in the suet, after she had torn the suet open so that the lean organ lay on the fat like an oyster on the half-shell. With this accompanied on the warm plate by lean back rashers of bacon, black and white pudding, two fresh fried eggs and well-browned fried bread, and the kidneys in their bed of crispy fat with salt and pepper and liberally doused with HP Sauce, 'You wouldn't,' as Mammy would say, 'call the Queen your aunt!' (Of course, in later years you could call the resultant pain in your chest 'angina'!)

Talking about lambs and black pudding (which I loved) and white (which I didn't) — two memorable learning experiences at the O'Briens' are connected to them in my mind. For days the talk was about the inspector coming for the sheep-dipping. As with the other important happenings on the farmer's calendar, the excitement built to a joyful frenzy. Maybe it was only me, but the talk of making the hay or dipping the sheep was more colourful and exciting, and the waiting more unbearable, than it was for the coming of Duffy's Circus or even the Christmas pantomime.

'Make sure you have rubber boots, an old cap, your oldest clothes and a thick pair of gloves. You don't want to get the sheep dip on your skin, and if you get it on your clothes you'll never get it out.' They were right. All the sheep on the farm had to be dipped once a year in a solution that would kill off the bugs and worms that were dangerous to them and to the large industry in Ireland that was dependent on them. So first of all we had to round up all the sheep and lambs, some of them grazing far afield on barren hillsides. I was allotted to the O'Briens' uncle — Johnny, his name was. We always called him 'Windy'. He was the spitting image of Windy, Hopalong Cassidy's sidekick, and he was just as funny and friendly and much wiser. I wasn't acting; I was living a part in a great cowboy (never mind that they were sheep) moving picture. I was totally preoccupied with the work to be done, giving my every sense to doing it, enjoying it with every fibre of my body; and yet, with my 'third eye', seeing myself do it, through the eyes of my family, friends, enemies, girlfriends, and favourite female film stars.

Every four-footed woolly creature accounted for, stragglers and wanderers chased back into the herd, we drove them into the 'haggard' by the farmyard. Then, one beast at a time, we drove them into the chute. They bleated pitifully as they slithered down the concrete slope to the churning, frothy red liquid dip, to be dunked under by a man up above with a long wooden gadget. By the first day's end I had tried my hand, more or less successfully, at every stage of the procedure.

Killing or sticking the pig is a more sobering memory. A hush seems to surround everything about it. 'Are you sure you want to watch it? A lot of blood flowing everywhere, and the screeching of the pig is pitiful, and it goes on for a long time,' Mrs O'Brien and her daughter, between them, warned me. Mrs Larkin really didn't want me to go, but stopped short of forbidding me. I don't think I really wanted to go. Somehow, though, I felt I had to, if I was going to be a farmer — which for years I had said I wanted, and which I now *knew* I wanted.

The butcher had already arrived when I got there. His little blue Ford van was in the farmyard. He was out in the shed, I was told, with Michael. I could go out there if I wanted, but no one would think any worse of me if I didn't.

There was a whitewashed shed. It had a cement floor with a drain in the middle and a section at one end raised about two inches above the floor, like a low stage. The butcher had a grip on a young pig, holding it steady while he shaved a large area around its throat with a cutthroat razor. I noticed the whole shed floor was still damp from a thorough scrubbing. There was a large zinc bathtub on the floor below the 'stage'.

When the shaving was done I was asked to get something in the kitchen — I've no idea what. When I came back blood was pouring from the screeching pig, like red water from a faucet, into the tub. The butcher, in a rubber apron and boots, had his blood-covered hands and arms around the pig's neck, which had gone limp. He was directing the blood flow steadily towards the tub.

The pig stopped screeching. The only sound I could hear was of liquid into liquid in the rapidly filling tub. Beside the butcher I saw the razor and a long-bladed, sharp-pointed knife with a black handle. It was bloodstained. This, I guessed or was told later, was the knife used to stick the pig.

I watched a little longer and went back to the kitchen. 'Why are they filling the tub with blood?' I asked Mrs O'Brien.

'To make the black pudding,' I was told after a surprised pause.

'What do you mean?' I asked.

'Black puddings are made up of pig's blood.'

'How could it become solid if it's blood?' I stammered.

'Well, they fill it into the pig's guts with grains and things, and it dries up there, in the smoke from the turf fire. We hang the bacon up there also, to smoke and cure. The butcher is getting all that ready now,' she said.

I was deeply shocked. 'I'll never be able to eat black pudding again.' And I didn't. Till the next morning!

In the year or two preceding my Crosspatrick holiday, foot-and-mouth disease had struck Ireland, first in isolated patches, then as a national epidemic. The government, when it moved, moved decisively: if the disease was discovered on a farm, all the herd on that farm had to be destroyed without delay and buried. Failure to report the disease brought with it heavy penalties. Farmers whose herds were destroyed were compensated. Foot-and-mouth disease was headline news in city, town, and country in those years of the 1940s. It was still a serious matter of concern when I got to Crosspatrick, and the particular farms and fields where the diseased or suspected cattle had been buried were tourist attractions and potent reminders to local farmers of dangerous times. I don't remember a single person who resented the government's action, and that surprised me; even at that age, I knew that being 'agin the government' was a national sport. Ireland has remained free of the dreaded foot-and-mouth disease ever since.

Other summer holidays were facilitated by Father Luke. He took a cottage for us at Bettystown, and subsequently for a number of years it was Destination Gormanston. He drove us there in his Swallow car. Mammy sat in the front with Father Luke and the baby, Sam; Paul and I, tucked in with rugs, sat in the 'dickie' at the back. Gormanston, less than thirty miles from Dublin, was about four hours' drive for us — through Dublin with its horse-drawn traffic, bicycles, trams, occasional cars, followed by stops along the lonely parts of the Dublin/Belfast road to relieve ourselves or get sick, which Paul always managed to do. All of this was worth it, for if Mount Merrion was Heaven, Gormanston was God's inner circle.

The Gormanston River — a tiny stream, really — marks the border between Dublin and Meath. A few small houses, a summer cottage or two, a dance hall and a modest, understocked huckster shop made up the village. To the north was a flat green airfield where red hangars housed the Irish Air Corps; there, with their Hawker Hectors and Gladiators, they did their summer training.

A small pub on the Dublin/Belfast road served most of the wants of soldiers, local farmers, labourers and occasional travellers. It was known locally as 'the Cock McCabe's', and a welcoming spot it was. The pub marked the turn-off to Gormanston Camp; the road continued along the north side of the airfield to the side gate, beside which was a green galvanised huckster shop, run by the McGuinnesses, that sold papers, cigs, matches, aspros, butter, milk, eggs and — most importantly — sweets and chocolates.

The farmland around there was mostly owned and worked with dedicated husbandry by the Shuttlecocks, whom we got to know. Their immaculately kept house stood beside the dirt road, with well-kept gardens, orchard, yard and farm buildings. You'd know from the look of it that the family was Protestant. It was with them that I eventually graduated from feeding chickens and calves to milking cows.

In a little nearby paddock, Father Luke had placed a well-converted three-compartment goods wagon from an ancient train, to house the Dowling family, visiting friends and himself. The Belfast–Dublin railway lines ran by within forty feet of us. We knew the name of every engine run by the Great Northern Railways. Slieve Gullion was my favourite. We laid halfpenny coins on the line if a train was due, in the hope that the iron wheels would make them look like pennies. They never did, only flattened and bent them so much that most shopkeepers wouldn't take them even as ha'pennies.

Each summer a short visit from the Irish Air Corps would be followed, in pre-War days, by a battalion of infantry with a company of cavalry. They would spend July under canvas across the dirt road from us. We'd wake up to the trumpet blowing reveille, and start home for bed after taps and the lowering of the Tricolour. We had the run of the camp and the field kitchen, to which we repaired at the first note of 'Cookhouse'. We learned to blow that call ourselves!

Come to the cookhouse door, boys,
Come to the cookhouse door.
Jolly wishes in the dishes,
Come to the cookhouse door.

No breakfast could compare with lining up alongside the 'buck' privates or NCOs for an enamel plate of greasy sausages or slices of bacon, with two fried eggs, a quarter of a loaf of batch bread, a hunk of butter, a spoonful of jam and an enamel mug of scalding, sweet, milky tea. Eat now, pay later!

We would go to their 'campfires', where Paul and I would sing and recite. The night before the battalion returned to barracks, the grown-ups were guests for dinner at the officers' mess, the tablecloths for this event being lent by us. One year, one of the officers of the élite battalion the Volunteers had several conversations with us about Ireland, patriotism, duty and purity. Our friends were impressed when we told them it was Major Vivion de Valera, son of the great Irish statesman and hero of the fight for Irish freedom, Éamon de Valera.

When the army returned to their city barracks, the boys from the reformatory school in Glencree, Co. Wicklow, would move in. Our family had some hesitation about our mixing with these reformatory boys. Paul and I, though, took every opportunity to continue our visits to campfires, concerts and games.

Then one day two boys came over to our carriage abode and asked us to lend our tablecloths — the ones the army had used — for a dinner for the Lord Mayor of Dublin, Alfie Byrne, on his annual visit to the Glencree boys at Gormanston. The Dowlings would be invited, and the three young Dowling boys could join in the entire Sports Day and festivities.

If they had said the Pope, Mr de Valera or Charles Chaplin, it would not have excited us more. Alfie Byrne was more popular, more loved, more written about, more photographed, more voted for, more caricatured, and more times Lord Mayor of Dublin than anyone alive or dead. To shake hands with this great handshaker of all time, this bowler-hatted, morning-suited, silver-haired, silver-moustached, smiling, generous, charitable dynamo, was a dream come true. But stop! The shame, the gossip, the humiliation if it was ever discovered that our famous tablecloths were actually well-washed, well-ironed, well-starched, well-slept-in bedsheets!

To hell with caution! Nothing ventured, nothing won. Of course we would be happy to lend our tablecloths to grace the Lord Mayor's table.

What a day! Three-legged races, sack races, relay races, sprints, high jumps, long jumps, soccer, Gaelic football, tug o' war, cans of boiled sweets, ice-cream in buckets, barrels of lemonade, lemon soda, sarsaparilla, mountains of cakes, sandwiches, crates of milk, and prizes, it seemed, for everything and for everyone.

From then on, and for years to come, the Dowlings were accepted as part of the reformatory family. I can still see the boys in their tan canvas shirts, shorts, wool stockings and ankle boots. Most of them smoked, though it was against the rules. They stood, one hand tucked into their shorts; then, after a quick look around, drew out the hand, cupping a cigarette butt between thumb and forefinger, hot end toward the palm; then a fast gulp to inhale, the hand returned to its hiding-place and the inhaled smoke would be blown sideways from the mouth.

Great hares shared the airfield with the old aeroplanes, but rabbits were everywhere then. They would make cheap additions to the Dowling dinner, if you could catch them. We failed miserably with stones, sticks, catapults and pellet-guns. Occasionally a friendly local would give us a plump grazer, but they refused to share the secret of rabbit-catching.

One day, one of them relented. We swore we'd never tell the secret if he imparted it. 'All right. Get a big stone, as big as a dray horse's hoof. Put it, just before sunset, outside the rabbit's burrow. Don't let him see or hear you. Put stones outside as many burrows as you want to catch rabbits. Then get a canister of pepper. Shake plenty of pepper on the top of each stone. Then go home to bed and get up at sunrise, when the rabbits does go out in the fields. You'll want to pick up your dead rabbit before some other person or animal gets him.'

'But how does he get killed?' we asked, wide-eyed.

'Rabbits are very inquisitive. When they come out, they'll see the stones that were not there the night before. They'll smell the pepper and it'll make them give a terrible sneeze. Their heads will crack forward against the big stone and kill them dead!'

It took many sunsets, sunrises, big stones, pepper-canisters and miles of walking before we gave up on catching them that way!

I learned to swim one of the first summers in Gormanston; the girls taught me on 'our' beach, on the south cheek of Ben Head. Any fear I had of the water was dispelled as we played 'Ring-a-ring-a-rosy, a pocketful of posies, asha, asha, we all fall down.' Sixty years later, in a small town in Derbyshire, I found out that that song was sung by the children of the town, all of whom perished in the Great Plague in England. The town is still there; it is called Eyam. They fell down dead. We fell with a laugh and a splash into the cold salt sea.

Certainly, for as long as I can remember, I had a healthy interest in sex. In Gormanston we watched roosters toppling hens, an eager heifer being brought to a powerful bull, and the distraught cow fighting to get back to him after a quick mounting that was satisfactory from the breeding point of view but only made the cow eager for more. In every field, and sometimes on roads, we saw four-legged animals mount each other — bullocks, cows, goats, sheep, dogs. We even understood the jokes: 'A man and a woman were riding along on a tandem bicycle and a dog came out and threw a bucket of water over them!'

No adult at home, in church or at school ever talked about reproduction, though. We were supposed to acquire the knowledge by osmosis, as they themselves probably had. It wasn't until I was twenty-two years old, when I told my mother I was going to England to break into theatre, that she said vaguely, 'You'll have to be very careful over there.'

'Don't worry,' I said, 'I know all about women.'

'It's not just women you have to worry about over there,' she said as pointedly as she could.

'Don't worry,' I laughed. 'I know about that too, I can take care of myself.'

I did somehow take care of myself, but I know now I was lucky. The repressed youths and men I encountered were not violent, nor did they frighten me. Still, I wish I had been warned about these possibilities and told how to deal with them.

There was a young man who worked on a farm near Gormanston. He was a grown-up to me, maybe seventeen. I liked him. He let me help with the cows and the horse, with cutting, stacking and, best of all, bringing in the hay. First we'd rake it into long lines about twenty yards apart; then we'd turn it with forks and leave it a few days to dry. Then, after making small trams or haycocks to dry it further, we'd build them into six- or seven-foot 'cocks' and tie each one down with a *sugán* or hay-rope, laden with two stones or bricks. When they were dry, we'd take a 'bogie' — a low, flat cart — back it up to the haycock, tip up the front and push the bottom under the hay, put a halter from the front of the bogie around the haycock and winch it up along the flat bottom. When it hit the balance point it would click the base back down flat, into position. At day's end, there was a slow drive home on the bogie, lying against the dry hay, singing cowboy songs and dreaming cowboy lives. To me, this work was the very essence of the joy of a farming life. I felt that loss of self-consciousness, that feeling of oneness with the world, that I would later feel only on stage or during sex. And it was good!

It was not, however, a romantic life to a strong young lad working long hours for little pay. He talked, out in a hay-field, of showing me something that was 'great to do'. When we'd had our sandwiches and milk, he told me to lie in the grass and he'd lie on top of me, like we were lying on the bogie, bouncing along. Fully clothed, he lay there bouncing up and down. When eventually he stopped, he said I should lie on him. I did, but I was bored with this 'game'. I could see no point to it, and so we went back to doing the hay. I don't remember him telling me not to tell anyone, but I told Paul. He allowed that the same had happened once with him. Next time, Paul said, he'd come along. Somehow I knew it was wrong, though I didn't have any sense of why.

Another day Paul and I went cutting thistles with the young man in a big field on Ben Head. We stopped for lunch. He led us under a hawthorn bush. It was like he had a little hideout there. After we ate, he joked about showing us something and took out his mickey. It looked awful, all veins. I know now he masturbated sitting in front of us. Whether I actually turned away or mentally turned off, or whether he stopped, I don't know; I have no memory of an orgasm. Nor would I have understood one then. It was a kind of stunning experience, put into a compartment in my memory and never opened. I didn't even associate it with two or three similar experiences in earlier and later years. What they all had in common was that I got out of the encounters with good-mannered evasion, without confrontation or blaming the perpetrator, and with no sense of enjoyment — and also with no under-standing at the time, no questioning of what drove these men. And, more astonishing to me now, with no damage to me. Gormanston and my love for it remain unscathed.

Soon, it seemed too soon, the family rumours that we would be moving out of Mount Merrion came true. Word was given to us that Mammy was selling the house and we were moving nearer to the city. It had to do with Marie (working in town and going steady with Jim O'Hanlon, a senior officer in the Civil Service) and Kitty, a receptionist to a chiropodist, being nearer their offices, and Carmel going to commercial college. More urgently, it was about paying debts and lowering living costs. We boys were to go to St Mary's

College, Rathmines, run by the same priests who had Blackrock College. Rugby was the game of choice there, and these colleges fielded official teams for every age group. We'd have college caps and college blazers with the college insignia on them. S-N-O-B! We'd live in Marlborough Road, Donnybrook, within walking distance of school.

We had regrets about leaving Mount Merrion, especially the woods, the lawn, the fields, and friends. Of course, we swore we'd visit them and they'd visit us all the time.... We seldom did. They seldom did.

However, that is not true of Mammy's or my sisters' friends. If anything, we saw more of them after the move; Marlborough Road was 'handier' for most of them. They were wonderful, truly friends in need and friends indeed. I especially loved, we all especially loved, Anne O'Reilly. Stylish, beautiful, with the whitest, evenest teeth I have ever seen, and great, smiling, sad, loving eyes. She adored us, especially when we were muddy, dirty, tousled, and sticky from playing, fighting, or stuffing ourselves with the chocolates and toffees she always brought with her.

She also brought her fiancé, Charles David Knox Pebbles — we always called him David — later her husband. They had no children; they wanted to adopt me and take me to their enormous sheep ranch in New Zealand, near Christchurch. At first my mother saw it as just a romantic joke, but gradually she realised that Anne and David were serious. She talked to me about it, told me that it would give me chances that she, in her circumstances, could not provide. I was enchanted with the idea of living a cowboy lifestyle on a sheep ranch! My mother came around slowly and painfully to agreeing to the adoption 'after the war' if Anne, David and I still wanted it. But David was killed stepping out of an aeroplane near the German border with France, the day before the war ended. The decision never had to be made.

There were so many others, too, who made music in my heart: Miss Nell Clarke, Brendan McGee, Kitty Gilligan, Vivien Dachus, Ernest Sutton, Nell Brogan, Dougie Haig and his father, Bunny O'Reilly, brothers- and sister-in-law, Jim O'Hanlon, Paddy McCarroll, Betty Kielty, and I'd have to say my favourite brother-in-law, Brian O'Daly, the pilot.

We made the move to 31 Marlborough Road, Donnybrook, in the summer of 1942. I was thirteen years old. We were not renting the whole house, but we weren't just moving into a flat — oh, no! We had, as we would quietly insist, half a house! Actually we had two-thirds, though one third of it was not quite a basement but a garden flat.

Marlborough Road began at Morehampton Road. A row of some fourteen two-storey brick houses on either side of our road gave way, a little humbly, to tall, red-brick, three-storey Victorian houses with impressive granite steps leading to recessed, fanlighted and brass-knockered heavy doors. We lived in the second of these houses. Oh yes, we were a step above buttermilk! Rows of houses continued on both sides of the road, interrupted only by the grounds and buildings of Muckross Convent for Catholic Girls on the left, up to Ranelagh Road and Sandford Protestant Church and Hall, which looked down, pleased with themselves, on our respectable road. For a time Sandford Hall supported the best Saturday-night dances ('hops', as we called them) for miles around. Neither the Catholic nor the Protestant clergy were too pleased with that kind of inter-sectarian action!

If you cross Morehampton Road towards the American Embassy and Ballsbridge, on the edge of the footpath you will find our telephone, in a public phone box! It was the only telephone we Dowlings ever had until my mother left Marlborough Road nearly twenty years later. Continue past the phone box and you are in Herbert Park, which stretches on both sides of a tree-lined railing and a gently curved road. Beautifully kept, it had tennis courts and a large duck-pond that also welcomed swans and toy boats. There were walks, flowerbeds, lawns, trees, and bushes, all of which we enjoyed over and over again through four seasons, year after year.

The bushes, of course, I came to enjoy the most. In one of these bushes, about a year after we arrived in Donnybrook, I lay with a veritable angel — I will call her Angel: pretty and my own age, about thirteen and a half. We kissed and hugged and pushed our bodies against each other so hard and so excitingly and so long that the unstoppable force met the immovable object and exploded in my trousers. It gave me the most uncomfortable, undignified walk home of my life as I tried to keep the sticky, cold mess away from my bare legs and out of sight of Angel, passers-by, and whomsoever I might find at home. I must have succeeded; I don't remember any remarks, scolding, or consequences of any kind.

I quickly learned that Angel knew more than I did. We did not, however, progress beyond those particular gymnastics. I swiftly learned to provide handkerchiefs for myself in convenient pockets when I went out with her — until confession and conscience moved me to 'give her up', little prig that I was.

Indeed, I didn't progress much past that point, sexually speaking, until just before my twenty-first birthday. Feeling bosoms and thighs led in time to touching 'the holy of holies' and to what we misnamed 'dry rides': climaxes without flesh contact! It never occurred to me for years that I would enter a girl until I married her. Contraceptive shields — 'French letters', we called them — might be joked about ('the grand old man of French Letters') or referred to in stories, but they were illegal in Ireland, they were condemned by the Catholic Church and they cost money which we didn't have. I don't think I actually saw one until I was married and in the Abbey!

It's not surprising, then, that when I finally did use one, it led directly to the end of my relationship with the Holy Roman Catholic Church — but that's another story.

Jack, who had joined the Irish Army as a private soldier early in the Emergency, had been working in Navan as a draughtsman and staying with family friends, the Kieltys. They had two shops, four sons and a beautiful daughter, Betty. Jack and Betty fell in love during this period, and Betty came to Dublin to work in Arnotts, and stayed with us. We adored her. In a real sense she became the fourth Dowling girl — if not actually a sister, one of the family.

Jack, who was stationed in Athlone with an Engineers Company, in some way acted very intelligently — we always said heroically — to put out a big fire in an Athlone woollen mill and to stop it spreading. This led him pretty directly, via corporal, to a Commissioned Officers' Course, which he passed with flying colours. Jack and Betty became engaged when he got his Sam Browne belt, officer's uniform and second lieutenant's single bar on each shoulder.

In the meantime, tennis had become a love match for my eldest sister, Marie (whose Civil Service salary had kept the wolf at our door from becoming a tenant), with a handsome, well-educated, likeable, quiet steady drinker and winning tennis player, Jim O'Hanlon. Jim, as a rising civil servant, would be able to keep her in the comfort she was not always accustomed to.

As it turned out later, he didn't. He drank his wages, almost all of them, in the first few days of every month for years. Eventually he beat the habit, though not till he had created, in all, eight brilliant, wonderful children. Truly, theirs was a wonderful love that lasted more than fifty years. 'Love,' Marie told me once, 'is shared experience.' They gave me my first nephew — made me an uncle at thirteen! I remember running down Marlborough Road with Sam, shouting out to the world, while leaping up and down on the footpath with sheer joy, 'I am an uncle!' They called their first Redmond, after the famous rapparee Redmond O'Hanlon. Anyhow, Redmond, now a professor of French and Theatre at University College Dublin, is one of my favourite people in the world. He is a wine connoisseur, from time to time writing a wine column, and he is still a joy.

On the theory that two couples can get married as cheaply as one, Jack and Betty and Marie and Jim were going to get married on the same day, early in February 1942, in the same church (the Sacred Heart in Donnybrook), and share the same reception afterwards in the Haddington House Hotel on the seafront in Dun Laoghaire. The hotel was owned by 'a lady from Trim', my mother's home town. I think Mammy had arranged a special deal, which she needed to, as the Kieltys had come out against Jack marrying Betty —

'much as they liked him'! But they wanted more than a bar on each shoulder of a second lieutenant for their only daughter. Now a bar in each town, or even one in either town — that would be a horse of a richer colour! Not that any of us blamed them. We did not agree with them, but we understood their feelings: what good are two bars if you can't sell drink in them?

Well, the Irish government decided that second lieutenants who got married after the end of January that year would not receive marriage allowances, so Jack and Betty hurriedly altered their sacramental strategy and set the splicing service for a late-January date. Jim and Marie finished second in the marital sweepstakes. Sam and I were the real winners: within two weeks we got two wedding breakfasts, two collections of coin of the realm from the well-wined wedding guests, and two days off from school! The Kieltys, Auntie Jo and Uncle Jack, changed their colours literally at the last minute and joined happily, to everyone's delight, in the race to the altar. They became great parents-in-law and grandparents.

None of them lived happily *ever* after, but the two couples lived happily often enough after. At any rate, they lived a deal happier than Brenda and I did in my first marriage, my mother and father in theirs, or my grandfather Sam Kelly and grandmother Agnes in their ill-fated disunion.

The next four years were taken up with two things: my new school and girls. Needless to say, I did not apply myself to the former in nearly as ardent or successful a way as to the latter!

What I did enjoy was rugby at St Mary's. Togged out in a white-collared jersey, white rugby 'knicks', knee-length blue woollen stockings with white turned-down tops and white-laced real leather rugby boots, with a white star on your left breast, you were spotless as you trotted out onto the field. Shoulders hunched, hands in pockets, you trotted purposefully until you were thrown a swift pass. You caught it effortlessly and whipped it expertly but casually to a teammate, or punted it high in the air, as the Mary's supporters clapped and chanted, and the sun's rays caught the brilliantined, perfectly combed sheen of your hair.... Better than being an altar boy! Nearly as good as a solo curtain call at the College play.

The only thing was, I wasn't on the under-13s team in my first term at St Mary's. I was the first substitute. As first sub, you put on your togs and joined the team for the warm-up; then, when the referee blew the whistle for kick-off, you retired to the sidelines, where you acted as linesman and secretly dreamed of the day when you would actually be on the team.

The first match of the season was against Terenure College, our nearest neighbour and therefore our greatest rival. As we togged out, word went around that Ulick O'Connor, our star player and scrum half, had not arrived.

Fifteen minutes before kick-off, our trainer, Father 'Freddy' Fullam, came in. 'Vincent Dowling, if O'Connor isn't here by the time we're ready to start, you'll play scrum half.'

Fifteen minutes later, on the big rugby pitch in front of the College, the surrounding walls and railings lined with spectators, the whistle was blown. Terenure kicked off, and the ball and fifteen giants were stampeding towards me.

I caught the ball, cried 'Mark,' dug my heel into the soft grass and hugged the ball to my breast. It seemed as if all fifteen of them tackled me at once! I emerged still holding the ball; the ref signalled that it was a good mark and I had a free kick. As I walked back the requisite ten yards I saw the puzzled face of Ulick. He was on a bike, his togs in a knapsack over his shoulder, supporting himself with one foot on the railings of the rugby pitch.

From then on I was everywhere. I couldn't do anything wrong. Long, smooth passes to get our back line moving; quick darts around the blind side; short kicks from the base of the scrum over the heads of the other team; catching, dodging, kicking, tackling, scoring.... St Mary's thought they had found another rugby star.

They hadn't. I never played that well again. However, I played well enough to keep my place in the Under-13s and went on to play scrum half in the junior cup team. And, more than fifty years later, I still have dreams where I am called from the grandstand in Lansdowne Road International Rugby grounds to play for Ireland!

Walking around the territory between home and school, I would be away in my own reverie, often having serial adventures accompanied by Gene Tierney. It must have been after seeing her with Tyrone Power, John Carradine and George Saunders in *A Son of Fury*, where she wore a sarong and a white flower in her hair. I made those stories last, sometimes for weeks. Once, as I passed Waterloo Road, with still a half a mile to walk home, I actually finished the Gene Tierney story. It had led me from getting word from Gene, in a bottle washed ashore on the sands beneath Ben Head in Gormanston, calling for help to save her from the wiles of a George-Saunders-like Hollywood villain, to stowing away on the *SS Irish Elm* to America, a Pony Express ride across the States, train robberies, cattle drives, stagecoach hold-ups, and Indian raids and maidens to be rescued in every instalment — right to a swimming pool in Hollywood, where I outwitted the crafty Saunders and drunken John Carradine and saved the saronged and beautiful film star, then dived back into the pool to save her white floating magnolia, to the music of 'Underneath the Blue Tahitian Moon', which swelled up as she melted into my arms.

Then came the realisation that the story was over and I had nothing to look forward to. I determined then and there that I must never again allow my story to end until I had found that one perfect girl I was sure was waiting for me. In the meantime, the search, not the arrival, drove me on.

Latin was taught by the President, the Very Reverend Father Peter Walshe — 'Pete', the boys called him behind his back. With his tiny head, his baby face, and his tall, fat body under the long soutane, he always reminded me of one of those pear-shaped dolls that, no matter how you push them over, always bound mindlessly upright again. His was the easiest of all our classes. He always gave good marks, and seldom, if ever, sent a boy out. He sat up in front of us and read from Virgil's *Aeneid*, in Latin and then in English. Sometimes he would ask a student to translate a line into English; if the student didn't know it, Pete would call on another boy. By that time, every student in the class had taken a quick peep at the key at the back of the book.

'O'Neill,' Pete squeaked. '*Forsam et haec olim menissere.* Translate!'

'Eh....' said Larry O'Neill, grimacing and squinting in an attempt to give the impression that he knew the English but it just wouldn't come out.

'Dowling,' squeaked Pete, as I tried to close the key innocently.

'Someday —' I started to translate.

He interrupted me harshly. 'What have you under your hand?'

Pete had never forbidden us to have recourse to our key — until a week earlier. Unfortunately, I had missed several days of school the previous week — including that one.

'My English key, Father,' I said.

'Your English key,' he repeated, slowly, incredulously. 'I told you in the last class that I would make an example of any boy using a key in this class, and by heaven I mean to. Now —'

'I never heard that, Father. I was —'

'You are a liar as well as a cheat,' he said witheringly. 'Get out of here this minute, boy. Go to my office and wait there. I'll teach you a lesson you'll never forget! *Out*, I said!' And I went.

His office was on the second floor. Big windows with lace curtains looked out over the senior rugby field, the Lower Rathmines Road, and the blue-domed church of Our Lady of Refuge — I believed implicitly in her in those days, but she proved to be no help. I thought to myself: *He's making a mistake; when I tell him about being away from school, it will be all right....*

The door opened and he was there. 'Father,' I said, 'I —'

'Lean over that chair.' He turned a mahogany chair's leather seat towards me, put down the books he was carrying, and picked up a long, slim bamboo cane.

'Father, on my word of honour —'

'Lean over that chair, I said. I won't tell you again.' And he flexed the cane.

I leaned over and grasped the sides of the seat. He slashed my bottom again and again, full force, till I thought he would never stop. I don't know if I cried out. I couldn't stop farting, and the humiliation of that, and the pain of the cane, had the tears flowing freely down my face.

Finally — from exhaustion, I think — he stopped. 'Go down to your next class,' he said.

I remember nothing until I came into the science room, slowly and painfully, and tried to explain my lateness to the science master. 'Never mind,' he said. 'I know.' I cried then, a little. The kindness after the injustice, I suppose.

Early on in my time at St Mary's, one brother cast me in the annual play as a young boy saint. It was hard to tell which of us were playing girls and which boys in this deadly dull piece of 'ancient' Irish piosity, as we all wore linen robes, painted with Celtic designs, that looked suspiciously like skirts. Apart from this, I did play a girl, in a skirt, for a Boy Scout Jamboree in the Main Hall of the college. I got a lot of laughs, but mainly where there should have been none. From these two inauspicious starts, no one would have thought I had a future anywhere near the stage.

It never occurred to us boys to report the 'sexual advances' of this brother. However, a year after I was 'encouraged' to leave St Mary's, I learned that a classmate of mine had told his older brother. The brother, realising that the teacher's goings-on were familiar from his own recent days at St Mary's, had the good sense to bring it to their father's attention. The resulting brouhaha must have been enough for the heads of the Holy Ghost Order to notice.

But no criminal charges ensued, no advice to parents or warnings about predatory behaviour; no, it led only to the transfer of the brother from our day school to Rockwell College, Co. Tipperary. I learned from my brother Sam, who went to Rockwell for a time, that the offending brother was put in charge of the boys' dormitories. There he, if not the boys, lived happily ever after.

It is ironic that during this period, the Very Reverend Dr McQuaid, Archbishop of Dublin and a Holy Ghost Father, forbade Catholics from attending the 'Protestant' Trinity College Dublin, on pain of mortal sin. Clearly he was more concerned with the effect on our souls of Protestant professors than with the effect of Papist paedophiles on our more physical properties.

While world peace was occupying all our minds, I did my Intermediate Certificate examination. I passed, with honours. I would be in fifth year; I would stand a good chance of two years in the Senior Rugby Team; I might matriculate the following June, and even if I failed that year, I would surely get the 'matric' with the Leaving Certificate, in 1947, and I would not yet be eighteen years old. Things were looking pretty good — for about an hour!

During my first class on the first day back after holidays, I was told to go up and see Father Murray. What could I have done now? Father Murray was the Dean of Studies and you were sent to him for corporal punishment (something I had had occasion to receive at least once in my time there).

I knocked, entered and was invited to sit down. That threw me. This was the first time I had been asked to sit down in this room. Kneel down for confession, yes; hold out my hand for three, six or even ten of the best, yes! I sat down gingerly.

'You got honours in your Intermediate?'

'Yes, Father.'

'Not in Irish?'

'No, Father, but I did well enough in Maths to make up for it.'

'But you'd want Irish for the Civil Service.'

'Yes, Father. I hope to get my matric in June, and any subject I don't get this time I can try again in sixth year.'

'What do you want to do when you leave school?'

'Be a farmer, Father.'

'Have you or your family got a farm?'

'No, Father.'

'Or the money to buy one?' He was very polite. There was no trace of sarcasm in his cultured voice.

'No, Father.'

'Well ...?' He raised his dark eyebrows quizzically.

'Get a good job, Father, I hope.'

'What would you say to a good job now, Vincent? A good job with a future?'

'Now, Father? ... Well, I'd have to ask Mammy. What kind of job, Father?'

'An office job. Junior clerk in a very prominent Scottish insurance company, in their Dublin office. Of course you would have to be interviewed first. But the father of one of our boys, Alan Baker, has just been appointed Manager for Ireland of the Standard Life Assurance Company. He has asked us to find him a clever, well-spoken Mary's boy with honours in math and English in the Intermediate.... They are not, being British, interested in Irish-language skills.' He gave a faint smile. 'You would be the first Catholic ever to be employed in their office. What do you say?'

'Thank you, Father, it sounds very interesting —' Already my imagination was racing wild on dances and girls. ' — but I'd have to see what Mammy says.'

It was arranged that I would rush off to talk to my mother, as the interview slot was the following morning. By the time I got to where she was, at a wedding in my cousin's house, I was completely sold on the idea. Thirty-two shillings and six a week, and at least two and six of that would be my own pocket money. No more school, no more of that brother making sexual advances, no more homework, no more slaps....

Mammy was, as I had thought she might be, dismayed. I spoke strongly in favour of the idea, talking about the help I could give our household budget, more ailing than ever now that the girls were married.

'God knows, Vin,' she said sadly, 'we could do with the money. It would be a big help. But to leave school at your age.... You're only a boy.'

'I'll be sixteen tomorrow,' I said, 'and it's what I want to do. Besides, I won't be leaving school altogether, I'll be going back to do the examinations for the Insurance Institute.' What that was, I hadn't the faintest idea!

'All right, Vincent,' she said finally and very unhappily. 'If it's what you really want.'

'It is,' I said, and kissed her. And I jumped on my trusty bicycle, waving and calling goodbyes, and sailed out across the tram tracks and downhill all the way to St Mary's, lustily singing, above the sounds of the trams, my favourite song:

I'm an old cowhand from the Rio Grande
And my feet ain't soft and my cheeks ain't tanned.
I'm a cowboy that never saw a cow,
Never roped a steer because I don't know how,
And I sure ain't fixin' at learnin' nooow —
Yippe-eye-o-ky-ayyy....

And I rode into the sunset on any hope of a scholarship or a university education. That nobody in the family even considered that I, as an honour student, might go to university was a typical 'sufficient unto the day' piece of Dowling non-thinking, blinkered decision-making.

Mammy, of course, had instantly made the connection between the Dean of Studies making the job offer and the fifteen guineas we owed the Bursar for school fees. I didn't. I just knew nothing! We paid off our debt to the Holy Ghost Fathers over the next couple of years. We owe them nothing. Can the same be said for them?

Ruth Smyrl was the loveliest thing about the office of Standard Life Assurance. About 5 feet 2 inches small, with long lovely black hair, very white satin skin, slim-built and small-bosomed. She smiled easily and often, with devastating effect on my vulnerable sexuality and sensibility. In the office of the Standard Life, like the five or six other female employees, she wore a navy-blue dust coat over her street clothes, though hers had style. Like everyone else in the office, she was Protestant — Presbyterian, to be precise. She was about the same age as I. Her elderly, pipe-smoking, easy-going father had a good job with a big Protestant merchant firm; her mother was a warm, loving, loveable, humorous, white-haired, hospitable woman; her sister Norma was overweight, shy, and really very sweet. They all lived together in a comfortable two-storey red-brick townhouse that opened right onto Windsor Avenue, in Fairview on Dublin's north side. They were Dubliners and proud of it; they were tolerant, but probably would have been happier under British rule. We never argued about this, though. I became almost one of the family. I think, with hindsight, the religious/political atmosphere of the time put them under a much heavier strain than I, or maybe they, realised.

I often slept over — always, of course, absolutely on my own, in Ruth's little room, while Ruth would move in with her sister. Their friends, until I showed up, were mostly Protestant, because that was the way things were. They loved me, as I loved them, and my mother loved Ruth. Both families shared the regret, and conviction, that 'it could never come to anything'. The Catholic Church's *Ne Temere* position, commanding that any children from a 'mixed marriage' *must* be brought up Catholic, was accepted without question on my side of the equation; it was never spoken about by Ruth and her family, but I know it was frightening to them. I didn't consciously think about it; 'sufficient unto the day' and so on. I found, though, that Ruth actually did.

I think I can say we fell in love, Ruth and I, shortly after I started working at the Standard, in September 1945. Before long we spent almost every waking hour of every day, including weekends, together. Promotion came quickly to me. It made some, but not a great difference in my salary. In the Standard Life, we called it 'a Scottish honour' — a better title, but little or no extra money.

Soon I had Ruth as my typist; later, when I was chief clerk and cashier, she was my secretary. After work I would walk her down to her bus, which left from the top of Talbot Street, beside Nelson's Pillar — an artistic, architectural, historical landmark and lovers' meeting-place, wantonly destroyed about twenty years later in the name of Irish nationalism — 'a hard wallop at the British Empire'!

For a time her people were my people and where she went, I went. It was because I didn't want her to do anything without me that I literally followed her to the Brendan Smith Academy of Acting.

As soon as I started acting classes, I was hooked. Acting was living! I was finding out what I was meant to do, why I was alive, what I was really *for*. In my first term, I was cast as George in Thornton Wilder's *Our Town*; the *Dublin Opinion* reviewer said, 'Vincent Dowling had the spirit of the thing in him.' Then I knew I wanted to go on and do the whole two years of the course. Ruth had found that it was not for her, that I must choose her or the stage. I chose the stage. I have never regretted it — yet!

At the end of my first year, Brendan Smith invited me to have breakfast with him in his flat on Fitzwilliam Square West, to discuss transport arrangements for an upcoming tour. The house was set in an elegant row of red-brick Georgian houses. The Smith place was on the second floor, nice, but modest. I had never been there before, and was never there again — usually, meetings would be at the Academy in South Great George's Street; and perhaps it was the out-of-the-ordinary venue for this one that prompted him to tell me of his own background, something he never told any other student or member of his company that I know of. It was a simple story, but it led me to see him in another light.

He told me this had been his parents' place. The father had died many years earlier. His mother, Gretta Smith, was still living there. I knew her and really liked her. She played the piano in Robert's Café on Grafton Street, and in 'the pit' (which was actually a tiny side stage with its own curtains) of the Gate Theatre. It was going with his mother to the theatre, as a youngster, that got Brendan into 'the profession'. He started with boy roles and later became stage manager — sometimes actor — for Micheál mac Liammóir and Hilton Edwards at the Gate Theatre Company. He left them to give his full attention to the Brendan Smith Academy of Acting when it took off. Even then, he told me, he had intended to have his own professional company and theatre in Dublin. I can see Brendan, sitting at the breakfast table, his chubby face and frame, his rueful smile, one forefinger twisting and stretching a single strand of brown hair from the balding patch at the back of his round head.

'My father was English, came over here to Dublin after the Great War,' he told me. I gathered he had had a respectable but not especially remunerative office job of some sort. He had met and married Brendan's mother; they moved into the flat and had Brendan and his sister. 'Somehow, Ireland completely killed his spirit,' Brendan said of his father. 'He couldn't function here. Eventually he just gave up working altogether.'

Only for his mother giving music lessons, playing at Robert's, and knowing Micheál and Hilton and getting the job at the Gate, he didn't know how they would have survived. 'Even as it was,' he told me, 'we lived hand-to-mouth.' A situation not unknown in the Dowling household! I could see it all, understand it absolutely. 'Nice people with nice manners but they got no money at all,' as the song says! It was as familiar to me as the back of my hand. I remember, clearly, thinking as I left, *That's why Mr Smith* (I wasn't yet calling him Brendan) *will never feel secure — never feel he has enough, no matter how much he has*. I realise now that I suffered from a somewhat similar insecurity, but found, or learned, what enough is.

Brendan and Beryl, with her red-gold hair, white lovely teeth, and sculptured profile (were they married then? Later, I think), became good friends to me. Really good friends.

The reason Brendan had wanted to talk with me was to have me find and buy a vehicle of some kind to transport his recently formed professional acting company on their second tour. The converted ambulance that I had previously found and purchased for him, though 'it had never let them down', was deemed by some of the actresses to be claustrophobic, having no windows on the sides and only two little square ones on the back doors. My instructions were to find something that would carry safely, and without too much discomfort, eight adults, including the driver; that had windows on the side; and that was reliable, of reasonable appearance and a good bargain — in that order. The company would number ten people, but the covered army lorry that carried the scenery, lighting, props, and our 'skips', trunks and cases was in good shape and would transport the other two.

I don't know exactly how much I paid, but I got what they wanted. It was cream-coloured and it had (for those days) a futuristic line, sliding windows almost the length of each side, twin-windowed doors at the rear, and a step up, or down, as the case might be. The engine, tyres, paintwork, driver's and passenger seats were all as good as new. In the back, there was adequate seating space for six people, but no seating of any kind! Brendan elected to have his 'man who made the scenery' fit the interior with secured wooden benches, with enough room for three on each side. The vehicle had been in its first life a spiffy mobile ice-cream van; its horn — or klaxon, as we preferred to call it — played high, childlike notes that could not have been more inappropriate to herald 'a cry of players' such as we, bent on catching the conscience of our audience.

Brendan was really pleased about the whole thing. Even the price — whatever it was. During my time as a student at his school, he had found that, apart from my primary interest in acting, I was a first class stage manager, a good organiser of people and events, meticulously attentive to detail, financially savvy, able to drive a car, dependable, eager, honest, and a quick learner, with a talent for directing — but also with a weakness for pretty girls. I could also, with a little notice, wangle time away from my work at the Standard Life Assurance Company. He used me in all these capacities — and I was more than happy to be used — at the Academy; in Butlins Holiday Camp, at Mosney, where he presented the legitimate theatre shows every Monday night during the summer for the jolly campers; and as his emissary to his professional company on tour through Ireland, on their first year on the road.

I was particularly happy about the last role. I had fallen in love with a beautiful girl, who, as an acting student, had 'starred' in a little independent film — *My Hands are Clay* — which I thought, though she didn't, made her a film star. Her name was Bernadette Leahy.

At the end of her second year as a student at the Academy, and my first, I was stage-managing one of the Monday-night plays at the holiday camp for Brendan, and Bernadette was playing in it. I had driven a hired car down from Dublin, that morning, to set up the show. It was my first paid job in the theatre. After the performance, while the company went over to the Ballroom for drinks and dancing, I persuaded her to come for a drive with me to the Nanny River Estuary at Laytown, which had been a haunt of mine as a child. Of course, romance was in my mind. Harmless romance, though, it was: as always with Bernadette, I got exactly nowhere!

It was about an hour and a half after we had driven out through the camp security check that we arrived back. I'd been told — wrongly, it turned out — by someone who had been to Butlins before, that they'd be dancing and drinking till the small hours. There was a cluster of people around a line of cars as we approached the checkpoint. 'What's going on here?' I thought — and then Mr Smith, unmistakable in his navy-blue blazer, stepped into the lights of my car and waved me down.

He came around to the passenger side, opened the door and said in an icy voice, 'Miss Leahy, get out of that car and get into mine immediately!' As she did, he came round to my side and told me in no uncertain terms what he thought of me and my behaviour in taking a young woman out of the camp on my own, for no good reason, at this time of night, through security, without saying anything to anyone; causing alarm throughout the entire camp, which had been searching for us; bringing him and his company into disrepute; endangering his relationship with Butlins, perhaps for ever. He ended by saying, 'Mr Black will drive back with you. See you go straight home. Return that car first thing in the morning, and don't bother coming to the Academy ever again. *You are expelled.*' As Eugene got in beside me, Brendan turned, got into his little Morris 8 and drove past me without even a sideways glance.

Eugene filled me in on the grisly details. We had been told wrong. Dancing had stopped and the bar closed in the Ballroom about an hour before. Non-campers had to be off the grounds no later than 10.30, and Brendan had to account to the gate security for the exact number who had come in. For visitors, which we were considered, exiting and re-entry was an absolute no. Worst of all was the panic that something had happened to us, when repeated calls put out on the loudspeaker system had elicited no response. We both agreed we had never seen Brendan remotely like that before. I never did again.

Next morning, I returned the car. I remember it well — a blackbeetle-like wreck that I had hired for ten shillings. I practically crawled up the carpetless stairs of 5/6 South Great George's Street to the Academy and shamefully devoured humble pie. I'd have done anything. I knew I wanted, more than I had ever wanted anything, to be taken back, to finish my course and become an actor.

Brendan listened. Expressionless. Slowly twisting strand after strand of hair straight up, then carefully putting it back into place again, so one became almost hypnotised. He believed me. Warned me. Gave me another chance. Never, in all the years that followed, referred to the incident again.

I learned a lot about professional theatre at the Academy, and about the discipline of theatre. The most important lesson, however, was never to take even one drink before a performance. That was one of Brendan's first formal lessons to us. Like many of my closest colleagues in several countries, even a few close friends, I would be dead now, only for it. I learned a lot about the craft of acting at the Brendan Smith Academy. There was never any talk of 'the art' of acting, though, which was a pity. It didn't become the question for me for at least another ten years after that.

And voice! We had a voice teacher, but it was all about 'el-o-cu-tion' and being heard — especially in Butlins, where over the loudspeakers *in the theatre during the performance* there were frequent announcements that 'There's a baby crying in Chalet Number X.' Still, as the poet Louis MacNeice wrote, 'God or whatever means the Good/Be praised' that I went to Brendan Smith. He was right about my weakness for girls, too. I don't think I ever told him that I had only joined his Academy because of Ruth at the Standard Life.

The two years as a student at the Academy were a breeze. Oh, I worked like two ends of a whore, as Patrick Kavanagh would say. I was more confident at the Standard, earned more salary and commission. At home, Jack, Marie, Kitty and Carmel were all married. Mammy and I had Marlborough Road to ourselves most of the time; I had a whole room to myself. Sam was at boarding school at Rockwell, under the 'bentevilent' eye of the infamous brother. And Paul had been callously, cruelly exported to the peace-time Royal Air Force. I played a mean part in that unsavoury playlet. Thoughtlessly, I acted as a decoy to lure him home from a dance at the Orpheus ballroom — only to be confronted, in our home, by a policeman. Paul had stolen and pawned almost everything of value Mammy had.

At the Academy, I was learning acting, stage management, the business of theatre; getting parts in the Academy shows; creating a student company to perform a play in the towns of Trim (Mammy's hometown) and Drogheda (where Eugene Black's people lived). Desmond Grogan — a young director of real promise, who, alas, gave up professional theatre to marry — directed, wonderfully. I produced and starred as the baby-faced Welsh killer Danny in Emlyn Williams's *Night Must Fall*. Eugene, Pat Dix, Madie Shanks, Michael Ryan, and my future wife, Brenda Doyle, made up the cast.

It was one of those periods you find in theatres and theatre classes everywhere: extraordinary talent on every side. Watching, learning from and with, scores of attractive, interesting, interested, young and not-so-young men and women. I could fill pages with their names, their looks, the parts they played; the girls I fell in love with; the ones who fell in love with me, and the ones who I wished had but who didn't! Talking, arguing, dreaming, in class, out of class; walking home in the small hours; sitting in Cafolla's on O'Connell Street, after class or rehearsal, over coffee, chocolate biscuits, pastries, Melancholy Babies and other exotic ice-creams. Planning and doing. Meeting Shaw, Chekhov, Shakespeare, O'Casey, Synge, Tennessee Williams, Priestley, J.M. Barrie, etcetera, etcetera, in play-books, in plays, at the Abbey, the Gate, the Gaiety, the Olympia. Acting! Acting! Acting! Parties! Dances! Picnics! Printing our own newsletter. I was even presented with a scholarship worth ten pounds, by the patron of the Brendan Smith Academy, for my work as a stage manager in the all-female *Children in Uniform* at the Peacock and Gaiety Theatres.

Then the rumours, the announcement, the excitement, when Brendan sent out a full-time professional company. The happy ones who were going, the disappointed ones who weren't. The silence when they were gone. Then the growing certainty, for me, that when my course was done, I was going to be an actor, and that nothing on God's earth would stop me. I wasn't the only one; but so many of them seem to have just vanished. Hard to believe, in Dublin. So many I never saw or heard of again. Some of them, maybe, were our audience over the years? I hope so. Most, I suppose, passed like snow long, long ago, like the gleam in the barmaid's eyes.

4

My Real Life Starts and I Lose My Virginity

If you want to do something like that, why don't you go to sea like your father?

'We are paid, at the Standard Life Assurance Company,' we used to say, 'weakly — very weakly, on the fifteenth of every month!' I got my final month's pay, plus three weeks' holiday money, on 15 June 1950. That same day I became a professional actor. I started rehearsals for a season of ten plays at the Town Hall, Portstewart, Northern Ireland, presented by Brendan Smith Productions. I was to play the 'juv', as the wanted adverts in the Stage column, on the back page of the *Irish Independent*, would say — the juvenile lead — in most of the plays, play the 'juv/char' (juvenile/character) in a couple, direct some others, and act as business manager-cum-public relations.

I got six pounds sterling as actor/director and another two pounds for the business end of things — a total of eight pounds per week. This had to cover lodging, eating, washing, cleaning, chasing girls, and other diversions. A month earlier, on 15 May, I had given my written month's required notice to the Standard Life and surrendered the small policies held there on my life, a bloody stupid thing to do. I should have increased the 'sums assured'; they were 'with profits', which were always high at the Standard. It was typical of my 'sufficient unto the day' way of responding to things.

When I handed my notice to HVB — Mr Henry V. Baker, the pinstripe-suited, natty-bowtied Secretary for Ireland of our illustrious mutual company, founded in Edinburgh in 1825 — I was the senior member of the office staff, next in order of importance to HWM — Harry W. Mullock, Assistant Secretary for Ireland. I, VGD (one did not have to use three initials, but after my secretary Ruth Smyrl used 'VD/RS' on my first batch of correspondence, it was suggested that I should use my middle initial!) held a permanent, pensionable position — chief clerk and cashier. I was undoubtedly in line for the next inspectorship, a position with company car, expenses, salary and commission. Mr Baker already knew what my letter was about, but he read it anyway, a small figure behind his huge mahogany desk in the centre of his luxurious, skylighted office.

'I should not have let you give your blood for transfusion to Mr Mullock last week. Maybe he'll want to be an actor now, too. Then what would I do?' he said, his eyes twinkling behind his thick glasses, and a tiny tightening of his lips, which was all he allowed himself in the way of a smile towards a subordinate.

'Thank you, sir,' I said, 'for all you did for me.' After all, he had brought me into the company, the first Catholic ever to be employed by the Standard Life above the level of porter.

'Good luck, Dowling,' he said. I always cringed inside when he called me, or anyone else, by surname only. 'Well, don't forget us when you are famous. Hope you do well,' said HVB, as he shook my hand.

'Yes, sir. Goodbye, sir!' I closed the door softly behind me, noting that he had turned the red light off and the green light on, allowing the next entrant to 'knock and enter'.

Like a special old photograph, I see in my mind's eye Mammy and me standing at the window of our damp dining-room, looking out at the uncut grass sloping up to the garden level, the black iron railings and gate, and beyond them the Victorian terraced houses across from 31 Marlborough Road.

'Well, I gave my notice today, Mammy. A month from now I'll be an actor,' I said, as I gave her my pay, less my pocket money. 'There's an extra three weeks there. Holiday money.'

'Thank you, dear.' She looked at me sadly, with much love. 'Oh, Vin,' she said quietly, 'you know I've never tried to stop you doing something you really wanted to do.'

'I know that, Mammy,' I muttered.

Then, after a short silence while she struggled to think calmly: 'If you want to do something like that, why don't you ... go to sea like your father?'

Considering her own feelings about him, and what going to sea had done to his body, his career, and their lives, it was an extraordinarily generous thing to say. Extraordinarily funny, too. I didn't know whether to laugh or cry, so I said, 'Don't worry about me, I'll be all right. I'll be great, if I don't die of hunger. I'm starving. Let's have our tea!' We did, and she never questioned my decision again.

Fuzzy images of rehearsals in a basement; a clear mental 'collage' of packing the company truck with everything we would need for our ten-week season of ten plays; the ruined stone storage space that Brendan Smith rented, over the Dodder River at Clonskeagh. Some twenty canvas 'flats', one side painted white for country-kitchen settings, the other side 'stippled' and reddish-pink for drawing-rooms; assorted windows; fireplaces; doors; one half-door; one French window; a set of stairs about six steps high; black masking flats; a sky-blue backcloth; heavy black velour drapes; 'legs', 'borders', and a 'skip' (basket to you) of set dressings would fill our needs. Then there was the lighting: a dimmer board with six dimmers; two wooden troughs for 100-watt lamps, which could be used separately, or plugged together, for footlights; three metal troughs, each about eight feet long, for overhead light; four 1,000-watt floodlights; about six 500-watt spotlights; six metal stands, with heavy iron bases; some thirty braces to hold the flats upright, and large hand-turned 'screw-eyes' to hold them in place on the wooden stage; and a grey canvas stage-cloth.

When we got to Portstewart, we weren't allowed to use the screw-eyes on their polished stage. We had to get sandbags and back-breaking weights. We provided our own modern costumes, including evening dress and accessories, but were supplied with 'period' clothes. Furniture, carpets, window curtains, and better set dressings would be borrowed from the shops, hotels and lodgings in Portstewart. Each actor was responsible for his or her own make-up, make-up remover, beards, moustaches, towels and soap. Wigs, if absolutely needed, might be hired, but only for very, very special needs. Talc, silver powder, or paint were the ageing agents preferred by management; they had the added attraction of being paid for by the artists! Brendan wasn't really mean, just miserly — in business, that is. He was a generous friend off stage, especially to me.

All this paraphernalia, except the actors' stuff, was stacked in the store, precariously perched between the large holes in the rotten flooring, twelve feet above the Dodder riverbank, and the smaller, frequent gaps overhead, in the slate roof, through which the June rain poured. Somehow we, the male actors, manhandled it all into the truck, neatly and securely, without losing any actor, box, or flat. And I loved every moment of the doing it, singing out of tune, indeed knowing no tune, but nevertheless singing the whole time, over and over — 'Hi-diddly-dee, an actor's life for me!'

Then, having picked up each actor and actress's personal skip at their homes, Des Perry, Eugene Black, Gerard Parks and I set out, via the Navan Road and Ashbourne, along the road some English king had made for his mistress, to Slane, the very place where St Patrick, in 432 AD, announced his arrival in Ireland with the Paschal Fire. Slane, too, was the birthplace of the poet, Francis Ledwidge, an unspoiled village with at the crossroads four identical period houses, one on each corner, for a rich man's four daughters. I still love to visit, even to think about that village.

Ever nor'-north-west we drove, a gallant band of play-acting pioneers, bringing our 'good news' across the Border between the Republic and Northern Ireland, a border manned by Her Majesty's Customs, backed up by The Royal Ulster Constabulary, augmented by the dreaded B-Specials, to the

Protestant seaside town of Portstewart. The first troupe of Irish Catholic actors in history to occupy the Town Hall for a summer season!

We arrived on the last Saturday in June. My first memories of Portstewart are of the ocean: the small pleasure-boats moored at the rocky inlet at the east end of the Promenade, where I would lose my virginity, after keeping it religiously for twenty years and ten months; the shops on the sea-front; a Dominican convent at the west end; the Town Hall sporting a poster announcing 'Brendan Smith Productions Summer Season'; a shop and restaurant called Black's — 'no relations of mine,' Eugene Black assured us; and the single bottle of Guinness we each had (except Des, who only drank orange) in the little bar further up the Main Street, Doherty's, 'The Anchor'. One drink was all we could afford.

Even now, as I write of our first day in Portstewart, I feel again the happiness in my veins, the anticipation tingling my nerve-ends. I can see the sunlight sparkling on the small waves. The good-humoured, happy, well-dressed holiday-makers jostling, joking, laughing and talking in their articulated, crisp North-of-Ireland accents, over the drums, trumpets, voices of the Salvation Army's uniformed men and women praising Jesus and collecting money for the poor. A single stanza from some obscure translation of 'Omar Khayyam', which was popular in my repertoire that year, comes back.

> *How green the sea, how blue the sky,*
> *And we are living, living, you and I.*
> *The sun shines and our love is near —*
> *How good it is to live, how hard to die!*

I, who have always felt free — except free of fear of being in bed alone in the dark, and of rats — had never felt more free. I was free, for the first time in years, of the longing for some young beautiful maid; yet absolutely confident I would find one, love one, be loved by one. Free, too, of the nagging, subconscious fear that Daddy's two pounds would not arrive on Saturday. Confident that I could earn my livelihood acting, directing, business-managing our little company, filling the seats at our summer place. Confident, above all, that I was where I ought to be — working in a theatre — now, and forever! As the poet T.S. Eliot wrote, 'It was you might say satisfactory.' No! It was bloody marvellous!

Of course, it was madness, too. A play a week for ten weeks! Thousands of lines to learn, and little time to learn them. Unload and store the scenery, props and costumes. Hang the lights. Turn a bare town hall into a theatre overnight. Lay the stage cloth. Make bare rooms into dressing-rooms, with lights and mirrors. Create a box office. Arrange daily visits to hotels, to take reservations. Borrow furniture, dressings and special props. Get a car with loudspeaker to trumpet our productions. Arrange newspaper adverts and interviews. Find somewhere comfortable, clean, and cheap, preferably on the front, where we could lodge and get all our meals. Every week till the end of the season, 'strike' the set, furniture, and props and return the borrowed ones. Erect the next set and do it all again. In addition, perform, direct, stage-manage or 'tech' a show, six nights and one matinée per week. We had Sunday free(!) to do our last work on lines for the Monday opening, do our washing, write letters home enclosing a postal order for two pounds, and have a lot of fun.

Before the first play even opened, Des came round about ten o'clock one night, after rehearsal, to see if we wanted to go for a walk. Eugene and I had found a haven at Miss McTamney's Bank House, smack in the middle of the promenade, across from the ever-changing sea. It wouldn't be exaggerating too much to say we had found heaven, run by a humorous, warm-hearted, white-haired, motherly Protestant angel without wings, prejudice or badness of any kind. It cost us two pounds ten shillings a week, 'all in'. Eugene and I shared a large, comfortable, scrupulously clean back bedroom on the third floor. We also shared a large double bed, which, coming from large families, as we both did, we took as a matter of course. Though we didn't know it then, we wouldn't spend that much time in it together!

'I'm going to have a bite to eat, and then a walk along the front, before bedtime,' said Des.

'Not me. I'm exhausted,' said Eugene. 'Besides, I want to go over my lines before I go asleep.'

'I'll go,' I said. 'Just what I need. Besides, I know —'

'Don't say it, or I'll knock your block off! You — know — your — lines! You must have a sponge for a brain!' he said with mock disgust. 'And don't wake me up coming in.'

'Come on, Des, let's go, or we'll be blamed if he doesn't know his lines.' We were gone before he could think of a good answer.

It was dark when we got outside. The lights were out in most of the shop windows along the front; streetlights were few and far between, making pink pools of light on the path opposite and reflecting in the still sea. Portstewart goes to bed early.

'I've found a little snack bar on the edge of town. It stays open till midnight. A very pretty girl works there. She's a smasher! Just your style.' Des smiled as he cupped his hands to light a cork-tipped Craven A cigarette — 'the man's cigarette that women like,' the advertisement claimed.

Knowing his sense of humour, I pictured a pinched, spectacled, Puritan old maid with her hair tied tightly in a bun. 'I believe you,' I said. 'Thousands wouldn't.' He smiled enigmatically.

Little it was, the snack bar. It had no name on it. A light-bulb without a shade lit the narrow window; a narrower door stood open. The place, which was empty of customers, had a few small white tables with matching chairs, and a counter at the back of the twelve-foot-deep room. The walls were as bare as a newborn baby's bottom, as my mother used to say. However, I had no eyes for any of this on that first visit, for behind the bar counter stood a tallish, slim, lightly tanned young woman with shoulder-length dark hair and a bright, intelligent and, I remember thinking — as we always did in those days — Protestant face. She wore a flimsy cotton dress, with a neckline that was not exactly plunging, but pointing in that direction. It was not see-through, of course, but I remember stifling the thought, *Has she anything on under it?*

'Hello, Desmond,' she said with that tongue-driven accent Northern girls all seemed to have, which sent my heart into dizzying rhythms, as she came out from behind the counter to wipe one of the tables, revealing long, bare, sun-tanned legs, feet with open sandals. 'Is this another actor?'

'Yes. Vincent, this is Heather. Heather, this is Vincent — Brendan Smith Productions' official heartthrob.'

'How do you do?' I smiled, holding out my hand. 'Don't mind Desmond. The sea air goes to his head.'

'I'm grand, thank you. Welcome to Portstewart, Vincent.' Her smile was frank and friendly, her handshake firm.

We ordered sandwiches. Des had tea, to which he was addicted. I had a glass of milk, because I rarely drank tea or coffee before bedtime; we had been told all our lives that they keep you awake. We certainly would have smoked several cigarettes. I smoked in those days: Sweet Afton, sometimes Senior Service, on which I had learned to smoke at the tender age of ten — stole them from the stash which Mammy always brought back when she stayed with Father Luke. Heather didn't smoke, that I can remember.

The snack bar closed at 11.30 most nights. Like most Northern businesses, it didn't open on Sundays in those days. Sunday was the only night we didn't perform. Sunday observance laws, I suppose. Heather didn't know if she would be able to see a play, but she would try. She lived a couple of streets back from the sea, up by the east end, we learned.

'Would you like to go for a walk some night after you close?' I asked.

'Yes,' she said. 'When?'

'Eh ... tonight?'

'I can't tonight. They're expecting me home.'

'Tomorrow night?' I laughed.

'All right, then,' she said, laughing too. 'You don't waste much time, do you?'

'No — with the way Des works us I can't afford to!'

'We won't get many in here at this time of night till the week of the Twalfth,' she twanged. 'The summer holiday season in Portstewart really begins next week. You could come around here about this time tomorrow night, if you like.'

'We'd like,' said Des, imitating her accent. Northern girls have a way of saying 'like' that's so liquid you want to swallow it.

'Sure thing,' I said, swallowing. 'Good night, Heather.'

'Good night, Desmond,' she said, as she came from behind the counter to turn off the lights. Then, putting her hand lightly on my arm: 'Vincent, pull the door behind you, if you don't mind.' I closed it.

'Jesus! Des, you're a genius,' I croaked, over the sound of my thumping heart. 'You weren't kidding — she's gorgeous! Yahoo!' I yelled, taking a run and a jump at a lamppost and hugging it.

'I thought you'd like her,' he said with a tolerant smile, when he caught up with me. 'But I think we better turn in, before you're arrested. Besides, it will be another long day tomorrow.'

'I wish it was longer,' I said. 'They're not half long enough to get everything done. But, Jesus, Des, it's great, isn't it!' It wasn't a question, it was a fact.

'Better than working,' he replied, in a perfect Northern accent, as he blew a stream of cigarette smoke through the top of his Craven A, making it glow in the now-unlit promenade. 'That's your place, isn't it? See you in the morning. God bless you.' The blessing was in the voice of Brendan Smith, and he was gone.

We opened with *Pink String and Sealing Wax*, a Victorian thriller written probably in the 1940s by Maurice Denham. It was set in England. Eugene Black played the Victorian father, Marie Litchfield (I think) the mother, Pauline Delaney a woman of ill repute, Gerard Parks a detective, and I played Albert, the son who gets involved with the woman. I think Des, who was company manager and leading character actor, directed this one. That's all I can remember about it, except that it was a well-made, gripping piece of English drama, and we did it well — very well. Even Des thought so, and he wasn't easy to please. I seem to remember that my character had a young sister. Laurie Morton played her. There may have been one or two other smaller parts in the play. The company would depend for the whole season on this core group.

It was a strong, experienced, versatile 'cry of players', although for Laurie, Eugene, and myself, it was our first contract. For most plays in the remainder of the season, two or three professional players (occasionally a student from the Academy) would be brought up from Dublin, where they were working with Brendan Smith's company at Butlins. One of these professionals was Brendan's wife Beryl, a very fine actress.

Pink String was well received by large audiences. The people of Portstewart, if they felt any resentment towards this South-of-Ireland Catholic acting company, never showed it. Well, they barely showed it, and only once: on the Glorious Twelfth. During the Saturday-afternoon matinée, the Grand Parade of the orange-sashed, bowler-hatted, Lambeg-drum-beating, brass-band-accompanied, anti-Papist-banner-carrying Loyalist Protestant Orangemen took a right turn off the promenade, marched past the Town Hall to the Convent and marched back again! On stage we just talked louder till they were gone.

However, I'm getting ahead of myself. I still had an ignoble role to play in my ordinary life before I arrived at that Glorious Twelfth. I am none too proud of it, but I can't ignore it!

'Bless me, Father, for I have sinned. It is three months since my last confession. I've missed Mass almost every week since Easter, Father. I didn't abstain from meat on ... I think four Fridays. I took pleasure in passionate kissing of girls about ten times, Father —'

'Girls? Plural?'

'Yes, Father, two. And once I — eh ... rode ... the second one. I mean —'

'I know what you mean,' he said dryly. 'Are you going to marry this girl?'

'No, Father.'

'Why not? She may be pregnant.'

'She said she was sure she wouldn't be.'

'Were you practising birth control?'

'No, Father. But she's a Protestant.'

'I see,' he said severely. 'However, I can't give you absolution unless you have a firm intention not to go out with her again.'

'I have, Father. I told her last night I wouldn't go out with her again.'

'Don't be missing Mass and staying so long away from Confession. They help you to resist temptation. For your penance say a decade of the Rosary. O my God ...'

'O my God, I am heartily sorry for having offended Thee [nothing about offending, humiliating, perhaps even damaging this girl]. I detest my sins above every other evil.' The real evil, of course, was that I felt everything was all right now that I had confessed it to this man — who, I firmly believed, had the power to forgive me! I went on believing it, even if for long periods I didn't keep up the practice of my religion. I believed it until my mid-thirties.

Heather had somehow arranged to see, I think, the first night of *Pink String*. Loved it, loved me in it. Came to the little party Brendan gave after it. He wasn't too keen on having a 'local' at the party, but he gave in to my pleading. Afterwards I walked her along the sea-front, around into the street that ran parallel to it, and we kissed in the shadows, passionately, till I said, 'We'd better stop. I'll see you to your door.'

'No,' she said. 'The neighbours would be talking.'

'So what? Let them talk.'

'I wouldn't give them the satisfaction!' She pronounced it 'satis-fahk-shun'.

Then she told me that she lived with her younger brother and sister. Her mother was dead, or had married a second time, I can't remember which, and their father lived away somewhere. She hardly ever saw them. Very occasionally they helped with a little money. That's why she was working at the snack bar; why she didn't want any talk from the neighbours.

The next night, or maybe the night after that, as I walked along the darkened prom, the lights all out, my arm round her waist, when we reached the east end, as if with one mind, we crossed into the rocks around the moorings. She lay down on a mossy patch between rocks. I knelt beside her, rolled over on top of her.

'You can make love to me properly,' she said, simply.

'I can't, it's not safe.'

'Yes, you can. I want you to. It is all right. Really.'

And it was! Until it was over. Then, of course — confusion ... remorse ... guilt. Fear, too. Though I didn't show any of it, she sensed it. She was gentle, considerate, loving, confident. I walked her to the corner of her street. I don't think either of us spoke.

I said nothing to Eugene, and as usual slept well, but woke up early. The enormity of what I had done lay like a sickness on my stomach.

I took Des Perry aside at the first opportunity. 'I've got to talk to you. In private.'

We were rehearsing our second play. We took the walkway along the sea, round the Head, past the convent, and over to the strand beyond. I told him the story of the night before. I told him what she had told me about her family. 'Why would she want to do it with someone she met only a few days ago?'

'Because she likes you. I'd say that she likes you very much. Thinks you like her. Probably thinks it's love with both of you. Maybe it is. Is it?'

'I like her. I like her very much. But why would she ask me to go the whole way?'

'Because she wanted you to go the whole way. Clearly you did too, didn't you?'

'I hadn't even thought about doing that! I've never done *that*, ever. I didn't think I'd ever be in a girl till I was married.'

Des lit a cigarette. He always lit a cigarette if he had to really think about something. 'Were you wearing anything?'

'You mean a French letter? No. I've never even seen one, let alone used one,' I said, truthfully.

'She must have been sure it was safe — her safe period.'

'I suppose.' I'd heard about all that but didn't really know how it worked; but I was afraid to ask and show my ignorance.

'So what's worrying you? A lovely girl likes you, wants to have sex with you. Most fellows would give their right arm for the chance.' He paused, looking at me — summing me up, I suppose. 'I'd get a packet of French letters, if I were you.'

'No. I'm not going to go out with her again. I think she ... Well, I'm not. I'm going to Confession on Saturday, and Communion on Sunday.'

'You think she *what*?' he asked, looking hard at me.

'I ... I don't know. I don't think I should go out with her again.' I couldn't bring myself to tell him what I really was afraid of.

'Far be it from me to tell you to go against your conscience. If you really think you shouldn't go out with her again, then you shouldn't. It's a pity you didn't think about it earlier. But, as the man said, there's no use crying over spilt milk; there's enough water in it already.'

'That's from *The Patsy*.' I said, laughing.

'Yes. But who's the patsy here? ... I'm sorry, I shouldn't have said that. Come on, we'd better be getting back. We'll be late for dinner, and we have only an hour's break. Let's step it out.'

When we got to Bank House, just as I was about to go in, he put his hand on my arm. 'Tell her what you're going to do. Do it nicely. She's a fine young woman. Adios, amigo!' He went on to his lodgings, which were next door to mine.

That night, after rehearsal, I went alone to the snack bar and waited till Heather closed shop. As we walked along the front, she did most of the talking. I answered questions about the day and the rehearsals in mono-syllables. I guess I wanted her to sense there was something wrong.

When we got to the east end, she slowed up as if to cross over to the rocks.

'I'm taking you straight home ... I mean to your street. I'm tired; it's been a tough day,' I said apologetically.

'There is something wrong, isn't there? If there is you should tell me, Vincent.'

I didn't answer, kept walking.

'You don't want to see me any more, is that it?

'It's not that I don't want to,' I hedged, stopping in the shadows, where I had kissed her those other nights. 'I just can't. You see ... I ... I'm a Catholic and you're ... you're not, and I've gone through this in Dublin with a Protestant girl for nearly three years. It's no use. It won't work. It's better to face it sooner than later, for everyone's sake. I know what I'm talking about.'

'I've known you for about a week, Vincent. I wasn't thinking about marrying you. Were you thinking about marrying me?' she asked in that straightforward way that Northern women have, which we Southern men, maybe all Irishmen, seem incapable of.

'No. That's just it. What we did last night is a sin for me, a mortal sin, unless I'm married to you. And I can't go on seeing you, after that, unless I'm going to marry you. And I can't do that, not only because of our different religions, but because I'm an actor. Just beginning. I've given up security, a career, a pension, forever maybe. I can't take on responsibilities, and I can't go on doing what we've done without a resolve to marry, and, as I said, I can't do that — and, to be honest, I don't want to do that....'

She was just looking at me, and I stopped talking. She didn't say anything for what seemed ages.

'I'm sorry you feel like that,' she said, absolutely without sarcasm. She swung round gracefully and walked up the short hill to her home. She didn't look back.

I felt sorry, but also, I had to admit to myself even then, relieved. I had no doubt that she genuinely liked me, and that I liked her; but I was afraid that, consciously or unconsciously, she wanted someone to help her take care of her brother and sister, and that I might be the one. If I went on having sexual relations with her — which I wanted to — sooner or later, I'd get her pregnant. Then, no matter what anyone else thought, I'd feel obliged, and be obliged, to marry her. It was a hell of an argument I was having with myself. And, of course, it was one I was going to win. And I did — at the time.

I know now, have done for many years — knew then, really — that I was wrong, shamefully wrong. I was the one thinking these things. They probably never crossed her mind.

Well, I never really spoke with her again. Des continued to drop by the snack bar, but he didn't talk about her to me. I knew he never would. The few times I ran into her in a shop, or walking along the prom, we exchanged polite, muted hellos and went our separate ways as quickly as decency would allow.

On the way back home, that night, I crossed over to the sea side of the prom. I stood a while looking out on the path the moon made on the still sea, as if I was watching myself on a film. Then, repeating quietly my mother's favourite saying — 'Sufficient unto the day is the evil thereof' — I flicked my cigarette end out into the salt water; and, feeling as if everything was settled, I crossed back and let myself into Mrs McTamney's.

In the big sitting-room on the second floor, someone was playing the piano, and Eugene's bass-baritone was pouring out 'McBreen's Daughters'.

I listened at the door, the actor in me waiting for the applause to finish before making my entrance.

The Twalfth had brought a tidal wave of young, lovely girls to our seashore. Our lodgings were flooded with the loveliest. My built-in lens zoomed in instantly and locked on a vivid, jet-haired, pale-skinned girl, her red lips parted over white teeth, her wide hazel eyes looking into mine.

'You must be Vincent,' said the softest Northern accent I had ever heard. 'I'm Rita.'

Not since the film *White Cargo*, when the jungle storm blew open the bungalow door, revealing the black beautiful face and figure of Hedy Lamarr huskily intoning 'I am Tondelayo,' had there been such a beginning to a romance! The ending would not be quite as tragic, but it would not be a happy one either — nor one that did me much credit.

'Paradise Regained' is certainly what I felt after my absolution for my 'sex sins' and the advent of Rita into my life. I wouldn't have expressed it that way, probably. Milton was not exactly on my reading list that summer!

Not only was this new relationship sexually within the bounds of my sixth-commandment sensibilities, but Rita was a Catholic! It was a relief, after the years of families on both sides of the religious divide lamenting the pity of it that Ruth's and my attachment for each other 'could never come to anything' — though the idea of marriage, in the summer of '50, was 'as far away as from here to Timbuktu,' as my mother used to say. Being an actor, having lovely red-lipped Rita who was mine and I was hers (for the time being, at any rate), plus the fact that Brendan Smith wanted Des Perry, me, and Eugene Black for an autumn and winter/spring tour south of the Border (the Irish one, that is) — that was as far as I could, or wanted to, look into the future.

From the coming of this crowd of young female holiday-makers till they left early in August, every night was party night at Bank House. Late supper for the actors after the show; then upstairs to the drawing-room for piano-playing, singing, dancing — if we kept it slow — 'resimatations' (poems to you), storytelling, and post mortems on the plays. Every actor in the company, plus Brendan, Beryl, Rita, her sister 'Slim' the nurse, her two pharmacist cousins, and Maureen McClure (she and Eugene had fallen in love at first sight), did their same party pieces almost every night. Mine were 'The Green Eye of the Little Yellow God' and 'Paddy's Dream', which ended up:

... And, peeping through the keyhole, said,
'I'm master now, you see,
But I'll give up heaven, keys and all,
If you'll set all Ireland free!'

I wouldn't say that one if Miss McTamney was there!

The actors 'up from Dublin' for one play, and rehearsal thereof, provided a welcome change in the entertainment, as well as in the holiday romancing. Miss Mac — our pet name for our adored and adoring landlady, hostess, friend, nay, surrogate mother — enjoyed it all as much as the rest of us

Well, on the second or third night after the coming of the young female 'flock', Eugene and I were ready for bed, in our pyjamas, toiletries done, and our prayers said. Oh, yes! Even in my most 'sinful' days, I always knelt down and in about two minutes flat recited a list of special intentions, three Our Fathers, three Hail Marys, three Glory Be to the Fathers, an Act of Contrition and God bless Mammy and Daddy and Marie and Kitty and Carmel, Jack and Paul and Sam and Uncle Paddy and Auntie Cis, and make Walter (her mentally handicapped son) better, and please God, let me die first. Bless Father Donnellan and all our relations and friends, in the name of the Father, Son and Holy Ghost, amen!

Then, just as Eugene and I got into bed and were about to take a last look at the lines of the scene we were rehearsing the next morning, the bedroom door burst open; two girls, impish in cotton nightdresses, rushed in, turned off the lights, pulled the blanket up over our heads, switched on the lights again and, laughing the whole time, were gone back to the room next door which five of them shared!

Eugene, a little over thirty then, was square-jawed and square-shouldered, with wiry, wavy black hair, a straight-backed military bearing, heavy black eyebrows over devilishly humorous eyes, and a wicked grin. 'Come on,' said he, his eyes flashing and his Drogheda drawl more pronounced than ever, 'we'll return the compliment.'

As he spoke, he rolled up the legs of his pyjamas above his rugby-forward's calves and knees, then put on his dressing-gown, so it appeared he had no pyjama bottoms on under it. 'Wait till you hear this,' says he, and was off without waiting to see was I with him or no. I wasn't! I was listening, waiting outside their door, wishing I had the guts to go in.

'May I come in?' says he, in a posh, innocent voice.

'I think so,' says one of the girls!

'It's ever so nice of you to invite me,' says my man, keeping up the act. 'Just move over, one of youse. I'll get in beside you when I get this dressing-gown off!'

Shrieks of girlish alarm, hush-hushings, and 'You'll have Miss Mac up here' — and Eugene is back, grinning from ear to ear, his dressing-gown over his arm. He closes the door and begins to roll his pyjama legs down again.

'What did you do?' I asked.

'Let on I was going to get into bed with them. Opened my dressing-gown. For a split second they thought I was going to expose myself. Then they saw my pyjamas rolled up, knew they'd been had. I'm always telling you: it's all in the timing! You should have seen their faces! That'll learn them!'

Well, it did. Over the next few nights we progressed to getting into bed with them. Under the bedclothes? Yes! But strictly aboveboard — cross my heart and hope to die!

On the Saturday night following — and by this time it was accepted that Rita and I were interested in each other — I fell asleep, and slept the whole night there, my arm around Rita. There were four of us in the bed, but all innocent as newborn babes. I know it was Saturday night because the next morning the others slipped off to Sunday Mass — early Mass and Holy Communion — leaving Rita and me asleep. 'Youse looked so peaceful together, we didn't want to disturb yez,' they said later, probably half-joking, wholly in earnest.

Suddenly there was a knock on the door. I was wide awake in an instant. 'Rita....' said a familiar voice — Miss Mac!

Her voice trailed away to nothing as the door opened. She stood there in the doorway, aghast! speechless! stunned!

'Miss Mac —' I started to say, to explain.

'You ... you can't stay in this house — either of you,' she said in a very small voice, and she turned and went down the stairs. I knew somehow she was afraid to say any more, in case she'd cry. I knew that.

Then I realised I was still in the bed. I got out and sat on the edge, numb, looking out on the promenade and the sea. 'How could I have been so stupid?' I kept saying. 'How could I have been so stupid?'

'What will I tell them at home, if I have to leave here?' said Rita.

'You won't have to. She'll believe us, if we just tell her everything the way it happened. She will. I'll get washed and dressed, then I'll go down and tell her.'

'I'll go with you.'

'Only if you want to.'

'I think so,' she said, and I remembered the voice saying that to Eugene. Horrific as our situation was, I laughed.

'Why are you laughing?'

'The way you say "I thank so". It makes me laugh.' It still does.

Well, we went down about fifteen minutes later. She was standing in her bright, spotlessly clean kitchen at the gas stove.

'Miss Mac,' I said, and she turned around. And we told her every detail of the goings-on; and she believed us. Really believed us. The relief — hers as well as ours — was beyond description. Extraordinary, but every moment of that morning feels like a play I have just done.

Oddly, I remember very little about Rita and me in Portstewart after that. She taught me to play 'Lavender's blue, dilly dilly,' on the piano, with one finger. To this day it is the only thing I can play. We promised to stay in our own bedrooms, and Miss Mac didn't want us to tell the others about her involvement. We kept our promise, of course. I had to tell Eugene, though — 'Singing and dancing but none of that!'

I know the girls' holidays ended shortly afterwards. I got some letters from Rita — stupidly, I didn't keep them — and I made plans to see her after the season, when I would visit Father Donnellan in Loughgall, which is quite near Coalisland, her home. She paid a surprise visit for my twenty-first birthday and put on a little party for me — a small cake that wouldn't take twenty-one candles, so we just used one. After the play we cleared a place for dancing. The only records we had were our pre-show and interval music, and though it included my favourite — the can-can from _Orpheus in the Underworld_ — it isn't great for dancing, unless you can-can, and I can't!

It wasn't exactly a memorable evening. In fact, it was a pretty dull coming-of-age. I didn't let myself think about that, of course! I missed Rita, though, when she wasn't there, and — surprising for me in those days — I didn't take up with anyone else!

Still, there's no doubt about it: the plays were the thing! Not that I didn't play; I played golf, most days, quite well, but never up to Eugene's standard — he had real style. I preferred the small rocky links along the seashore; Eugene liked the Championship Course at Portrush. No, for me the plays were the thing. I did well as a business manager, too. Brendan was a very fussy taskmaster, but there was not one complaint or question about my bookkeeping or bank-balancing all season.

The Rotary Club in Coleraine sent word they wanted someone to address the Members' Weekly Luncheon on 7 September, my birthday. 'Sorry, Vincent, it's you,' said Des Perry. It was. For me, this was the shape of things to come for the next fifty years!

They invited me to be a guest at the lunch on 31 August, to see what went on and what would be expected of me. I got the bus from Portstewart and walked from the edge of Coleraine to the small hotel restaurant. No expense accounts for us!

I remember distinctly the Rotary motto — 'Service Above Self' — in blue lettering on a small silk banner, on a flagpole next to the Union Jack — the Union Jack, symbol of British rule. The guest speaker that day was Sir Norman Stronge, Speaker of the North of Ireland Parliament at Stormont. I liked him. He was friendly, unaffected, encouraging. 'An actor is someone who, if you ain't talking about him, he ain't listening,' Marlon Brando is supposed to have said; obviously, Sir Norman Stronge's talk was not about me, and I don't even recollect what it was about. I was too busy thinking about what I would say the next week.

Well, I used 'Service above Self — A Motto for Rotary and the Theatre Too'. The political eminence alone of Sir Norman Stronge made him quite an act to follow. I think I did well. Everyone said so. Fortunately, I was absolutely unaware of the incongruity of this Catholic republican youth lecturing these worldly-wise, hard-nosed Protestant unionist businessmen. Everyone was very nice to me on both occasions. They toasted me, for my twenty-first birthday — after I had joined in the toast to 'His Majesty the King'! That was a hard toast for a republican to swallow; but my mother and sisters had taught me well. I also had to stand for 'God Save the King'. I had my own secret fun with that, using our boyhood parody of it in my head: 'God save our gracious cat, feed him on bread and fat, God save our cat....'

Unaware of my duplicity, Sir Norman invited me to visit him in Stormont. The one time I was there, alas, he was somewhere else. I always got a kick, somehow, out of seeing his name in the papers — until about twenty-five years later, when I read he was killed by the IRA. As Seumas Shields says in *Shadow of a Gunman*: 'I'm a nationalist right enough. I'm a nationalist, right enough, but, all the same...!'

Brendan, never one to miss an opportunity, arranged a matinée performance in Ballymena, on the way home from Portstewart, to wind up the season in the North. We liked that it added an extra one-sixth to our salaries. I think we did *The Patsy* — a light comedy — and we played it in a kind of ballroom. Maybe Liam Neeson and the Reverend Ian Paisley saw the play! They were born in that very Protestant town, I believe, where they speak a Scottish kind of dialect.

My next stop was the Catholic Parochial House in Loughgall — well, outside the village of Loughgall: there were no Catholics *in* the village. The motor vehicle carrying the scenery dropped me off at Father Donnellan's late that evening. The thought uppermost in my mind: Rita, down the road a few mile! (In that part of the country they drop the 's'!)

They are much more different from us Southerners than from each other, those Northern Catholics and Protestants. Therein, I felt even then, was a hope for eventual unity. In general, I like Northerners better. They are refreshingly direct. We Southerners are so oblique.

Notwithstanding my tolerant attitude, the Portstewart Local Council majority voted against inviting a Free State, Catholic theatre company to their Town Hall the following year! Independent Ireland was called the Irish Free State until the Republic of Ireland Act of 1948 was passed, and it still is by many Northern Protestants. 'No surrender!' as Randolph Churchill taught them to say.

I had spent vacations with Father Luke before, but now, in Loughgall, with a new parochial house, things were utterly changed. His Reverence now had a bathroom next to his room on the second floor, so gone were the days of cold baths of seawater brought in barrels from the seashore — of him stalking stark naked through the unheated house calling 'Coming through!' so my mother, sisters and any of us staying there would remain in our rooms till he had passed to and from his ablutions. Gone, too, were the sun-ray lamps which he would sit in front of every morning. Still, to me, it was the self-same Father Luke Donnellan waiting to greet me.

I was in a small room on the ground floor and heard him going out to say Mass every morning. Being me, I attended only the Sunday one. We would breakfast together on half an orange each, the peeled skin of it soaked in the hot teapot to flavour the china tea; toast with country butter and marmalade; rashers of bacon, and eggs — boiled or fried, scrambled or poached. Then we would drive to Armagh, Portadown, or Newry, to shop or to make business visits. During these I would do chores for him, or just wander about, or both. Coming and going we passed through 'a very Protestant village' called Rich Hill. I loved the look and the name of it, always.

We would have dinner when we got back in the early afternoon; sherry before it, then wine — Graves, Sauterne, or Beaune claret, depending on the main course. Always there was one of his ritual salads. These he made as ever, only now I might be allowed to slice the lettuce thinly, using a wineglass to hold it down, chopping it fine with his razor-sharp bone-handled knife. We usually had boiled, roast, or mashed potatoes, cabbage, carrots, turnips, parsnips or peas to accompany the meat or fish. I would have dessert. He would not.

After meals he would hand-roll one cigarette, and smoke it. Then we would walk in the area of the old parochial house and gardens, or drive to some special place where he liked to walk. We would talk about what I had been doing, family, the apple trees (this is apple country), weather, local people, books, music, mathematics, food, wine, his inventions, or favourite stories of his that I would prompt him to tell. He would punctuate his and my stories and remarks with 'Capital! Capital!' He always put 'Miss' before the names of my sisters, or other young women we knew, even if they were now married — 'Have you seen anything of Miss Nell Clarke?' Any reference to my brother Sam was followed by 'Dam is the best man'; any mention of the actual village of Loughgall or of the Orange Order — which was founded there, certainly — led to his telling this story, which I loved him to tell:

'As you know, the Twelfth of July' — he never said 'twalfth' — 'is the day the Orange Order celebrate the victory of William of Orange over James II of England, in the 1690 Battle of the Boyne. They march the length of Loughgall to the sound of brass bands and Lambeg drums, wearing black bowler hats and orange sashes, carrying elaborate banners with slogans — "To Hell with the Pope", "No Surrender", "No Pope, Priest, or Holy Water" — and singing "The Sash my Father Wore", "Lilliburlero" and "The Protestant Boys".' And he'd hum a tiny snatch of each. 'Some of the marchers then repair to hostelries, where intoxicating liquor might sometimes be consumed! Well, a group of these stout fellas, a couple of years ago, came late at night to the church here and tarred some of their more colourful catch-cries on the walls. The next morning, at the crack of dawn, a group of decent Orangemen asked at the parochial house for an audience with me. This I granted at once, and invited them into the front room of the new parochial house, which I suspect they were eager to see. The little committee formally apologised, and requested my permission to clean the church walls! This being granted, they not only removed the tar and left the walls cleaner than I've ever seen them, but at the next Orange Order meeting in Loughgall, I was advised, passed the resolution: "If they'd make Father Luke Donnellan Pope, there would be no more trouble with the Orange Order!" Isn't that capital?' Father Luke clearly enjoyed it all hugely, and laughed loudly whenever he told it.

'What do you do about sex?' the survey questioner asked a Northern farmer's wife. 'We does have our supper about sex,' she replied. Well, we had dinner at sex o'clock at the parochial house — another gourmet meal, with wine, perhaps a brandy after. Father Luke was rarely not in bed and asleep by eight o'clock, summer or winter. When he visited us in Dublin, he and Mammy would stay up till ten or even eleven o'clock, drinking and, to our alarm (us pretending to be asleep in the next room), arguing violently — mostly, it seemed, about my sisters having married! Whether this was the real cause I don't know. I suspect it had more to do with his sexual frustration. Carmel always held that she had had to fight off his advances. Many years later, Marie and Kitty confirmed this.

After dinner, I would read, potter about and listen to the wireless, my eye on the clock. Then, after about eight o'clock, I would listen carefully and quietly on the stairs and then exit, through the kitchen, to the garage behind the house. In the growing darkness, I'd push the circa-1934 Austin 10 to the end of the house, in a precisely curved move, so that it was facing down the slightly sloping cement pathway. The gate was always left open, which helped, though I would not have been deterred if it hadn't been. Then I would open the driver's door; with a tiny push, it would start to roll; and I'd hop in. The car would gather a little speed as I turned right onto the deserted country road. Down a further slight incline, past the front of the church.... I'd switch on the ignition, put it into second gear, ease out the clutch, put on the lights. Then, bursting into a raucous, out-of-tune 'I come, I come, my heart's delight', I was on my way to see Rita. Life was bloody marvellous!

Actually, my evenings in Coalisland were quite disappointing — not that I admitted that to myself, much less to Rita. I have vague memories of talking to her behind the counter in the empty bar in Dorman's Public House, on the Square; walking with her to an undertakers', across the road, which they also owned; supper in the kitchen with her, once; and walking the streets of Dungannon after going to the pictures together.

What are utterly vivid are my memories of getting the car back into the garage of the parochial house without discovery! The first thing was to make sure I had the car filled up. This I did at Dorman's — yes, they owned a service station, too; well, in those days it was a local garage and petrol pumps. I would aim to get back to Loughgall about midnight. I'd rarely, if ever, see another car after leaving Coalisland. About half a mile from home, before coming to the hill leading up from the Catholic graveyard to the church, I'd make sure to get some speed up — 35 or 40 mph. Then, as I came to the church, I would turn off the headlights, leaving on the side lights, rev up the engine, switch it off, and freewheel the twenty or thirty yards to the gate; I would switch off the side lights as I made the turn in, the impetus taking me easily up the path, round behind the house, and silently into the garage. A touch on the brakes was enough to bring it to a silent stop. Easy as falling off a log!

Half a century later, it struck me for the first time ever: what if Father Luke had had a sick call on one of those nights? I think he might have killed me! On the other hand, he might have loved the whole idea. He was an extraordinary man.

Father Luke drove me to Belfast, from where I took a train to Dublin. We had lunch in a pub called the Club Bar, owned by Michael and Julia Agnew. One or both of them had been born in the same village as Father Luke; 'decent people,' he would always say about them and their parents. That day I also went with Maureen McClure, who was now Eugene's 'steady', to visit her father, one of the few Catholic senior civil servants, at Stormont. I missed Sir Norman Stronge, who was away.

As I pulled out of Belfast in the Great Northern Railway train that day, I was not, I know, looking back on Portstewart, Loughgall, Rita, my priestly patron Father Luke Donnellan PP, or my loveable landlady Miss Margaret McTamney. As I still do today, I broke from those pleasing thoughts to catch a glimpse of the Irish Sea and Mornington Lighthouse as I crossed the bridge over the Boyne River at Drogheda, and again minutes later to watch out for Bettystown, Laytown and the Nanny Estuary, eagerly viewing every inch of sea, green grass and white powdery sand, till Ben Head was almost upon us; then I would have lurched to the right-hand window for the split-second sight of where our rail carriage and hut used to be in Shuttleworth's haggard. But my head, my heart, my imagination were spinning around to the rhythm of iron wheels on the iron tracks, taking me to Dublin, new roles and old roles, and life on the open road — an actor! It wasn't Hollywood calling, or London — or Dublin, even. It was the Irish towns, villages, crossroads, a different play every night, different digs and audience every week, sometimes twice a week, for the rest of my living life. That I — Vincent Dowling from Mount Merrion, who couldn't pay the fees at St Mary's College, who might still have been pen-pushing and figure-totting at the Standard Life Assurance Company — had been for three months, was now, and would be for ever earning my living *acting on the stage*, was an impossible dream that already had come true.

5

The Fit-ups

We're not used to playing to hooligans, the likes of you!

The two oldest professions in the world,' an older actor, Paddy Mallon, said to me, 'are spoiled by amateurs.' We were handling long pieces of light timber from the street, through the lobby and onto the stage of the cinema in Tullamore, Co. Offaly.

'What are they?' I asked.

'Acting and prostitution,' said Paddy sadly. 'What separates actors from ordinary people is the tabs.'

This was the first date on my first fit-up tour with Brendan Smith. Paddy was one of two old pros that Brendan had engaged to teach his young company.

'What do you think is the most important equipment we have with us?'

'The actors, I suppose.'

'Apart from the actors.'

'The plays.'

'No,' said Paddy. 'You can always make up a play from another play, or a story, or even a film. I'll tell you: it's these four-by-twos, a handful of screws, those wires, some curtain rings and the front tabs that we brought in the wooden crate.'

'Oh, the red curtains,' says I.

'Tabs,' says he, emphatically. 'I'll show you how to put them together into the fit-up frame. With them, you can turn any hall, room, barn or tent into a theatre. That's the reason a company like us is called a fit-up company.' He was right: the 'fit-up' frame, complete with 'tabs' that can be pulled open and closed, is really a portable proscenium.

John McMahon, about forty-five years of age, the other old pro, always shared digs with Paddy on these trips. Everyone shared; it was cheaper. John was meticulous in everything he wore, said or did, both on and off stage — unlike Paddy, who dressed like a Midlands farm labourer, in a hand-me-down suit made for a man nearly twice his height and girth. John had a beautifully articulated North of Ireland accent, fine features, wavy dark hair and a strong leading-actor build. They were an original 'odd couple'. I learned a lot from them.

Des Perry and I were sharing the play direction, playing the leading character and juvenile lead respectively. We claimed we were able to get a legitimate laugh on any line in a play, and we could prove it. We got a laugh a line in *Paul Twining* by George Shiels. Des was still the company manager, and I the business manager.

Gerry Burke, young, dark, energetic, who had worked with Des in England, had joined us, with his fiancée Mary Minchin. And Eugene Black, Laurie Morton and Pauline Delaney had returned to the company after Portstewart. Along with these were newcomers Mae Long — who went into every role hair first, much to the delight of the local hairdressers — and Ruth Durley, a married woman with a grown family who had fulfilled a lifetime ambition to become an actress later in life. Then there was Dermot MacMahon — no relation to John — who was big, humorous, good company, attractive to and attracted by women. Last, but not least in my life, was Brenda Doyle. She had a very strong 'thing' for Dermot. He reciprocated in a cavalier kind of way, which led me to 'protect' her — a mistake on my part.

Brenda was a splendid, talented, versatile, energetic, and very fine all-round company member. She had auburn hair and a trim, sexy body, which she liked to show through tight sweaters; she could sing and dance, and she had a great smile and sense of humour. She was kind and helpful, always good for a loan of five or ten shillings — she always insisted that it be returned on the next pay-day. In a past life she was probably a squirrel; saving was a compulsion with her. She took responsibility for costumes and volunteered to do the laundry for Des, Dermot, Eugene and me, which we accepted. We made a collection at the end of the tour and bought her a present, something imaginative like a box of chocolates. She seemed to have everything a tour needed — oddly enough, inherited from her father, who opposed her going on the stage.

On this tour we had five plays in our repertoire and one, *To Kill a Cat*, to rehearse on the road. We looked upon ourselves as a step above most of the fit-up companies touring the smalls. We did only recognised, published works; no music, dance or comic skits. Furthermore, we played on Saturday nights; that was the late-night-shopping and bath night in the country, when most of the travelling companies didn't waste energy playing. We, however, had the Abbey Theatre sensation, *The Righteous are Bold*, with its shocking smashing of a statue of the Blessed Virgin Mary on stage! We filled the house to bursting point with it on one weeknight, and did very respectable business every Saturday night too.

It was absolutely necessary to do a comedy or farce if playing on Sundays. Against our advice, Brendan insisted we put on the highly dramatic *The Righteous are Bold* for a Sunday matinée in Carlow. He wanted it to be in top shape to open the next day at the most prestigious venue of our whole tour — the Theatre Royal, Wexford. Swank!

The hall in Carlow was packed to the back wall, where the cheaper seats were. As at Mass, that was where the 'boyos' congregated. I can still see the young men sitting up on the high window-ledges, with the daylight behind them shining through the gaps in blinds and window-frames.

From the moment that Nora, the possessed girl, began to speak with the devil's voice in Act II, the boyos hooted and jeered. The shushings and glares of the establishment adults kept this more or less in check until the third act, when Nora breaks from the exorcism off stage and rushes on, broken ropes trailing behind her, her perm dishevelled, her blouse torn, shrieking triumphantly, 'We have beaten God, his angels and his priest!' She throws herself screaming on the floor while the priest (John MacMahon, who later played another priest in *The Riordans*), his hair turned white from the ordeal (and liberal handfuls of flour), staggers in, kneels beside the girl, and says 'Nora Geraghty, do you believe?' Off stage, Brenda and Laurie are running from side to side, shaking the set and screaming in diabolical tones, 'We will not leave, we will not leave.'

They were joined, unrehearsed, by the boyos out front jeering, laughing and yelling, 'Jaysus, she's down again! Christ, will you look at her blouse!' Then John MacMahon, still kneeling in priestly posture, turned out front and boomed, in a voice like a North-of-Ireland God, 'Will you shut up, you ignorant gets! We're not used to playing to hooligans the likes of you.' And without missing a beat or changing his tone, he raised his right hand in blessing: '*In nomine patri et filii et spiritu sancti, Amen.*'

Not another sound broke the silence until the curtain call. It was John MacMahon's finest hour.

Our tour was a mix of the hair-raising and the hilarious, with each new venue and audience demanding all our ingenuity and our acting skills to ensure that we kept up the quality of the plays and playing. Then, in December, it was the rest period for Christmas. Though we were not paid then, the company needed a break. Rehearsals were to start in mid-January, and most of us had saved enough to get us over Christmas. Personally, I would rather have stayed on the road. Somehow I never liked going back to Dublin when I was away.

On arrival home at Marlborough Road, I discovered I had a letter from Rita, asking me to the Annual St Vincent's Hospital Nurses' New Year's Eve Ball. Rita knew I was 'resting'. We had stayed in touch, though getting and writing letters was hard, we were so moving so much. I could not afford the tickets, nor the hire of tails. They were her Christmas gift to me. It was arranged that I would pick her up at her sister Slim's flat — she was a nurse at Vincent's.

Mammy and Sam were living at home. Sam was an apprentice to the quantity surveyor Paddy McCarroll, who worked with my sister Carmel's husband. Marie and Jim, still drinking, lived in Glenageary, and Kitty and Brian (now a captain with KLM) were in Holland.

I hope that I may have sent Rita a present. I do know I agreed to go to the dance with her. That didn't stop me taking out a pretty blonde girl with a dimple, whom I met at a city dance hall. I brought her to the Savoy Cinema a couple of days after Christmas; bought her a small box of Black Magic chocolates, which we ate while watching *The Lady or the Tiger* in the supporting programme. I took her for a coffee afterwards; we got a bus to Rialto, walked along the Grand Canal and, parked up against a tree, had a hot 'coort'. It was a long walk home to Donnybrook alone after midnight. Why can't I remember her name? Her face, figure and presence are as clear as consommé.

It was no surprise to find Mammy awake when I went in. 'I can never sleep, Vin, when you are still out,' she would always say to me, or to any of us when we were at home, no matter how long we had been living away from it. This time she had an extra reason. A message had come to the Kellys, next door, that I was to ring a number in Waterford, no matter what time I came in, about an acting job with Anglo-Irish Productions. I felt like Andy Hardy, or someone in the films, except that I had to walk down to the phone box on the corner of Morehampton Road with all the coins I could find in the house.

Early next morning I was on a train from Kingsbridge Station, bound for Waterford. I was met by two actresses, Pauline Flanagan and Pat Turner, *avec* script — well, sides, in true Shakespearean manner — of Paul Vincent Carroll's *Shadow and Substance*. I was booked into the Munster Hotel; thence I went to the Theatre Royal to rehearse the part of Father Corr. The priest's suit worn by the actor who had left the company, without notice, fitted me. Later, I would hear that this was Billy Quinn, who preferred to play female roles. I was relieved he was not in the company. In my ignorance, I was wary of anyone who might be what we misnamed 'queer'. Though I was not to know it, I hadn't heard the last of Billy.

I walked through my scenes once with Joe Nolan, who was playing the Canon, then went back to my hotel and learned my lines. Pauline and Pat ran me through them. I had high tea and did the show. I got through without a hitch until towards the end of my biggest and last scene, which was with the Canon. I walked confidently up to him and said, out of the upstage side of my mouth, 'That's as far as I know.' Joe talked me through to my exit. He was better than any airport controller that ever talked down a plane.

That night, after a drink and supper, I learned the next play. I did the bad guy, Brent, in *Peg o' My Heart* the next night; the older brother in *The Winslow Boy* the night after that; and then played in *The Wise Have Not Spoken* by P.V. Carroll on New Year's Eve!

At the party afterwards, the New Year bells of 1951 rang out. Rita — Rita Dorman! *Jesus, Mary and Holy Saint Joseph, Rita is in Dublin. I am supposed to be with her at a ball tonight!* After a long, anguished silence — 'Sufficient unto the day,' I thought, and went on drinking champagne.

Before going to sleep I called St Vincent's Hospital and left a message for Slim. Next day I heard from her that Rita would never again speak to me. Though I wrote to Rita to apologise, it would be seventeen years before I laid eyes on her again. I did hear from Eugene's girlfriend, Maureen, how deeply wounded Rita had been, and how Rita had told her she had hoped to marry me, that it wouldn't have mattered that I was an actor without any money or security. She had more than enough for the both of us.

The second part of the Brendan Smith tour went on the road in late January. We added a new play to the repertoire: Micheál mac Liammóir's *Ill Met by Moonlight*, a kind of Irish *Tempest* in a teacup, in which Brenda played opposite me. Of course we knew Micheál and Hilton Edwards and Lord Longford's companies at the Gate Theatre; but, like the Abbey, they were in Dublin — as removed from us as Hollywood, but as glamorous.

In terms of digs, Des Perry and Pauline Delaney had a sleeping arrangement which led to long night journeys for Des from his to Pauline's bedroom. Within a short time, this became a crisscrossing traffic that included Brenda and me. My first excursion of that nature took place in the home-town of Percy French's redoubtable creation, Paddy Reilly of Ballyjamesduff. It came about because Des and Pauline were unable to secure two single rooms in the best digs in town, which were run by two sisters in conjunction with a women's hairdressing salon. The idea of two unweds openly sleeping together was just not an option in those days. Pauline, I think, sounded out Brenda about sharing with her; Des, I know, sounded me about sharing with him. The relationship between Brenda and me had been progressing nicely since we had started rehearsals for this leg of the tour, and we both agreed happily to the nightly bed-swapping performance.

This entertaining activity continued through the remainder of the tour, which ended in the town of Banaher on the River Shannon. Banaher had the best digs of the whole six months of touring. We paid two pounds a week each for a shared room, four good meals a day, plus a glass of hot Tullamore Dew Irish whiskey every night before bed — our landlord was a caretaker of that distillery's store in the area. As the traditional Irish compliment goes, 'That beats Banaher and Banaher beat the devil.' I never stayed anywhere that beat Banaher.

One of the nights there was a chimney fire in the small hours that almost led to the discovery of our secret. Des Perry's straight, sensitive nose led him to the fireplace in the kitchen, the source of the fire, just as our tall, bald, handsome landlord's nose led him there too.

'Wake the women,' said he to Des. 'I'll wake Vincent.' And before Des could think what to say, the landlord was in my room. Fortunately, I can hear grass grow, and I was out of bed with the bedclothes piled on top of Brenda's sleeping form, completely camouflaging her.

'Okay,' I said, 'I'm coming.' It was lucky I wasn't! Our sexual activity never advanced beyond the undercover contortions of my teens — but with rather fewer impious ejaculations and subsequent handkerchief and pyjama launderings. It is fair to say that a sexually active teenager today would not have called what we enjoyed so regularly and thoroughly 'sexual activity' at all. An Irish farmer was heard to say about abstinence of my kind, 'He must have had a mortuary quiet tool!' I hadn't, but I had control of it. That was fortunate, because it was the only birth control available then in Catholic Ireland — well, except our Latin friend *coitus interruptus*, with whom I was not working at that time.

We played seven performances a week, sometimes with a matinée. We moved from place to place once or twice a week. Good digs were difficult to find, and sharing a room, sometimes even a bed, was normal. We loaded and unloaded everything for the get-in at every venue, in winter, carrying in sets in sleet and rain. Try carrying canvas flats that turn into sails trying to bear you off, as you stagger up the steps in somewhere cold and blowy like Loughrea. Loughrea, however, was one of our favourite dates — not only because we did tremendous business there, but because the audience was one of our best. I would choose it, nearly twenty years later, to try out *The Shadow of a Gunman*, the first play I directed for the Abbey Theatre.

We were on the road performing for about six months. For all that time, Brendan Smith did something very simple, but unique in my experience, which contributed to our happiness and well-being and to the quality of our work. Every actor and actress had to stage manage and assistant stage manage. This meant 'running' the show and changing the set, resetting the lighting and borrowing — often begging — the props and furniture after each performance. Salaries varied from six to eight pounds a week; I got nine because of the business management and directing, and Des ten because he was the company manager as well as an actor. But any week that we took a total of more than £110, we got a bonus of one pound each. Only once in the whole six months did we fail to make the magic figure, and Brendan gave us the bonus that week anyhow. It is a policy I recommend without reservation.

From time to time in my fifty-year career on stage, I may have been as happy in other companies, but never as constantly happy as I was from June 1950 to the end of April 1951. I took off in the month of May with a return sea and rail ticket, twenty pounds in my pocket, some copies of my only theatrical portrait, taken by Bobby Dawson, and two introductions, to find fame and fortune in London. I was following the lead given by Des Perry, Gerry Burke and Mary Minchin. They had sown the seed of the idea when I realised they had their sights set on England. If they could do it, so could I. In fact, I arrived there before them.

I was on the mail boat, bound for the Isle of Anglesey, as millions of my countrymen and women had been before me. I had exactly twenty pounds sterling in my pocket. As the ship pulled away, everything I knew — my friends from Marlborough Road and the Brendan Smith Academy and Productions, Brian Kelly, Frank Barry, Brenda herself, Des Grogan, Clare Mullen, Ritchie Whitty, Joan Bearshaw, Laurie Morton, Beryl Fagan — grew smaller. Behind them, I could see the Town Hall clock-tower, below which the Christian Brothers had beaten some learning into me and brainwashed me with Catholic soft soap — alas for me, I was not aware of this at the time. Further upstage, the steeple of St Michael's reminded me that I had been confirmed there, a strong and perfect Christian.

There were not many, maybe, as imperfect as I. Even fewer held to the absolute belief that Jesus was God and that Pope Pius XII, John Charles McQuaid, Archbishop of Dublin, and Cardinal McRory, Primate of All Ireland, were directly in the line of succession from the apostles on whom Jesus had built the one holy Catholic and apostolic Church and, *ipso facto*, were infallible in matters of faith and morals — which, I thought, covered about everything that was any fun. I held these beliefs, realised I couldn't always live up to them, but determined not to disavow them. Oh yes, I was confidently prepared to face the dangers of life in, if not godless, at least misguided England.

Having left, I have no recollection of missing anyone, including Brenda. I had no apprehension, though I was very conscious of every penny I was spending; my premise was that I had a round-trip ticket so I could go home if I ran out of money and got no work, but the longer I could make the twenty pounds last, the better my chances of breaking into the London theatre and film scene. My backup was that Brendan Smith would use me for the Mosney summer camp season, and was anxious to send out another tour in the autumn.

By about eight the next morning I was at Euston Station in London, fresh and focused. 'London,' I thought. 'Gerry Burke and Mary Minchin! Wouldn't it be great if I got work in London before them!' There was no malice in this, just zest.

Years later, on BBC Radio — or the wireless, as we called it then — I heard a wit say, 'So many Irish settled in Camden Town when they came to London because it was the furthest they could walk from Euston Station with a large, heavy suitcase!' I knew the truth of this. Not that I carried my suitcase there, only to the bus that would pass through it on the way to Crouch End. I lugged my case — everything I owned — upstairs to the front of the bus; I wasn't going to trust it in the luggage space under the stairs. Besides, I wanted to look out on the way for Bed & Breakfast signs in case I drew a blank at Crouch End. Camden Town was a busy shopping street; nothing for me there, except a church that looked like it was a Catholic one — a cross on top. Camden Road, north of the town centre, produced two B&B signs in the windows of four-storey red-brick town-houses with gardens in the front and black iron rails and gates — like Marlborough Road, only bigger and better kept. I took a note of two possibilities, one opposite a nice-looking, old-fashioned grey stone pub — the Brecknock Arms. I noted this pub, too, as a landmark.

There was no answer to my knocking on the door of a town-house that had no front garden. I had already checked with the conductor the difference in fares from the West End, the Mecca of all actors, to the Brecknock Arms and Crouch End. The saving was substantial: several pence, each way, each day! Back with me to Camden Road, marvelling as I went at the number of churches that had most of their steeples shorn off by German shuttlebugs and bombs. It was as if the Nazis had used the church steeples for target practice.

I paid ten shillings a night for a single bed in a room shared with another man, breakfast, and a bathroom-cum-toilet used by all the tenants on that floor. Twopence in the gas geyser paid for a hot bath. The breakfast was my first culture shock: tea, toast, porridge and Spam! Other mornings we had cheese and a half-tomato, or baked beans on toast. Sundays were better — bacon, egg and sausage. Shock Number Two was my roommate, a pleasant middle-aged man, mad-professorish in appearance. He was a full-time student of 'form', as relating to race-horses. He worked six to eight hours a day studying that form and making bets based on his acquired insights. Even more amazing, he made a fair living out of doing it. It was less risky than being an actor!

I went, my first Sunday morning, to that church I had seen from the bus. I was a tad late getting there. Mass had started, I thought, but I couldn't quite get the hang of what point it was at. I forced myself to concentrate. *What's going on? There's something different ... the Latin with an English accent? No. No! It's English with an English accent! Christ, it's a Protestant church! What am I going to do now?* I slithered to the end of the empty pew I was in, lowered my head, praying no one would catch my eye, and tiptoed out into Camden High Street. A quick glance at the notice-board out in front told me it was an Anglican church. It was as if I had seen an attractive female friend of my Mother naked by mistake: pleasurable, but not to be acknowledged!

I went looking for a *real* Catholic church, and found one. The last Mass was well under way. The consecration was past. Technically I had 'missed Mass'. Oh well, I had tried. That made it all right. I waited till the very end; no skipping out after the last blessing. God — an accountant by profession, I reckoned — would give me more points for half a Mass than for one whole service of Protestant hymns and prayers.

Feeling virtuous, I made for a pub I had spotted opposite the Anglican church, had a couple of glasses of Guinness and chatted with some Cork lads. In the men's toilet, newly painted and a lot cleaner than most Irish pubs of that period, was written in large letters over the pissoir: 'The Pope drinks Beamish'. A message from a homesick Corkman, lonely for the Lee river and a taste of a good Cork stout, I thought, washing my hands!

Through my Uncle Vincent and Mammy, I had an introduction to Carmen Dillon. She had worked, some years earlier, as an architect in his office in Merrion Square, and knew and liked us. By 1951, she was a most respected production designer at Denham Studios. She invited me there to lunch during the filming of *Robin Hood* with Richard Todd in the title role. However, the day led to nothing in the way of work. It was probably pretty hard to help me, an inexperienced youth with a suburban Irish accent. I really didn't expect much, and I wasn't disappointed.

Richard (Dick) Carrickford was a friend of a different hue. Dick had toured with Des Perry, and was the son of Lilian Carrickford, actress/ manageress of a well-established Irish fit-up company. He lived down Camden Road from me, with a girl he was going to marry. Strange, I thought, but this is England! He was a struggling actor who got small film parts now and then. He was really struggling to get scripts of plays and documentary films accepted. Well known and liked around the West End, he certainly didn't need to take on the likes of me to help and mentor!

I survived in London because of his unselfish, generous camaraderie and brotherly care. He introduced and recommended me to agents, managers, actors, actresses, and his and their favourite coffee shops. He took me to auditions; he taught me how to find out where they were being held, what to do at them, how to talk off stage in an English accent, and when to use my Irish or my assumed American. He brought me to meet Molly, the saintly, practical lady in Soho who ran the Interval Club. He got me free into the Windmill Theatre, to meet the girls who posed naked there in continuous performances twelve hours a day. The Windmill's proud boast, even during the war-time bombing, was 'We never closed!' The girls sunbathed between shows on the theatre roof in two-piece bathing costumes, so on stage, they showed tanned bodies and white breasts to an endless stream of men. Richard shared his money when he had it, his table when he hadn't. He made me at home in and with London. He didn't look for return. We had the fit-ups binding us.

Maureen McClure was a trainee manager for the North of Ireland Housing Trust, getting experience in London. She was staying in quite a lovely girls' residential club. Because I was her boyfriend's best friend, not her boyfriend, and very young and innocent-looking, she was allowed to have me to dinner. The wonderful free dinners — free to me; Maureen paid — were truly a godsend.

Meanwhile, with Dick Carrickford's help, I had moved further north, just past Holloway Women's Prison, to a nice suburban house quite near Holloway tube station, under the strict but benevolent discipline of a London landlady straight out of Central Casting! Ma 'Iggins, she was always called. She was kind and protective of me. It was a pound a week cheaper than Camden Road; the food was at least as good; I had my own bed in a room with four other young men, all good fellows. For a short time Des Perry stayed there, before going to work at a repertory company in Penge. One night, before he left, he had been to see a show in the Lyric Hammersmith — *Monserrat*. I remember him sitting on his bed, next to mine, and telling me about this brilliant young actor who had played the title role — 'Remember this name, Vincent; you are going to hear of him again, if I know anything. His name is Richard Burton.' I felt vaguely resentful, somehow, but as usual did not say it, even to myself. Des Perry, blowing the smoke through the smouldering top of his last Craven A before sleep, as he had done night after night in the fit-ups ... the curious curve of his fingernails always dominates my image of him!

I eked out my meagre resources with two days clearing tables at Lyons Corner House on Coventry Street, playing, for my own edification and morale, the part of a charming, ebullient foreign waiter. I got thirty shillings a day; the three pounds lasted me a week. In the meantime I was doing the rounds. 'You'll have to get rid of that brogue, Paddy!' 'Sorry, nothing for an Irish actor in this play/film/season.' Then, when I got the courage, I learned to talk to a new agent, director, or casting director in the accent the part required. Then it would be 'Sorry, nothing for your type today' or, worse, 'Can't you do anything except a brogue, Paddy?'

On a tube one day, coming back from some unsuccessful interview, I spotted a huge advert for jobs on the night shift at Wall's Ice Cream Factory. I got the phone number down and called it.

'Start tonight,' said the voice at the other end.

'I'm an actor; what if I get an acting job?'

'Just give twenty-four hours' notice when you come in of an evening; tell the supervisor you won't be back next night. You'll get paid at the end of the night. Then give us twenty-four hours' notice when you want to come back to us.'

This is heaven on Earth, I thought, *and at thirty-four shillings per night!* Actually, it was more like freezing to death for ever in hell. The night went on and on, a gradual speeding-up of a production line of ice-cream-laden zinc trays, whose frozen underneaths had to be manually pulled outward and fitted into a four-tier trolley beside you, in one fast movement. If you were a beat too slow, the continuous stream of trays, ice-cream and all, piled up on the floor under your rubber-booted feet and ridiculous white-suited, chef's-hatted body. Then, shame of shame, the production line stopped, the foreman shouting foul racial epithets at you — 'You bog-trotting Paddy, go back to your bleeding pigs in the kitchen!' Eventually, there was an even more demeaning, but less demanding job: washing trays in lukewarm water.

At the 'dinner break', around midnight, I discovered that so many actors worked the shifts it was known as Wall's Repertory Company. Well, maybe tomorrow night I'd get a cushier job.

The last straw that night: 'No. You can't tike yer firty-foor shillings for the noight! You mast give twenee-foor owehs noteece *befoh* yeh start wurk, mite!' I couldn't eat ice-cream for decades after.

Next day — *Thank you, God, I never doubted you* — a call from Maud Spector's office: a two-day 'Special Artistes Contract' at Nettlefold Studios, on *A Christmas Carol*, at eight pounds sterling per day! A 'Special Artiste' is an Equity member who is capable, if required, of speaking dialogue or of on-camera acting — unlike Crowd Artistes, who in those days were treated, and often referred to, as 'cattle' and were paid two pounds per day.

The cast of the film included others apart from me. If you see it on a largish TV screen and know what I looked like fifty years ago, for a split second you can spot me, in my turn, breaking from the line of Scrooge's apprentices and dancing blithely with a young female towards the cameras! Alistair Sim was a great Scrooge; Michael Dolan from the Abbey Theatre (the best and most dedicated small-part actor I have ever known) was as the Ghost of Christmas Past, and George Cole was Scrooge's nephew. 'Why him? Why not me ?' I asked myself. 'Pull!' I said. I knew it wasn't. I think I was laughing, a little ruefully, at myself. I hope so.

Things were looking up. My London life had been extended by some weeks. Sixteen pounds for two days' work!

Richard Carrickford married his girl. I was a witness. They slept together the night before, got up together and went to the wedding ceremony separately. I was shocked, and said so to Richard. He just laughed at me. I was all ready to give him my 'The Catholic Church is the only true....' speech; fortunately I didn't get the chance. I was invited to breakfast with the best man, the bridesmaid and the bride and groom, and a great day was had by all. I suppose I grew up a little that day.

About this time, I came back to my abode in Holloway about nine o'clock one night. I was met at the door by 'Ma'.

'I've put you in the front room upstairs, with your actor friend from Ireland,' she said.

'What actor friend?' I asked.

'It's all right, I'm not going to charge you any more for sharing with only one. I've moved your things in. Good night, dearie!' she said as she disappeared into her own quarters.

I opened the bedroom door. It had two beds in it. Standing bent over a ship's trunk was a figure in a startling blue off-the-shoulder dress. 'She' straightened up with an elaborate blonde wig in hand, turned to look in the mirror on the wardrobe, saw me and smiled. I saw that 'her' clearly dyed hair had a short, boyish haircut. A well-spoken male Irish voice said cheerfully, 'Don't be afraid, love. I won't touch you. You must be Vincent. I'm Billy Quinn.'

And he never did. My third guardian angel had arrived, to join Richard Carrickford and Maureen McClure. Billy was over to do an audition for a drag show with Danny LaRue at the Dominion Theatre in the West End. Billy didn't get the job. I learned years later that Danny LaRue was Irish!

Billy and I became real friends in the following weeks. He was fantastic company, a great storyteller, a wickedly funny mimic and commentator. His sister was a manageress at a hotel in a square near the centre of London. Over the next few weeks she sustained us, generously, with good nourishing lunches. We walked (to save fares), talked (a lot about Ireland), laughed (at ourselves, the fit-ups, the English and the Irish) and dreamed of Utopias for Irish actors, on our way about London. Billy was married to a daughter of a Member of Parliament, Hector Hughes, I believe. They had a family. Billy's *tour de force* was a brilliant, accurate impersonation of Siobhán McKenna as Saint Joan. He sang, improvised brilliantly, convincingly acted men, children and Madame Arcati, loved life and people, was without an ounce of self-pity. I was privileged to be his friend. From him I learned not to judge a man or woman by their sexual preference, only by their humanity. And, though he disappeared from the picture for a time, he would make welcome, though too infrequent reappearances, all unexpected, of course.

Then the morning came when I had five shillings left. My rent was paid up to and including breakfast that day. If I didn't get work that morning, I would take the evening train from Euston, the night boat from Holyhead and go home. Thank God I had bought a return ticket! Whatever else I spent that coming morning, I would keep a half-crown for the journey. I was determined about that. Billy had gone back. Des Perry was in Penge. I couldn't go on scrounging on Maureen. This was it!

I visited a couple of small agents who would see me but wouldn't take me on yet. I met Dick Carrickford at Legrands and bought him a coffee. We ran around to a theatre in the Covent Garden area. We had heard they were seeing people for a musical; maybe there would be a non-singing part. We had no appointment made for us by an agent, nor anyone else, but we were adept at getting confidently past stage doorkeepers or other impedi-men placed to separate the milk from the cream.

That morning — maybe it was an omen — we found ourselves in an unfamiliar rich red-upholstered auditorium. We were approached respectfully by a gentle morning-suited male. He would take our music to the director.

Music? We hadn't brought it.

He was a little taken aback, but would we take a seat?

We approached a beautifully attired young man with a music case, obviously waiting his turn. What were they auditioning for?

The Sadlers Wells Opera Company.

Dick and I looked at each other and, with all the dignity we could assume, quietly slipped out. 'Well,' I said, 'at least I was offered an audition at Sadlers Wells!' And I told him of my decision to go back to Dublin that evening.

As we walked back through Covent Garden, Dick insisted we look into the Swan in case there was anyone in there — that meant any job-giver. I waited outside. I now had only one half-crown and my bus fare to Holloway and back to Euston. Dick was 'stony broke'. He reported that there wasn't 'anyone' there, though it was full with the lunchtime theatre crowd!

As we crossed St Martin's Lane, opposite the passageway between the theatre and the Salisbury Hotel, which was no longer a hotel, he said, 'Let's go into the bar there. A lot of people I know will be there at this time.' Before I could repeat my piece about what I was keeping my money to do, he said, 'I really think something's going to click, Vincent, and if it doesn't, I promise I'll get a half-crown somewhere for you. There's a little emergency cash at home.'

It would be churlish to say no, I felt. 'All right, one half of bitter each,' I said. That would leave me enough for a cuppa on train and boat.

I can see it all now. The gorgeous cold meats and pies on the mirrored shelves below the polished counter. The man drawing the half-pints of light-brown, soapy-looking, almost-headless, bubbly bitter. The shilling and tuppence change, safely in my pocket. Dick — his high forehead, his strong nose, his receding, well-groomed hair, his navy-blue suit, his white starched collar and plain dark-red tie — calmly surveying the lunchtime drinkers, picking his target.

'Come on,' he said quietly, moving towards four men standing smoking and sipping pints or 'small ones'. Two of them I knew from an office they shared with a small agent across from the Garrick Theatre. A tall, un-prepossessing man, sad-eyed, with thin ginger-and-salt hair and thick glasses on a bumpy nose over a ginger moustache, relaxed on his slightly bent knees, was listening to a man I didn't know talking about photos of a naked Hedy Lamarr, which could make a lot of 'bees' — bees and honey, the Cockney rhyming slang for money. 'Jesus,' I thought, 'is this what I've sacrificed my food money for?'

I was introduced to them by Dick. I immediately liked the sad-looking red-haired man — Dominic Roche, actor, playwright, producer. I was an Irish actor 'having a go' at London, Dick told them. Though they shook hands with me, they were signally unimpressed with my credentials. That was clear.

Very soon after that Mr Roche excused himself. Dick and I sipped slowly and infrequently on our bitter beers. I smoked a cigarette from time to time. The lack of food, and the sheer boredom, had me dizzy. *I'll have to go, whether Dick likes it or not, when I've finished this drink,* I decided, starting to take larger gulps of the almost-untouched 'half'.

Suddenly Dominic Roche was back. 'Have you ever done stage manage-ment?' he asked.

I told him I had done a lot, and had won a scholarship to acting school for it.

'Can you do a North Country accent?'

'Yes,' I said, very quietly, not really knowing what it was.

'Well, take this script. Look at the part of Norman. Come in here at ten tomorrow morning, to the rehearsal room upstairs, and read it for me. If it passes, you have a job. Good luck.'

He shook my hands, and left again. Who said the age of miracles is past!

Dick must not have known the accent, or I didn't want to admit to him that I didn't. The next thing I remember is calling Maureen; going to her place for dinner; meeting an attractive, friendly blonde resident; being permitted by the club manageress to go upstairs to Maureen's sleeping cubicle with my new Lancashire friend and Maureen, and reading the scenes with her. The play was called *My Wife's Lodger*; it was low knockabout Lancashire comedy.

Norman was the 'gormless' son. As it got later, and it was time for me to make my long journey to Holloway, I asked my accent coach to give me a phrase in the accent that I could hold on to — that would be my touchstone, my reference sound, if I felt I was losing it. She said without hesitation, 'Eee, bah gum!' She got me to repeat it over and over — 'Keep it flat as you can!' She finally pronounced me perfect. Eee, bah gum!

My accent must have been good enough. They had probably been let down at short notice by someone else, I reckoned, and the fact that I was Irish may have helped, as Dom was originally from Ballymahon. I got the part. I got the stage manager's job, I got twelve pounds per week, I got one week's rehearsal and one week playing *in a real theatre in London* — the very edge of London, on the sea, at Southend, but *in London* — Gerry! *In London* — Mary! There might be more weeks to follow, certainly at the end of August!

Actually we got one other week, following the first, at a huge theatre in Walthamstow, another London suburb. Then I went home to Dublin, confident that there would be a tour coming up soon. The audiences had flocked to the play, and local papers had loved it. Dom was a brilliant comic actor.

The only slightly worrying thing was the company manager, a gentle, elderly actor (he played a very small part as a police inspector; I doubled as his assistant, as well as playing Norman and stage managing), Jack McCaig by name. In the old days he had been a very successful provincial leading man. He took a very friendly interest in me; I was a little afraid that he was too friendly! Shame on me. In order not to offend him, I talked continually of my girlfriend in Ireland and the tour we had done together. He encouraged me to get her to apply for assistant stage manager and understudy for the almost-certain upcoming tour. I did, and he supported the idea. Thus our lives are shaped!

I used my return ticket to go home for a holiday — as a success? Yes, as far as I was concerned, absolutely.

A week later, a telegram arrived at Marlborough Road, sealing Brenda's involvement:

OPENING IN THE COMEDY THEATRE LONDON WEST END. COME AT ONCE. BRING YOUR GIRLFRIEND AS ASM AND UNDERSTUDY. DOM ROCHE.

We found Brenda a bedsit near the Brecknock Arms. The landlady knew her parents. They opposed her going to London. My feeling was that her mother, a joyless woman, opposed everything except going to church, school, boring work, cutting the grass, and domestic drudgery! I went back to Ma 'Iggins. She only took men. That was just as well: the Doyles would have, at best, had conniptions if their daughter was in the same house, even, as an actor.

The excitement at the Comedy Theatre in London's West End was intoxicating! I introduced Brenda to the company and met the new director. It was felt that Dom, who had directed the original production, needed to concentrate his energies on his exhausting leading role, twice nightly, six nights per week — a schedule normally reserved for revues and variety shows, not legitimate plays; though calling *My Wife's Lodger* 'legitimate' was stretching it a fraction. As the stage manager, I had to establish immediate credibility, authority, and means of communication with the stage doorkeeper, the night fireman, the light and sound control, the house manager, the stagehands, and the front-of-house staff.

Our stage director, Jack Martyn, who also played Roger the Lodger, was a big, fat, ugly, greasy-haired, smelly man, on and off stage. I never warmed to him, but we had quite a good working relationship. Dom knew it and I knew it: Jack, as was the custom, 'fiddled' a little off the top of the stage-management expenses. He never could believe I didn't. I did most of the work. He allotted the dressing-rooms to the actors in order of their billing and supervised the one simple set going up, the Higginbottom dining-room. Meanwhile, I acquainted myself with house rules and practices.

As I went on stage for a final check before going to lunch, I bumped into our new director, Vivian Hall. He was small, skinny, straight of hair but not of sexuality; a Londoner in early middle age, he had a prematurely grey face. 'Do me a great favour, my dear,' he said. 'I want to see the lighting from out front. As you know, I'll be doing Norman. Would you do it for this afternoon's run-through? My first time to see it, you know. Thank you, dear,' he added squeezing my arm. Norman was the part I had played.

I don't know if I said anything. Probably not. Brenda was at lunch, or on an errand. Stunned, I walked in bright sunshine to the pub. Dom was there, with Alan Sedgewick, a big, handsome Canadian actor who played the GI romantic lead. Already we were quite good friends; he was like my big brother.

'Ah, Vincent. Have a drink, son. What'll it be?' said Dom.

'Is it true the director is playing Norman?' I asked.

'Oh, Christ, Vincent, I meant to talk to you myself. With everything happening so quickly, it went clean out of my head. I'm sorry, lad. The people with the money thought we should have a director. Hall said he'd have to have ... eh ... someone English in the part. We thought you were smashing in it, but ... eventually, I just had to give in. But you'll be still playing the other detective, and you'll understudy Norman, of course. Come, let's get you a drink.' That's pretty accurately what was said.

I made some excuse about not having the drink, and somehow left them thinking I understood. I walked up the street towards Lyons Corner House. Bright, bright sunshine.

Inside I was crushed, beaten. Dull images and lines, passing blackly through my head. The people in the company knowing I wasn't good enough to play the part. Brenda, Maureen McClure, Dick Carrickford, everyone at home whom I had told. I'd be a laughing-stock. *Gerry and Mary — they'll have the last laugh....* I knew, somehow, that I had never felt so hopeless before.

I stopped to cross over to Lyons. Buses, taxis, cars flashed past into Piccadilly Circus. There was that awful emptiness in my stomach, like when Mammy went to Father Luke's or wasn't there when I came home to an empty house. There didn't seem to be any point, now, in going on with life. Cool and calm, I decided there was one thing to do: step out in front of the next bus. I wasn't afraid. I thought: *It will hurt for a moment. There will be one awful bang, but then it will be over.* That seemed awfully good. Get away from this shame, this betrayal.

I took a step. Stopped. But it was a near thing. Only once ever again would I feel quite like that.

It wasn't fear. It wasn't religion. It wasn't thought for others, even my mother. It was the face of Vivian Hall that turned me around. *I'm not going to let that little fucker drive me to do this. Fuck it, I'm not.*

Well, I didn't. I went over to Lyons, had something to eat, went back to rehearsal, and did the best Norman I knew how. And I never stopped working on the part and the accent!

As it turned out, nobody laughed. Nobody thought it strange that, going into the West End, they'd want an English actor in an English part. Nobody liked Vivian, on or off stage. That helped, but I would be the perfect stage manager even to him. My time would come. I knew it, somehow. I didn't say it to anyone, even Brenda, but I knew it.

Dom got fantastic reviews for his performance and even some for the play. The drunk scene between Alan and Dom was said by Beverly Baxter to be the best drunk scene since Shakespeare's *Twelfth Night*. The night that Carol Reed, the hottest film director of the time (*Odd Man Out, The Third Man*), came to see it, Dom was so drunk and tired that he really fell asleep on stage, and it was obvious to everyone, including Reed, that Dom's wife in the play, Queenie Barrett, was really trying to keep him awake. The director of *The Third Man* and *Odd Man Out* did not return after the intermission. Though Dom was never quite sober in the play, I never saw the drunkness showing again during the run.

Dominic Roche was born in Ballymahon, and looked it; went to Sandhurst, and sounded it. He rose to the rank of Major in the British Army. He served in India during the Second World War in ENSA, the entertainment wing of the forces. He smoked, drank, and fornicated too much. Ate too little. Acted beautifully and lived for it. He was funny on and off stage and generous to a fault. His ambition was, and I quote what he said to me, 'to die of sexual exhaustion *and* on the stage'. He came as near as damn it to achieving it!

The play ran for over three hundred performances, to really great business. Vivian Hall turned out to be a disaster in *my* role, I'm glad to say. I got it back for the last week of the run and for the wonderful twelve-month tour of every major theatre in England, Scotland and Wales, including the Memorial Theatre in Stratford-on-Avon, that was ahead.

Brenda had a letter from her parents saying they were coming over 'for a holiday' — read, 'to see for themselves'. I don't know how long they stayed. Whatever it was, it was too long. I was able to plead work and keep out of the way as much as manners would allow. One whole day we spent together, showing them the West End.

The strain, inside, got so unbearable that about noon I suggested that we have a drink. Mr Doyle reluctantly agreed. As we were coming into Leicester Square from Soho — where we had shown them St Patrick's Cathedral, where Brenda and I went to mass on Sundays; probably the only thing Mrs Doyle enjoyed in her whole visit — I suggested a good lounge bar, up some steps, beside the Empire Cinema. He and I, ahead of 'the ladies', who kept a respectful few paces to our rear, stopped on the bottom step; he turned to his wife and daughter and stated, 'You wait here. We'll only be a few minutes!' Before I could say anything, he entered the licensed premises.

I followed him, and suggested that it was not a good idea to leave two women standing on a street corner in these parts. I didn't actually say that it was the territory of prostitutes, who were very protective of it; the very word 'prostitute' might have given him a heart attack. It was the shortest time I have ever spent drinking in a pub in my life. I was out in about two minutes flat! I must have done something right during their sojourn, however, for after that, I apparently became *persona* a little less *non grata* with the elder Doyles!

I very soon woke up to the fact that being in a longish run, even in a capital city, is — apart from the steady work and wages — a bore compared to the fun and excitement of touring to new places, seeing new faces, land, sea, city and especially countryscapes. But, meantime, I was saving enough money for a good visit home for Christmas. I liked the walks in Clapham Common, the talks with Des Perry, the movies just round the corner in the Odeon in Balham, the digs which we had moved into, Brenda, Des and myself.

Each night I made the long journey and the even longer return in the early hours between my room and Brenda's. Apart from the fact that we did not have actual sexual intercourse till our honeymoon, some seven months ahead, we enjoyed the intimacy, comfort, and excitement practised, nay perfected, frequently. Once, in spite of all that, Brenda had a very late period; greatly fearing she might be pregnant, she had a doctor's examination that proved she couldn't be!

Various friends, families and friends of friends visited. Eugene Black, who had given up the stage and was working for Heiton's Coal in their Westmoreland Street Dublin office, was one of them. He was living, a lodger and almost an adopted son, at Mammy's in Marlborough Road. Mostly we went to the Hand and Racquet for drinks, darts and stories. Occasionally there were parties on stage, for the fiftieth, the hundredth, the two hundred and fiftieth and the three hundredth performance. Then, often, there were drunken nights and even weekends at Alan Sedgewick and his English wife's large garden flat on Fairfax Avenue — Fairfax Gulch, we called it affectionately. There, working film and theatre people would join our merry band, mostly from the Embassy Theatre in Swiss Cottage. Clare Mullen, Oliver McGreevey — both ex-Brendan Smith — and little Dermot Kelly of the Abbey, standing straight and stiffly drunk, blinking his eyes, his flat peaked cap on head, always with a cigarette, tapping the ash on the shoulders of his long, too-long, shabby overcoat....

At the house in Balham, one week, a delegation of trade union officials from the North of England came to stay. We had great talks together every night at supper, after our show and their conference, on Ireland, England, trade unions, politics. One of them told me that what they were doing, as trade unionists, was making sure that the 'good old days' whose passing I was bemoaning never came back! They told me in no uncertain words what those 'good old days' had meant, even in their lifetimes, in the way of hunger, working conditions, unemployment and disease. It was the beginning of my awakening to some social realism and responsibility.

In the last week of the run, when I was playing Norman, I learned that the Dents — the smiling Dents of the shining white teeth and of Adelphi Films, who were going to make the film of the play — had seen me, and wanted me to play the part of Norman in the film!

We ended a short post-West-End tour in Bristol, and broke for Christmas. The tour would resume at Stratford-on-Avon in January. Dom said that historians would be watching the burial place of the Bard on our opening night, to see if Shakespeare turned in his grave!

Just after New Year's Day of 1952, I went back to Loughgall for my last visit to Father Luke. I was there at the request of my mother, who felt the good priest could do with the company, particularly as he hadn't been well.

'You have driven my car,' Father Luke stated rather than asked. Pushing the images of my carjacking to the back of my mind and concentrating on the few times in the autumn of 1950 when he had let me drive from Armagh or Newry, I acknowledged that I had, a few times. Did I think I could find my way alone to Dundalk, by the 'unapproved' roads? he then wanted to know. Well, yes, I was sure I could, if I was given directions, to remind me. I probably would have said 'yes' to any chance to drive anywhere.

We had just finished one of his gourmet dinners, preceded by Williams and Humbert sherries and accompanied by a fair share of a bottle of Beaune, and at this point we were sipping Hennessey brandies while I was puffing a Senior Service cigarette. He was running very short of wines, spirits, and a number of essentials, all of which he only bought 'across the Border in Dundalk'. What if I was stopped by the Customs on either side, I wanted to know? If you were a Southern Catholic, you didn't fool around with things like that in 'the Protestant British North', especially on 'unapproved' roads, where the trigger-happy B-Specials held sway!

But he had thought about that. In his car, which everyone knew well; wearing his great black overcoat, collar turned up, and his unusual black high-brimmed hat; sitting upright on a cushion, looking straight ahead, as he always did; if a Customs officer came to the gate-house at all, which was rare, I was to raise my right hand 'just so' and *keep going*. He demonstrated that little half-salute, half-blessing I had seen him give a hundred times. 'I hear from your mother that you are a capital actor!' he said, in a tone that, for him, settled everything!

About 9.00am, in spite of a slight hangover, I was ready to set off. I had been extravagantly breakfasted by the housekeeper; I had a list of items to be collected, a few pounds in English money, and a written description of my itinerary tucked in my back pocket; my clerical costume was folded in the back seat; all the directions, cautions and good wishes had been repeated. I pulled out the choke, clicked the wooden clothespeg on it to keep it out, pressed the hidden ignition button, and the Austin 10 spluttered into a kind of life. I nursed it into movement, backed out of the garage and bucked down the drive as the engine fought to run, waving to a strangely forlorn priest and housekeeper, and sputtered out of their sight in an unhealthy cloud of exhaust. I was headed for a range of hills, through one small town, on tarred but little-travelled roads. It was cold, very cold, in the car.

By the time I got the heat going, I was approaching the first of the hills. I started to speed up, to nurse the old crock up the steep incline. Fifty yards up, suddenly, I was waltzing from side to side. *Ice! Don't brake!* a voice was shouting in my head. *Turn into the skid!* And I did — left, then right, then left again. I was still on the road — straight — going in the right direction for a split second ... then slowly, slowly, *sufferin' Jesus*, slipping backwards down the hill. A car coming up, in the rear mirror! I leaned on the horn. He swerved outside me.

Nothing coming the other way — *thanks be to the crucified Christ.* Thump! and I was in the grass verge. The engine had cut out. Still, I was all in one piece.

Very gingerly, I edged my way back onto the little empty country road. The tyres wouldn't grip. Slowly, I backed onto the verge again; it narrowed up ahead, but it did continue to the top. *Well, at least I'm still on an approved road. No contraband aboard. Probably still in Father Donnellan's parish....*

The thought of going back flashed through my mind. I pushed it out. I edged my right wheel on to the road ... one, then both ... *keep the left ones on the frosty grass ... keep it in first gear ... ease up to second ... that's enough....* And a hundred years later, or so it seemed, I crested the hill. Then slowly down a long, long, road to a small village, where I stopped for petrol and a bar of chocolate. The sun was out and the road thawing, but night must fall, and I had a long way to go, so on I went. One more stop to answer nature's call, put on Father Luke's hat — which was a better fit than I had expected — an old pink cushion under me, the frieze coat on, the collar up; and then, at the 15 or 20mph at which His Reverence always drove, I entered the narrow 'un-approved' road and sailed without sight of a single soul across the border for which so much blood was spilled in the names of Ireland, Britain and religion, into the Irish Free State.

My shopping done and tucked in the space where the other front seat had once been, I was driving north towards the County Armagh border by about three o'clock — not as early as I would have liked, but not too bad. I crossed the actual Border on the same unapproved road, without incident, having put my costume back on.

The Customs officer on the Northern side didn't have an actual customs post; a small farmhouse residence served. Father Luke had described it in detail, particularly the gateposts, by which I would recognise it. It would be on my right going back. That meant there would be nothing but the window between me and anyone who might come to the gate; I would be slightly more visible than I would have been if someone had been at the gate on my way down. I was torturing myself with this sort of convoluted conversation as I drove up the very straight section before and after the driveway. *So far so good. Please, God, be nice now, keep the nice man inside his little house.... There's someone ... in some kind of uniform — don't let it be a B-Special, God.... Don't think about it. Think Father Luke Donnellan, parish priest of Loughgall, whistling tunelessly, eyes straight front, watching the road, 15 to 20 mph.... It's a Customs officer — don't breathe! He's touching his hat. Raise your right hand — almost a priestly blessing — pleasantly, casually.... Don't look back ... don't speed up ... don't relax ... yet.*

At the top of those hills some time later, I don't know how long, I stopped and saw the sun set on this beautiful, peaceful-looking part of Ireland. I can still feel the deep breath of happiness and relief.

It was dusk as I drove up to the parochial house. Father Luke was pacing back and forth before the hall door. He walked forward to meet the car as I came through his always-open gate. I stopped and rolled down the window.

'Everything go all right?'

'Yes, Father,' I said.

'Capital! Homeric! Vincent is the best man!'

He died early that spring. I was on tour in England, of course. Father Luke Donnellan. Father he was to us; not a perfect one, I suppose, but without him I doubt if I would be sitting here now writing this book. His life is, I believe, an unassailable argument against enforced celibacy for Catholic clergy.

6

My Invasion of Britain

Here come the fish and actors!

In spite of the predictions, in January 1952 there were no signs in or about Shakespeare's burial place that he was less pleased with *My Wife's Lodger* than any other citizen of Stratford-on-Avon. The reviews and responses to our presence were more favourable than anyone, from the Bard of Avon to the Ballymahon Boozer himself, dear Dominic Roche, had a right to expect.

The Shakespeare Memorial Theatre was a once-nightly venue, with two matinées — eight performances a week. To us, this was almost a holiday. Brenda and I spent days photographing historic buildings, shops, streets and cafés, and exploring the banks of the Avon River, where the gliding white swans know that they are the real attraction. The Swan Hotel and Bar was an major attraction for our company, as were the Dirty Duck and the Red Lion, where we (except, it has to be said, for Brenda) spent our nights and much of our earnings. The telling of stories, the singing of songs, the reciting of poetry and Shakespearean speeches, and the frequent consumption of frothy pints of beer, tart rough cider and stiff Scotch whiskies, occupied our energies night after night.

Brenda and I stayed in separate, adjacent rooms at a nice little hotel, the Barwyn, which was surrounded by well-kept gardens. Though we did not have bathrooms *en suite*, I remember being keenly disappointed that Brenda refused to have a bath with me down the hall. I sulked for quite some time, to no avail.

We travelled on Sundays, and usually had the trains to ourselves in those days of observed Sabbaths — except for the fresh cargo. 'Here come the fish and actors!' was our cry, as these two undervalued commodities were almost the sole Sunday occupants of Britain's iron horses. Time ruled our actorial lives. Train times, and distances between dates, were usually chosen to allow the company to arrive in a town in time to find digs and get to their 'home' for the week, in time to have dinner — and, most important, in time for several drinks before the ten o'clock Sabbath closing time.

Kidderminster, famous for its carpets, certainly didn't put out a red one for me. Brenda and I had failed to reserve digs in advance. Everything recommended was too expensive. By dinner-time we had nowhere to sleep. What we did have was a row, and dinner, separately. She went alone to find a place. I repaired to the pub, 'to find out if any of the others had spare room in their place' — of course, having a few drinks that kept me there till closing time! Brenda came by to see if I had found somewhere. She had, but they had only one room, and she had taken it. No, I could not stay in her room. They knew we weren't married because she had asked for a room for me, and 'that was that'! Eventually, I talked her into talking her irate landlady into letting me sleep on a kind of sleeping-chair in the dining-room, with my feet up on another chair. It was January in England, they had never heard of central heating (nor had I), and to add insult to injury, in Kidderminster, capital of carpet-making, the dining-room floor was covered with cold linoleum! Well, I never arrived in another town without having arranged digs.

From Bournemouth on the south coast to Edinburgh in Scotland, from Swansea in Wales to Hull on the shores of the North Sea, and nearly everywhere in between, we had a 'Number 1' or 'Number 2' touring date in 1951 and '52. The Number 1s were the best provincial theatres; the Number 2s were just as good, really, but a little less prestigious.

'Direct from the Comedy Theatre in London's West End!' sang our posters! During the get-in and the set-up, on forty or so Monday mornings, I was told by a stagehand or the driver of the truck (occasionally, horse and cart) as we went to pick up our sets at the railway station, 'This is the hardest audience to please in Britain. If you get by here, you'll get by anywhere!' He invariably added, to prove the point, a litany of top-line music-hall artists who had said it. Well, of course they did; Dom said it in his nightly curtain speech, if he was sober enough to remember the name of the town. Drunk or sober, he never missed a laugh, much less a line or a piece of stage business. It helped that his character, the easy-going, older private soldier back from the war, ignored by his wife and two children, had got gloriously drunk with a uniformed GI and stayed that way for the whole play.

Brenda, Blair Aiken (Pat Davis's very pretty, highly strung, very funny, nephew) and I were kept pretty busy on first days, doing light and sound and giving the resident stage manager and his crews their assignments. We were usually finished by lunch-time. Then we joined Dom, Pat and Jack Martyn at the chosen pub for that week, and reported on problems peculiar to that particular place.

The tradition in England was that 'half an hour', 'fifteen minutes', 'five minutes' and 'beginners' calls were given. A call boy who was late or early with those calls was likely to be reported. An actor who failed to indicate that he heard the call would be reprimanded by management. All this was observed by the cast of *My Wife's Lodger*, except that after the half-hour call, all subsequent calls for Dominic, Patricia, Alan and Jack Martyn were made in the nearest bar!

Saturday nights, I supervised the get-out. The men put everything, in the order I told them — last thing in, first out — into our railway wagon. Next day, that wagon would be hitched to the train that would take us to our next destination, sometimes a considerable distance away. There were ten of us in the company: eight actors plus my two assistants, Brenda and Blair. I understudied Alan and Jack McCaig, Blair understudied me and all the other men, and Brenda understudied 'Grandma', the ingenue, and the neighbour. Yvette covered the mother. If certain people had got sick, it could have been a theatrical domino effect! If more than one got sick at the same time, Dom said, he wouldn't allow it! Brenda went on a few times, and did very well, but that was about the extent of the cast problems. As Mammy used to say, 'The divil's children have their father's luck!'

The ten rail tickets purchased for the company entitled us to two reserved third-class compartments and a goods wagon about thirty or forty feet long. If food and drink were not available — and they weren't always — we brought our own sandwiches, and scrambled for drinks during short stops at stations where they were loading more fish and actors. You'd think that, at least, they would have given 'actors' top billing!

On the train, the company was about equally divided between those who didn't and those who did play, for small stakes, a great game of cards called Solo — some call it a poor man's bridge! I loved it, and mostly won money. Those who didn't play read newspapers, wrote letters, gossiped, and slept.

Most of the company's conversation was peppered with 'Ben Lang' — that is, Cockney rhyming slang. It was like learning a new language. For example, for the word 'stairs' they'd say 'apples'; actually it is 'apples and pears', but the Lang-uist only uses the non-rhyming word in the phrase. To make it more difficult, practitioners will invent new phrases, instead of using the traditional ones. One of my favourites was 'Pope' for 'home': 'the Pope o' Rome' equals 'home'! Get it? No, don't try; you'll get 'cat'! Cat what? Cat and kitten — bitten! And, like me, once bitten you'll be using the Ben for your carving! 'Carving knife' — 'life'!

For me, memories are images, moving pictures that carry with them feelings and dialogue. I don't think that was always so. I started to work in images, as an actor, thanks to that strange little genius Frank Dermody, at the Abbey

Theatre, about 1956. Now I find that when I use or entertain memories, even infrequently, they will 'obey my call', and often, unexpectedly, evoke other images that have lain dormant. The resulting excitement and nourishment is palpable!

Brenda's father and I had one thing in common, anyway: VD. Our initials. He was Valentine Doyle. It is not altogether surprising that the idea of Brenda and me marrying was first mooted on Valentine's Day. We were playing a once-nightly date in a college town — Reading, I believe. Dom and Pat suggested we should get married. We had a week out — a free week — coming up after Southport; Dom would get the Archbishop of Liverpool to marry us, and we could have a honeymoon in the Lake Country.

I was a few months more than twenty-two years old at this time. Brenda was a few months older.

I had felt real misery and jealousy when Ruth Smyrl had gone out with some Protestant man with a car for a time. I had felt real stabs of jealousy when Brenda had told me about being 'mad about' Dermot McMahon, and would again in later years when she would compare me unfavourably to him. At this point my premise was: Brenda is my girlfriend. I am her boyfriend. I am very attracted to her, physically. I like being with her. As far as I know, she feels the same about me. We are the same religion. We like the same people. Above all, we have the same interest, the same passion: the theatre. The theatre is our lives. We are two Irish people in England. We have a real future in this country, and with this company. We are the only ones in this company who are right for each other, culturally, religiously. I am going to be in the film of *My Wife's Lodger*; I will be in the Coronation play that Roche-Davies are doing next year, which will probably go to the West End and then tour. There will be work in stage management, and most likely a part for Brenda too. We are earning over *one thousand pounds a year* now, between us. What more could we want! Love? Love is wishing well, said James Joyce. Love is shared experience, said my sister Marie. Yes, we loved each other. In love? That's just kid stuff. We never talked about that, never said it to each other, never thought about it. Well, at the time, I didn't, anyway. I honestly don't know if Brenda did. I was in love with love. No, I was in love with being loved. The fact is I thought I knew it all, and I hadn't a clue!

The Doyles, Brenda's parents, wasted no time in shooting down the idea of a Southport wedding while we were on tour. She was their daughter, and it was their responsibility to make and pay for all the arrangements. That was understandable, and accepted without argument by all concerned.

I was disappointed at the loss of a theatrical-cum-publicity event, in which we would star, surrounded by our families, old friends, Irish colleagues, and the *My Wife's Lodger* family. But I kept my disappointment strictly to myself. Then, because the week after Southport was filled due to a change in the dates for filming, the wedding was postponed to the end of April.

Aldershot spelled army and 'the Tattoo' to English people of those days. To me, it spells the news that Father Luke had died. I was sad that I would not see him again, and glad I had gone up to be with him during the Christmas holidays. It wasn't something I dwelt upon. Incongruously, my other impression of Aldershot is that Brenda, Blair, and I went to the pictures every day we were there, and that every cinema there let us in free, without any hesitation. The tradition in Britain and Ireland was that professional artists were offered 'the compliments of the house' at the cinema manager's discretion, on the artist presenting a business card. If a show was doing very well, the manager might refuse admission. It is even more interesting that at the famous London Palladium, the foremost variety venue in Britain, for the Wednesday matinée, even if the world's most famous star was appearing, the professional artists lined up in a special queue; a uniformed usher came down the line, collected the cards and brought them to the box office; and we, the artists, were seated before the paying customers in the best seats. Our cards were returned as we collected our tickets at the box office — free! Of course, it is the least that should be done, in all theatres and cinemas.

Blackpool — an enormous ballroom packed with dancers, music by a famous radio orchestra, Brenda and I in our element. One morning — 6 February 1952 — on the way to the theatre, in a tram, reading the latest news headlines in lights, along the sea front: KING GEORGE VI IS DEAD. Saturday afternoon, walking along Blackpool Strand, scene of so many 'funny' and 'dirty' picture postcards, with Alan, Edna, Brenda, and Blair; a child swinging on a swing, crying pitifully, 'I want to get down'; the gaunt, weary, angry mother, savagely pushing the swing, screams in a flat Lancashire accent, 'You cum ear tu 'njoy thysel ant thou is bluddy well goin' ta!'

Southport — not getting married by the Archbishop of Liverpool! Going to a jazz concert on the Sunday night we arrived, in the theatre we were going to play, because Brenda wanted to go. I didn't want to spend the money; they were people I had never heard of — Chris Barber and his Band, Johnny Dankworth and Cleo Lane! Ouch!

Bradford is in Yorkshire. I knew from family history that my mother's mother, who had been banished from Trim by my grandfather, was buried here. We spent a chilly, sunny morning in the cemetery, but we failed to find any trace of my beautiful, tragic grandmother's resting-place. We were playing Holy Week there. I thought it the grimmest town we had seen in the tour. Underneath the theatre we were playing was another empty, deserted, cobwebbed auditorium, seats and stage. It was the creepiest place I have ever been in. I couldn't wait to get out of it.

Leeds — we were at the Leeds Empire, a huge Moss Empire House seating over two thousand, one of many of these we played. A pit orchestra, mostly brass, played in all these, and the excitement, the overture, and our *My Wife's Lodger* theme to take up and bring down the curtain never failed to set my nerves a-tingle.

Dom's friend, star comedian Eddie Reindeer, drank with us. He invited us to the famous 'City of Varieties — Leeds', where a continuous nude show punctuated with great comedy ran all day. I can still see Eddie, in his moth-eaten fur coat and ridiculously small felt hat, counterpointing tall, beautiful naked girls swinging on large cut-out moons.

On a different end of the dramatic scale, I saw Michael Redgrave, Kirk Douglas, Raymond Massey, and Rosalind Russell in Eugene O'Neill's *Mourning Becomes Electra*. The theme music was 'O Shenandoah'. In Sheffield, playing another Moss Empire, we were all invited to see two Western movies made by 'Slapsie' Maxie Rosenblum. Even though they satirised my favourite kind of movie, I loved them! Sheffield had always meant table knives to me. 'Slapsie' Maxie changed that forever!

I was playing my first role in a feature film, albeit a low-budget one. Not all the members of our theatre company made the transfer to screen. Edna Hopcraft was replaced by a blonde bombshell who became a star afterwards, Diana Dors. The lodger was played by a well-known Cockney actor, Leslie Dwyer, and quite a big name character actress — Thora Hird, I think — played the mother. Come to think of it, only Dom, Alan Sedgewick and I made it from stage to screen.

I was nearly sacked on the first day. Having worked all morning, and seeing I was not on the shooting schedule for the afternoon, I asked the production manager if I could leave, especially since I had a show to do that night. He should not have agreed, as I was told in no uncertain terms next day by the director, David Dent. I was being paid a total of sixty pounds sterling for three weeks' filming, and I needed the money for a wedding suit, among other things. I took his threat to sack me seriously and stayed on set all day, every day, from then on. Well, it bought my suit, which was used in a film made with the Abbey Players ten years later and made several splendid appearances on several splendid actors on the Abbey stage for more than two decades. That was probably the most good that my first film role did me, or anyone else.

Back in Dublin before the wedding, I was aware of a certain vibe from Brenda's father. I had had to reassure him already, in not so many words, that his daughter was not pregnant. Our relationship was not easy, so when he suggested that I should no longer call him 'Mr Doyle', I thought things were looking up!

I was about to say 'What do you suggest?' but he got in ahead of me. He said, 'Why don't you call me Dad?'

I made myself smile and nodded. I never did go that far! It wasn't that I didn't like him; I did. He was a funny man who should have been on the variety stage! It was a shame.

Brenda and I were married in an imposing neoclassical church on Griffith Avenue, Drumcondra, on Dublin's north side. There was a nuptial Mass, of course. Brenda, in a fitted gold dress and a feathered golden skullcap, looked radiant and happy. Eugene Black was my best man; Maureen McClure, later Mrs Eugene Black, was Brenda's bridesmaid. Most of our families and special friends from Marlborough Road, St Mary's, the Brendan Smith Academy and the fit-ups were there. *The Evening Herald* featured the bridal party on the front page that afternoon.

The reception was at Jury's Hotel, then on Dame Street. The food, wine, speeches, dancing and party pieces were all just what the doctor ordered. I don't remember anything but laughter and good feelings. I didn't want it to end.

In fact, I had to be told to go — practically ejected — by my pals. My wife had changed her dress; the coach (a car on loan from Uncle Vincent, who also lent us his cottage in Brittas Bay for our honeymoon) was awaiting us. Fond farewells, confetti, cheers, jeers, hugs, kisses, and *sotto voce* advice from the boys — and we were on our way.

A left at Jack White's Cross; a mile or so of narrow country road; and then the familiar, longed-for sandhills of Brittas Bay.

The bedroom was on the ground floor, at the back of the cottage. The sheets were green, well-aired and smelled fresh; there was a little lavender bag in the bed, arranged by my mother! We made love fully, for the first time, but Brenda's period was due, and duly arrived. We laughed about that. There was no panic. We had a lifetime before us, so we thought.

Back touring in the UK, one of the first stops was Swindon, where we had no doubt that our first child, Bairbre, was conceived.

I had a fear of embarrassing men who might be mistaken about my sexual leanings. So when I met with the stage manager of the Palace, Torquay, on a sunny Monday morning at the railway siding outside the town, I was a little anxious that he kept calling me, with a disarming Devonshire drawl, 'my dear'.

After we had set up, I went to see the theatre manager about tickets for the current show. 'Of course, my dear-r,' he told me, 'whenever you want!'

Brenda had asked me to get a roll of film while she was settling us into our self-catering digs. There was a white-coated, middle-aged man behind the counter of the chemist's shop. Before I could speak, he asked pleasantly, 'What can I do for you, my dear, this fine day?'

I'm safe nowhere in this town, I thought, going back to Brenda with the film.

'Don't be such a conceited idiot,' she told me. 'That's what everyone calls everyone here. Don't you call everyone "darlin"?'

At last it was Christmas 1952, and the *My Wife's Lodger* tour, still packing them in, was over! Brenda and I found ourselves back on the mail boat from Holyhead to Dun Laoghaire, across the Irish Sea. It was the worst crossing in living memory. It was the night an English tugboat, the *Enterprise*, sailed into world headlines and fame, and the name of Captain Carlson was written in wind, wave and salt water into the history of marine heroism. Brenda, being Brenda, though six months pregnant, struggled to the rail again and again to throw up, while the waves lifted the boat like so much nothing, hoisting it up on giant waves, then throwing it down with a sickening thud into the trough. Me, running after her, hanging on to her and to whatever there was to hang on to on the ship, helping her back to her seat to lie down, then flinging myself flat on a low table to keep myself from throwing up.

Our visit to Ireland was followed by my return alone to touring in Britain. I was playing and stage managing in *To See a Fine Lady — A Coronation Play*, which was a hasty adaptation by Dominic Roche of a Lancashire play by Armitage Owen named *Up for the Cup*. Enough said. I had been able to get Des Perry into the company. That made it less lonely. Leaving Brenda pregnant in Dublin with her family hadn't been easy for either of us.

Our first date, which we hoped would lead to a London production, was Brighton. We played in a lovely intimate theatre, in a town famous as a London 'try-out'. Our production called for a travelling clock, on the mantelpiece of an almost-unfurnished room, which a working-class Lancashire family had been given to see the Coronation procession go past. Brenda and I had received several travelling clocks as wedding presents. Indeed, except for some welcome money and a couple of travelling rugs, we got next to nothing but travelling clocks! The red one was on the stage at Brighton, when it wasn't in my lodgings, set to wake us in the mornings at ten o'clock for eleven o'clock rehearsals.

On the first night, the critics were all there, some from London. We were all in high hopes that *To See a Fine Lady*, as it was called, might emulate its predecessor — *My Wife's Lodger* — and go to the West End.

Any hope the show might have had was taken care of by Dom Roche. He was drunk, and fell asleep during the very loud playing of 'Land of Hope and Glory' in the final scene — sitting on his false teeth, which were in his back pocket, wrapped in a piece of toilet paper, and splitting the plate neatly in two. When the curtain fell I awakened him; he rose to his feet, inserted his teeth in his mouth, and started to make his curtain speech — 'This humble theatrical tribute to our dear little Lady, who will soon be our Sovereign....' — blissfully unaware that the alarm clock had started ringing on the mantelpiece! As he spoke, the left side of his dental plate would drop down, and as he pushed it up with his left thumb, the right side would fall down. Again and again it happened.

Somehow he kept speaking. He ended by saying, 'How happy we are to be back here in ... eh ...' He could not remember the name of the theatre or the town. '... back in this lovely theatre and this great theatre town, with the most discriminating audience in the entire British Isles!' The audience responded with good-mannered applause. The local reviews were quite good, the London ones not good enough. We didn't get to the West End.

The highlight of the week, for most of us, was seeing Katharine Hepburn in Shaw's *Millionairess*, next door in the Theatre Royal at a matinée. We did have to pay a shilling for her autograph, a notice at the stage door had told us.

I will never forget her entrance. She blew in the door of the law-office setting, upstage centre, like a fresh breeze. The audience burst into spontaneous applause. Perfectly in character, she gave a look that said clearly, 'Oh! I am in the wrong office,' and stepped out, closing the door in one graceful move. Then, as the applause died, she came back in, with a smile that seemed to say, 'How stupid of me, I was right the first time' — and went on with the play. Robert Helpmann, the actor and dancer, played opposite her.

I reckon I had at least twelve 'weeks out' during the *My Wife's Lodger* engagement, between July 1951 and December 1952. In the short *To See a Fine Lady* tour, from the end of January to the beginning of May 1953, we had about four 'out'. For most of these, we came back to London and stayed at the Interval Club, on Dean Street in Soho. It was a club for actors between engagements. There was a Catholic connection: it was run by Mollie Hewitt, a practical, devout Catholic saint with a halo of white hair and a sterling character. Married couples could have a room there, same-sex singles would share. You 'did' your own breakfast, but an excellent midday dinner and afternoon tea were provided for residents, and available to members and friends. Room and board, in the very centre of the West End, was a real bargain. Brenda and I were members. There was a constant flow of fellow travellers from Ireland and the fit-ups — most notably Joan Beardshaw, who met her husband, John Phillips, at the club.

When Brenda had gone home to have Bairbre, I shared with Paddy Scharuk, a.k.a. Paddy Joyce, an actor and singer, nephew of James Joyce. We shared more than a room: we shared food, at night, that he would bring from his evening meals with a sister of his living in London. He was an actor and I had no money either, but we shared it when we had it. We never starved, but we were often hungry! When working I was sending Brenda half my salary. Out of work, I lived on unemployment insurance while Brenda, in Ireland, saved on expense by living with her parents.

The weekly pilgrimage to the Employment Office at Victoria took me through Leicester Square, past old Nelson on Trafalgar and the Whitehall Theatre, where I had seen my first London play — *Reluctant Heroes*, starring Wally Patch, whom I got to know, with Dom. Then right on Downing Street, just to check on the Prime Minister; turn left at the end; and work my way by small streets, lanes, and bits of parks to Victoria. Occasionally I would give the House of Parliament and Big Ben the once-over, to make sure they were still there. Being out of work wasn't all that bad! Then....

The public phone in the passage outside our bedroom rang one morning, before breakfast. Paddy answered it and told me it was for me. Now, the phone ringing at the Interval Club at any normal time of the day was a long-running tragicomedy. The young actors and actresses nearest the phone in the lounge area, who were expecting or hoping for a call from an agent or producer, leaped at the glass door to the phone box, while every single head in the room, twenty to thirty of them, turned, hope that this one would be for them shining for a moment in every face — then all but the lucky one slumping momentarily, before bravely recovering and carrying on with tea, scones, reading, or conversation.

'Was it from Ireland?' I asked Paddy, a little afraid.

'No, it's an English accent. He said his name was Bullock.'

The dispassionate voice at the other end confirmed this, adding, 'From Victoria Unemployment Office.' He told me that I was to come to see him, that morning, to discuss my National Service obligation.

I was taken aback for a moment. Then I thought, *This is a joke some of the lads are playing on me.* 'What did you say your name was?' I asked.

'Bullock,' he said impassively.

'Bollox, you mean,' said I, derisively.

'Mr Bullock. And I want you to come here to Victoria at 11.30 this morning,' he went on, just as impassively as before.

'Good try, Dick. I'd know your voice anywhere, Dick Carrickford. Now I haven't had my breakfast yet, so call me later, mate.' And I put down the phone.

It rang again before I reached my room. I picked it up. The same voice, in the same tone, repeated the same instructions.

'All right,' I said, very politely, 'if you are who you say you are, read me my insurance number.' He did. I apologised and, later, went to his office.

He was a really nice man. The long and the short of it was: I would have been two years in England in May 1953; my wife being pregnant was not relevant; neither was the fact that I had served in the FCA Irish Free State Second Line Reserve. Unless I was medically unfit, I would have to do two years of National Service in the British Army, commencing in May, or leave the country before that date. In answer to my question, he told me that I could work in *To See a Fine Lady* up to a short time before the second anniversary of my arrival in England. 'Good luck to you and your family,' he said, as I left.

Well, I was OK for the rest of the tour. I knew, after the Brighton reviews, that the play wasn't 'coming into town'. My re-enactment of the phone call that morning was added to my repertoire of stories forthwith. My only regret was that I could not do the National Service, see the world in the army entertainment wing. It would have been the end of the Doyle connection to even suggest it ... though if I could have read the future, who knows what I wouldn't have done!

While playing in Exeter, on a lovely summer-like March day, I got word by phone that Brenda had given birth in the Rotunda Hospital, Dublin, a little ahead of expectations, to a baby daughter. Her name was Bairbre, after Brenda's character in *Ill Met by Moonlight*, and 'mother and child were doing well'. It would be some weeks before I would see my Fine Ladies. That was hard for everyone.

We ended the *To See a Fine Lady* tour in Doncaster – appropriately, I thought, in pretty nearly the middle of England. Our good friend and fellow actor, Jack McCaig, lived there with his wife. As always, they were wonderful to me.

I left the morning after the play closed, on the mail boat from Holyhead. I said goodbyes to the company. Some few, like myself, had been with both plays. The usual 'nice to have worked with you'; admonitions to stay in touch; hopes to work together again; wishing each other well – all sincerely meant, but, in the nature of our work, we were already thinking about finding, or, if one was lucky, doing the next job.

I was going home, twenty-three and a half years old, to a new daughter, a fairly new wife, probably a hundred pounds' savings in the Post Office, no fixed abode, and no immediate prospect of work in Ireland. England was closed to me, because of the National Service. As far as I was concerned, however, I hadn't a worry in the world! What I did have was a phoney 'adopted' English accent, which would make many in the Irish theatre think I was 'camp' and make more of them wince. I had lived among the ancient enemy for two whole years. No one had done me wrong – on the contrary: the enemy, I was learning, was within!

I bought a copy of the *Irish Independent* at Dun Laoghaire railway station and scanned the always-short column under 'Stage'. There was one 'character couple' needed urgently by a drama/variety fit-up. That left me out on three counts: the other half of my 'couple' would be busy nursing our daughter for some months; I was not 'character' by any stretch; and I had no talent (particularly without a singing voice) that a variety company would be interested in — or so I thought. The last small ad read something like: 'Wanted — juv. lead; drama only; immediate tour; quick study; salary according to experience. Telephone Frank O'Donovan Productions for interview.' It quoted a Fitzwilliam Street address and telephone number.

I knew Frank O'Donovan was a brother of Harry O'Donovan, Jimmy O' Dea's scriptwriter and partner. It meant 'quality' and it could be made for me, I thought, but I'd wait till later before phoning. I knew not to call anyone in Dublin before 9.00 a.m. — an actor, not before 10.00 a.m.

Brenda had rented a small Corporation house off Collins Avenue East, half a mile down the road from the Doyles. Not where I would have chosen, but Brenda wanted to be near her family, and they wanted that too. I'd have to make the best of it, and I easily persuaded myself it was what I wanted, too. When the gods want to punish us they give us what we ask! Oscar Wilde said so, but I didn't know that at the time.

The baby was lovely, I thought. Strange and wonderful to hold. Part of me! The surprise: a head of black hair. 'That will fall out and be replaced, probably, by something very different,' I was told. It did; it was replaced by blonde curls.

As Brenda showed me our new home, she brought me up to date. The baby hadn't been baptised yet. They were waiting for me, Eugene, and Maureen, who would be the godparents. We had already agreed on Bairbre as the baby's name. The front room downstairs was our bedroom, and also housed a basket rocking cradle for the baby. Later, she'd move to Brenda's cot; her parents had kept it, of course. Brenda was breast-feeding, which meant she'd be up during the night. The baby wasn't ready for a pram, but we'd start looking for one soon. Oh, I had plenty of experience with those things, with all my nephews and nieces!

There was also a dining/sitting-room with a fire, sparsely but nicely furnished. Brenda's parents were giving us the deposit on a house, two hundred and fifty pounds. That seemed great and wonderful of them. Of course, they hoped that we would live somewhere near them; there were nice three-bedroom houses near Santry that they wanted us to look at.

I told Brenda about the job and that I needed to find a phone box, right away. The nearest was at Malahide Road and Collins Avenue. I would call Frank O'Donovan, and if he wanted to see me right away, I'd take the bus in to town. I'd see Brendan Smith, too. He had left word with Brenda that he wanted to meet me before I made any decisions.

I met O'Donovan in a big, comfortable living-room on the first floor of a large house on Fitzwilliam Street. It was just opposite Tommy and Nora Coleman's, Mammy's friends. Kitty had worked as Mr Coleman's secretary/receptionist. He was a very successful dentist, a dapper, intelligent, kind man. Mrs Coleman was like your very favourite 30s film beauty. We were all crazy about her and liked him a lot. They had a special affection for me. Their little daughter, years younger than I, had developed a terminal disease when I was fifteen or so. I would visit her often, coming home from St Mary's and later from the Standard Life, tell her stories, and read to her. She was going to marry me when she grew up, she told them! She had the loveliest long, red-brown hair I have ever seen on a child. Darna was her name. She died before she was even ten. All of this I thought about as I ran into Mrs Coleman on my way to the interview. Having seen my own daughter for the first time only an hour before, seeing the loss and the new lines in Nora's lovely face, after all those years, brought it all very close.

The meeting couldn't have gone better. I could have closed the deal there and then, but I had promised Brendan that I would see him first. I realised, too, that I had learned a lot and gained a lot of confidence in my worth over the years in England.

Brendan got straight to the point. He didn't want me to take the touring job. He would be doing a two-month summer season at the Little Flower Hall in Bray. He had had a very successful one the summer before. I knew the venue well; I had seen the Ronald Ibbs Company do *Hamlet* there, and loved it. That production, a modern-dress *Hamlet* directed by Tyrone Guthrie, had started off at the Gate and then moved to Bray for a summer season. I was offered a part in it — Rosencrantz or Guildenstern, I think — but it paid much less than Brendan was offering. So I turned down Tyrone Guthrie!

And Brendan had several very good roles for me. I would be playing the Playboy in *The Playboy of the Western World*. Of course, there would be Butlins at Mosney every Monday, and he had in addition a permanent job for me with 'Radio Publicity'. That was an expanding little company doing all the sponsored radio programmes on Radio Éireann for McConnell's Advertising Agency. I would start right away at eight guineas per week; there would be another eight pounds during the season, and two pounds for the Mosney Monday show. In addition, I would get two guineas per week for each new sponsored programme. The fact that I would be at home was an additional financial attraction; the fact that I wouldn't be acting immediately, a minus. Deep down I knew that not being on the road was, for me, another minus.

The fact that I knew nothing about writing, creating, administering and producing radio programmes Brendan dismissed as of no importance. I would pick it up in no time. 'No time' is exactly what I got! The die was cast, even if this cast could die in the attempt.

I didn't! Radio is one of the truly great gifts given me in my life. It would subsidise me as an actor for the next decade or more. Strange: most of my childhood, we couldn't afford to have a wireless, but radio would make me a 'soap star' as well known as my mother's proverbial 'beggar's ass'!

Signature Tune: 'Lovely Lady'. After 30 secs, fade for:

> FRANK: *'Lovely Lady' and Colgate Palmolive are on the air!*
> BONNIE: *From now until 2.15 the makers of Palmolive Toilet Soap bring you a programme of music and song featuring....*

'Frank' was Frank Purcell, an architect who augmented his practice with fees for broadcasting and acting. He had numerous young daughters, and seemed always to be adding to them. I suppose he needed the extra money. He was a nice, quiet, pipe-smoking man with a pleasant voice, absolutely reliable — important in a live programme. 'Bonnie' was Bonnie O'Reilly, married to Sean O'Reilly, a pawnbroker. She was a sister of Beryl Fagan, Brendan Smith's better half. She was a warm-hearted, warm-voiced, delightful woman on and off the microphone. Nepotism is all right, they say, as long as you keep it in the family! I thought at the time she was 'oldish'; she was under forty!

The lines quoted above, and the format, were my first attempt to put together a script for a sponsored programme. Five records would follow, the fifth always an instrumental or orchestral piece which could be faded and the parting message spoken over it, cross-fading to the signature tune. We were allowed thirty seconds of commercials and an identification of the product at the beginning and end, in a very limited number of words. This formula, which I hit upon, with something like the knowledge of radio and music that the famous 'monkey at the piano' enjoyed, was to serve me and Colgate-Palmolive and various products of theirs for a very long time. For example, with Cadum, their French toilet soap, the signature tune was 'I Love Paris' played by Michel Legrand and his Orchestra, followed by four French popular vocals, a lot of Jean Sablon and another Michel Legrand to close. *Gladiator*, their hard kitchen soap, had 'Entry of the Gladiators' played by some English symphony orchestra.

The voices for *Gladiator* were done by Beryl Fagan and one Marie Mulvey, a woman with a nice down-to-earth Dublin accent. She was also known as Marie Kean, one of the finest actresses at the Abbey Theatre. She became, a few years later, the best-known woman in Ireland, excluding only the Blessed

Virgin. She became Mrs Kennedy, five days a week, for nearly twenty years, on the most popular radio show in Ireland — *The Kennedys of Castlerosse*. When John F. Kennedy came to Ireland as the President of the United States, the big question among thousands of Irish country people was 'Is he any relation to the Kennedys of Castlerosse?' Marie Kean went on to play many major character roles in film, too; her last was in John Huston's lovely adaptation of James Joyce's 'The Dead'. To keep the record straight, she had another name. Unless you had become a member of the Abbey Theatre Company *before* Ernest Blythe (he preferred Earnán de Blaghd) became Managing Director, you were forced to have your name in the printed programme in the Irish language. Marie Kean was known in the Abbey by her Irish name — Máire Ní Chatháin.

'You should audition for the Abbey,' Marie said to me, the second or third time I produced the *Gladiator* programme. I told her I didn't have any Irish. From my first month at the Academy, I had learned that the Abbey offered no hope for the likes of me who didn't speak our native Irish tongue. Blythe, the ogre at the Abbey, counted fluency in Irish as more important than acting talent. Marie — who, off stage, always sounded to me as if she was in an O'Casey play — considered that 'that was true and it wasn't true.' All the juveniles brought in in recent years — Ronnie Walsh, Mick Hennessey, Joe Lynch, Ray MacAnally, to give them their names in English — had put on weight and didn't show any sign they were going to take it off. Marie explained that it wasn't enough to bring in a young fellow from the Gaeltacht (the Irish-speaking areas of Ireland) — 'Blythe will do that anyway. They need someone experienced for a whole range of Abbey juvenile parts, *now*.' She suggested that I was 'made for them'. In fact, she had already spoken to her friend, Ria Mooney, the producer at the Abbey, and she was prepared to audition me. Then, if she liked me, Marie would get me someone to 'coach' me in an Irish-language audition for Mr Blythe!

And so I got coaching in Irish from Seamus Kavanagh, head of children's programmes at Radio Éireann (RÉ). He looked like a fifty-five-year-old, hungover Irish W.C. Fields. He had a nose that must have cost him thousands, and a bag of gravel where his tonsils used to be. He had a heart as big as his head and was a marvellous storyteller and actor. He had been a schoolteacher in an earlier life, and he must have been a wonderful one. He chose a scene from Micheál mac Liammóir's *Diarmuid agus Gráinne*, and for a couple of hours, five days a week, for four or five weeks, he took me through every sound, every letter, word, sentence, thought, and emotion of two good-sized speeches, until he was satisfied I could have walked into an ancient Irish encampment and passed for a native-born son of the Gael. Then, and only then, did he let me phone Mr Blythe and make an appointment for an audition in Irish.

One of the mornings we worked together, Seamus, who was a bachelor, arrived with little pieces of tissue paper stanching myriad tiny, bloody razor-cuts. I had enough sense, even then, not to ask him what had happened. However, he volunteered that he had had 'a terrible night the night before'. He had wakened that morning with 'the father and mother of a hangover, and the shakes'. As he had a meeting with the Director General of RÉ after he finished with me, he had thought it safer to go to his favourite barber for hot towels and a shave. The barber, always a good talker, talked and talked, fussed about with this and that, until Seamus's nerves could stand it no longer. 'For Jaysus' sake, Paddy,' says Seamus, 'will you give me the fuckin' shave!' 'I'm sorry, Mr K,' says Paddy, 'you better do it yourself. I had a terrible night last night, and I've got a fierce attack of the shakes!'

'You're looking at my handiwork,' said Seamus, pointing to the blood-stained papers. 'I'd better go the men's room and see if I can get this stuff off without bleedin' to death.'

My Irish audition was held on the stage of the Queen's Theatre, the Abbey's 'temporary' home — for fifteen years! Another monument to Celtic indecision. (I must give credit for that line to my friend Frank the Friar, priest brother of the great Abbey actor Philip O'Flynn!) The audition went well, I thought. Tomás Mac Anna, who directed the plays in Irish and the annual Irish pantomime, was very encouraging. Ria Mooney, who 'hadn't a word of Irish', to quote Mr Blythe, thought he had looked pleased. However, he didn't wait to speak with me, but had Tomás tell me to phone his secretary, Maureen McCormick, who would arrange for him to meet me. So far so good. I wasn't counting on anything; I had a season lined up in Bray with Brendan Smith, and there was no way I would let him down. I was sure about that.

Meantime, with Brenda, I went about buying a pram, looking at houses, inquiring about Corporation loans and government grants, and learning as much as I could about records new and old, spinning discs, and the jargon, customs, rules, and personnel pertaining to all aspects of sponsored radio. I was greatly aided by the ace disc-spinner Gene Martin, a charming, multi-talented fellow about my own age, working on both sides of the RÉ world — the sponsored and the non-commercial. They coexisted in an uneasy relationship in our national radio station, which was situated over the General Post Office, its entrance at No. 1 Henry Street watched over by the singular eye of Lord Nelson, who was still atop his pillar on O'Connell Street.

My days were pretty full, and I loved it that way. Leaving the house at 7.00 a.m., I cut across a small field to the Malahide Road to catch a 42 bus to the city centre. Passed the time of day with Tommy, the uniformed porter at the front desk, sole guardian at the gateway to RÉ's administration, studios and cafeteria. Got my recorded programme, and/or 78-rpm records and scripts, at the SPO (the Sponsored Radio Office), and a copyright form or log to complete, detailing artists, composers, arrangers, publishers, and duration each disc had been played. I hated that niggling job! Then proceeded along the long, tiled, toilet-like corridor of power to the other end, climbed the short set of stairs to the old studios. Gave the balance and control engineer, sitting behind the control panel, his or her copy of the script, went into the studio, put on my earphones, cued up my discs on two or three turntables — speech on one, music on one or two others — tested each table and the microphones, listened to the news on the non-commercial side of the operation until 8.15, then put my programme on the air. If there was no live show following me, I rehearsed my next show for that sponsor; otherwise I did it in the Record Library, which shared space with the SPO.

By nine o'clock I was usually on my way to a pot of tea — or a full breakfast, if I had got up late — at the RÉ cafeteria. This was the place where you wouldn't know who you'd bump into or sit down beside — announcer, producer, director, comedian, actor in the RÉ Rep, writer, advertising-agency type, B&C officer, or one of a constant flow of famous or at least newsworthy people in for interviews on Niall Boden's *In Town Tonight*. Within a few weeks, I was on nodding, talking, breakfasting terms with everyone from waitresses and porters down!

About ten o'clock, I would saunter up O'Connell Street on the way to the Brendan Smith/Radio Publicity office on South Great George's Street. I'd be going over my lines, inventing new radio programmes, window-shopping, and daydreaming. The daydreaming was sparked by the sight of some actor or actress I had seen in a play, or whose picture I had seen in a newspaper. I remember, as if it were this morning, one of my very first days doing this walk, crossing from O'Connell Bridge to the Ballast Office; and halfway across the road, coming towards me, in a creamy-brown tweed coat with raglan shoulders, was the tall figure (getting a little heavy) and handsome face of one of the Abbey Theatre's leading young actors — Ronnie Walsh! As we came abreast, he gave me that friendly 'flick of the head' Dublin greeting and a smile, and was gone. If the Pope had stopped to ask me to tea at the Vatican, I couldn't have felt better about myself! I actually said to myself, in a kind of amazement, 'God! I wonder will some young actor ever walk past me and be so elated because *I* gave him a friendly nod?'

At the office, I would read the Colgate programme file — particularly old scripts — write new scripts, play records for future programmes, and work on my auditions for the Abbey. Then, about noon, I would have a cheap lunch at Bewley's Café next door, the Stag's Head, or, across the lane, the Stag's Tail.

Tuesdays and Thursdays I would go back to RÉ to do the Colgate Palmolive. In the afternoon I would walk up Grafton Street, take a turn round St Stephen's Green, then go into May & Co. music shop to read their catalogues and play the latest records on their turntables. The manageress, Joan Smith, helped me from the start with news of new releases and advice about recordings, music and musicians. Go, then, next door to Peter Hunt Studios, to leave off or pick up something for Larry Morrow's programme for one of Radio Publicity's clients. Peter Hunt, an uncompromising, not gentle English gentleman, and his darling wife Iris recorded most pre-recorded sponsored shows on RÉ then. The quality of his work, his relentless pursuit of perfection, and his angry contempt for anything less, shamed me into raising my eyes from easier visions towards excellence.

Larry Morrow! Dear, dear Larry Morrow. I admit not many would say that about him, but I do. 'Good morrow, good people' — the opening line and name of his witty, substantial, satirical, disturbing program. He and his partner-in-life, Sheila — sister of genealogist extraordinaire 'the Pope' O'Mahony of Cork — taught me so much about radio, literary and theatrical Dublin. Gave me friendship, time, advice and encouragement. Shared with me, not only drinks, but stories, gossip and outright slander. Introduced me to interesting hostelries. It was from Larry I first heard of Brendan Behan — 'the poor man's Paddy Kavanagh,' he dubbed him. Larry roared with delight when I said innocently, 'Who is Paddy Kavanagh?'

The nights we weren't seeing a play, or I 'an old friend I hadn't seen for years', I went home to dinner, to a sleeping baby, Brenda, and often the presence of one or both of my in-laws, with their always-implied and often-expressed criticism of my way of life. My response: a bland smile. 'No prowoke!' as I had learned from Akim Tamiroff as the bandit chief in *For Whom the Bells Toll*. It took me twenty years and a stomach ulcer to break through my imperturbable smile and shout and show my feelings — in public, that is. At home I rehearsed quite often those outward manifestations of anger and frustration. *Mea culpa*.

Eric Gorman, a gruff, shy little gnome of a man, opened the side door in the lane of 'the old Abbey' and led me up the stairs, through his office, where he handled the day-to-day money matters of the world-famous Irish theatre, in Dickensian style. He muttered something like 'He's in there,' flicking a forefinger in the direction of a tiny cubbyhole of a room, where dwelt the ogre of the Abbey.

The dreaded, infamous managing director swung around to face me, from his desk at his room's single window, and indicted the bent wood chair dangerously close to the electric fire, barking quite pleasantly, in a strong North-of-Ireland accent, something that I took to be 'sit down' in Irish. I already knew what he sounded like. Everyone who had anything even remotely to do with the Abbey, from Marie Kean on, impersonated him all the time when they spoke of him. I already knew him by repute, not a wholly reliable image but one which informed my approach to the man:

Blythe had been born in the North of Ireland, a Co. Antrim Protestant. Had learned to speak Irish as a child from a maidservant, joined the oath-bound illegal Irish Republican Brotherhood, been jailed in England during the 1916 Rising, taken part in the War of Independence against the British. He came to Dublin as a supporter of the Gaelic League, perfected his Irish and wrote as a journalist for *Sinn Féin* newspaper. He turned to politics and was elected to Dáil Éireann (the Irish Parliament); in the ensuing Civil War he sided with Michael Collins and the pro-Treaty forces, against de Valera and the republicans. He became Vice-President in the first Irish Free State government, and held various ministerial appointments, including Minister of Finance in 1924. He was instrumental in giving the first government subsidy to a theatre in the English-speaking world. The story was told of how he had ordered the execution of seventy-seven prisoners, former comrades, in the Irish Civil War, and some said that he was a Blueshirt (I also heard he was not). Not long before the General Election in 1932 he cut one shilling per week off the ten-shilling-a-week old age pension, losing his party control of the government for several years.

Blythe left active politics with the defeat of his party, and W.B. Yeats brought him onto the Abbey Board. In 1941, on the death of the poet F.R. Higgins, Blythe succeeded him as Managing Director, where through devious dealings he got rid of all opposition on the Board. Before long he became a not-too-benevolent dictator. Blythe controlled the Board, company, stage staff, front-of-house, administration, artistic, language and financial policies of the Abbey Theatre. The driving idea of these policies was his oft-repeated 'The Abbey is not an art theatre, it is an instrument of national defence!'

As a rule, he only engaged fluent Irish-speaking performers. He compelled actors to use Irish forms (often invented by him) of their names. From the day after Christmas, for several weeks, he presented, in the English music-hall tradition, an annual pantomime, in Irish, loosely based on — others would say debasing — some ancient Irish myth or legend, peppered with pop songs and contemporary political and social comment! Whatever their position on the revival of the Irish language, even the most fair-minded lovers of the art of theatre, of the Abbey tradition, and of our native tongue had reservations about Mr Blythe's use of that theatre to further the language's restoration at the expense of artistic excellence. I slowly came to realise that any wilful use of the theatre for any purpose but the making of theatre art would inevitably be corrupting.

When he turned to me that morning, what I found myself facing was a smiling, bespectacled, pleasant, charming gossip. He was captivating, totally disarming — engagingly, nay, scandalously frank about the great people past and present who had written for, acted in, directed, managed, praised and criticised this venerable institution. No, he told me, the Abbey didn't bother about contracts. They used to, but on one occasion Cyril Cusack had asked permission to be released to do a film. They wouldn't let him go, because they particularly wanted him for the leading role in a new play coming up. 'Well,' he told me, laughing delightedly, 'Cyril played the part so badly — and there was no way we could prove it was intentional — that we decided there was no point in trying to keep someone against their will. So we' — he meant he — 'decided to do away with contracts altogether!' Amen!

Among other titbits, he illustrated some point by using the great short-story writer Frank O'Connor's *affaire* with the wife of fellow Abbey Board member Robert Spaight. Meantime, I was burning down the left side from the electric fire, freezing down the right because of the open door to Eric Gorman's much colder room, and wondering if we were going to talk about me and my Irish audition.

Eventually I got it in that I was committed to a summer with Brendan Smith Productions in Bray. He wanted to know what I was playing. I told him: *The Playboy of the Western World*, *The White-Headed Boy* and Joe Hession in Louis D'Alton's *Lovers Meeting*. Then he asked whether was I prepared to go to the Gaeltacht to learn Irish each June, during the annual holidays when the theatre closed down, if they decided to take me. I said yes, of course, but that I had done 'school Irish' for ten years. That clearly didn't impress him.

Harking back to the plays I would be doing, he said he would get Lennox to see *The White-Headed Boy*. I assumed that he meant Lennox Robinson, who wrote the play. Then, if Lennox liked me, I could come back in September and we would discuss it in more detail. As an afterthought, he enquired if I sang. I said I didn't. He seemed a little regretful about that, I thought. And I was out in the lane, and making for the 42 bus, before I realised that I didn't have anything settled at all.

Always an optimist, I thought it had gone pretty well. As the days went by, I wasn't so sure. But before long I hardly thought about it, so hectic were my days, between travelling to Bray and back and keeping up the radio programmes.

'In the name of the Father, and of the Son, and of the Holy Ghost — St Teresa, Little Flower of Lisieux, help me....' And I turned up the narrow drive, took a left through the wooden gate and drove the motorbike up the steep, grassy slope, turned it sharply as I reached the little flowerbed and let myself fall off the bike, pushing away with my foot as I touched the soft earth. Not a scratch on me or my brand-new 125cc James. I figured there must be a better way of getting off a motorbike … still, I had arrived at the Little Flower Hall in Bray, our summer theatre, in one piece. Not bad for my first ever motorbike ride!

I had told Brenda, 'I can't do all I have to do and spend an hour each way, six days a week, on the Bray bus, arriving at Donnybrook at half past midnight, the last bus gone, and walk six miles from there to here or get a taxi!' 'All I have to do' meant being at Henry Street studios for four radio programmes a week — two at eight o'clock in the morning, two at two o'clock in the day — and everything else that went with them. That had really been a full-time job in itself for the past two months — *and* I was learning, rehearsing, playing and publicising a different play every three days for the Bray season, and one other play on Mondays at Butlins auditorium, where I would perform and do the set-up with one helper! This for the next seven or eight weeks! 'Publicising' entailed driving around in a hired car with a loudspeaker attached, trumpeting something like:

COME TO THE LITTLE FLOWER HALL TONIGHT AT EIGHT O'CLOCK AND SEE THE GREAT ABBEY THEATRE TRAGICOMEDY LOVERS MEETING, *PERFORMED BY BRENDAN SMITH PRODUCTIONS' COMPANY OF IRELAND'S FINEST PROFESSIONAL ACTORS AND ACTRESSES! DO NOT MISS THIS THRILLING LOVE STORY, WHICH PLAYS ONLY TONIGHT, TOMORROW AND THURSDAY!'*

So it was agreed between Brenda and me that, as we couldn't afford a car — that went without saying — I should get the little motorbike. Soon I was motorcycling to and from Bray in daylight, moonlight, starlight and flashlight, as I rode learning my lines for play after play. During the whole season I never fell off, hit anyone or anything or lost a line on stage.

No longer reliant on public transport, I lingered longer after the shows in the lounge of the Royal Hotel. This led me, I am ashamed to say, into dalliances with a red-headed distressed damsel who came to see me in the plays, after playing a small role in one of them, I think. I mention this, not because it was the first of my lapses — it wasn't — but because she was the first who I was aware pursued *me*, relentlessly, humorously, and very provocatively! I found her open expression of her sexual desire for me, and her delighted, declared awareness of her ability to arouse me, startling, shocking, refreshing and maddeningly desirable. She was frequently and frustratingly a 'teaser' of satanic cunning. She was also married; she knew I was too, but thrust herself into my life. She had a car. Liked a drink. Always paid her share. We had great fun, and, however unjust, it was one of those things. I just accepted it was 'par for the course' in an actor's life. She soon departed from my life, or I from hers — I know not which, why, how, or when. I never ran into her around Dublin, afterwards. We came and went!

The company included Pauline Delaney, a good Pegeen Mike, and a young doctor, Austin Daragh. In principle, I had already developed strong views against semi-professionals 'taking the bread out of the mouths' of people who were prepared to give themselves completely to the insecurity of a life on the stage. That didn't stop me liking him personally, and he gave it and more back later as an Actors' Equity Medical Adviser. He also became an extremely rich man, which I didn't envy in the slightest. Even then I liked the good things in life, if they came with doing what I wanted to do. I never thought of being rich as something worth going out of my way for.

Apart from Pauline, Austin and myself, Beryl Fagan, Marie Conmee, and Dermot MacMahon played in the Company. I remember the hospitality, friendship and props that the pharmacy close by gave us all summer. It was owned by first cousins of Eugene Black. One of the girls married a Jordan, and gave birth to a son — Neil. He in his turn created several outstanding films — most notably, for me, *The Butcher Boy* from Pat McCabe's astounding novel.

The work was good in Bray — most of the plays well worth doing, the range and variety thrilling. It was much more exciting and fulfilling to me than *My Wife's Lodger* — the West End, Edinburgh, Stratford-on-Avon, Malvern, the film and Diana Dors notwithstanding! Priestley's *Dangerous Corner* and Coward's *Blithe Spirit* coexisted peacefully with John Millington Synge, Louis D'Alton, Lennox Robinson, American comedies, English farce.

Our notices were thoughtful, and very good. The critic on the local newspaper, the *Wicklow People*, 'knew his own know', as they say. A few years later he became the critic for Ireland's largest daily, the *Irish Press*. Michael Mills was his name. The publicity work I was doing introduced me to the theatre writers on Dublin papers: JJF, John Finnegan, in the *Evening Herald* — if ever theatre had a true and modest lover, it was he; R.M. Fox of the *Evening Mail*, another man of the 'old' school. The loudspeaker and I led to a visit from an English critic from *Theatre World* magazine. He was doing a story on Dublin, but staying in Bray. He was tickled at hearing, on a mobile loudspeaker in this working-man's seaside resort, the unusual combination of 'the Little Flower' and *The Playboy of the Western World*. We stole the limelight from the big Dublin companies — he gave us and our production the raves in his article on Irish theatre: 'Christy Mahon was beautifully realised by Vincent Dowling.... It was the best performance of *The Playboy* I have seen and the most enjoyable play that I saw during my stay in Eire.'

Lennox Robinson came to see me in *The White-Headed Boy*! Nobody told me. He didn't come around after the play, or leave any message. I don't think

I even thought about him till the season was over; I was simply too caught up in the work with Brendan. It was all I had hoped the theatre would be, all I had hoped life would be.

I had no doubt that Brenda and I would soon have our own house. There would be plenty of work for her, too, when she was ready. An exciting, interesting future, at home, at work and at play — that was the premise I bought into. When this season was over, I would either go into the Abbey or, if they didn't want me, take out a tour for Brendan and do radio; and there would be Bray again next year. I was quietly confident about all this. Of course, I always knocked on wood if I said so!

7

The sh Abbey Theatre

Oh, the Abbey Players make them up as they go along!

In London, they bury the queens in the Abbey. In Dublin they bury the Abbey in the Queen's' — or so went the music-hall joke of the time. The 'old' Abbey, as the original on Abbey Street was called, suffered a devastating fire in the early morning of Wednesday, 18 July 1951. Some people connected with the theatre thought that the fire could lead to better things, that now the government would honour the promise they had made at the outbreak of WWII to build a new theatre. Others maintained that the old building itself should be restored. It is clear that the loss of the old Abbey was to affect the acting style and the kind of drama performed for decades, perhaps forever.

The first move was to the Rupert Guinness Hall. Then, in August 1951, the Abbey moved to the Queen's Theatre on Pearse Street. The Queen's had been opened in 1829. In less than a hundred and fifty years, it would be demolished, rebuilt, restored and demolished again, to make way for an office building. It was a theatre famous for presenting a wide spectrum of dramatic and musical work and a huge array of great talents. In the early 1900s, a popular young actor named Tyrone Power played leading roles there in the melodramas *Rory O'Moore* and *Theobald Wolfe Tone*. By my reckoning, he was the father of the film star. His father's father had also been an actor with the same name. 'More Power,' said old Power when young Power was born!

The 'old Abbey' was not completely evacuated. Seaghan Barlow, stage manager in Yeats's time, and a master carpenter, continued to make the scenery there, a law unto himself. I found it delightfully ridiculous to see the scenery for play after play at the world-famous Abbey pushed in a handcart by a daydreaming stagehand, in hail, rain and snow, along the quays, across Butt Bridge, up Tara Street, over Pearse Street, under the arch and down the lane to the loading dock, for the company that William Butler Yeats and Lady Augusta Gregory built! You could synge that if you had an air to it!

Eric Gorman — 'Uncle Eric', as he was called affectionately by the older actresses — continued as company secretary and bookkeeper in the undamaged office upstairs. Very occasionally, he emerged, a pleasant and happy, friendly but shy man, to act in one of his famous roles. Ernest Blythe — or Earnán de Blaghd, as he termed himself — retained his cubby-hole there too, whether to keep an eye on the money or the building, or just to irritate Eric, I don't know. Probably all three!

As at my first interview, I sensed there was something bordering on dislike or contempt in Eric's voice as he flicked a finger towards the cubby-hole with 'He's in there.'

It was a warm September day so the electric fire was mercifully unlit. Pleasantly, Mr Blythe got straight to business. Lennox Robinson had 'thought I was quite good'. I hated that expression then, and I hate it now. I know it's supposed to be a compliment, but to an actor it's insulting. 'Ria' (Ria Mooney, an actress, then the producer) had liked my audition. 'Tomás' (Mac Anna) thought I had done very nicely in *Diarmuid agus Gráinne*, Blythe said. But while he was prepared to make an exception to the rule about actors being able to speak fluent Irish, he had to have an unqualified commitment from me that I would spend the annual four-week summer holiday practising my native language in the Gaeltacht of Connemara, in Spiddal. The Abbey would assist me financially to do this, he indicated. This I had already agreed to, and apart from the fact that I wanted to be able to speak and understand Irish, the thought of four weeks in Connemara every June was heaven on earth to me.

Now there was the question of money. I made the case that I was married with a baby, and though I was new at the Abbey, I was coming as a very experienced actor, having trained at a school of acting, toured Ireland, performed at resident seasons in Portstewart and Bray, featured in a West End production, played in a feature film and completed two national tours of England, Scotland and Wales. His answer to all that was, 'Well, we have another actor about your age who has applied. He has buckets of experience, better Irish, and he can sing, but we think he will get fat. We think you will be like Cyril Cusack, able to play juveniles until you're forty. So we are prepared to take you, and give you ten pounds a week.' The other actor was T.P. McKenna! He didn't get fat, either!

From Blythe's tone, I knew that was an offer I had to take or leave. I took, and joined the Abbey Theatre company in September 1953.

The Queen's is the only theatre I've ever known where the fleas were so big they drove out the rats! Early in my first decade at the Abbey, one of my favourite actresses of all time, Dame Margaret Rutherford, was playing the Olympia as Lady Bracknell in Wilde's *The Importance of Being Ernest*. She cheerfully agreed to let me interview her for one of my sponsored radio programmes. It would be a live interview from two o'clock to 2.15 in the afternoon. I met her and her husband at Henry Street in the studio, having come straight from my rehearsal at the Queen's. Right from the start we got on like a house on fire, and even as we sat before the mikes, voice checks done, she asked me if I could come to her Saturday matinée. When I told her we didn't have matinées at the Abbey, she — apart from being 'so jealous' — insisted that she would come one night by taxi during her second act, in which she didn't appear, and see me as Johnny Boyle in *Juno and the Paycock*. As the minute hand on the large electric studio clock began its final round to 2.00pm, I said 'Stand by' and was leaning out with my right hand poised to spin the signature-tune disc, when the largest flea I have ever seen leapt off my hand onto the turntable counter beside Margaret Rutherford's microphone! I got it with one deadly smack and we were on the air. She thought it was hilarious.

She did arrive at the stage door that night, in the full regalia of Lady Bracknell; she was escorted up the back stairs from stage right to the anteroom and slipped unnoticed, even by me, into the Royal Box. At the intermission before Act III, I met with her and walked her to the stage door, as she swept out into her taxi and back to the Olympia. Oscar would have loved it! I went to see her, of course, at her Saturday matinée, and went back afterwards to her dressing-room. I've never seen a better or funnier Lady B., not even Micheál mac Liammóir or myself, who both played her in one-man shows about Oscar. I am sure the Wilde Dubliner would have agreed.

I only saw one rat — a four-legged one, that is — in my thirteen years in the Queen's. That was on stage during *The Righteous are Bold*. Fortunately I saw it from the front, while watching a dress rehearsal for a revival. If I had been on stage, I would surely have been the one 'driven out'. I made the point to our stage manager, 'Red' Sean Mooney, that if a woman in the audience saw the rat, we might as well close down the theatre. My point was taken; I was very relieved to observe that a plethora of poisons and traps began to be used to good effect. They didn't eliminate the fleas, though.

I did once share the Queen's stage with a mouse, during a melodrama called *Copper-Faced Jack*. I was playing a swashbuckling, devil-may-care character. I was terror-stricken at the sight of the tiny mouse. I stamped my booted foot on my first line and, thanks be to God, it bolted! The old bricks of that theatre building, particularly those of the back wall, snuggled into the walls of Trinity College. We knew that they housed the nests of rats and mice, probably undisturbed for the best part of a century. I would try not to think of that rodent life going on, as it were, in parallel to our own. But such thoughts still invaded, and still provide the setting for my recurring dreams.

Another problem with the Queen's was the dust. One of our leading actors, Joe Lynch, claimed that when he went to a specialist with laryngitis, the doctor diagnosed him with black lung disease, silicosis, known only in coal-miners! On the other hand, as anyone who knew him would admit, Joe — who *never* failed to claim that his prowess and experience capped everyone else's, even Ray MacAnally's — had a still more irritating habit of being proved right! Joe was one of those juvenile leads whose growing *avoirdupois* was beginning to come between Mr Blythe and his vision of what constituted a romantic figure. To his credit, Joe never, in over forty years, admitted to any truth in Blythe's view. 'No, not an ounce of fat,' he'd say, thumping his powerful chest, 'that's pure muscle' — in a voice with enough Cork in it to bung a barrel of Beamish.

The perennial complaint of actors at the Queen's was that there was no contact with the audience in the stalls, because the raked stage was so high above their heads. In addition, the rake was so steep that our legs became, as scenic artists say, permanently 'rake-adjusted', so that on flat surfaces we appeared to limp. I bought into this particular line of thinking, for a while, anyway: that was what the older, experienced Abbey actors said, so it had to be true. What is certainly true, however, is that the actors who had played at the 'old' Abbey never adjusted emotionally, even though they did technically, to this 'shAbbey' — the Queen's. Neither did the 'old' audiences, who had become accustomed to challenging drama that would stretch their idea of what a play could be. Now much of the audience began to expect — even demand — all year round, the kind of easy laughs and shallow sentimentality that we provided in the pantomime and the John McCann plays.

Money should have been spent on the Queen's — its seating, dressing-rooms, and equipment. Then the 'old' Abbey's stone façade, which was and is extant, should have been used to house a redesigned auditorium, stage and back-up spaces. In that way, the National Theatre could have had two historic theatres, with every modern convenience. See what the Moscow Arts did with a theatre very like the Queen's. These two theatres would have served Dublin and drama a lot better than the cement-and-glass box that the late Michael Scott, former actor and friend of our family, and Ernest Blythe dreamed up for us. Of course, Ernest Blythe would still have been in charge all those years; and that, I believed and still believe, was the root of most of our problems.

The morning after I joined the Abbey, I was backstage looking at the call board. Ria Mooney, who was the producer (they weren't yet saying 'director') of all the plays in English, saw me.

'What are you doing here? You're not needed this morning,' she said, in her posh, rather English way — I was already losing mine.

I told her I was just checking the call board, to see if there were any calls for me. She was very moved. She wasn't used to the 'act-*ors*' coming in unless they were sent for; even then, she suggested, they didn't always come, or if they did, they came in late. For months after that, I was embarrassed at the number of times she saw me repeating my conscientious action. It wasn't long, however, before I learned why the actors came only when they were called.

About a week later, Brenda and I, in bed but not asleep, were rudely startled by a knocking on the front door about midnight. I went to the window and shouted down, as quietly as one can shout, that I was coming. If you have a new baby, you don't want her wakened in the middle of the night.

A very tall man standing beside a parked car told me in precise, clipped sentences that there was no need to come down. He confirmed that I was Vincent Dowling, introduced himself as Frank McCann and told me that it was Michael Hennessey knocking on my door. They had come to say that I had a rehearsal next morning at ten o'clock. I'd be playing Ronnie Walsh's part in *This Other Eden* the following night! Michael, in an undulant Cork accent that always made him sound as if he were asking a question, added that he had pushed Ronnie's script through the letterbox — 'with the moves and everything on it, you know'. Even in my dishevelled state, I asked them if they would like to come in and have a cup of tea. Luckily, they hadn't the time. Frank had still to drive Michael home and then go out to Howth.

We mostly used the English versions of one another's names off stage. For those who knew them from the Abbey programmes, Frank McCann, producer of works in the Irish language, was Tomás Mac Anna; Micheál Ó hAonghusa was one and the same as actor Mick Hennessey. They were part of a group, in the Company, of native speakers who usually spoke Irish to each other. A second group spoke Irish when necessary but used English as a first language. I aspired to being one of those. A third, older group, pre-Blythe, didn't speak our ancient language either on or off stage. They had their names in English in the programme. I had suggested that I should have my name in English, as I had established it before I came to the Abbey. My suggestion was ignored, and I became Uinsionn Ó Dubhlainn in the programmes. Even my mother often didn't know who I was in the plays. It would not be the end of the matter, but it was symptomatic of what was wrong at the Abbey.

While the 'Irish names' question wasn't something that improved the creative climate, still, the company feeling and pride remained strong. Broadly speaking, Dublin, where the Abbey Theatre was concerned, was divided in two: the 'besieged' insiders, fighting off the 'besiegers' outside, who were trying to get in and were prepared to bring it down in any way they could if they were repulsed! One day soon after I arrived, Brian O'Higgins, a wonderful character actor and a sad and witty eccentric, said dryly as we passed the statue of the melodious Thomas Moore, atop the public toilet in College Street, 'It is my ambition to see actors at the Abbey paid as much as lavatory attendants. The number of actors trying to get into the Abbey is only equal to the number trying to get out.' There was a lot of truth in what he said.

This Other Eden was a play by Louis D'Alton, being put on posthumously. I was taking over the part of a sensitive young man in a small country town, who suddenly finds he is the 'bastard' of a hero of the War of Independence. The moral forces in the community combine to try to conceal the fact that their idol has fathered a son out of wedlock. These include a canny hotel-owner, a whining politician, a super-conservative priest and Sergeant Crilly, who interprets the law as needed. *This Other Eden* combined political satire, well-observed characters and clever, witty dialogue. In the manner of Shaw's Broadbent in *John Bull's Other Island*, it had an Englishman — Roger Crispin, superbly played by Christopher Casson of the Gate Theatre — who charmingly moves the locals towards resolving their problems with his relentlessly romantic interpretation of Irish life as 'this other Eden'. Casson was ably equalled by Harry Brogan, angry and outrageously funny as the republican die-hard. Audiences and press loved it, and rightly so. I had seen a performance of the play, and I felt I was better cast than Ronnie, who looked too mature and heavy, though he played it well.

It took me days to get up the courage to approach Harry Brogan. He had a face that seemed carved from granite, but it turned out that this actor was as insecure as a harlot at a hockey match, and ten times as innocent. After a couple of drinks he would assume a very drunken, superior pose, threaten to tear up ten-shilling notes, claim kinship with the Countess Markievicz and mutter darkly about the English trying to get him. Harry and his drunken poses informed one of my best performances — Phil Hogan in *A Moon for the Misbegotten*, nearly fifty years later.

Before my first and only rehearsal for *Eden* began, I was sent up to 'the wardrobe'. I introduced myself to Miss Devoy, a tiny little lady all dressed in black, who had been the wardrobe mistress for ages past. There was no such thing as a costume designer at the Abbey at this time. One would be brought in for the pantomime, or for new historical dramas not already in the Abbey repertoire. Ria told you the kind of thing you would wear; you went through the stock and picked out what went with her view, and with your own sense of the part. If you were unlucky enough to want something that had been used regularly by Barry Fitzgerald (gone to Hollywood many years before) or by F.J. McCormick (always considered the best actor ever in the Abbey, by this time several years dead), Miss Devoy would exclaim, 'Oh, you can't have that! That belongs to Mr McCormick' or 'Mr Fitzgerald'. It was even worse if you needed a button on the fly of your trousers, even in an emergency situation. She simply refused to acknowledge that such a thing as a fly in a man's trousers existed. Your request would just be ignored. Fortunately, none of these impediments arose in dressing me for *This Other Eden*.

It is not surprising that the first time Brenda came to see me in the play, she told me she heard a well-spoken, knowledgeable-sounding Irish woman saying to a group of American visitors, in absolute seriousness: 'Oh, the Abbey Players don't use scripts of plays. They are so used to doing these kinds of plays that they make them up themselves, as they go along.'

In fact, the Abbey actors were only supplied with 'sides' — that is, scripts showing their lines only, preceded by the last few words of their cue. When a series of cues, as often happens, are monosyllabic, it makes things very difficult. Oddly, when we fought for and won the concession for a full script from a reluctant management, the 'old guard' of Eileen Crowe, May Craig, Michael Dolan, Eric Gorman and Harry Brogan clung, I discovered, to typing or writing up their own sides. The custom of giving sides to actors was a throwback to Shakespearean days, when theatre managers feared their scripts would be stolen and sold to competitors. This fear did not influence Blythe's reluctance to give in to our demands for full scripts for study purposes. He just didn't like 'change' — especially coming from actors, whom he considered wilful children.

There was a ripple of shock when I walked on without a script for my one and only rehearsal of *This Other Eden* and went through the lines and almost all the moves without a major problem. At the end of each scene, one or other of the actors — mainly Bill Foley, who had most to do with my character — would supply me with some tiny idea or suggestion that would solve a little problem in timing or positioning and help me not to kill a laugh. I felt as much at home as if I were with Des Perry, Eugene Black or Dom Roche. Better! This play had so much more quality than *My Wife's Lodger*.

My first night of *This Other Eden* went without a hitch. However, it stirred no interest outside my friends and family. A few days into the run, Christopher Casson, who was the son of Dame Sybil Thorndyke and Sir Lewis Casson, surprised me. He suggested delicately that I shouldn't cry at a certain point. I was shocked. I was very pleased that I was able to cry there. He hinted that perhaps it would be better if the audience were moved to tears by my character fighting not to cry! It took me quite some time to understand how right he was.

For me, this Louis D'Alton play, and the actors in it, laid down the first of many stepping stones towards an understanding of the craft of true Abbey acting, towards seeing how drama could mirror and illuminate modern Ireland, towards gaining my own understanding of modern Ireland, warts and all, and towards an understanding of myself.

Mick Hennessey had a 500cc motorbike. Knowing where I lived, he asked me one day if I wanted a lift home. As we roared up the Malahide Road he shouted over his shoulder, asked if I'd like to go for a spin. Of course I would, and we swung over to the Howth Road, cut across to the coast by the Bull Wall, went up around Howth Head, into the village of Howth and home to Donnycarney. As he dropped me home, I asked him to come to dinner the next Sunday night. We had Sundays off.

If I had made the invitation for even a few Sundays later, it might have made an important difference in my marriage. In the three months and more since coming home from England, I hadn't had a whole day alone with Brenda and the baby. Yes, it could have made all the difference in the world.

We had a fire lit in the sitting/dining-room. Candles on the table. Sherry before dinner. Mick brought a half-dozen bottles of Guinness. Brenda had roast beef with Yorkshire pudding, which we had become fond of in Britain, roast potatoes, vegetables, dessert and coffee. Mick was relaxed, funny, and clearly enjoying himself. There wasn't a sound from Bairbre during the really nice dinner. After dinner, Brenda fed the baby in our bedroom, and Mick helped me to clear, wash and dry the dishes. I have no doubt that we smoked our share of cigarettes, as was our unfortunate habit in those days. I was learning to like the Irish-manufactured Sweet Afton, thought that they made me cough less. Then Bairbre was brought in, fed, changed, powdered and smiling. Mick was wonderful with her. I was surprised and pleased by that. Why surprised? I don't know.

At some point, I lifted Bairbre and held her up, proud and happy, yet with that sense of wonder that babies can give you — the feeling that it never happened to anyone before, though you know at the same time that it's been happening for millions of years.

'It's like I *know* for the first time she is mine,' I said to Mick.

It wasn't the most profound statement I ever made, but I think it caught something of the feeling that had come up in me. I kissed her and put her down.

Brenda, soon after, excused herself and took Bairbre to bed. Mick and I finished the Guinness, I am sure. We certainly wouldn't have left it. We smoked some more, and soon after that I left Mick to the door and saw him roar off. A good night was had by all — or so I thought.

I don't remember any 'attitude' from Brenda that night or the next day. I know Mick talked, a number of times, about how much he had enjoyed himself.

Quite a long time after that, we had moved to our own house at 24 Shanowen Road in Santry. We must have been having a pretty nasty row, which culminated in Brenda saying something like: 'And after I had carried her for nine months, given birth to her by myself with you in England, minded and fed her, night after night, month after month here, with you gone from early morning and coming back after she was gone asleep, you, in front of a total stranger, have the gall to tell me, "It's like I know for the first time she is mine!"'

The intensity of her anger and resentment stunned me. I hadn't exactly been holidaying those eleven months, especially since coming back to Ireland. Besides, my comment had been a response to being *home* with *my* family at last.

I didn't feel angry, just utterly hopeless. I was stunned. As at most times when something really shattering happens to me, I went cold — an instinctive response, but one that always seemed to upset Brenda even more.

'I believe it was a reasonable thing to say, in the circumstances,' was all I said. Somehow I know I must I have sounded like my father.

Our house, Number 24, was in a row of new houses with five others on Shanowen Road, which runs east to the Airport Road and Santry Village, and west towards a plant where cars were assembled. Small front gardens and low brick-and-cement walls, with an iron gate, separated us from the cement footpath and road. Opposite was Shanliss Road, with a Number 16 bus stop on either side. There was a tobacconist-cum-newsagent beside the 'into-town' bus stop. Each house had three bedrooms, two reception rooms with fireplaces, a kitchen, one bathroom and one separate toilet. We had a long garden behind, with which, as in Mount Merrion, we did the minimum required to keep it from going wild. We had a play-cum-storage shed built there. Wooden fences separated us from neighbours to the sides, and a lane ran behind.

The house cost £2,250, to be repaid over thirty years. Dublin Corporation gave us a low-interest loan at two and a half per cent interest, and a government grant had reduced the sale price by two or three hundred pounds. Our new home was on the north side of Dublin, which was hostile country to me culturally and emotionally. I only realised this fully when I left it, thirteen years later.

It housed us and we had good neighbours. It was, in the early days, within walking distance of open country and nice little country roads and villages, which I made good use of. We could afford it, but it was far too near my father- and mother-in-law for anyone's good. That was serious. I should never have agreed to go there. I did, and nobody would have shot me if I hadn't. There was only myself to blame.

If some thought D'Alton's *This Other Eden* had echoes of George Bernard Shaw, John O'Donovan, the author of the first play of 1954, a brand new work, seemed to see himself as kind of reincarnation of the great Irishman. They had much in common. John was a writer, a wit, a Dubliner, and a delightful but, like most of us, sometimes irascible man. He did not endear himself to the cast of his play *The Half-Millionaire* by insisting, on the first morning, that he should read aloud the whole play, clearly with the intention of showing us how it should be done. He took up the whole three hours' rehearsal time, one-twelfth of the entire rehearsal period. We were bored to distraction.

John O'Donovan had been schooled at Synge Street Christian Brothers, where he was encouraged to be interested in theatre by Francis MacManus, then teaching there, along with another future Abbey writer, James Plunkett. He was a journalist for many years but is probably best remembered for his radio programme, *Dear Sir or Madam*, in which he took satirical swipes at Irish mores. His first plays had been rejected by the Abbey, though with encouraging noises, so it was a relief to him when *The Half-Millionaire* was accepted and ran for two weeks. Synge Street was where George Bernard Shaw had lived with his family. John later wrote *The Shaws of Synge Street*, which we produced at the Queen's.

My part was small. I was playing a slightly moronic Dublin printer's apprentice on a newspaper, who made about three or four entrances in the play. His answer to any remark made to him was, 'I'm only telling you what Paddy said.' I realised that this could be a show-stopper. I was a little disappointed that neither Ria Mooney nor John O'Donovan had anything in the way of direction to give me, nor did the cast ever laugh during rehearsal. However, I was strangely confident that the audience would get it. They did. I brought down the house on my line every time, got rounds of applause on exits, and had really satisfactory notices. For years after, people would greet me with 'I'm only telling you what Paddy said.' More important, my standing at the Abbey quietly rose. I had something confirmed for me, too, that I had suspected for some time. It is dangerous to pay attention to the laughs other actors give to lines in rehearsal, as they very often don't come in performance. I found that true wherever I went.

It was the actors who restricted the rehearsal hours to two or three hours a day, except for the two dress rehearsals before an opening. Sandwiches and tea were supplied in the stalls bar on those days when the actors were full-time at the theatre. There was one glorious exception to this particular food tradition: the play *A Riverside Charade*, which was put up a little later, in July 1954.

Everything about this particular play was exceptional. It was an exceptionally bad play. Indeed, you couldn't call it a play at all; the author didn't, though he intended it to be performed as one, and he submitted it to the

Abbey. It had no discernible plot, a huge cast, expensive costumes and a live goat. Or was it an actor in a goat-skin? It had the shortest run of any play in English in my time; it was perhaps the only one to be withdrawn before a week was out — after three days, if I remember correctly. This was in spite of it going on in Horse Show Week, the best week of the year. The exception to the 'sandwiches and tea' was that the author brought to each dress rehearsal buckets — buckets — full of strawberries and fresh cream. He was the only member of the British House of Lords to have a play performed at the Irish Abbey. He was Lord Moyne of the Guinness family, otherwise known as Bryan Guinness. The piece was aptly titled a 'charade'; that it was, and it was also Blythe's gesture of gratitude to the Guinnesses for the loan of their Hall after the fire.

The twelve days' rehearsal per play was management policy. Most new plays ran for two weeks at the Queen's, as did revivals. Among the notable exceptions that ran for longer were *Home is the Hero* by Walter Macken, *This Other Eden* and, later, *Twenty Years A-Wooing* and the other Dublin comedies by John McCann, who had been a journalist and Dublin's Lord Mayor. In 1954, during the eleven-month performance year, there were seven 'new to the Abbey' plays produced; one of these was a full-length costume play in Irish. Furthermore, the annual pantomime played for four weeks. In addition, one-act plays in Irish were prepared and presented. English revivals were also mounted continually, often with cast changes.

The company was more or less twenty people strong, when you count actors released for films, compassionate reasons, or illness. When actors were free, which wasn't often, they kept as far from the theatre as possible. Ria, herself under attack from some commentators in the media, had at least once complained about the onerous task of the seventeen productions she had to do in one year. She was given little support by the management, and on one occasion was derogatorily referred to as 'menopausal' when she attempted to deal with some of the issues facing the company.

Later, when I was on the Players' Council, Blythe was quite open with us concerning the fact that he had given Ria her job as producer in order to silence the criticism that arose in the newspapers in 1947 in the wake of Valentin Iremonger's outburst from the stalls of the Abbey. It was before the final act of *The Plough and the Stars*, and he lambasted the artistic policy as utterly incompetent. Iremonger's views were endorsed by *The Irish Times*.

'Ria was behind it, you see,' Blythe asserted. 'Grasp the talon and the bird is lost!' He quoted this same line with great glee when he told us that he was appointing to the Board the arch-critic of the Abbey, the *Catholic Standard*'s Gabriel Fallon. I don't believe Gabriel ever wrote a bad word about us after that! Interesting, is it not, that Blythe should have used Tolstoy's subtitle for his play *The Power of Darkness, or If One Claw is Caught, the Whole Bird is Lost* as one of his guiding influences. The other dominant saying he invariably used if asked to concede one of his blindly held positions was 'I'd rather die fighting than commit suicide.' I am ignorant of the origin of that one, but it carries in it Blythe's Spirit!

Actors, however they might feel about management, did have security. It was said you had to commit murder to be sacked, and it was nearly true. The job security is what really made 'the besiegers' see green. We were paid very badly. I, like Joe Lynch, had started at ten pounds a week. That was a big deal! May Craig, after forty-seven years with the company, had seven pounds a week. Eileen Crowe had maybe twelve. While she richly deserved to be in the top echelon, it was because she was the widow of the great 'F.J.' that Blythe deigned to put her there. Players, especially married players, unless married to someone gainfully employed, constantly needed to augment earnings by working on radio or film, adjudicating at drama festivals or directing amateurs, to keep their heads above water. I even posed a few times for 'prestige' advertisements in American magazines. An hour a day travelling, an hour or two studying, three hours' rehearsal and three hours' playing — before my radio work — was routine. The remainder of the day was my own.

I believed all of this was worth it to be in the Abbey. That same feeling was shared by almost everyone there. No matter what insensitive, hurtful actions or attitudes the theatre hierarchy took against the company or its members, the Abbey Theatre itself held the love and loyalty of almost every one of us. Slowly I began to realise that it wasn't necessary, nor was it the right of the management and indeed the nation, to take advantage of the actors' love of the company to the extent that they did. This realisation would lead slowly to another time-consuming and far-reaching obligation that some had already undertaken and which I soon would seek: election to the Players' Council.

Around this time I joined the Labour Party. Again, it was on my brother Jack's suggestion, and though I supported and support its ideals, most of my political friends were in Fianna Fáil. During my years at the Abbey, my personal political attitudes were respected by all government parties.

Blythe's commitment to the Irish language was palpable in all he did; but what were his criteria for choosing plays in English? I began to see that they included the following: an Irish subject by an Irish writer, one set, three acts, preferably ten actors or less, realistic, observing the unities of time and place, with a logical series of events and no foul language. All of these combined to meet his oft-stated belief that the Abbey was 'not an art theatre but an instrument of national defence'. And, in addition, plays should definitely have *no ghosts*! He would certainly have rejected *Hamlet*. He did reject Hugh Leonard's *Madigan's Lock* and lose us this important playwright for too long.

'Move down right on that line, Joe,' I remember Ria telling Joe Lynch at an early rehearsal of *Twenty Years A-Wooing*.

'Why am I moving down there, then?' Joe asked incredulously.

'Because I want you there,' was the answer, and she went on to say something to someone else.

'I'll tell you why she wanted me down there,' said Joe, after the rehearsal. 'Typical Mooneyesque bloody move. Cross down right because someone is coming in centre on the next page.'

And it was true. 'She couldn't direct traffic' was the common complaint from the actors. As it's the poor what helps the poor, so it was the actors what helped each other. I also began to hear the name of Frank Dermody mentioned as a true dramatic artist, especially by Philip O'Flynn and his wife Angela Newman, both of whom I grew to like and admire more and more on stage and as friends. Philip continually attacked and articulated the factors, the causes, the insensitivity, the wrong thinking and the stupidity that were threatening to erode the creativity and the joy that is essential to good work. His enemies in the company — and he had made them mostly with his outspoken, often tactless criticism — called him 'Cribber' Flynn; but then, so did his friends. With Philip's encouragement, I ran for the Players' Council and was elected by a good margin. 'The thin end of a very long wedge,' Blythe was to term my election, twelve years later. I joined Ray MacAnally, Bill Foley, and Philip O'Flynn, an Olympian!

Ray MacAnally spoke in a clipped, fast Northern Ireland accent with hard consonants — a far cry from my ex-girlfriend Rita's soft 'I thank so....' Ray ended almost every sentence with a rhetorical 'you know?' He hardly ever waited for an answer, just kept rattling on.

Ray was inclined to do this on stage too, to the annoyance of Michael Dolan, the doyen of the Abbey Players, a former manager. Michael was the best small-part actor I have seen anywhere and a perfect gentleman. I had met him during the making of *A Christmas Carol*. One morning, at the break in rehearsal, Michael took Ray aside. (Ray, to give him his due, told me this himself.)

'Eh ... eh ... eh ....' Michael always began. 'Where are you from, Ray?'

Ray was taken aback. The unexpected question threw him. 'I — ah — from Buncrana, you know?'

'Eh ... eh ... eh ... what county is that in?'

'Well, I — ah — thought everyone knew that. Donegal, you know?'

'What does your father do?' asked Michael, who knew very well the answer, and Ray knew he knew.

'Um ... bank manager ... Ulster Bank,' stammered Ray.

'Ray,' said the old actor, very gently, 'I've asked you a few questions that you have known the answers to all your life. Yet you had to stop and think about them, and why I was asking them. Now stop bouncing cues off me on stage like they were table-tennis balls!' With that, he shuffled back to the rehearsal, eh-eh-eh-ing.

Ray knew he had learned a valuable acting truth. Typically of him, and of the Abbey actor in general, he shared it with the new arrival. Around this time Ray was released from rehearsal for a few days to be with his father, who was having an operation on his penis for what I now take to be cancer of the prostate gland. He arrived back after a couple of days. Before anyone could ask him how his father's operation had gone, he announced to the entire rehearsal, 'My old man's old man's all right!'

In the vernacular of Catholic rural Ireland, Ray MacAnally was a 'spoiled priest'. He wasn't popular with the company at that time. He covered his insecurity with an aggressive assurance. He never seemed to listen. Like Joe Lynch, but without his charm or humour, he suffered from verbal diarrhoea. Like Joe, he would claim the impossible, and eventually seem to pull it off. He became a powerful actor, though not a generous one to be on stage with. The play often lost while Ray won. I didn't fight with him, nor did I let him away with anything. I faced him with what he was doing to me and to the play, told him how he was making things difficult on stage. I kept doing that until he stopped with me in that particular play. It was a long, long time before we became friends. Eventually, I'm glad to say, we did.

Work, Oscar Wilde said, is the curse of the drinking class; but if he had lived in the Ireland of my day, he would have found an even greater curse. It was called 'the round'. The round was the obligation of each man in turn, in any gathering of two or more, to buy a drink for everyone in the group, whether they wanted it or not.

My friend at the Gate, Dermot Tuohy, told me he knew he was back in Dublin after a long stay in London when he was approaching the Shakespeare Bar on Parnell Street one afternoon and saw a little 'Joxer' of a Dublin man run out the door. After him came a big 'Captain Boyle' figure. He grabbed the smaller man and hissed at him, 'I just bought you a pint.'

'I know,' said the little man. 'I've had enough. I don't want any more.'

'I don't care if you want it or not, you're going to drink it.' And he dragged his boozing companion back to the pub.

I have known a man dying of thirst to walk miles to a pub where he was not known, sometimes making a journey to another town, because, though he had enough money to buy himself a drink or two, he had not the wherewithal to buy a round if he fell among friends or acquaintances.

A poet on the Abbey Board, Roibeárd Ó Faracháin, had a reputation for being 'slow on the draw' in the matter of his round (we always claimed that Roibeárd had written his own version of Earnán O'Malley's *On Another Man's*

Wound — but Roibeárd's version was called *On Another Man's Round*). But I only ever met one drinking man in my Ireland years who steadfastly refused to take a drink on any man's round. Like many of my friends, he had nothing to do with theatre. 'I'm on my own, actually,' I heard the man say a thousand times, if I heard him say it once. He was a Kerry man from Cahirciveen, who taught wood and leather crafts at a vocational school in Dublin — not a highly paid position. His name was Sean O'Shea. We'd call him Sean 'I'm on my own actually' O'Shea, to differentiate between him and the singer Sean Ó Sé. Our Sean was a great storyteller. I have dined out around the world on the stories he told us in his deep, r-r-rumbling Kerry voice, which matched the deep humanity of his sense of humour. I am indebted to Sean for a story that captures the style of the great Irish poet Patrick Kavanagh, who stalked through our lives barely noticing us — or me, anyway. Sean, who knew and admired him, met the great man some months after Kavanagh's marriage, late in life.

'"How are you enjoying married life, Paddy?" I asked him,' said Sean. '"Well, Jack," Paddy declared — he always called me Jack,' explained Sean. '"If you get married you'll be disappointed, and if you don't get married you'll be disappointed."' And he continued on his way into MacDaid's, his spiritual home.

One night, before Paddy got married, T.P. McKenna invited our crowd over to his place to meet the poet. Kavanagh, like the man who came to dinner, only worse, had moved in on T.P. and stayed some months.

'You're all mummers,' said the poet, breathing as if he had a stage thunder-sheet in his chest. 'Make me laugh, if you are any good. It's a black night for me.'

T.P., Pat Layde, Phil O'Flynn, Angela and I all told our best stories. We laughed at each other's efforts, in varying degrees, but Patrick Kavanagh never cracked a smile. He only groaned the louder. 'It's a black night!' — and he went sadly, coughing and groaning, to bed. We all agreed that he was a wonderful poet but the worst audience we had ever played to. T.P., we learned then, had told Paddy earlier that night that he would have to leave or T.P.'s wife, May, would.

T.P. McKenna, one of our crowd, and Pat Layde, another, had followed me into the Abbey in fairly short order. T.P. was from Mullagh, County Cavan. He was born at the same time, on the same day of the same month, in the same year as I was — 7 September 1929, about 2.00 p.m.. I always gave my age as of my next birthday, he as of his last birthday. T.P. gave out hell to me every time I gave my age, especially as we got older, because everyone knew we were 'twins'. 'You are not forty, Vincent Dowling. You are thirty-nine!' he exploded, I remember, his lips pursed on the 'f' of 'forty'.

Strongly built, with a magnificent head of wavy hair, which he never lost, he had an aristocratic straight nose. 'Your head'd look great on a ha'penny,' an actor had ad-libbed about T.P. as Robert Emmet! His accent was a small-town refined by his time as a bank official. He was a brilliant mimic; his Patrick Kavanagh was better than the poet himself. He was, and is, a marvellous, versatile actor. Apparently an extrovert, he had a worry-wart gnawing in his vitals that was balanced by a rich sense of humour. He hated the country; he totally embraced city life, manners, and tailored clothes. 'Jesus, Dowling, if you'd lived for eighteen years in Mullagh, you wouldn't want to be going to Connemara for your holidays!'

On one occasion, he rightly accused me of being 'a Victorian Puritan, in spite of your sexual goings-on'. I was shocked. I realised he was right. He married a few years later than I, and was wholesomely frank with everyone he worked with about his worries in the matter of his prowess on his honeymoon. This led to an English actor, with whom he had done a Scotland Yard film, ending a letter to T.P. thus: 'I have found a new pill that will solve all your problems. It is a mixture of aphrodisiac and tranquillizer. It makes you want it, but if you don't get it, you won't care!' T.P. laughed loudest of all. That was another of his charms. He always laughed at himself.

Patrick Layde was a tragedy in one actor. Born to a poor family in Mullingar, his father, he told us, had been a 'spalpeen fanach' — a travelling farm labourer; he had lost one leg in an accident with some farm machinery, and had a wooden leg. I don't think I met him, though I did know Pat's mother, a tiny 'Juno'. Pat was a little over six feet tall, slim (when I met him first), with a beautiful speaking voice and the stance and walk of a dancer. He, too, had an aristocratic nose and profile. Even in his early twenties he was losing his hair. Sensitive, talented, he had already made a little mark in Dublin with a semi-professional company devoted to verse drama, the Pilgrim Players, led by a wonderful lady, Josephine Albericci. As a youth Patrick had been the national step-dancing champion. He had a reel named after him and earned money, as well as fallen arches, at concerts in Ireland and England. He suggested that his father had forced him to dance for his drinking friends, to the tapping of his wooden leg. This had been traumatic for Pat. Very rarely, he would consent to doing a few steps at a party. When he did, even after he had put on weight, he seemed to move on air, not on the ground at all.

He had a very good mind, a deep need to succeed, and an inclination to put on weight. He had real talent as an actor. His problem, I think, was that he hadn't the will or, perhaps, the energy. Maybe he didn't believe it was necessary to work hard at it. Quite early in his time at the Queen's, I suggested something more he should do with a role he was playing. He answered, in that lofty way he had of speaking, 'I am giving an eight-pound-a-week performance. I will give a ten-pound one when they pay me that much.'

At the time, he was earning quite a lot in radio, and this continued for a long time to come. He was wise with what he made and bought a house later in Nutley Road — very posh! He always had the best car of anyone in the company in those days. He loved literature and famous writers. Thereby hang two tales — but those will come later.

Pat amused and frustrated us all by becoming a 'sitting-down actor'. No matter what moves a director gave him, he seemed to end up sitting down for most of any scene he was in. In Hugh Leonard's first play, *The Big Birthday*, he had only one very short entrance through a door down right — in, speak and out! It got a big laugh. Pat made up only the downstage half of his face, the half the audience could see. Patrick Layde was an artist. The pain of that and of his childhood, perhaps, drove him to rely on drink. The Abbey of those days was not the place for him, yet he was much loved and admired — not least by me; not most, either. He died too soon. He did not fulfil his potential.

Philip O'Flynn was the person I got to know best at the Abbey and, with the possible exception of Frank Dermody, the one who influenced me the most. It was always 'Philip and Angela' — that is, Philip O'Flynn and Angela Newman, or Philib Ó Floinn and Aingeal Ní Nuamain. He was very tall, well over six feet, with hair very thin on top. He had white, even, strong teeth, and used them to smile with and to chew chicken bones before swallowing them! Because of his height, his evenly distributed weight and his balding head, he was cast in character parts in his early twenties. He complained of this all the years I knew him. He was a Dublin man through and through, a wonderful, truthful actor who reflected the perfect Abbey approach to the art: the maximum of the interior, the minimum of the exterior.

What Blythe had done, was doing and would do to the Abbey was a continual offence to Phil's sensibilities. He had a gift for storytelling and seeing through to the primary question, except sometimes in himself. He had a wholesome, delightful sense of humour. I don't know of any actor I would rather be on stage with than Phil. He suffered from depression and went to a 'shrink' (as he called him) most of his adult life. Speaking for myself, I didn't understand it, or what he was going through, at all. Like the others in our group, I loved him. I also drove him, at times, to despair. I suspect that deep down he never forgave me for going to and staying in America. I have never stopped regretting that he stayed at the Abbey. It didn't make him happy; it wounded mortally his love of acting. He died in 1999, though he was probably glad to go. I like to think that his last words were a griping 'They might have let me see the fucking millennium!'

Of course I loved Phil's wife, Angela Newman, as did almost everyone who came into our group and its orbit, and as did audiences year after year in the Abbey. For one short period, I perhaps loved her too much. As we used to say, I 'copped myself on' in time, and no harm was done; nor did anyone notice — except Angela, who enjoyed it, encouraged it to a point, and stopped it short. I wouldn't have had it any other way. She was the best actress in Ireland in my time, bar none. She was a Dubliner, too. Comedy, tragedy, young, old, peasant or lady of the manor, in English or in Irish, she was magic. Her Juno Boyle in my production of *Juno and the Paycock* was the Juno of Junoes.

In the morning, at rehearsal, she might look a hundred years old, as if she had slept in a ditch all night. Then, as the part developed, she would become translucent, beautiful. Off stage she was funny, wicked, a sport — 'one of the boys', but always a woman. She was the only full-time female in our group. Others might float in or about, but they passed on like ships in the night. She excited love from those who liked her, hate and resentment from those who didn't, in and out of the theatre. Some wives, I think, resented her. She had no children, so she went everywhere with Philip and the rest of us, while the other wives were at home nights minding babies, children, houses. I remember a Welsh actor saying, 'Actors need wives, but they should not get married!' The good die young, they say; the great never die. Angela, though she can no longer walk the world, having been taken far too young, will live as long as I live, at least.

Dubliners call countrymen 'culchies'; culchies call Dubliners 'Jackeens'; the English call all Irishmen 'Paddy', as I knew. One of the brightest lights in our crowd's orbit was Paddy Long. Long, he wasn't: he stood a sturdy five foot nothing. Paddy he was by name, but he was a quintessential Jackeen. He was not educated in the formal sense; he had hardly, if ever, up to that time, voluntarily read a book. I believe he was born and brought up in Donnybrook, in 'the cottages'. Probably left school at fourteen. We could have walked the same paths, played in the same Herbert Park, prayed in the same church and travelled on the same bus, but I don't think I ever saw him in my teens. He told me later that he was very aware of me and my pals. Because of his size in the tough world he lived in, he had developed his tongue as a weapon of defence and offence through vitriolic, withering name-calling, and he had cultivated a stance and a stare that demanded respect from the bigger boys and bullies.

He was stand-in and double for James Cagney in *Shake Hands with the Devil*; he looked exactly like him, but two inches shorter! Brenda doubled for Glynis Johns. That's how Paddy manoeuvred into our orbit.

He was a house-painter, an odd-job man, and — when there was a part for him in a play, as there was in Behan's *Borstal Boy*, and later in television — an outrageously funny actor. He was a loyal, dependable, generous, supportive, friend and court jester to all of us, all our lives. At one period, when we were all having fun inventing our epitaphs, his choice was a naked statue of himself as Cupid, one hand on hip, the other with the limp-wristed 'camp' gesture and the line, cut in stone, 'He was great fun but he was just one of those things.' Later, he decided he wanted simply 'LONG GONE'. Long is, alas, gone. My epitaph, I blush to admit, was 'He has loved much, much is forgiven him.' I think it was more in hope than in contrition.

1954 saw a string of plays with little in them to make them memorable for their dramatic content. *John Courtney*, by John Malone, was followed by John O'Donovan's *Half-Millionaire*. Then came *Twenty Years A-Wooing* by John McCann, which, with its sequels, concerned an impecunious Dublin middle-class family — a widowed Mrs Kelly (Eileen Crowe), a responsible older brother (Philip O'Flynn) and a second son (Bill Foley) who had a band, the Yellow Tigers. Their vocalist (Joan O'Hara) was my girlfriend in the play. They were the 'good' fellows. I was the 'bad' fellow, the youngest son, Iggy, a congenital liar and his mother's pet! The moral of the play was that the real virtue in the 'good' fellows was their luck in picking horses that won races at great odds. Philip hated those plays with a passion. I saw the shallowness of them. They were, I thought, stage soap operas. I regretted that better plays were treated by audiences, and by some reviewers, much less favourably. These, however, found a huge audience. No doubt about that.

Still, it was an interesting dilemma. The Abbey desperately needed box office to survive. There is and has always been a demand in European theatre for 'the witty man and his joke aimed at the commonest ear', as Yeats wrote contemptuously. Blythe, who claimed to be, in his own words, 'in the apostolic succession to Yeats and Lady Gregory', had an obligation to reject that demand. I realised during the next few years that one of the three great lies is the excuse that 'if you get them in for the shallow stuff they will come back for the deep'. They won't and didn't. Comedy or tragedy, it makes no difference. We may have all differed about what the other two lies are, but we all liked John McCann, the man.

Nothing succeeds like success, we are told. I believe the great popular success of the McCann 'Kelly family plays' succeeded in distorting the very real contributions to Irish drama of the Abbey Theatre at the Queen's. I know Iggy actually did me harm, artistically. I played the liar convincingly by acting the lies as if I were speaking the truth. On stage, many actors like to signal to the audience that they are lying; I refused to do that. This acting lesson I had learned at home from my brother Paul, by example. He was a brilliant practitioner of the art of technical logical inexactitude. Later, as a director, I discouraged other actors from tipping the audience off in any way either. The play is supposed to do that!

My sister Kitty, home on a long holiday from Holland, introduced me to a woman friend of hers. At the end of the afternoon she said to Kitty, 'You are right, Vincent is really a nice man.' Kitty told me, afterwards, that her friend had told her that she'd been watching me for several years in those McCann plays, and that she 'wouldn't trust the Hail Mary coming out of that fellow's mouth'. Angela Newman, for the rest of her short life, right up to the last time I saw her in the new Abbey in the 1980s, never called me anything but 'Iggy'.

After the holidays, in mid-July (the Abbey went dark in June in those days), *Knocknavain* by J.M. Doody made a brief, inauspicious debut. The play had received a joint first prize, along with John Malone's, in the Abbey's play-writing competition. The torture to actors and audiences that comprised this kitchen-sink drama ended in the curtain coming down — we thought! But the author rushed on from the wings, grabbed the hands of two actors, saying, 'We have a hit,' and, still holding the unfortunate actors' hands, gave the speech he had prepared on the assumption that this sadly wide-of-the-mark 'miss' would be a hit.

This was followed by that flat Bryan Guinness, *A Riverside Charade*, which, despite having me dressed in a kilt, still didn't run! Later that autumn, I played the part I had done in my Irish audition for Blythe in the revival of Mac Liammóir's *Diarmuid agus Gráinne*, directed by Frank Dermody. I took that as a compliment from Blythe. However, I was never cast in a full-length play in Irish again. That, I took to be an act of kindness on our manager's part towards the true lovers of our native tongue.

All wasn't lost in 1954. Joseph Tomelty's *Is The Priest at Home?*, a resounding success with the Belfast Group Theatre, for whom he had written it, in distinctive Northern idiom, got an Abbey production. To everyone's surprise and delight, the laughter and applause resounded even louder at the Queen's for Harry Brogan's brilliant sexton and Philip O'Flynn's sympathetic priest, with every other role a gem of character writing and acting. Joe Tomelty was a man of the theatre, radio and cinema, from his toes to the tips of his teddy-bear thick white hair. As a writer, Joe had created a brilliant, successful radio family called the McCooeys and many fine plays. As an actor he was a stage star in London, Belfast and the provinces. In film he had attained star status in a movie with Ralph Richardson, *No Highway*.

Apart from those around and on the stage, an almost endless stream of extraordinary people came to the Abbey, saw our work and met with us on stage after the plays, or in the bar after the curtain fell, as well as at parties, receptions, embassies and homes. We met them all as different but equal.

The first memorable meeting for me was after a performance of *This Other Eden*. The international P.E.N. was meeting in Dublin. They took a whole house at the Abbey for themselves and their guests. Afterwards the cast was invited to the Gresham Hotel for a reception. Maurice Walsh, my favourite writer since my teens, was prominent among them. I asked if I could meet him, to get his autograph. It was the first time since becoming a professional actor that I had asked such a thing. Before I was even introduced, he congratulated me warmly on my performance. I thanked him, told him how much *The Small Dark Man*, *The Key above the Door* and *Blackcock's Feather* had meant to me, and asked for his autograph. 'Yes,' he said. 'On one condition: that you give me yours first,' and he pulled out the programme from his pocket. The John Ford film *The Quiet Man* was adapted from one of his short stories. I didn't tell him I had written a letter to Arthur Shields asking him to get me a job on that film.

During this period the lack of satisfaction, fulfilment, appreciation of their work, and quality of many new plays in English and Irish was straining the enthusiasm of the Players. Ria's inability to provide inspiration in either new or proven plays was even more frustrating and more damaging to the reputation of the Abbey. These two issues became major grievances at the Players' Council, to which I had recently been elected. Ria's tragedy was that she was a magnificent, experienced actress who hated her position as producer under Blythe. She was terrified that, at her age, she would lose the security that provided a home for herself and her ageing father, for whom she was the main financial support. Blythe saw the role of producer as that of a facilitator, who kept the actors from bumping into one another and the furniture, and who ensured their speech could be heard and understood. He would concede, in a puzzled kind of way, that 'Frank Dermody got extraordinary things out of Máire [Maura O'Donnell] in *Righteous are Bold*.' But before my stint at the Abbey was over, he would be conceding more than he might have imagined.

In the Council's first big success, we got him to bring back Frank Dermody. Our pressure on Blythe to use guest directors led to his asking us if Frank Dermody would be acceptable. Frank returned, initially as a guest director and then as a permanent one. He had left the Abbey in 1947, the same year that Siobhán McKenna, Denis O'Dea and Cyril Cusack left, to work with Gabriel Pascal's film company. It led nowhere for Frank. He directed a few shows in England onstage, but was very unhappy there. He came back now to stage Tomás Mac Anna's play *Winter Wedding*, and later he would be appointed senior play director when Ria Mooney resigned.

Being able to work with Frank was to be the most important thing in my artistic and professional life. Blythe admired Dermody because he was a 'native speaker' and had created the first Irish-language panto. He may have also thought in some way that bringing in Frank evened the score with Ria Mooney, who he believed had prompted the Val Iremonger protests against his control over play choice and the hiring of actors.

From then on, though it would take me seven or eight years, with help, support and education from many sources, I was working to identify what Jack called the 'primary question' as it existed at the Abbey, and then to answer it, with back-up from the Players' Council, Dermody, and Jack — and, to be fair, with the stimulus of a worthy adversary like Blythe to spur me on.

8

Queen's Theatre Moonbeams

Mr Yeats told me in a dream that this is what he wants.

In December 1954 we celebrated the fiftieth anniversary of the opening of the theatre on Abbey Street with three short plays, one mistress and two masterpieces — *Spreading the News* by Lady Gregory, On *Baile's Strand* by W.B. Yeats and John Millington Synge's *In the Shadow of the Glen*. Lennox Robinson directed the Yeats. I see him uncoiling his long thin body, like a gentle, friendly snake responding to the music of a snake charmer, to drawl a direction in the kind of English accent Cork people acquire. Then he'd re-coil himself into his seat.

Though he was not inspiring as a director, the company enjoyed him immensely as a change from Ria's uptight, defensive approach. Directing a Yeats or Synge, she stood behind the production table or the brass rail of the orchestra pit and monotonously thumped out 'the beat', as she called it. When Philip O'Flynn and Brian O'Higgins suggested, in different ways, that this regular 'beat' would put the audience to sleep, she dismissed their opinion with 'Mr Yeats himself told me in a dream that this is what he wants, that the beat is all that matters!' Brian went away muttering something like, 'Why not give the audience sleeping pills? They'd have a better sleep and save us money and energy.'

I was in the crowd in *On Baile's Strand*, and I played and enjoyed Shawn Early in the Lady Gregory, who fortunately didn't talk to Ria through dreams. On the afternoon of the opening we had Gort cake, a kind of currant cake Lady Gregory made on her estate near Gort, for the workers and inhabitants, at Hallowe'en. At the Abbey she distributed it to the Players. It was brought, served and shared with us on the stage by Lady G's charming, shy granddaughters. Frankly, at the time, I knew next to nothing about Lady G, other than that she was a playwright. Yeats, I knew, had written some strange plays, and a poem I had had to learn at school — 'The Lake Isle of Innisfree'. I didn't share my ignorance with anyone. I wasn't that stupid. I listened hard, kept my mouth shut on subjects I knew nowt about, and gradually learned.

On the night of 27 December, 1954, to the cream of the Dublin political, literary, and Irish-language revival establishments, while the actors and stage crew waited behind closed curtains, Ernest Blythe told a long fairy tale, in Irish. It was about the success of the theatre's Irish-language policy. He recited endless numbers and figures for attendance at pantomimes and one-act plays in Irish. What he didn't tell them was that the attendance figures he was giving them were for *all* the patrons who attended the *English* plays, with no mention of the fact that seventy to eighty per cent usually left before the little Irish plays began.

Whether Lennox knew what his fellow director was saying, we can't be sure. What I do know is that, when Mr B eventually finished, Lennox — who, we used to say, was not as green as he was cabbage-looking — got a huge laugh and applause on his first comment: 'Now for a few *facts!*'

Most memorable, however, was the letter that Lennox read from the Minister for Finance, Gerald Sweetman. It announced government approval for the rebuilding of the Abbey on the old site, with Michael Scott (a one-time Abbey actor himself) as the architect. The Peacock would be used for plays in Irish and more experimental drama. It had about as much immediate interest for us as a Doomsday prophecy!

It is only fair to say that during this period, most of the one-acts in Irish were well acted, beautifully spoken, and decently costumed and set. Some of them, I was reliably informed, were very well written. Actors like Maura O'Donnell, Bríd Lynch, Mícheál Ó Briain, Mick Hennessey, Geoffrey Golden, his half-brother Eddie, later Eoin O'Sullivan, Eithne Lydon, Máire O'Neill, and many others, found something even richer and deeper when they were performing in their native language. Even I did, once or twice. Over the years there were certainly actors brought into the company because of their fluency in Irish who should not have been there, but these were few and far between. The real damage done by these Irish policies of Blythe's was that good actors, whom the Abbey needed and who needed the Abbey, were locked out and saw no point in even trying to get in. If it had not been for Marie Kean, I would have been one of them.

Madame Pandit represented the Government of India to Ireland and the Court of St James in Britain. She was a sister of Pandit Nehru, India's first Prime Minister, colleague and successor to Gandhi. Later, she would become Indian Ambassador to the United Nations. She saw, from the Royal Box at the Queen's Theatre, *Is the Priest at Home?* I played Karl Marx O'Grady, a North-of-Ireland country Catholic turned communist. She asked if she could meet the cast at the end of the play! That I found astonishing. I would have gone to the end of the earth to meet a sister of Pandit Nehru, and someone who knew

Gandhi, and here she was asking to see and then to meet us! Friendly, relaxed, interested and warm, she captivated us all. She put us absolutely at our ease. Dignity, humility and a beauty were within and about her; yet, if I was to say, then or now, what I felt, I'd say, 'It was like my mother coming home from Loughgall and being amongst us again.' She asked us, before she left the stage, if we all could have lunch at the Shelbourne Hotel with her next day.

At the lunch, she asked me to sit beside her. We talked about trying to find a way to bring the play to India. She said how much she would love her brother — Mr Nehru — to see it. I can still feel myself walking on air through Saint Stephen's Green, after lunch, to pay my respects to the three Fates and the bronze busts of Countess Markievicz and James Clarence Mangan — who gets more like Robert Mitchum every day!

In early 1955 *Is the Priest at Home?* was revived. One night we were asked to stay on the stage at the end of the performance. The curtain was raised. The house lights were on in the empty auditorium. Two forms came towards us from the stalls entrance doors halfway back. The familiar morning suit, the butterfly collar and tie, the red beaming face (perhaps a modest Irish whiskey or two at the interval?) under thin, well-groomed white hair — the President of Ireland, Sean T. O'Kelly. He was linking the taller, immaculate, white-linen-jacketed, strong yet fragile figure of Pandit Nehru. His dark eyes, his crème de café skin, his peacefulness, and a sense of being at once there and in some other state are what stay with me. He said, in answer to a question from Philip O'Flynn about the play, that he recognised every character. Each one had a counterpart among his own people in India.

We never did get the play to India, though Madame Pandit's brother did see it! I can look at my right hand now and say, as I said to Brenda that night, 'There's the hand that shook the hand of Pandit Nehru, that shook the hand of Mahatma Gandhi.'

T.P. McKenna might easily have been left outside the Abbey looking in, though not for want of knocking on the door. Fortunately, Ronnie Walsh got stuck down the country. His car broke down at a race meeting, I think. T.P. was called in to read his part in *Is the Priest at Home?* T.P. was kept; Ronnie was let go!

When I discovered that I had done thirteen pantomimes in Irish at the Queen's, my first instinct was to not write about them at all. I avoid thirteens like they were ... well, thirteens. On Friday the Thirteenth I prefer to stay in bed all day. I am not superstitious; I just can't afford to take chances! My mother had a superstition for every thought, not to mind every deed and day, and I admit to having a few myself. One of my more stupid ones is that if I accidentally hit one elbow I must then hit the other. You should see me in a shower — well, maybe you shouldn't. If things go well for me one day, the following day I will try to do everything exactly the same way, from what I wear to the exact order in which I approach my toiletries. Olwen, to whom I have been married for twenty-five years, says that if she had known how stupid I was about that sort of thing, she would have never married me. 'Superstitions are catching,' she says. 'Just look at my bruised elbows.'

Our group at the Abbey had very mixed feelings about the Irish pantomime. It was like late-night drinking and extramarital sex: it cost a lot of money and was not good for the constitution or the institution. But it was fun! I recall a line indicative of the whole experience. The prince was being played by a fireman from Tara Street Fire Station, across from the Queen's. His name was Jesse Owens. He had even less Irish than I had. His *fuimeanna* was ferocious, even when he learned his part parrot-like with all dialogue cut down to the bare bones. This handsome, humorous, manly figure, bare-legged in a toga and sandals —a fine singer, too — spoke our ancient native tongue in a flat, toneless Dublin accent. His unforgettable opening line sounded like 'Kaw-will-muh-van-prune-sa?' In English, 'Where is my princess?' In Irish, '*Cá bhfuil mo bhean phroinnsa?*' I used to answer, '*Tá sí ins an Queen's*' — in English, 'She is in the Queen's.' Big laugh! It might be called low comedy. Like me, most of the audience were, in a way, laughing with relief that they understood what was being said!

Because I didn't sing and never fully mastered Irish, but knew how to get laughs — visual, bilingual, or in such simple Irish that our mostly school-age audience could understand it — I was given the freedom by the producers (Frank McCann and later Frank Dermody) to invent my own dialogue and insert it wherever it would work. Of course, I always — well, nearly always — rehearsed it.

Our brilliant pit orchestra composer, conductor and pianist was the great Sean O'Riada. We called him John Reidy or 'Squire', because he wore tweed, a fishing-hat and a cloak, comported himself like a squire and smoked small black cigars. Sean took delight in adding brilliant, sometimes wicked, musical comment to my onstage jokes or 'funny business'.

In most years, I — second to T.P. McKenna as the prince — usually developed the biggest rapport with the kids. T.P., with his fine singing voice, gift for comedy, thick wavy hair and strong well-shaped legs, was the ideal prince for a record-breaking six pantos. The girls loved him. The lads wished they were like him. Blythe, who had at first rejected him on the erroneous ground that his nose was half an inch too long, had to eat his words — in Irish!

In one panto, I played the devil. He was a humorous, sexy devil. I manufactured my first appearance with our special-effects man, my good friend Ronnie McShane. At the end of a drum roll, in a flash of light from a flash pot, I appeared. A moment grinning wickedly at the audience; then I would say the traditional greeting, in Irish, of course: 'Dia 's Muire dhaoibh' — 'God and Mary be with you.' It brought the house down. At one perform-ance, the house full, in the momentary pause before I said my line, my daughter Bairbre, then aged about three, cried out clear as a bell, 'That's my daddy!' It got an even bigger laugh! Alas, I could hardly ask her to do it at every performance!

From 1955 to 1960, about thirty-seven new plays in English were played by our little company. I was in all but three or four of them. John McCann wrote six of the new works, and we revived his *Twenty Years A-Wooing* as well. His plays were all popular fare, loved by large audiences and successful at the box office.

The Galway playwright Michael Joseph Molloy, a solitary, sensitive little figure with a limp, had taken Dublin by storm, and went on to London, New York and Cape Town with his stirring historical drama, *The King of Friday's Men*. He had been hailed, not without cause, as a successor to John Synge. He gave us, in '55, a good comedy, *The Will and the Way*. It gave Bríd Lynch an opportunity to show the great talent she had when cast in the right part. It also gave her a moment where she had to quaff a tumbler of Guinness in one gulp. This she did every night, to thunderous applause. Of course it was a trick. Of course I am not going to tell how to do it! Molloy's next play for the Queen's was a semi-unsatisfactory melodrama, *The Right Rose Tree*, in October 1958. A serious and poetic writer, Molloy would go on to write *The Daughter from Over the Water* (staged by Siobhán McKenna in the Gaiety in 1962), and *The Wooing of Duvessa* for the Abbey (1964), among other things. He will be remembered as someone able to dramatise in a real way the outlook of rural people, and someone unafraid of numbering among his pet hates touring showbands, popular music and foreign play producers adapting Irish plays.

A marvellous woman, who owned her own pub in Cahirciveen and who brought fun, laughter and Kerry into our lives, was Pauline Maguire. I played the juvenile lead, named Vincent, in her play *The Last Move*, October 1955. Not a great play, it dealt with young people hoping to modernise Irish country life, but it did earn a staging. Then Walter Macken — a former Abbey actor, whose star qualities as Bartley Dowd in *The King of Friday's Men*, and in other plays, had been recognised in Ireland, England and America, and a brilliant novelist and successful playwright — gave us all good parts, and Mick Hennessey a superb one, in his well-made tragedy about a former guerrilla in the War of Independence, *Twilight of a Warrior*.

I played my first character part, successfully taking over from Harry Brogan, in an emergency, the leading male role — opposite Eileen Crowe, who was my mother's age — in *The Glorious Uncertainty* by Brindsley MacNamara. A good title, seeing that I got eight hours' notice to learn the part. I ran through it once on stage with the cast, went to the Radio Publicity Office, did a few necessary chores, and spent the rest of the day learning the part. I didn't miss a line, cue, or laugh! I acted, too, that year in my first Sean O'Casey play at the Abbey, *The Shadow of a Gunman*. This, coincidentally, would be the first play I directed at the Abbey, more than a dozen years later. In both productions Philip O'Flynn played Seumas Shields while Micheál Ó Briain took the part of Maguire. For my money neither of them could be bettered.

From June 1954, when I spent my first month in Connemara, a beautiful, barren, rocky land alongside the wild and wide Atlantic Ocean, I wanted to live there. If ever I have to make my home in Ireland, that is where I will do it. Outside Spiddal Village, *An Spidéal*, some ten miles west of the historic city of Galway that gives its name to the county and bay, was where the Abbey actor Micheál Ó Briain was born and reared. This, for me, is the heart of the Connemara Gaeltacht, one of those few areas where Irish is still the first language for some if not all of those native to the place. When Micheál came to the Abbey through the Irish-speaking Taibhdhearc Theatre of Galway, his English was far from fluent. To a great extent, he had to do in English what I had to do in Irish — that is, get help with meaning, speech patterns and pronunciation.

Denis O'Dea was one of the leading actors in the Abbey Company when Micheál — direct, you might say, from Connemara — arrived there in 1947. Denis later became a fine film actor. In the men's dressing-room, Denis noticed that his tooth powder was disappearing from its little can at an alarming rate. Just before going on stage one night he found it empty.

'Who is using my tooth powder?' he asked, as much in wonder as in anger.

'I'm sorreh. I t'aught 'twas telcum powdher,' answered Micheál through closed teeth, in his Connemara English, shamefaced.

'I see. How long are you here now, Ó Briain?' said Denis, trying not to laugh.

'Arount six monts, I t'ink,' replied Micheál.

'Well, why the hell don't you get talcum powder of your own? And, come to think of it, your own make-up as well? You're always borrowing something!'

'I'm waitin' to see if I'm goin' to be kept,' said Micheál seriously. Not as seriously as Denis thought. Micheál was a very subtle and humorous man.

My first June in Micheál Ó Briain country, Connemara — the first of twelve Junes I spent there over the next twenty-three years — I stayed alone at *teach Phadraic Ó Tuathail*, Patrick O'Toole's house. It was in a tiny village called Inverin, about four miles west of Spiddal. The house stood about a hundred yards back from the seashore, on the narrow tar Coast Road. It was a two-storey, cement, slate-roofed building, with no paint of any kind to brighten it, but clean and very sparsely furnished. The lavatory was an outhouse with no plumbing; the priest's house, the national school, and the two pubs in the village had the only running water. Washing and shaving were performed with jugs of water; hot, if required, came from the black kettle on the open turf fire in the kitchen. That was no surprise. What were a surprise and a constant worry to me were the attacks from the flock of geese who seemed to have appointed themselves daytime guardians of the 'one-holer' in the back yard. At night the hissing feathered 'hoors' were locked up. Fortunately I had brought my little 'James' 125cc with me (by train from Dublin to Galway), and I learned quickly to park it right beside the back door, so when I was 'short-taken' in the early morning, I wheeled the motorbike around the flock, using it as a moving shield, while shouting imprecations at the horrid beasts, until the privy door was within reach; then I blocked the entrance with it as best I could, and slipped into the sanctuary of my unholy of holies. Coming out, I would start the engine, roar it, hop in the saddle and — if no O'Tooles were watching — scatter the hissers in every direction as I zoomed out on to the road.

Unexpectedly, one day, 'Red' Sean Mooney, our stage manager at the Abbey, arrived on his 350cc. Only one other man I ever knew in life had a bigger laugh. Over a week or so we waltzed and wove our iron ponies from Inverin by a winding coast road and all over the terrain. The brown, seaweed-covered, rock-lined inlets of the Atlantic on our left, now blue, now green; over the little stone bridge on the Costello salmon-filled waters to Carraroe with its coral beach, Lettermore and Lettermullan. High lonely roads over mountains, low roads through valleys, fast-flowing frothy trout streams, still blue lakes, and Clifden. St John Gogarty's haunted hotel, Kylemore Abbey, Leenane fjord, no better sunset in the world, Leenane Cross — 'Is that the cottage of *The Quiet Man*?' — Oughterard, the lake with an island for every day of the year. Seanafesteen and the Falconry, or Moycullen and Bothar Uaigneach, Derraherc and Ból Uisce, Spiddal and Tadhg Folan's, Tommy Hughes's or Martin Standun's pubs for drinks, the very names making better music than our songs or shouts of 'Look at that! and that! and that!' — the words whipped away by the wind. Always, near or far, a tiny thatched cottage, a tinier field, a castle, or another pub with advertising signs in Irish; ruined cottages, too, and black-faced sheep high on the slopes, black Connemara hornless cows nearby, black-and-white-spotted collie dogs barking and snapping by your wheels, hens, geese, turkeys scattering as the road cuts though a farm yard. Everywhere the smell of burning peat! All this enormous quilt of ever-changing green, purple, blue, gold, silver, black and white, stitched together with mortarless miles of man-made stone walls.

That first year, I spent several days over the month up on the Ó Briain bog with Máirtín, Micheál's father, cutting turf, footing it to dry it in the wind and sun, stacking it, and finally loading it on the donkey cart and bringing it home. At first they thought I was only a tourist, a Dublin fella wearing black glasses — 'Ah, God help us, is the poor lad blind?' But Máirtín found me a help, and was glad of company. I was talking more in English, I'm afraid, than in Irish (if only Blythe knew!) but getting close to the people and the place.

One day, cutting turf with Máirtín on his turf bank, Galway Bay below us, I picked up a seashell from out of a sod of topsoil and weeds. 'You know,' he said, 'everything on the land has an equivalent in the water.' Then he told me the story of the *Eac Uisge*, as we sat on a bank of dry earth, eating our soda bread and drinking milk from a Lucozade bottle that had been corked with a rolled-up piece of newspaper. They always took something to eat going up the mountain to the bog — '*sliabh gortach*,' they'd murmur, 'mountain hunger. A person could easily die with the hunger, in these mountains. Some of these fields are enchanted. You'd get a weakness and be going round and round the field and not find any way out. If you didn't have something to eat, you could wake up dead!'

Máirtín took a big bite out of his soda bread, washed it down with a swig of milk from the Lucozade bottle, wiped the top of it with his hand and passed it to me.

'Well, the *Eac Uisge* lived in a big lake up there in Mayo, God help us, on the estate where I used to work as a boy,' he told me. 'It came out of the water, a black shining stallion with a coat like a seal, and serviced one of the thoroughbred mares in heat, then returned to the water. The foal of that mare grew up to be a champion racehorse.

'Then one night the champion disappeared. You see, it had gone back into the lake to live beneath the waters. The loss to the lord of the estate was great, so he told his gamekeeper to lie in wait for the *Eac Uisge* with a shotgun and shoot it dead, for fear it would do the same thing to another mare.

'The man waited night after night. The stallion did not appear. Then, one moonlit night, when another mare was in heat, the stallion appeared out of the lake. The man waited till the stallion was well within range; got him in his sights; pulled the trigger; and — flash — the gun exploded in the man's face and killed him dead. The *Eac Uisge* disappeared back into the water; it was never seen again. You see, it was enchanted, that *Eac Uisge*,' Máirtín said with great seriousness, as he rose to get on with cutting the turf.

Because Micheál was cast so much in plays in Irish, or in Irish 'country' parts in English, his talent as an actor didn't get anything like the recognition it deserved. Nor was he helped or encouraged to extend his range. In comedy or tragedy, and all those areas in between, Micheál was a rock of truth, credibility and reliability — as the brother of the 'possessed' girl in *The Righteous are Bold*, in the title role of M.J. Molloy's haunting *The Paddy Pedlar*, as Maguire in O'Casey's *Shadow of a Gunman*, 'catching butterflies in Knocksedan', and as his incomparable Shawn Keogh, on both stage and film, in *The Playboy of the Western World*. For me, as the father in *Famine* by Tom Murphy, he reached greatness. In any other company, in any other city, any of those parts would have earned him fame and rich rewards. What they brought Micheál was a small house in a working-class area of North Dublin, a wonderful wife, an education for his children, and a bicycle with a three-speed gear, on which he cycled the five miles down and back up the hill to and from the National Theatre of Ireland till he retired at sixty-five, about a decade before he died. The heartbreak for an actor at the Abbey was — I heard Phil O'Flynn say it first — that no matter what you had done or how well, what reviews you had got at home or abroad, ten or twelve times a year, year after year, it was as if you were appearing here for the first time ever, a beginner. Unless you had been 'canonised'. 'Then, no matter how much of a balls you make, they will never take your halo.'

There used to be a lot of discussion with theatregoers as to the merits of the Gate and Abbey theatres — 'Sodom and Begorrah,' as some Dublin wit described them, respectively, if not respectfully! Dermot Tuohy, a Gate Theatre actor — a kind of Anglicised Irish Charles Laughton — and Micheál Ó Briain met on the top of the bus one morning on the way to their rehearsals, and got to talking about technique, or lack of it, in the Abbey. Dermot, as he'd be the first to admit, did most of the talking. As Micheál stood up to get off the bus at Abbey Street, he patted Dermot good-naturedly on the shoulder — 'Ah well, Dermot, ye have the technique and we have the talent. Good luck now!'

The difference between the two theatres lay not only in the difference between the kind of play the Longford Company and Mac Liammóir and Edwards did at the Gate and the kind we did at the Abbey, but in the purpose of playing. Ours was to hold the mirror up to Irish life, to reflect it realistically; the Gate's was to hold it up to the world and Anglo-Irish life, to reflect it theatrically. In general, the Gate actors wore 'costumes', 'moved' and spoke beautifully. The Abbey actors wore 'clothes', walked and talked. The Gate acting gloried in its technique. Abbey acting hid it.

'The Playboy', we at the Abbey always called Synge's great play — until the late, and sometimes great, Siobhán McKenna played Pegeen Mike at the Gaiety and in London. Then, a little cynically, or perhaps enviously, we called it for a time 'The Playgirl'. From the time my brother Jack first brought me to see it at the Abbey Theatre (I thought I was going to a cowboy play), *The Playboy of the Western World* has been my most reliable, helpful, and happy stepping-stone across the physical and theatrical worlds.

There was one exception. There was word out, about a year after I joined the Abbey, that *The Playboy* would be our offering the next spring for An Tóstal — a festival in Dublin for which Brendan Smith was organising the performing arts side. I was still, and would be for another ten years, a very bad (on the sexy sixth-commandment side), completely believing Catholic. My belief that *anything* you asked in the name of Jesus would be granted to you was absolute.

So for six or more months, no matter what sexual divilment I was up to at the time, I got down on my knees by my bed in Shanowen Road before sleep and prayed simply, childishly, and with real faith, that I would be cast as Christy Mahon in *The Playboy of the Western World*. It wasn't an unreasonable request. I had played Christy, to high critical praise, for Brendan Smith in Bray in the summer of 1953. It had been the audition piece which got me accepted into the Abbey by Ria Mooney, and she would be the producer of this production.

From January on I scanned the call list day after day, week after week, for two months. Then I heard: 'The *Playboy* cast is up!' I donned my blank mask, stilled my trembling heart as best I could, sauntered up to the call board.

I was not cast. Ray MacAnally was Christy.... No, I am wrong: I *was* cast — in the crowd! To have played Christy, and now to have to rehearse and play an extra, was, you might say, harsh. I felt like Lucifer, cast not only out of Heaven but into Hell. Of course, I said nothing; I just re-learned Christy and rehearsed it by myself, and prayed that Ray would have to drop out of the play — nothing fatal, mind you; just something painlessly incapacitating for a few weeks!

I prayed till opening night, but Ray was stronger, healthier, more sure of himself than ever — miscast and awful in the part. I hated every moment that I was on the stage, every night. I learned something from the experience, though, that has stood me in good stead as an actor, director, and teacher of acting. Saying nothing on the stage is not having no lines; it is a decision, which the character makes continually, *not* to speak.

That is the Abbey tradition of acting at its best: the leading role today, the crowd tomorrow. There are no small parts, only small salaries!

Mammy's beautiful friend Anne O'Reilly married John Belton, a second marriage for both of them. John was an Ambassador for Ireland, posted variously in London, Sweden, Canada, and Spain. They were home during that *Playboy*, saw it and invited me to a party after the performance.

I loved and admired both these people. Even when I was a teenager John had engaged and encouraged me in chess and in discussion of world affairs. He was impressed with my knowledge of and interest in things that interested him. His approbation had been important to me.

To my dismay, at the party, when the conversation turned to the play, John and Anne were vehement in their dislike of John Millington Synge's plays, and in particular *The Playboy*. All the old stuff that the 1907 *Playboy* riots had thrown up from the pulpit, press, and political arena was rehashed. 'Try to represent Ireland in the outside world as a modern, emerging economy — with the savage idiocy of an Irish peasantry worshipping a young man because he killed his father popping up to discredit you every time the National Theatre comes to town,' said John, the Ambassador, supported by Anne. The National Theatre is not, I argued, and should not be, a public relations agency for the promotion of the Irish image abroad, any more than it should be what Blythe sees it as, an instrument to revive our ancient language — worthy as both those objectives are. I went home thinking that, if intelligent people like this could be so wrong about dramatic art, live theatre was in real trouble.

That was Dublin near the mid-1950s. More than thirty years later, in Manhattan, among enlightened, educated, theatre-loving, affluent Irish and Irish-Americans, I met the same gut rejection of another powerful piece of Abbey poetic drama, Tom McIntyre's *The Great Hunger*, for the same kinds of reasons. *Plus ça change, plus c'est la même chose!* — Well, not quite. These same people had loved the *Playboy* I brought them a year earlier.

While we were doing Brendan Behan's *The Quare Fella*, a call came to Brendan Smith's office asking me to meet with the Manager of Colgate Palmolive (Ireland) at their offices in Aston Quay. Of course, I went.

If the Pope of Rome had unexpectedly arrived in a country convent, there could not have been more delight and dismay than I encountered among my sponsored radio clients. The International President of Colgate Palmolive would arrive next Monday from New Jersey on his whirlwind tour of Europe! Three nights, he was staying! Would I come to lunch with him and the senior staff? Perhaps I could suggest something interesting he could see or do while he was in Dublin?

'Why me?' I asked. 'Isn't it business, financial, and government people he would want to see?'

'His daughter is an actress. He loves the theatre.'

'Well, I'll ask him to the Abbey, introduce him to the company, have a drink with him in the bar afterwards, if he likes.'

Their relief was palpable. For once, I felt like the learned man, they the boys. They had been warned by New Jersey that He — Ralph Hart — was a holy terror. He would turn the place upside down, change everything he didn't like. Not to put a tooth in it, the whole Dublin office was in a blue funk.

Ralph Hart was a small, bright, intelligent man with a big hat. You'd know he was American and he astride the moon. He and I got on like a house on fire. He knew and was interested in the Abbey Theatre; he would love to come, love to meet the actors, love even more to have several drinks in the bar afterwards. In short, he met me in the bar every night of his three-night stay. I enjoyed him as much as he, apparently, enjoyed me. I saw it was a relief for him to be treated like a person, instead of like the Pope of Soap.

On his last night we were having a last drink, just the two of us. Ralph wanted to know how much I earned at the Abbey. I told him ten pounds a week.

'And from the radio?'

'Another eight pounds.'

He translated that into dollars.

'I'd like you to come to Jersey City and be my personal assistant. You'll make ten times that, to begin with. We'd bring your wife and daughter, of course. You'd have a great future with us,' he said, or words to that effect. He said them quietly and simply.

I thanked him. I don't know exactly what I said, other than, 'I am an actor at the Abbey Theatre, one of the great theatres in all history. That is what I want, more than anything.'

I had a couple of letters from him, a few goodwill messages through the Colgate Dublin office. Alas, I didn't keep things in those days. Some time later, I heard his daughter, the actress, had been kidnapped and a large ransom had been demanded. Then I heard a boyfriend was involved in it. Soon after, Ralph Hart resigned from Colgate Palmolive. It would be thirty years before I'd hear his name again.

When I told my friend Michael O'Duffy, the golden-voiced tenor, that I was going to Paris with the Abbey to play *The Plough and the Stars* at an international theatre festival, he had said that I must see his friend Dick Driscoll, director of the Voice of America radio broadcasting in Europe. Michael was doing a weekly radio programme for me in Dublin at this time — he, singing and introducing his favourite songs to the accompaniment of Norman Metcalf, a brilliant cinema organist; I, writing the scripts and directing the show. Michael suggested that 'Dick would probably lend you a wire recorder if you wanted to get some interviews over there, or maybe do a show on the whole trip.'

Even before we opened the play in Paris I brought our crowd to Avenue Hoche, one of the streets that run out from the Etoile, to the Voice of America office, to meet Dick. We were all, literally and figuratively, embraced by him and his small staff — particularly Pat Layde and me, by his two beautiful secretaries: Pat, then unmarried, by the English one; I, married, which did not inhibit me at all, by the Breton beauty. I gravitated towards her and she towards me, and an *Alliance Française* seemed to be born at first sight. We all decided to meet, the night we returned from our two-week holiday on the French Riviera, at a party for us at Driscoll's small mansion in Villene-sur-Seine outside Paris, and to stay the night. That was something to look forward to!

The Plough and the Stars (*La Charrue et les Etoiles*) opened at the Sarah Bernhardt Theatre with the French stage manager thumping three times with the traditional heavy wooden *boule*, I think it's called, on a section of the stage, down right, worn down from countless thumps. In Michael O'Herlihy's four brilliant sets, which caught both the Georgian grandeur of an earlier age and the poverty of the present slum-dwellers, the company, at their very best, swept through this masterpiece, from the young married couple's struggles in Act I to the street outside where the Rising of 1916 intrudes into their lives; then on to the great comic and dramatic mix of the bar scene, with prostitute, posturing political speeches, and the toast in red port to the blood sacrifice; to the ending, the tragedies of Bessie Burgess (Eileen Crowe) and Nora Clitheroe (Maura O'Donnell), the nobility of Fluther Good (Philip), and the oddly sympathetic singing by the British soldiers (myself and Ray) of 'Keep the Home Fires Burning' as Dublin outside the window burns and the Rising is quelled. The slow curtain fell into complete silence in the auditorium. Then, as we lined up for the curtain call, the whole company, shoulder to shoulder, filling the proscenium, the packed house exploded in applause, then cheers; then they swept down from their seats, waving their white handkerchiefs and banging their fists in rhythm on the stage at our feet! The reviews next day in every major Paris paper and journal joyfully supported the Parisian audience's response. One reviewer even mentioned the love with which Michael O'Herlihy had painted *every* brick on the Georgian house-front in Act II.

We had a month's holiday every June at the Abbey. That the Paris festival took place in May couldn't have suited us better. Our fares paid to and from Paris for the Festival, we could have three weeks' holidays on the Continent that even we could afford. With the help of T.P.'s fiancée, May White, who worked with the *Alliance Française* in Dublin, we were going to have our first Riviera holiday in style — well, in modest comfort.

I used to have a fantasy in Mount Merrion about going to Paris and ' hailing me a woman from the streets'. I'd have to have money to pay her, I knew that. I had settled on two half-crowns, five shillings; I got that from a dirty version of the song 'Camptown Races' we had learned — 'I gave her a crown and she lay down, oh doo-dah-day.' I didn't know, then, exactly what

I would do when she lay down, but I knew it was something forbidden and desirable. Little did I know that I was going to have my fantasy fulfilled in the South of France, and by accident, not design.

Cassis was a small seaside town where the French vacationed. We liked the hotel but were shocked at getting little fishes, for our first lunch, with heads and eyes that we were supposed to eat. This was the first time 'on the Continent' for Angela, Phil, Pat, T.P., me, and Michael Coffey — a friend of T.P. who had 'a good job at Guinness' and was a fine musician into the bargain. At pains to impress the pretty waitress with red hair, I overcame my shock and ate the fishes. I was the only one.

Days we all would go for walks in the town or on the hills above it, ride the *pedalos* on the sea, and swim on the beach; and one night we went to a dance in a pavilion on the pier, where a very handsome, very popular Moroccan recording artist sang French love songs. His name was Moloudji — I won't vouch for the spelling. T.P., with great *sang froid* in his well-cut bank official's leisure suit — a bum-freezer — swept a beautiful French mademoi- selle onto the dance floor with a perfectly mimicked Charles Boyer French-accented '*Voulez-vous danser, Mademoiselle?*' The rest of us watched in envy and caution, except Phil, who was pushing Angela around the floor, try- ing to look as if he enjoyed it. At the end of the second encore the girl left T.P., like a whore at a hockey match, standing alone in the middle of the dance floor. She returned to her friends. Wearing an indifferent mask, he came back to us. It seems that when it became clear to her that his fluent invitation was all the French he could speak — except *pardonnez-moi* — she abandoned him for a known quantity. Our *courage*, which had been almost nonexistent, drained completely away, though the hotel waitress made a late appearance and my bravery in the matter of the fish was rewarded with several rounds on the dance floor and an hour or so of pressing myself against her, us both leaning against the Mediterranean sea wall of the pier by moonlight.

Out little entourage paid a visit by bus to Marseille, and another by train to Cannes, where we missed the last train home and stayed in the Railway Hotel. The harbour was full of American warships, and the town of American sailors. Our most memorable experience, and one that gave us a quotable quote for years to come, happened as we were passing a small hotel near the Railway Station. Two young sailors emerged, 'adjusting their clothes'. A little drunk, one of them complained hopelessly, 'Twenty bucks! Jesus Christ! Two strokes and I blew my top!' We laughed to ourselves.

Our daily budget was so small that one drink, one ice-cream, or too much Ambre Solaire on your skin as you sunbathed would mean doing without some necessity of life further down the line. That half-inch on T.P.'s nose that Blythe complained of was costing T.P. sorely in the Riviera sun.

Le Corsair was the name of the bar/*pension* we landed in at St Raphael. May White, in Dublin, had booked us into a hotel outside the town of St Raphael. Phil had serious reservations about the place after we had lunch served by a wild, witchlike woman. I was elected, because my school French was 'better', to find a place in the town — cheaper if possible, certainly not dearer. Michael Coffey decently offered to come with me, while Phil dealt with the disgruntled hotelier.

Le Corsair was very near the sea-front and had a well-painted sign featuring a swarthy pirate. The price list in the window showed a price less than we had budgeted, the bar through the window was plain but clean-looking. An old lady with short dyed-red hair, a mouth full of gold teeth and a Bohemian style of dress was pleased to show us the accommodation. Four men? Yes. No, we would not mind being in one big room. If necessary two would sleep in each bed. But did we say a man and his *wife*? Yes. Well, she had one small room with a small double bed. That looks fine too, we said. Breakfast was included. So we went and collected the others and we all moved into *Le Corsair*.

After dinner that evening, we bargained with the Arab boys selling rugs along the sea-front; unable to bring them down to our range, we ambled inland to the edge of the town.

'Let's see if this road will bring us round to our side of town. I think it will,' I said. I've always preferred to find a new road rather than go back the way I came.

It was starting to get dark. We turned the corner. The others were down the narrow street, about twenty yards ahead, waiting for us. When we were within about ten feet of them, a snarling German shepherd — *chien méchant* if ever I saw one — was there between us. Before the beast could make up its mind who to tear apart first, we were back on the other road. When we looked over our shoulders there was no sign of the other four. The dog held the pass. Michael being as much of a coward as I am where strange dogs are concerned, we decided to press on in our original direction. Less than half an hour later, we entered the small town of Frejus — Bejasus, as I have called it ever since.

There were two bars side by side — more like road-houses. One of them had an American cowboy name — *El Rancho*. We checked our money; enough for a few wines. There was slow dance music playing as we entered. Tables with check tablecloths, wooden chairs, the walls newish pine. A small bar on the other side of a small dance floor. About twelve ravishing young women, in threes or fours, sitting at tables. Not a man in sight. Heaven? No: a brothel!

Les Girls were disappointed that we did not accept their offer of sex, even after the selling price was lowered enormously and we were offered a special bargain for 'sucky-fucky'. We didn't even know, either of us, what that meant. We told them what we were doing in France; that we belonged to the other oldest profession in the world, like theirs, spoiled by amateurs. They were delighted with us. When we told them we were staying at *Le Corsair* they mimed, hilariously, effeminate male movements and putting on more than one pair of pyjamas. No wonder the gold-toothed Madame had been puzzled by Phil and Angela's presence there! Some of the girls danced with us, to the tune of, I swear, 'Someone to Watch Over Me'. We promised to return the next night and take advantage of their specially reduced prices.

A promise made is a debt unpaid! I don't know who came back with me. Certainly not Phil and Angela. Nor do I remember who did or did not make the journey upstairs. I guess I had other things on my mind. It was my first, and only successful, professional engagement of that nature, anywhere, ever. I was relieved that the very beautiful young girl, Laura, was extremely thorough in her examination of me for any signs of nasty things. At the end of the engagement she told me, sweetly, how much she enjoyed my passion, and my speed. I did better than the Cannes American sailor, but not by very much.

Later that year, I read with dismay that a faulty wall in the reservoir at Frejus had given way, with serious loss of life and property. I was really disturbed by that news, yet powerless. Worse still, at the time I thought it was some kind of divine judgement!

'Of all sad words of tongue or pen, the saddest are "It might have been".' This from my beautiful Breton lady friend with the short blonde hair and the faintly tanned skin. It was our last day in France; we had come back to Paris for one night on the way home to Ireland. We were being driven from Villene-sur-Seine, never to meet again. She wrote the words hastily on a scrap of paper and pressed it into my hands. It was signed 'With love, Jacqueline'.

The whole situation, I felt, was happening in the film *Casablanca*. Only the music in our heads was different. The night before, as we danced on the balcony of Dick Driscoll's small mansion home, she had kissed into my ear, in broken English, 'That is my favourite song.' The record playing was 'Begin the Beguine'. Before the dancing ended, Jacqueline and I, Pat Layde and the English secretary had planned trysts in the guesthouse in the garden.

Dick's wife, a staunch Catholic, had other ideas. She ensconced her mother in the only downstairs room that commanded the entrance to the girls' room upstairs, while Pat and I were tucked away in the upper reaches of the main house. Next morning Pat, T.P., Phil, Angela and I flew home to Dublin. I never saw Jacqueline again. We wrote for a while, and I mooned around Dublin for a month or more with 'Begin the Beguine' torturing my heart!

After the holidays, we came back to Dublin with this justly hailed production of *The Plough and the Stars*. The *Irish Times* reviewer, Seamus Kelly, having slighted every major performer, ended with something like, 'Only Eileen Crowe, as Bessie Burgess, survived, in the face of a music-hall Corporal Stoddard, played by Vincent Dowling, badly in need of a No. 1 army haircut!'

That's how it was, much of the time, with the Abbey, from its birth and for most of the twenty-five years I spent there — not with the Irish papers in general, but with the Dublin ones. As my mother would say, 'The nearer the Church, the further from God!' Compare this with the supportive treatment of institutional theatre in London by the best British papers, and the very positive effect that has on British theatre imports to America!

9

Anno Dermody

Christ, one Dowling is enough for any company!

'How dare God move when Dermody stands still!' Frank Dermody, as he spat through an almost toothless mouth at the Supreme Being, was a sight to behold — standing there on the stage (or in the Upper Circle bar, where we also rehearsed), a worn black overcoat on his five-foot-nothing frame, a felt hat covering his bald head or thrown purposefully on the floor at his feet, two nicotine-stained fingers pointed at a sixty-degree angle towards the ceiling.

Frank Dermody was demonstrating to us what he wanted at all times from the actor on stage: divine authority. 'Don't *tell* me! Take me there!' he demanded, over and over. For him, some of us, boys and girls, would stand on a terrazzo floor, hands by our sides, totally relaxed, no bending at the knee or swivelling round, and fall forward flat on body and face. He did it, time and time again; so we did it too. I can see a girl, now as I write — her name was Maureen Cook, I believe; thick black curly hair, white teeth. We are standing in front of the fireplace, in the dining-room of Groome's Hotel, talking to someone about Frank Dermody. To prove a point she falls flat on her face on the tiled floor, again and again. None of us ever hurt ourselves in doing it. Would I do it now? Not for all the tea in China.

1956 saw the launching of Hugh Leonard as an Abbey playwright. Hugh Leonard was the pen name of John Keyes Byrne (or Jack, as we called him). He was a civil servant then, with the Land Commission. In typical Dublin fashion, when the professional premiere of his play *The Big Birthday* was presented, the Abbey was slighted by many because it had been already performed by an amateur company! I loved this comedy of modern Dublin and Dun Laoghaire life. It gave me my first ever opportunity to play a character that I thought of as *myself*. The play did well and so did I. *The Big Birthday* was followed by new plays in English by Frank MacManus, John McCann (not a Kelly family saga, but a political period piece) and Denis Johnston, and two full-length plays by writers of stature John O'Donovan and Sean O'Tuama. Then the Abbey was scorned again for presenting Brendan

Behan's *The Quare Fella*, which had earlier had been rejected, and which the Pike Theatre had already produced in Dublin! 'Better never than late!' Brendan was at every performance of the play. He always waited for us in the theatre bar with his wife Beatrice and came with us to O'Neill's and to the theatre club afterwards, but never took a drink during the entire run of the play. What a lovely man that made him!

At the little Pike Theatre, it was a great year. The Pike was a small club theatre housed in a converted mews at the back of Herbert Street; founded by Alan Simpson and Carolyn Swift, it presented new Irish plays of quality that had failed to find a place in larger and commercial venues, as well as cutting-edge works from around the world. It filled an important gap in the Irish theatre experience for nine years. They gave Ireland *Waiting for Godot* for the first time. Lucky for Beckett the Abbey hadn't done it first; it would never have been heard of again! Brenda played at the Pike, that year, in *The Respectable Prostitute* by Ernie Gebler, who at that time was married to Edna O'Brien. Brenda was praised by the press but 'read from the altar' by our local priest. She never went to that church again!

The Globe Theatre also played an important role in Dun Laoghaire and Dublin theatre. It had a strong, often brilliant director in Jim Fitzgerald, and it attracted the best young freelance acting talent in Dublin. When the Abbey rejected Hugh Leonard's *Madigan's Lock*, the Globe did a brilliant production of it.

However, for me, 1956 was *Anno Dermody*. On 26 November his production of *Winter Wedding* by Tomás Mac Anna (Frank McCann) opened with me in the lead. Being directed by Dermody was the beginning of a long day's journey into acting as an art — 'the finest of the fine arts,' Yeats once said, according to Professor Denis Donoghue. It can be, but, alas, is not always. 'Don't stage-manage your emotions,' was one of the first lessons Frank taught me. 'Spit on your finger; touch the hot iron — sizzle!' It was his graphic way of calling for spontaneity!

For Vincent Citizen, Saturday night was party night, mostly at the Pike Theatre. It was 'bring your own drink' and keep your eye on it! There were one or two regulars who were 'freebooters' — they'd drink it out of any kind of boot as long as it was free. Brendan Smith was usually at these gatherings with a bottle of Cork Dry Gin; most of us were lucky to have three beers, or stout. At one party given by some American students, in a flat off Stephen's Green, the place was pretty packed. Brendan tucked his round frame into a tight corner in the kitchenette, facing the partygoers. Glass in hand, he poured himself a libation, then raised the bottle over and behind his head and eased it onto the shelf. Nobody, you would think, could get to the bottle without moving Brendan out or standing on his feet. 'I am monarch of all I survey,' he seemed to say.

Above (top): *The cast of* The Kennedys of Castlerosse — *left to right: Geraldine Plunkett, Desmond Nealon, Philip O'Flynn, Angela Newman, Patrick Layde, Bill Foley, Pamela Mant, Vincent Dowling ('Christy'), Kathleen Barrington*
Above (bottom): *Vincent as a boy scout (front row, second from the left) with friends Larry O'Neill (front row, first left) and Pat McCarthy (front row, first right)*

Previous page: *Vincent Dowling, Guest Director, Missouri Repertory Theater. A promotion for his public lecture: 'The Irish Agony — An Artist's Perspective'* (Courtesy Michael Mardikes)

Above: *Vincent gives an after-dinner speech. Ronald Reagan, is to the left of the fireplace, and to the left of him is Tip O'Neill*

Left: *The author enjoying a trip on the Midi Canal with Hugh Leonard.*

Philip O'Flynn as James Tyrone and Vincent as Edmund in Long Day's
Journey into Night
(Courtesy G.A. Duncan)

Above: *The author (far right) with (from right to left) Roma Downey, Frank McCusker and David Kelly, outside the Abbey Theatre during rehearsals for the 1990 American tour of* The Playboy of the Western World

Below: *Vincent and family at Westfield College after he received his doctorate in Fine Arts. Also present were Colm Meaney (first left) and Ken Tigar (second left)*

Above: *Cast of* Nicholas Nickleby *outside Ohio Theatre, 1983*

Below: *Vincent as a schoolboy at St Mary's College, Rathmines. Vincent is in the centre with his arm around his best friend, Brian O'Kelly*

Opposite page: *Patrick Laffan (left), Vincent Dowling (centre) and Clive Geraghty (right) in Alan Simpson's production of* At Swim-two-Birds

Vincent and family

Top left: *Vincent's mother Mai, and Olwen*
Top right: *Vincent and Cian*

Centre: *Valerie*

Opposite page: *Olwen*
(Photo: *Evening Press*)

Below: *(left to right) Bairbre, Rachael and Louise on the set of John Huston's adaptation of 'The Dead' by James Joyce*

Vincent's first theatrical portrait
(Photo: Bobby Dawson Gallery)

Above: *Vincent as Donal Davoren and Philip O'Flynn as Seumus Sheilds in*
The Shadow of a Gunman *in Mullingar*
(Courtesy Leo Daly, Mullingar)

Below: *Vincent and Bono backstage after a benefit performance at the Abbey Theatre*

Above: *Vincent receives an honorary doctorate from John Carroll University from President T.P. O'Malley*

Below: *Vincent in* Lady Windermere's Fan *during the Brendan Smith Academy season at the old Peacock Theatre. Left to right: Paddy Slattery, Brendan Delany, Eugene Black, and Vincent as Cecil Graham*

Above: *Cast members of the Abbey Theatre Christmas pantomime, 1954. Left to right: T. Hennessy, T.P. McKenna, Bill Foley, unknown actor, Vincent Dowling, Milo O'Shea, Maura O'Donnell and, at the piano, Gerard Victory* (courtesy *The Irish Times*)

Below: *The cast of* Is the Priest at Home? *with Madame Pandit*

Above: *Vincent in the Ohio Theatre*

Below: *Cast of* Do Me a Favourite, *Vincent's play about Anew McMaster. Left to right: Mary Kay Dean, Jody Catlin, Tom Hanks and Robert Elliott*

Above: *Éamon de Valera with cast and crew of* Long Day's Journey into Night. *Éamon de Valera is in the centre of the picture; to his left are: (front, left to right) Ernest Blythe, Angela Newman; (centre front, left to right) Philip O'Flynn, Séamus Wilmot; (centre back, left to right) Tommy Woods, Leslie Scott; (back) Tomás Mac Anna. To the right of Éamon de Valera are: (front) Frank Dermody, Deirdre Purcell (behind him); (centre) Gabriel Fallon; (centre back, left to right) Vincent Dowling, Micheal Ó hAodha, Rhona Woodcock; (back, left to right) Pat Laffan, Patrick Kelly, manager*

Below: *Vincent and Brenda's wedding photo. On the left is Eugene Black and on the right is Maureen McClure (later Black)*

Vincent as W.B. Yeats in I am of Ireland *by Edward Callan — Miniature Theatre of Chester, 1999*
(Courtesy of Michael Donovan)

He asked me if I wanted a gin. I said, 'No thanks, I'm drinking beer.' I moved on — in search of 'crumpet'! I was chatting up an American girl. She wasn't interested in a beer, or in me; but I thought Brendan might extend his offer of a gin to her. As I approached, he emptied his glass, then raised his hand to the shelf, feeling around carefully with his fingertips, then flapping them in growing panic. He turned around to the shelf. It was bare as a new-born baby's bottom. Brendan's face, when he turned back, was like the baby's: his mouth open, making gurgling sounds, unable to speak.

'It's gone,' he said finally, in a tiny voice, totally disbelieving. 'It's gone!'

We never did find the bottle, nor discover how or by whom it was taken. There was one actor there that night who might not have been able to resist the challenge of outwitting Brendan Smith, but I won't say it was Charlie Roberts. Let me say I hope it was. With the coming of Irish television, Charlie, a good actor, became a great television floor manager.

This freedom with other people's drink extended, for ever-increasing numbers of actors, me included, to sexual relationships. We were the artists, the spearhead of the movement to shatter the lingering Victorianism and hypocrisy that was stultifying Irish life! We each had different ways of saying it, and a lot of us came to believe in Free Love. It was liberating and healthy, we thought. Needless to say, we didn't like it when our own spouses or girl-friends were 'liberated' by some other arrant rover. As Paddy Long quipped, 'The actors are complaining to their wives that their girlfriends don't under-stand them!'

At a party in our home on Shanowen Road, around this time, I found our bedroom locked and my wife inside with 'a very good friend and colleague'. A few days later, in town — Bairbre, then only a tot, was with us — we had words about something else. Of course, deep down it was resentment, jealousy maybe. 'In our own bed!' I said, in outrage. I was leaving her, I told her, and jumped on a bus going in the opposite direction.

I had been seeing a girl called Violet, a Protestant — I had still not broken the instinct to describe someone in those terms. She had recently graduated from Trinity. Our sexual relationship had advanced rather quickly. She had her own flat, where I had visited her, and her bed, a number of times. I really loved her, though maybe not enough; and she, perhaps, loved me too much. I had always left her in the early morning hours, and gone home.

That first night I left home, I stayed with a male pal. The second night, after the bar in the Queen's closed, I went to see Violet. She came down to the door, which opened onto the street, and invited me in. I said that first I wanted to tell her I had left home. She said I could stay with her.

I balked at that — not because I didn't want to, but because I somehow realised that would be a commitment. I told her I had a baby at home, and not enough money to be living apart; there was no divorce in Ireland, and I didn't really believe in it anyway — or words to that effect. We talked for a long time, though it was raining. The image of Brenda's stunned look, and the minute figure of Bairbre waving as the bus moved off, had stayed with me.

In the end I went home. Violet said, 'If you change your mind, I'll be here.' At that stage of her career, she didn't want any commitments either. I owe her a great deal. She taught me a lot about undemanding love, friendship between man and woman, enjoying a relationship, taking the guilt out of sex. She introduced me to the joys of *soixante-neuf*. In the end she was directly responsible for my real liberation, though I don't think she ever knew it.

Brenda did a few other roles at the Pike. She did them very well. It paid even less than the Abbey, which meant that, what with paying for help — even though Brenda's parents often took Bairbre to their house, or babysat at ours — it was a financial loss.

Brenda was very good about money. I wasn't. 'Sufficient unto the day,' provided we had enough, and we had. At least I saw to that. But money was a cause of friction. Brenda thought I spent too much, but I think what really made her unhappy was not working regularly as an actress, in a regular company. She blamed me for that. *They've got everything — her husband is permanent and pensionable at the Abbey; give the job to someone who needs it!* was the attitude — or maybe it was *Christ, one Dowling is enough for any company!*

Over the next several years, interspersed with occasional 'legit' work, Brenda developed a niche for herself in the variety world — the 'illegit', as they called it. She did wonderful work with Hal Roach, then with Cecil Sheridan, and finally with Danny Cummins, all talented old-time music-hall comedians.

My most vivid image of Brenda is of her in the huge three-thousand-seat Theatre Royal, making her entrance down the gangway from a very real-looking Aer Lingus plane, with Jimmy Campbell ('Who put the black lead in Jimmy Campbell's hair oil?') and his full Theatre Royal Pit Orchestra backing her as only they could. This was a mink-coated, diamond-laden, platinum-blonde Brenda, superb as Marilyn Monroe singing 'Diamonds are a Girl's Best Friend'. Then whistles, cheers and the sound of three thousand and one pairs of hands clapping wildly! I was very proud and glad for her.

1957, and Dermody cast me in another Hugh Leonard play, *A Leap in the Dark*, a tightly worked political thriller. It dealt with the partition of Northern Ireland and the border raids by those who opposed it. Hugh Leonard's gifted craftsmanship made the play work on many levels. I remember a party at his house in Sandymount; Phil O'Flynn and I were encouraging him to write 'heavier plays', and he was saying he was using the 'lighter' ones to get known — then would come the serious stuff. He knew then, but I didn't, that 'tragedy is only unrealised comedy', as the poet Patrick Kavanagh said.

'Acting is the shy man's revenge' is a Dermodyism and a true one. I think it goes for good writers as well. Particularly it goes for Jack Keyes Byrne. It's that shyness, apparently conquered — it has really been heavily masked — that confuses people, makes them think some artists are extroverts and super-confident. Jack is so sure of his opinions, his likes and dislikes, his loves and his hates for people, institutions, attitudes and things; but I believe he has paid, and goes on paying, a price for his stance and convictions. Behind his mask he is wounded, insecure, often unsure of himself. In short, this funny, sometimes hurtfully outspoken, brilliant, successful playwright/scriptwriter/ journalist is a shy man. He is also a kind, generous, loyal friend. That I know. I suspect he is a formidable enemy.

When Blythe turned down Hugh Leonard's next play, *Madigan's Lock*, a beautiful fantasy, because it had a ghost in it, Phil and I were distraught. We tried to get Blythe to change his mind. He wouldn't. At Phil's suggestion, we got Godfrey Quigley to use Leonard to write the daily radio serial *The Kennedys of Castlerosse*. I remember Phil and I called on Jack at the Department of Industry and Commerce on Kildare Street, to tell him he had the job. He left the Civil Service soon after that. Jack's stage, newspaper and television successes suggest that Blythe did him a favour.

In 1957, my years of practising an upper-class accent in England paid off when I played the British Foreign Minister in John O'Donovan's hilarious political satire *The Less We Are Together*. Marie Kean was an outrageously funny first lady Prime Minister. Nature imitating art, Oscar! This play ran for twenty-seven weeks. Audiences loved the way it depicted a Taoiseach of the future who had just won an election by selling the voters the novel idea of forgetting about Ireland's history. It allowed for another Queen's Theatre first: a television set made its première appearance on stage in Ireland. After a performance I met and fell for a beautiful English cosmetic sales repre-sentative. We were more than friends, less than lovers. The night Irish televi-sion opened, I took her out instead of taking television in!

Niall Carroll, drama critic of the *Irish Press* and brother of Paul Vincent Carroll, provided a play set in Blackrock entitled *The Wanton Tide*. In my youth, we had spent two summers with Father Luke in indoor, salt-water swimming baths. This play centred around attempts to replace the tide, which goes out three miles from the shore at Blackrock, with swimming baths! The play was only a little more successful than the attempts to build the baths: it had a decent run of four weeks. I loved the feeling of authenticity I got playing in it. I also liked Niall Carroll, a good man and a clever writer, who went on to have his radio plays broadcast on Radio Éireann.

After that, John McCann again set the box office humming, and Iggy Kelly lied his way through another two hours of easy laughter in *Give Me a Bed of Roses*. T.P. McKenna and Pat Layde effortlessly replaced Ronnie Walsh and Joe Lynch, who had gone to big success, and a lot more money, in Radio Éireann's *Living with Lynch*.

That same year, Brenda played a good supporting role in the famous production of *The Rose Tattoo* at the Pike, starring Anna Manahan. With the dropping of a French letter, Tennessee Williams's play brought the police to the theatre — not to see it, but to close it. Not satisfied with that barbarism, they cast the producer, Alan Simpson, in jail. It was not only a mortal sin to use one of those 'yokes': it was a crime to import, or even advocate the use of, one. Alan triumphed in court and with the production in the theatre.

Brenda and I made another of our periodic but absolutely sincere attempts to 'start again and make our marriage work'. Without the help of any birth control other than abstinence, 'rhythm', or the tried-and-true *coitus interruptus*, she was pregnant again before the end of the year.

Two years earlier she had had a miscarriage very early in the pregnancy. She had thought her period was late; then one afternoon she, in bed, asked me if I would mind cleaning up the toilet. She had had an 'accident'. I cleaned it up with paper. Later the doctor told me it was a foetus! We were extraordinarily innocent, for all our experience.

1958 saw O'Casey withdraw his plays from *An Tóstal*, the festival run by Brendan Smith. Jim Fitzgerald — 'Fitz' — had been going to direct *The Drums of Father Ned*, a new play by Sean O'Casey. That in itself was a major event. Jim was a declared Communist. How real that was, I don't know. He thought the play needed some rewriting. That I know was real. The Archbishop of Dublin, John McQuaid, did not like the idea of a play by O'Casey (a Communist) and a play adapted from James Joyce (an avowed anti-everything-McQuaid-stood-for) being presented at a festival that his Archbishopship was opening with a Mass. So there was no Mass, no city funding, no *An Tóstal*. Someone threw its symbol, a burning light, into the River Liffey.

Fitz had asked O'Casey for rewrites in the play, for theatrical reasons. O'Casey, not knowing Fitz and his leanings, assumed religious pressure and withdrew his play and *all* performances of his plays from Ireland, thus dealing a kick in the solar plexus, or lower down, to the poor innocent Abbey!

Probably unconnected to this, I got acute appendicitis. I missed playing in a beautiful witty comedy by Niall Sheridan, *Seven Men and a Dog*. Thus I missed meeting the director of *On the Waterfront*, Elia Kazan, whose work I revered, when he visited the Abbey and Groome's Hotel.

Then I played Endymion, a true-life Dublin character — my brother Jack thought it was my best performance ever up to that time — in Denis Johnston's beautiful, flawed *The Scythe and the Sunset*. The play, which Ria Mooney directed ineptly, was written from the point of view of an Anglo-Irish British Army Officer looking at our Easter Rising.

The great 'American' artist August St Gauden — born in Dublin — sculpted the figures on the Parnell Monument on Dublin's O'Connell Street. Pointing towards the Rotunda Maternity Hospital, Parnell, 'the uncrowned King of Ireland,' warned women in labour and their husbands, 'Thus far thou shalt go and no farther!' — or so the Dubliners joked. On the morning of 8 May 1958, I heeded this and, bursting with excitement, arrived at the maternity ward to see my tiny, still-pagan, perfect second daughter. I kissed her and kissed Brenda and told her that a song I'd played on the radio that morning had not stopped playing in my head. It was 'Louise', sung by Maurice Chevalier, and so we called the baby Louise.

When I would ask my mother if she regretted ever having met my father, she would say, 'If I hadn't met Willy, I wouldn't have had you, and you never gave me a moment's unhappiness since you were born.'

I can say the same of my Louise. If I had any unhappiness about any of my children, it was through no fault of theirs, but mine own; and, like my mother, I would not be without any of them.

At the Queen's, during tea-breaks we gathered in 'the Spot', a shabby little shop and snackery that two Miss Dunnes ran next to our box office on Pearse Street. It had a counter, and wooden Pullman-like seating arrangements badly in need of a fresh coat of paint. The great problems of the day — artistic, political, romantic, financial and sporting — were settled, or at least aired, in the Spot. 'The Method or not the Method' was the heated question. Abbey acting by another name *was* the Method, was my thinking. That provided fodder for our continual arguing and searching. My arguments were always about truth and beauty in acting, to the point that Phil O'Flynn finally baptised me 'Truth-and-Beauty' Dowling!

Noel Purcell happened by one morning. Pantomime dame, music-hall comedian and successful film actor, he was no acting theoretician — well, not to us, in our lofty position as Abbey actors. 'Excuse me, lads,' he said in his flat Dublin, 'I couldn't help hearing what you were saying. But do you know what I do? Of course, I'm not even legit; but I pray every night for *con-cen-tra-tion!*'

I used to tell that as 'a mocking tale'. Now I teach it!

Ernest Blythe would not tour, at home or abroad. By dint of continual Players' Council pressure, however, we got him to do occasional visits to Belfast and

Cork, and at last he let us go to Paris. That was more to curry favour with the government, through the Department of Foreign Affairs, than from a belief in the value of touring.

'He who condemneth with small things shall fall by little and little,' said the penny catechism. The Players' Council had applied that to Blythe, with Sunday-night performances in provincial towns. We called them 'run-outs'.

The first of these was to Mullingar, Pat Layde territory. We brought *The Shadow of a Gunman*. It gave me my first shot at the title role. More importantly, it gave me the experience of being on stage with Philip, as Shields, all through the play. There is no truer, no more generous actor that I have ever worked with. No matter who I see in *Shadow of a Gunman*, or where I see it, his Shields provides the images that make contact with reality for me. That marvellous comic irritation with the world that has landed all its ills on his back! Phil had that quality in life, too. Then to work with Michael Dolan as Mr Gallagher, and May Craig as Mrs Henderson, was a thrill. They had been twenty years a-growing in the parts. Always the same, yet always fresh; the minimum of movement; listening as if for the first time; never taking away from the other actor. Tradition is an accumulation of skills, not of tricks.

The week in Belfast, with *The Shadow of a Gunman*, Michael Dolan was giving his farewell performances. He wasn't retiring, he was dying. A gentle, humorous man, he had given his life to the Abbey. I used to walk him from the Opera House to our digs, over the pub where *Odd Man Out* was made. I really got to like him. I think he liked me. He certainly appreciated my seeing him home.

I remember waking up early one morning, in the room over the bar which I shared with Bill Foley, and, feeling slightly hungover, putting down my foot to slip into one of my slippers, to go to the toilet — and, just in time, seeing a small, breathing family of newborn mice curled up in it. Bill said I literally hit the ceiling as, in one backward bound, I leapt onto my bed. I believe him. Some of the company said the mice weren't real at all, that Bill and I were in the DTs. True, we never during that week went to bed till after we had breakfast. We didn't drink that much, though. We couldn't afford it.

On another front altogether, while *Gunman* was playing in Belfast, I was acting as one of the British Auxiliaries, who behaved not unlike the B-Specials who were terrorising the Catholics in Northern Ireland at this time. An hour into the play, I would go to the stage door to escape the ear-bursting sound of a small bomb being exploded, in a bucket, as part of the play. It was at exactly nine o'clock. Remember, we are talking about being in British-held Northern Ireland.

Boom! went the bomb. Even over the intercom, it was deafening. Then Red Sean Mooney's voice told us to 'stand by for curtain call'.

As I turned to go through the connecting doors to the stage, the stage door burst open and four Royal Ulster Constabulary men crashed in, guns drawn, pointing at me. 'Put your hands up! What's going on here? What was that explosion?' It was like my own dialogue in the play, except that I was at the other end of the guns, and these were loaded with real ammunition.

'It's a sound effect in the play,' I said. They looked relieved, politely apologised for the intrusion and left.

A Royal Command Performance in Belfast was taking place that night in the cinema next door. England's Queen Mother had arrived at one minute to nine o'clock. She was just stepping out onto the red carpet when our bomb went off — *boom*! The security men pushed her back into the limousine, and it drove off at full speed! I was lucky I hadn't carried my 303 army-issue rifle with me to the stage door! Those fellows in Belfast were wont to shoot first and ask questions after.

During these years, we played in Armagh and Maherafelt, and when Brian Friel started to write plays, we played Derry City twice. There I got a heavy, innocent crush on a lovely little blonde hotel receptionist. That brought no harm or heartbreak to anyone. She married that great Irish musician, Phil Coulter, some years after.

No matter what the political climate of the time, we always did well in the North. We were well reviewed and wonderfully treated by everyone, Catholic and Protestant. On one visit, the whole company — Mr Blythe included — was entertained at the Governor Lord Wakefield's mansion. I suggested to Blythe at a Players' Council meeting, when we got home, that the Abbey should have a permanent presence in Belfast. The Irish international rugby team was drawn from both sides of the Border, and played its international matches on both sides alternately; why not have the National Theatre of Ireland do as much? He thought it was an interesting idea, he said, but not practical. I still think he was wrong.

A strange mixture, that man. He dominated the Abbey from 1935 to 1967. Driving to and from the run-outs, which he loved to go on, I learned a lot about him. His intimate stories of actors, writers and Board members were mostly funny. His candid personal experiences of the Irish Civil War and the great names associated with it, I found fascinating, sometimes disturbing, and always revealing. 'In war it is better to execute ten innocent men than to allow one guilty one to go free. In peace, better to let ten guilty go free than to execute one innocent one.' It began, very slowly, to dawn on me that he had developed a series of 'solutions' to all problems while he was in a British prison after the 1916 Rising, and that he had not rethought them since. I kept that discovery to myself, for the time being. It was, I told myself — half-joking, wholly in Ernest — my secret weapon!

'What do you do all day?' was the puzzled question T.P., Brenda, and others often asked when year after year Phil, Angela and I announced our annual departure to Connemara. The two of them usually stayed at a well-kept guest-house with every modern convenience in Spiddal village. Opposite was the Catholic church, where gender apartheid was still in force — the men on one side of the church, the women on the other. I took sinful pleasure in going to the women's side, with my baby daughter, later daughters.

One year, I rented a large old house in a dip in the boreen between Jim Faherty's pub at Knock and the sea. I called it 'Wuthering Depths'. Jim Faherty, who had the pub-cum-shop at Knock, had an always-smiling face like a friendly pet monkey's; he loved telling wicked, unmalicious stories of his friends and neighbours, who were also his customers in the pub, the shop and his hackney business. He drove them in his old car to and from the mental asylum in Ballinasloe, and to their final laying to rest in one of his coffins.

One day Jim's wife, Bea, when alone in the pub, locked herself in their new indoor lavatory. Oh, dear, what can the matter be, one old lady locked in the lavatory, she was there from Monday till Saturday, nobody knew she was there! It wasn't quite that long, but long enough to be frightening for Bea, and for her to be pleased to see me when, having heard her forlorn cries for help when I was in the shop, I followed her voice and rescued her.

Other years, I took Paddy King's cottage beside *Trá na mBan* — the strand of the women — in Spiddal. It was frequented by nuns from the convent, as well as by tourists and by Bairbre, Louise and me. When Bairbre was very little we lodged in a small house overlooking Galway Bay. Mrs Walsh was the *bean an tí* — woman of the house. She had two children. She supplied our meals and babysitting for Bairbre. Irish was spoken there — not, I confess, too much by me.

In none of these places had we every modern convenience, but I loved every moment I was in Connemara, and hated going back to 'dirty Dublin'. Spiddal, in my first years there, was a completely Irish-speaking village. The people living round it walked or drove donkey carts or cycled, mostly from thatched cottages. The women wore shawls and red skirts; the men, in peaked caps, looked and drank like characters in Synge's *Playboy of the Western World*.

I can see the Rolls Bentley owned by the American writer Paul Gallico parked outside Mrs Walsh's, bikes and donkey carts parked or hitched all about it. Inside, after a party, we gave our American friend, in return for the hospitality, Guinness, stories, songs, dances, fiddling and tin-whistling. He enchanted us all with his story of going in the ring and fighting the great Jack Dempsey. When Paul's book on Saint Patrick, *The Steadfast Man*, was published, he told how that night in Spiddal had given him the grasp on Patrick that had eluded him during all his research and writing!

It became a tradition that each week Phil, Angela, and I would have a really good dinner with wine in one of the big old hotels in Galway city or county. Often Walter Macken and his wife Peggy would invite us to their lovely house on Lough Corrib, then take us to Sweeney's Oughterard House Hotel, or the Zetland. Most years Kate O'Brien, one of Ireland's finest writers — novelist and playwright — would give us a marvellous night at her house in Roundstone: drinks, good talk, a spectacular sunset on the sea from her garden wall, then a gourmet dinner. Lord Michael Killanin and his lovely wife, Sheila, if in residence, would invite us to the Big House of their estate on the Spiddal River — also called Ból Uisce River — for drinks, good conversation, and dinner, which we would eat on the patio if the weather was good. Earlier, we would have watched from the harbour with their two sons as Killanin's man, Mick Dillon, directed the netting of the salmon coming in from the Atlantic and up the river to spawn.

Mick Dillon, gamekeeper, bailiff and chauffeur, lived with his family in a house on the estate. Mick had gold eyebrows and a white head of hair; square-jawed, powerfully built, with blue sailor's eyes and a dazzling smile, he was a handsomer Spencer Tracy. He could talk, sing, drink, and laugh infectiously with any man or woman on an equal footing. He claimed he always drove Killanin's big car to Dublin from Spiddal in two hours flat. It took us at best three and a half. He drove in the middle of the road. He claimed it was safer!

I would go fly fishing with him. 'Any sthrikes, Wincent?' he'd call out now and then as he flexed the fly rod that seemed to grow out of his hand, arm, and body. If there were no strikes, though that wasn't often, later that evening a large, fresh 'sahl-mon', as he'd say, wrapped in bloody newspaper, would be lying outside the door of my rented house or cottage. No doubt who had left it.

When taxes and costs drove the Killanins to sell the Big House and estate in Spiddal, the American who bought them retained Mick as part of the bargain. The Killanins retained the pink house near the harbour. Soon Mick and his family moved out, or were moved out. They left Spiddal. The new régime had not proved compatible with Mick's old ways.

One morning after rehearsal in the Abbey, to my surprise and delight Mick was waiting for me. He was on his way to the mail boat for a job in one of the big cities of England. 'I'll save a few pounds, and when I've something in the bank, I'll come home!' Mick said cheerfully, dismissing my dismay as we walked to my car. Spotting my two-tone cream-and-maroon Ford, Mick threw his hands in the air, in a gesture of mock horror, and at the top of his rich western voice cried, 'Chrisht, Wincent! And you hev the same cer the whole time!'

An hour or two later, as I waved to him from the platform of Westland Row Station, a broad smile on his tanned face, the air stirring his white hair, he called again, 'Chrisht, Wincent! You hev the same cer the whole time!' I never saw Mick Dillon alive again. Whatever else killed him, it was also a broken heart.

If I was asked to name one place in Ireland where I could live out my life, it would be Derraherc, a small wooded hillock in a vast lonely bog between the Coast Road and Bóthar Uaigneach — the lonely road, the road that stretches for miles between Spiddal and Moycullen on the Galway-Oughterard highway. To the west of Derraherc is a range of hills, mountains almost, topped by Seanafesteen; a high road indeed. There is a small lake fed by a sparkling, tumbling river at the foot of Derraherc. There I took my rod, flies, sandwiches and a beer, morning after morning, June after June, year after year. Rarely a soul in sight unless the children or a friend had come with me.

I first discovered Derraherc in 1957 or '58. Its two small farmhouses had occupants in the little houses by Lough Derraherc: one person in each house, both men. The younger 'black-Irish' man was the water bailiff. He spoke English slowly, translating in his head from the Irish, as he walked ahead, striding with wide steps in his rubber boots, to show me a pool upstream that had better trout in it.

'We haff a great gobberment,' he said, without any introduction. For a moment I thought it was sarcasm; who ever heard of an Irishman praising the government? But no! He went on, 'My daddy worked for the Blakes at Furabo. There was walls arount the big house and the fields, so high the birds could not fly over them. My daddy worked there for twelve hours a day pullin' tuirnips and at the ind of the day the agent would pay two pounds of tuirnips to him. But if the schales showed more than two pounds, he would slice off a piece till it was exactly two! Christ, we haff a great gobberment now!'

Another day, when I told him I was from Dublin, he nodded his dark head knowingly. 'Aye, Dublin. The gunboat *Helga* shelled Liberty Hall.' He said it as if that had happened yesterday, not on Easter Monday 1916. The next year I went there, the men had moved 'into town'.

In Derraherc I found that, for once in my life, I was not longing to be in that magic place miles away across the valley. I was in it. Of it. Part of it. Before and now. Years later I said goodbye, in this wild beautiful place, to one of the two or three women in my life I have really loved.

I chose this place to say goodbye
chose well, intuitively, this place that night
with sounds and smells and geasa that might
insulate our love from separation....

10

Long Day's Journey into Light

Glory, boy. Glory!

On 24 April 1956, *Long Day's Journey Into Night* by Eugene O'Neill had its world premiere in Stockholm, and very shortly afterwards *Life* magazine published a story on it. I picked up that particular *Life* and read it cover to cover, including the story of how this play about his Irish-Catholic family had caused O'Neill such anguish in the writing that he had left instructions that it should not be produced for twenty-five years after his death. Now his widow, in gratitude to the Swedish theatre, had allowed this production.

The article must have suggested that she felt the play was so important it should not have to wait so long for a production in English. Otherwise, why should I have felt instantly that this was a play that the Abbey could and should do? I also saw that it was a play that could fit even inside the Blythe 'narrower-than-the-founders' interpretation of the kind of play the Abbey was permitted by its charter to do — 'plays by Irish authors, on Irish subjects' (he conveniently ignored 'or such works as would tend to elevate and educate the audience'). The Players' Council agreed with me that this was a play for us to do. We did some research and found that O'Neill had paid public tribute to the Abbey when they first visited the States and showed him that there was a theatre that was doing the kind of play he was writing. We presented the *Life* article, and our case, to Blythe at the next Council meeting. He did not dismiss the idea!

We heard nothing for several months after applying to Mrs O'Neill. Then we heard that we could go ahead, but without the cuts allowed in the New York production. In the meantime José Quintero had premiered it in English on 7 November 1956, at the Helen Hayes on Broadway. Fredric March played James, Florence Eldridge was Mary, Jason Robards was Jamie and Bradford Dillman was Edmund. It played three hundred and ninety performances. Quintero cut over thirty minutes, I am told, from this four-hour-and-fifteen-minute masterpiece.

In *Long Day's Journey Into Night*, with Solomon-like wisdom as well as enlightened casting, Ria Mooney, a brilliant actress, was to be the drug-addicted mother of the Tyrone family. So she couldn't direct it! Philip O'Flynn (*avec* wig) would be the actor father, T.P. McKenna the damaged son Jamie, and I the tubercular writer Edmund. Kathleen Barrington was given the part of the Irish maid, Kathleen. Frank Dermody was the director.

The Players' Council asked that none of the cast should be cast in anything else until we had finished this epic work. To our surprise, Blythe agreed. We heard that he had informed the Board of Directors that as the new McCann play, *I Know Where I'm Going*, was clearly in for a long run, and as there were only five in the O'Neill cast, we could be spared to do this 'harmless rubbish'! He revised that opinion, long before it opened.

For thirteen weeks, three to five hours a day, six days a week, we worked on stage. Even after the official rehearsals, in pubs or restaurants or walking the streets, afternoons, evenings, and even nights, T.P. and I and often Philip went on teasing out this long, tightly woven, profoundly personal, painful material of O'Neill's with Frank Dermody. In our work together and alone, we all searched through every word, line, scene and silence, and into the deepest, most private recesses of our own lives, families, and imaginations. Talking, searching, arguing, learning from Frank. He was extraordinary, a mystic, whose insight into the true magic of theatre and acting was unsurpassed by anyone we had ever worked with. This was matched by his practical demands and help, in movement, listening, the very speaking of the poems in the text, and always in finding *the right image*.

His real difficulty was in slowing down his tongue from the speed of his mind. The old two-week rehearsal schedule, which the Council had negotiated to three, had often panicked Frank and made him totally inarticulate. Dangerously fearful of failing to realise the vision he saw so clearly, because he wasn't given time to achieve it, he was often driven to lash out cruelly at actors, or simply to disappear from rehearsal altogether. This time he had the time. He used it brilliantly.

Any physical or emotional 'pressing', as he called it, even for truth; anything in movement, emphasis, volume that was not absolutely necessary; any sloppiness in speech, thought, or action was anathema to him. Anything shallow or indulgent would earn a scathing 'Piddling realism, boy!' But if you got it right — which wasn't often, because 'right' was 'perfect' — it was worth it when he said, 'Glory, boy. Glory.' He talked about Greta Garbo, Kieron Moore, F.J. McCormick, and another whose name escapes me, as some kind of gods of acting, rattling off a role that each had played. Holding up the tobacco-stained fingers of one hand, 'Four,' he'd splutter, 'only four, truly great!' This, though he never said it precisely, we took as a challenge to reach their dizzy heights.

For me, as the tubercular son, the text called for outbreaks of violent coughing, from the top of the play on. The time he spent on that! His fear was that the audience — most of them, in those days, heavy smokers — would start coughing when I coughed, and for four and a quarter hours we would have a coughing chorus accompanying us. Who was it who said, 'People with coughs don't go to the doctor, they go to the theatre'? Then one morning, beaming, he came up on stage. He had the answer and he did it for me. A hard little cough, no chest sound in it, no breath — *hack! hack! hack!* — on and on. Frightening for the father and mother on stage. Totally convincing to the audience. Wonderful for the actor playing it. Not hard on the throat, either.

Never the easy answer with Frank. Always a search for the true answer. Get to the essence. Down, down, down. Get to the original meaning, and maybe, too, to a new meaning! Dylan Thomas said something like that about words. Dermody said it about words, feelings, moves.

I remember him describing 'walking all day around Dublin after a young pregnant tinker woman'. Even as he told you, you could see him do it. Then, when he did her walk, you could see her and every other pregnant women you had ever seen.

'Man or woman, you walk from here, and here' — he'd point to his forehead, for the mind, and to his nipples. Amazing, the feeling of rightness and confidence it gave you. Whoever, whatever you were playing, it soon became second nature to just fall into the right walk. That was what he wanted: second nature, the subconscious. 'Red raw,' he'd say with relish, to describe the sort of acting he wanted. Again and again, he'd spit on his finger; 'Touch the hot iron!' he'd remind us, then make a sizzling sound, prod and withdraw the 'burnt' finger with a yelp — and the emotion was there instantly.

Lord, he was generous, too. Always the first and the last to buy a drink. Straight up to the counter, no matter how many in the group — 'Come on, come on, come on! What are you having?' — putting crumpled notes, from pocket after pocket, out for the bartender. I don't think he owned a wallet or purse. Then, when a barman gave me the change, as they so often did — 'Christ, what's wrong with me?' he'd splutter. 'I pay. They give you the change!' I'd tell him that if he got himself a new coat and hat, and put in his false teeth (which he only wore on first nights in the theatre), they might give him his change. He had no interest in material things. He had the same coat and hat as long as I knew him. That's about twenty years.

Of course there were terrible days, for him and for us. 'Give it up, boy!' Or, 'You're stage-managing your own performance. For Christ's sake, trust yourself.' And when we had to say 'Jesus' and 'Christ' and 'Jesus Christ', which all the men in the play say over and over again, he would go very quiet. In those days, in Ireland or England, plays were closed for using 'the Holy Name'. But that's not what worried him. 'Now don't be afraid of it! Tear him down from the cross! Put him there beside you on the stage. He'll love you for it, boy!' One day, early in rehearsal, he said to Phil, T.P. and me, very calmly, very rationally, 'Tear him off the cross. Tear the thorns off his head. It's a prayer. Not a piddling, pious prayer. But a prayer torn out of their pain, for Christ's sake! We can redeem the souls of Eugene O'Neill and all his family — it doesn't matter that they are dead, time doesn't matter to God — if we *realise* this play, the implications, the pain and the love that are in it!' Those may not be his exact words, but that was his exact meaning.

He rarely talked this way with Ria. He gave her notes and direction quietly and privately, in deference to her age, her sex and her position as producer of the Abbey.

On mornings close to dress rehearsal, one or another of us would suggest, because we felt tired, or not too well, that we should just walk through. Soft-pedal. Save ourselves. He'd make no objection. Two minutes into the play, it would take us over. Hours later we'd remember, with a laugh, what we had said.

One of those days he came up to me, after he had let everyone else go. I was sitting on Edmund's chair, upstage left at the oval table. 'Glory, boy. Glory,' he said, going past me. He stopped. 'Oh, one thing: you blinked once in Act III.'

Later I asked him if he was joking. No, he wasn't. I said that everyone blinks all the time in life.

'This is not life,' he said. 'This is art. Anything that doesn't add, takes away.'

He asked me if I had seen the Russian film at the Astor Cinema. I had. It was called *The Cranes are Flying*. I loved it, particularly the actress. He wanted to know if she had blinked anywhere in the film. I realised she hadn't. Not once. 'If it doesn't add,' he repeated, 'it takes away!'

At the final dress rehearsal, we had the usual invited audience: seminarians from Maynooth and St Patrick's Colleges, as well as priests and nuns. They were allowed to attend rehearsals, but not performances where the laity were present. That was the law as laid down by the Irish bishops.

These clerics were our best audience for works in Irish or English. Educated, and hungry for theatre, they missed nothing. Four and a quarter hours was not long enough, they told us. They wanted it to go on forever. They crowded round Dermody when it was over. He was the happiest I have ever seen him.

A particular group of young priests asked Frank how he got the fog onto the stage and then off. They had *seen* it. There was no fog on the stage at any time, I told them. There was a foghorn *off* stage, and I as Edmund talked about the fog I had been in, and what it was like.

Well, they could have sworn they had seen it; but what about the sailing ship with the sails in the foaming sea? They had all *seen* that on the stage. Was there some kind of film projection?

No, we told them! It was an actor describing his greatest moments at sea, and another actor listening to him, and seeing what he was describing, and feeling what he was feeling. Nothing else!

But they had *seen* it. All of them in the audience had seen it — the ship, the sails, the foaming sea.

Dermody held up the tobacco-stained fingers of his right hand as we walked together down the lane to O'Neill's pub. 'You were with them today, Vincent. With Garbo and the others. Glory, boy.'

That night at Groome's Hotel, with Phil, Angela, T.P. and Dermody, I said, 'I wish we didn't have to do the play to the public. Just go on doing it in rehearsal. I know what Christ felt like. Why he said, "If it is possible, take this cross away."' Nobody disagreed.

The play went well. The notices were as good as we could have hoped for. London's *Sunday Times*, which didn't usually review us, was my personal favourite. It talked about my 'listening', in Act IV, to Philip as the father, in his speeches about his childhood poverty and his acting in Shakespeare. Most important of all, I felt and I knew that I was changed by the play. By playing it. By Dermody's direction of it.

Over and over, he had quoted Julien of Norwich: 'When mankind knows all and understands all, he, too, will see that all things are good.' I didn't understand that fully, but I sensed it was right.

I have never been in or seen any production — except the Moscow Arts's *Seagull* — of the quality of *Long Day's Journey into Night*; except its second revival in 1967, with Angela Newman as Mary and Patrick Laffan as Jamie. There are two reasons why this is so: Frank Dermody, and thirteen weeks' rehearsal! In my fifty years a professional actor, it is the *only* time I have experienced enough rehearsal with a great director. 'Oh, the crippling paralysis of the bottom line,' as I heard a speaker describe it.

On a very practical front, I wished I had done Edmund before I starred in one of four Abbey films made by Emmett Dalton Productions at Ardmore Studios. I had two big disappointments with regard to these films: Norman Rodway was cast in 'my' part in *This Other Eden*; and *The Big Birthday*, in which I had played the juvenile lead on the stage, was so mutilated by a film scriptwriter, Patrick Kirwan, assisted by a lovely Irish actress, Blánaid Irvine, that my part shrank to one line. I didn't have time to be bitter, however; I was acting non-stop. I had taken over from Derry Power the part of Christy in *The Kennedys of Castlerosse*, a character who had become known to millions over twenty years. I adjudicated at amateur drama festivals (Ireland's national sport in those days) and, at home, chaperoned Bairbre through her ballet lessons and modelling career and, for a number of extended periods, oversaw everything at 24 Shanowen, while Brenda worked in Belfast and London as well as round Dublin.

The fine Irish patriotism that motivated Emmett Dalton to make the Abbey films and to found Ardmore Studios did not extend to the casting of his Abbey Films. However, he and his imported directors brought us two wonderful actors, both of them with Irish backgrounds. Julie Harris played Sally; and Fielder Cook, who directed the filming of *Home is the Hero*, brought Arthur Kennedy with him. The two men made many friends among us.

I am particularly indebted to 'Johnny', as we called Kennedy. He came round to the men's dressing-room after a performance of Denis Johnston's *Strange Occurrence on Ireland's Eye*. It was doing well and had even received good notices. He sat on the old sofa at the end of the dressing-room, that Arthur Kennedy curl to his lips.

'Did you not like it?' asked Phil.

'Twelve blackouts in twelve scenes. Nothing could survive that! And ... eh ... the performances are kinda obvious.' He was clearly pained.

'Of course, you know we have only two weeks' rehearsal for a play here?' said Phil.

'Are you gonna have that on your tombstones — "We didn't have time"?' He wasn't joking.

The only one of the four Abbey Films to have no 'foreign' stars was St John Ervine's *Boyd's Shop*. But it had Vincent Dowling in the lead! I played opposite a beautiful, tall, slim young woman who had joined the Abbey Company. Her name was Aideen O'Kelly. Geoff Golden was the Boyd of the title, and Aidan Grennell the young Protestant minister; he wore that grey suit that I had had made for my wedding. The director, Henry Cass, had a good reputation. He had directed a successful British film, *The Legend of Glass Mountain*, whose theme music enjoyed great popularity. Most of *Boyd's Shop* was shot on location around Enniskerry, County Wicklow. The studio work was done in London.

I was awful in it. I'm not being modest. I saw it once and never had the courage to watch it again. I saw it one more time than almost anyone else in the world!

On the last day of shooting I had to do an eight-minute take, ending up with the set going on fire and me being hauled out by Geoff Golden. A little excessive, I thought. The money pressure must have been on. *Boyd's Shop* won no Oscars, nor did it get any of us any other film work. I have been intending to try and get a copy and look at it now from a safe distance, but I am, as Wilde said, 'a devout coward'.

In August 1958, Brenda got an offer to play in Dominic Behan's play *Posterity Bedamned* at the Metropolitan, in Edgeware Road, London. She would have to be there early in September. Louise would be about four months old. I was playing a leading role in *A Change of Mind* by John O'Donovan at the Abbey, and rehearsing nearly as big a part in *The Risen People*, a splendid piece by James Plunkett, which would follow. We would have to get a maid, and a reliable one. Bairbre, aged five, was at school, and would have to be taken there and home five days a week. We got a maid four days before Brenda had to leave.

Her name was Carmel. She was from a village in Co. Wicklow, one of a big family, used to looking after children and a house. She had a boyfriend, John, whom she was going to marry. He was a soldier, a bugler, stationed in Portobello Barracks. It was a tall order to take over a house and two very young children with their mother in another country, their father out six mornings each week and every night except Sunday.

Not to put a tooth in it, I was pissed off with Brenda for going away at this stage at all — and, worse still, leaving it so long to get a maid. However, she went, and I knew how much working in a play meant to her, so I determined to make the best of it. And, of course, I myself was occasionally on tour, augmenting the income.

Things were going along smoothly when a message came from our doctor for Carmel. He wanted her to phone him. There were tests he wanted to do. But I could not help noticing that Carmel, in spite of the white overall she wore round the house, was chubbier now than I had first imagined. Indeed, the thought which I had quickly put aside — *Could she be pregnant?* — kept rearing its suspicious head.

The doctor's message had hit me where unpleasant news or loud noises always hit me: right in the stomach. Knowing Dublin, I could hear the cracks, the innuendoes, the rumours, and eventually the story that while my wife was away in England I had got the maid 'up the pole'! Never mind that she had been only a month in our house; what have the facts to do with the gossip!

When I gave her the message before going up for my afternoon snooze, she blushed to the roots of her hair. In fairness, Carmel blushed at almost anything anyone said to her that was vaguely personal.

'Carmel,' I said very gently, 'are you pregnant?' I added quickly, 'It's all right if you are. I'm not going to put you out. It's just that with two little ones here and me out most of the day and night, I need to know.'

'Oh, Mr Dowling, I'm so embarrassed!' she said, red as a beetroot. 'I'm seeing the doctor because I have a cyst in my womb and it makes you look pregnant, which, I must tell you, I couldn't be — if you know what I mean?'

Muttering that I knew what she meant, I went up to my room and, with that truly great talent I have, put it out of my mind and slept soundly for my allotted hour. That night, after the performance of *A Change of Mind* — for which I had lent Father Luke's antique swivel chair to the Abbey, to be used as set dressing — I telephoned my mother, now living in Sandymount. She confirmed that such cysts in the womb did exist.

But that relief didn't last long. Each day, Carmel looked more pregnant. I had kept Phil O'Flynn up to date, and a week later he suggested that he should spend Sunday evening with me at Shanowen Road. He'd know, sure; wasn't his sister a nurse!

Dinner was served in the sitting-room. Carmel did us proud. And at the end of the night, Phil confirmed that I hadn't a thing to worry about. 'Carmel is no more on the road to Galway than I am,' he said, using his favourite metaphor. 'Take my word for it!' I did. I wiped the whole idea clean out of my mind.

But no matter how early I was a-stir, or how late I left to go to the theatre, John the bugler was sitting shyly in the kitchen. The image of John and Carmel in bed, in my house, haunted me. It wasn't a moral concern. It was about what the Doyles would say, and maybe do, if they found their two grandchildren were in the same house as a maid and her man 'living in sin' — under the roof on which the Doyles had paid the deposit!

So I decided I would lodge a bus ticket under the iron latch on our front gate, on my way to the Abbey. If it was still there when I got home, it meant John was sleeping in my house, billeting himself without leave from the commanding officer — me!

I told Phil on the way home in his car. I got out casually but quietly, stepped to the gate, lifted the latch, took out the crushed white paper bus ticket and held it up, with a mixture of triumph and dejection. Phil waved a sympathetic good night.

I knocked at Carmel's door and said — loud enough, but not so loud as to wake the children — 'I'm coming in, Carmel.' And I opened the door and switched on the light.

From the far side of the single bed in the maid's tiny room, John, in his shirt, was struggling to pull his trousers on and get out of bed at the same time, saying, 'I'm sorry, Mr Dowling! It will never happen again!'

Over a cup of tea, some minutes later in the kitchen, their sorry tale was told. They were from the same village, in Wicklow. They had been courting and were now engaged. Due to some ridiculous Army red tape, they had to wait a couple of months more to marry or they would lose his Army marriage allowance, something they could not afford to do.

There would be no repercussions, I told them. Not only did I hope Carmel would stay, I needed her to stay. All quiet on the northern front! For a while, anyway.

A week later Brenda returned. I had reserved a table for two at the Golden Orient, a favourite haunt of Dublin actors. I told Brenda the happenings of the past month, at home and at the Abbey. I told her how happy I was to see her again, how I had missed her. I didn't have to tell her how much the children had missed her and how happy they were to see her. They had shown that. I touched on our relationship and how I felt that something of a new beginning was needed; that I had done a lot of thinking — for once — and thought we should approach it gingerly, maybe even get some expert help. We agreed we shouldn't rush into anything. Mike Butte bought us a 'welcome home' drink, on the house. We talked a while more and ordered a taxi.

When we opened the door of 24, we found Bairbre sitting at the top of the stairs, half-asleep and weeping. 'Carmel has been crying but she won't let me go in to her,' she said.

While I put Bairbre to bed in our bed, Brenda went in to Carmel. She wasn't long there.

'You'd better phone the Rotunda and tell them to send an ambulance immediately while I get Bairbre to sleep. I'm pretty sure Carmel has started into labour,' she told me calmly.

From a public phone box opposite I called the Rotunda Maternity Hospital.

'Is she in labour?' the nurse asked.

'My wife thinks so,' I replied.

'We can't take her into hospital if labour has started.'

Before I could explode, she followed with, 'Are you Christy Kennedy?'

I said, 'Yes.'

'Christy Kennedy! I can't believe it!' was her amazed reply. 'Don't worry about a thing. We'll have an ambulance and two nurses out to you in two shakes of a lamb's tail!' And they did.

While the nurses, one male and one female, were with Carmel, we made tea and boiled water in every receptacle we had. The two nurses — maybe one was an intern, I'm not sure — came down shaking with laughter. Happily accepting the tea, they told us, 'She's in labour all right. It started a couple of hours ago. But she insists she couldn't be. She keeps saying, "It's impossible, I can't be! I never!" Then she looks up at the wicker cradle on top of the wardrobe and says, "Oh, isn't that a lovely cradle!"'

With promises to Carmel that we would call John, we saw her off in the ambulance. Calling from the public phone on the corner, hoping I had enough pennies, I got the Orderly Sergeant at Portobello Barracks. He instantly closed ranks when I said the words 'maid', 'baby' and John's name!

My army reserve training came into rescue. 'Get me the Orderly Officer on the phone and get him *now*, Sergeant!'

'Yes, sir. Hold on, please,' was the prompt response.

A dry North-of-Ireland voice came on the line. 'This is the Orderly Officer. Can I help you?'

'Yes,' and I took a deep breath to calm the trembling in my voice. 'My name is Vincent Dowling. I am an actor at the Abbey Theatre. My wife has just returned today from working in England. Our maid, who is nurse to our two very young children, has been taken to the Rotunda Hospital in labour. The father is the bugler in your barracks. Will you please —'

'You dirty bastard, Dowling, you should be ashamed of yourself,' the voice on the phone said.

'Please!' I said sharply. 'I'm gone beyond seeing any humour in this situation. Will you —'

'Keep your hair on, Vincent,' said the voice, 'I've already sent the sergeant to wake the bugler.'

'Who's that speaking?' I asked, relieved.

'Captain Kelly on Annual Reserve Training, Orderly Officer for tonight, alias Quidnunc and drama critic of *The Irish Times*!'

'Seamus Kelly,' I said, 'I never thought I'd be so happy to hear your voice.'

I told him the story and he said he'd see to everything. He did, too, and many is the night's drinking and talking we did after that. It didn't make my reviews from him any better. Nor did I expect it would.

When I arrived at the Rotunda, John, proud as Juno's Paycock, took me up to see their new son through a glass wall. Then we went down to see Carmel. Propped up on her pillows in bed, in a flannel nightdress, happy, relaxed, she was really glad to see me.

'Have you decided on a name for him yet?' I asked.

Carmel blushed furiously. Then, with a lovely shy smile, she said, 'We wanted to call him Vincent, but we thought we'd better not!'

Carmel and John were deeply in love and committed to each other, and only Army regulations had delayed their marriage. A short time after the birth, we were there to see the knot tied, and had a modest wedding breakfast at our house. I often saw them in Rathmines and when they brought the baby to see us.

For me those months had another outcome, though — a lasting and wonderful one. Those few months I spent playing both parents to Louise, at her very early age, bonded us so strongly that the bonds withstood — and strengthened under — the strains of my separation from Brenda, and even of my later emigration to America.

Although I went to an enlightened, saintly Dominican priest and marriage counsellor, Brenda could not bring herself, I think, to expose her private life to a man and a priest. That, I suppose, gave me all the excuse I needed; and our relationship slipped back to emotional separation, though we lived and slept together for several more years. To both of us the reality was: 'It is better for the children; and anyway, we can't afford to keep two homes, or even to get a bigger one.' Weird and wonderful are the ways of woman and man.

11

You're Losing the Prince

Jesus, Mary and Joseph, mind the baby!

Brenda arrived home unexpectedly one Sunday night, early in 1960. She was playing in Belfast in a variety revue written by produced by and starring Danny Cummins. Everything was closed in the 'black' North of Ireland on a Sunday in those days, except churches, chapels and meeting houses. As the old joke went, 'First Prize, a Sunday in Belfast; Second Prize, two Sundays'!

Carmel's place in our household had been taken by Josie, who had short, thick, straight, jet-black hair and a wrestler's physique. Josie wasn't likely to be found in bed with a young man, or to surprise us with the sudden appearance of a baby! She was reliable, capable and honest. She, I, Bairbre and Louise got on famously, without any closeness developing with any of us. Brenda had taken no chances this time round.

Brenda's unheralded arrival was joyfully received by the 'kiddos' the next morning. I was pleased she had given up her day off to come home. She would have to leave Monday, by mid-morning, and would have two shows to do on reaching Belfast, as they were playing twice nightly.

Over the previous few years she had gained experience and notice in the variety theatre, with Cecil Sheridan and Hal Roach. Danny, a wonderful, multi-talented performer and writer, had been moving from main supporting male comic, especially with the great Jimmy O'Dea, to starring in his own shows. Perhaps learning from Jimmy's success with Maureen Potter as a stage partner, he found a versatile comedienne-actress-singer, for his straight woman or 'feed', in Brenda.

I was actually in bed, or just going to bed, when she arrived. She looked in on the children asleep, but didn't waken them. She was full of chat to me about what she had been doing. In bed she was unusually affectionate; and, more unusual, she made the overture to the sex symphony, which we both played in full.

I had, from the first, found Brenda physically attractive. As a matter of course, I had, as our marriage deteriorated, turned off desire at will. I did it for months, then years. Brenda being away caused me perversely to miss her, and to determine to make our marriage work, for the children's sake as well as our own. Besides, there was no way we could divorce in Ireland, or afford to legally separate and have any sort of decent life. As it was, we got by pretty well, with the occasional help of Brenda working and my sponsored radio, a little freelance directing, drama-festival adjudicating, and very rare, badly paid 'bits' in foreign films made in Ireland. I remember one playwright saying to me, 'I always know the actors in a pub on a Friday. After being paid, one actor hands a pound note to another, saying, "There's the pound I owe you." Then that actor says and does the same to another. Sometimes the pound changes hands five or six times, usually ending up back with the barman!'

It soon became apparent Brenda was pregnant, which strengthened my resolution to 'make it work'. That same year, I played the male lead in *Boyd's Shop*. I lodged most of the fee in a savings account, against the new baby's birth. In the summer, I rented 'Wuthering Depths' in Connemara for the month of June. It was almost cheaper than living at home! Josie came with us, but Brenda didn't. She was working, or looking for work. Anyway, she hated Connemara — 'outside loo, cooking on a turf fire, and all that drinking in pubs every night!' Louise got the measles while we were there, I remember. The District Nurse looked after her, and there were no complications. We thought it fortunate that Brenda, 'with child', wasn't with us.

As Brenda's time approached, I was playing in Bryan MacMahon's *The Song of the Anvil*, a historical/political pastoral piece set in Kerry. Brenda really surprised me by wanting to have the baby in a private nursing home. She had some reason, which I didn't understand, why she shouldn't go to the Rotunda Maternity Hospital. It had proved satisfactory with Bairbre and Louise, had a great reputation, and cost next to nothing; in those years money meant more to Brenda than to me. She was booked into the Pembroke Nursing Home, on Pembroke Street — on the south side! An unfriendly foreign country to Brenda! I wanted one of my Abbey friends to be godfather; Brenda said that Danny very much wanted to do that, and as she was working with him, she thought it would be a good idea. I agreed, reluctantly, to Danny, too.

The baby was a girl. Mother and child were both well. She was called Valerie, after her grandfather Valentine Doyle. That, as you can imagine, delighted me!

Two powerful images of Valerie's early childhood come to mind. It was daytime. I was at home. Brenda wasn't. Valerie screamed, a stomach-dropping scream of pain. She was on the floor, one of her tiny fingers clamped in the fully closed legs of her wooden folding stool. I opened it slowly. Her finger was still in one piece — just barely. I took her to Temple

Street Children's Hospital. Amazingly, she didn't lose the finger. Extraordinarily, she allowed them to work on it without a tear.

The second memory is from some time later, certainly more than a year. Strange: it is so vivid, yet the exact details not related to the event are lost.

Our marriage had dropped back to one of accommodation, in every sense. More and more, Danny was about our house, coming, going, rehearsing gigs, developing and planning new shows. I was involved on the periphery, which I enjoyed, as I loved music hall. I took it for granted that Danny and Brenda were more than an onstage team! They had led the resident variety company in Butlins holiday camp the previous summer, and would be doing so for some summers to come. The kiddos went with them. Apart from the fact that it was thirty miles away and cost money, being regimented with 'jolly campers' and constantly assailed by amplified English voices, with no privacy, was not my style.

Well, the night in question at 24 Shanowen either was a Sunday night or came at a time when I was not in the play at the Abbey. I had gone to bed early, and was reading. Voices were raised in angry argument downstairs, followed by quiet, then more outbursts at intervals. Then a door banging. Exit Danny.

Brenda came into our room. I didn't comment, went on reading. She went to the dressing-room table in the shallow bay window. I realised she was crying. I remember thinking: *She's probably giving out to him about his drinking.* The tone of the argument had sounded oddly familiar. I was wrong.

'What's the matter?' I said with some concern. I was conscious of the need to tread softly.

'Danny said he's going to take Valerie,' she said, trying to control her tears.

'What are you talking about? How can Danny take Valerie?' It really didn't make sense to me.

'Oh, don't give me that. You know very well,' she said scornfully.

As if it were my brother Jack talking, I heard myself say, calmly, almost tonelessly, 'Oh.' I turned over, ostrich-like, and buried my head in the sands of sleep.

Next morning, in my mind, at the moments between sleeping and waking, where my problem-solving even as an actor and director is clearest, I was in *Lovers Meeting* by Louis D'Alton. It was the scene where the young girl finds out she is not the daughter of the man she has always loved as her father. She consoles him, telling him that he is her father because he is the one who protected her, took care of her, and loved her. *That's it! There's no more to be said*, I thought.

What I didn't count on was Valerie feeling different. However, a lot of water, a lot of streams, would have flowed under the bridges before I would know about that.

Harry Brogan had delighted Dublin audiences since 1944 in return for security, the honour of being an Abbey Player, and a pittance for payment. He had, at this time, never left Ireland. He wasn't afraid of travel, oh, no — he would never admit to that; he claimed he was still wanted by the British authorities for his exploits during the Troubles! Harry was a faithful husband and devoted father and a great comic actor. He was also, behind his mask of remote dignity, a gentle, insecure man with little formal education. Now and then he would make infantile little stands in defence of his pride and self-respect.

There was a bus strike during rehearsals for *All the King's Horses*. Harry lived at the foot of the Dublin Mountains, quite a distance from the theatre. He had never owned a car and was too old to cycle, and for him to pay for twelve taxi journeys to and from Tibradden out of his week's wages, with a wife and children to keep, was simply not possible. So he requested that the Abbey should pay for taxis for him to and from the theatre for the duration of the strike. Blythe dismissed the request out of hand.

The morning of the first dress rehearsal, Harry, who was playing the solicitor reading the uncle's will, failed to appear. It was decided to skip that opening scene, which could be picked up when we finished the first act.

At the break, Harry arrived with a rambling story: he had left home at eight o'clock, had failed to hitch a lift from passing motorists, and had walked the five or six miles.... There was no mistaking the smell of whiskey on his breath. If he hadn't been in a pub ever since opening time at ten o'clock, he had gone to one to bolster his courage for being deliberately late. Ria, who was producing, made no comment except to tell the stage managers to set up for the scene we had skipped.

While the house lights were still on and Geoff, Harry and I were taking our positions, Blythe came into the auditorium. This unnerved Harry. Again and again, he tied himself in knots with the lawyer's legalese. Unfortunately he started muttering, between mistakes, about the bus strike ... the weather ... the motorists who had ignored him ... the theatre's refusal to pay for a taxi....

One of these asides was rudely silenced by an angry outburst from out front. 'Cut out that nonsense, Brogan. You don't know your lines, you were an hour late, and you are drunk!' And Blythe slammed up his seat and stamped out of the auditorium, the stall doors swinging noisily behind him.

Every speck of colour drained from Harry's face. It was like seeing someone die sitting up beside you. *All the King's Horses* and all the king's men never completely put Harry back together again.

In April 1961, the Abbey put on Bryan MacMahon's *The Honey Spike*. I wanted the lead so badly. It was a romantic lead, a young Kerry tinker with passion, imagination, poetry, and balls — but he had to sing. He sings a love song — an old Irish song, 'Mary of Loughrea' — to his beautiful bride. Frank Dermody, who was directing, wanted me in the part. Bryan MacMahon was very happy about my playing it. It was up to me. Had I the courage to risk failure on the stage before my colleagues — including the beautiful young newcomer to the company, Fidelma Murphy, who was playing the tinker's bride?

Deep down I felt that I could sing, that it was my brother Paul's 'You're only a crow' that was sticking in my gullet. I had never tried to sing in public since.

I turned to John Reidy. 'I'll have you singing,' he said, after he had had me do, very painfully, some scales. 'You just need to practise and extend your range. All you're going to do is this: from morning till night, every moment you're alone, sing, "Do, re, mi — mi, re, do." Then add a note a day — no forcing, ever. In no time you'll be in charge of your whole range. You are not "tone deaf". You have a bad musical memory. Purely psychological!'

Over the following three weeks, I sang 'Mary of Loughrea' till I was blue in the face. Dermody's direction was, 'Sing it like you're singing it to put your daughters to sleep.'

Well, I did it. I didn't always get the note right, but I got the scene right. I got the play right, too, and so did Dermody. Maura O'Donnell as my jealous ex-girlfriend, Geoff Golden and Bríd Lynch as my wild drunken father and mother, could have been plucked from any tinker encampment from Killorglin to Kilcock. Fidelma won the hearts of audiences and critics — and, for some time, my heart.

Dermody, I'm afraid, gave her a hard time. I think he got an amazing performance from such a young, inexperienced actress, but somehow he grew dissatisfied.

I remember one night, near the end of the play, he came backstage from out front. Fidelma was on in her death scene; almost everyone else was on stage. Frank had some drink taken. When I came down to the side of the stage, a little before my entrance, he was standing, swaying, almost on the set, projecting a penetrating whisper: 'Give it up, girl. Go home. Give it up! Jesus!'

I stepped up as close to him as I could without being seen, and practically spat out, 'I'll knock your fucking head off, Frank, if you don't get out of here now!'

He looked blankly at me for a moment and shuffled out, sputtering God knows what. We never spoke about it again, but he also never did it again in my presence.

Mammy brought my eight-year-old Bairbre to see *The Honey Spike*. Mammy told me that by the end of the first act she was worried that the plot, which was violent and driven by the pregnancy of a young tinker girl

(Fidelma), would be too much for little Bairbre. The second-last scene of the play has a vicious fight between the pregnant girl and her husband's former lover. At the climax of the fight, as Fidelma was flung across the stage, Mammy heard Bairbre's tiny voice cry out a warning: 'Jesus, Mary and Joseph, mind the baby!'

One of the summers that the family was in Butlins, during the Abbey annual closure for June, I went to England with Pat Layde. To be accurate, I went on the ferry from the North Wall to Liverpool, with Mammy, in Pat's car, a Fiat — IYI46. How do I remember the number of the car? I always linked it to the air of a well-known song: 'I — Y — I couldn't I love you too? O, the pity of it all, O, the pity of it all.' I only have to think of Pat, and it starts to play again.

We drove via Stratford-on-Avon, where we stayed a couple of nights. I don't think we saw a play; just talked, walked, ate and drank in moderation. Mammy was so easy to be with. It was a wonderful time for both of us. Then I dropped her off with my cousin Patsy Coldrick and her husband Gordon, a doctor, in Oxford, and joined Pat Layde in London. He had arrived by Aer Lingus. It was a matter of money. He had recorded in advance a month's supply of radio programmes at Eamon Andrews Studios in Dublin. His girl, later his wife, worked there. She was Eamon's sister, Kay, a delicate, gentle, humorous girl, madly in love with Pat.

Both Pat and I had arranged to link up with my old friend Dominic Roche of *My Wife's Lodger* infamy. He had returned to London after some years in Dublin, mostly in my house, and he had offered to get us beds for the night. The link with him was effected about nine o'clock that Sunday night, at a party in West London. The party had a domino effect: I slept with an actress with an insatiable sexual appetite; Pat drank through the night into morning, alone in a Covent Garden pub, and lost IYI46 and all our possessions; we spent the next day with the Bow Street police and recovered the car and everything in it! The devil's children have their father's luck!

As I had neither the wish or the stamina for my new actress friend, we set out towards our holiday destination, St Ives in Cornwall.

Pat had played in Sean O'Casey's new play at the Gaiety Theatre in Dublin, *The Bishop's Bonfire*, directed by Tyrone Guthrie. We didn't know O'Casey, but Pat thought we should stop by Torquay, near where he lived, on our way to St Ives, and telephone him. I was all for it. This whole trip would be a happy retracing of former touring trails for me.

In a telephone box in the large Torquay General Post Office, Pat called. I waited. The call lasted about a minute or so.

PAT: Hello. Is that Sean O'Casey?

MAN AT OTHER END OF LINE: This is his son Breon.

PAT: Mr O'Casey, this is Patrick Layde. I was in the première of your play at the Gaiety Theatre, directed by Tyrone Guthrie.

MAN: This is his son Breon.

PAT: I have the Abbey actor Vincent Dowling with me. We're on holidays.

MAN: This is his son Breon.

PAT: We're on our way to St Ives. We would like to stop and pay our respects.

MAN: This is his son Breon.

PAT: Well ... eh ... Breon, could we stop by and have a few words with your father?

MAN: Not today.

PAT: Tomorrow?

MAN: No.

PAT: On the way home from St Ives?

MAN No.

PAT: Then when?

MAN: Next year, or the year after, or the year after that again!

And he hung up!

We walked out into the sunlight of Torquay's Main Street, straight into Siobhan O'Casey, Sean's daughter, whom we knew well.

'Hello,' she said, surprised and pleased. 'What are you doing here?'

We told her we were on our way to St Ives.

'Oh. One of my brothers has a studio there. You must meet him. As a matter of fact, he's in the post office right now. Come on, I'll introduce you,' she said, leading the way. 'Here he is. This is Vincent Dowling and Pat Layde from the Abbey. Pat was in *The Bishop's Bonfire*. This is my brother, Breon.'

We said nothing about our phone call to Sean O'Casey, then or later, to Breon.

Pat Layde would be at the centre of another brush with fame in Paris, in 1964. We were doing O'Casey's *Juno and the Paycock* at the Sarah Bernhardt for the *Théâtre des Nations* Festival. Maura O'Donnell and Philip O'Flynn had the title roles; Harry Brogan was Joxer; I was Gerry Devine, the Socialist hero with feet of clay; and Pat had a couple of small parts. Dermody directed, in a set designed in and sent from Iceland by Tomás Mac Anna. It wasn't the greatest *Juno* we had done. But it wasn't the worst I have seen, by any means. Paris liked it, though not as enthusiastically as they had the earlier *Plough and the Stars*.

On the last night, Pat Layde sidled up to me before the curtain call and whispered conspiratorially, 'There's a very small, very private, party after the show, being given by a *very important* writer — I can't say who. I can bring *one* of the cast with me. Do you want to come?'

I knew Pat's preoccupation with famous writers, and I was genuinely appreciative of the offer. I actually considered, for a moment, saying 'yes', but realised I couldn't. 'I can't. I have a date with a girl from a foreign Embassy for supper — and breakfast! Thanks all the same, Pat.'

He pointed his aristocratic nose upwards, sniffed slightly, and stalked towards the door he would enter for his curtain call.

Late next morning, we got on a Caravelle jet bound for London. Pat was sitting across the aisle from me.

'I hope last night was worth it!' he remarked airily.

'It was,' I said, truthfully.

'Good,' he said.

'How was your party?'

'Very small. Very interesting. The most interesting I ever was at! Just our host and a few friends. No one else from the company.'

'Who was the host?'

He gave me a long, penetrating look. 'Sam Beckett,' he said, a little smugly, I thought, and went back to his reading.

Well! That's the true history of how Sean O'Casey and Samuel Beckett missed meeting me!

'We ought to be able to give the children of the poor as good an education as we give the children of the rich,' said W.B. Yeats, one of the founders of the Abbey Theatre, in the Senate of the Irish Free State.

Joseph Groome, the proprietor of Groome's Hotel, was National Chairman of the Fianna Fáil party — mostly the governing party in those days. Patty, his wife, was the real boss. They and all belonging to them, especially Patty's sisters Joan and Clare, were generous, close friends to our crowd at the Abbey Theatre. Most of the theatre companies playing at the Gate Theatre, directly opposite Groome's, were welcomed too. For the future political stars of Fianna Fáil, like Charles Haughey, Brian Lenihan, Donogh O'Malley, and other 'young Turks', it was the place to go. A few older back-benchers, like Paddy Clohessy and Paddy Collins, actually resided at the hotel when the Dáil was in session. Paddy Long christened them 'the Sundowners', the name of a popular Australian film at the time. A few judges and journalists stopped by from time to time. In spite of different political allegiances, we all talked, drank, and argued on very friendly terms. It would have been a courageous police sergeant that would have raided the premises after hours. The unspoken question would have been, 'Will you have a drink, Sergeant, or a transfer?' Fair is fair. One policeman did once raid Groome's, that I remember. He found that all of us, about thirty in total, were 'registered' guests there that night — including District Justice Donagh

MacDonagh. This meant, of course, that we could legally drink there at any hour.

Charlie Haughey would later become Taoiseach (Prime Minister); Brian Lenihan rose to Deputy Prime Minister and Minister of Foreign Affairs; and Donogh O'Malley, after a Parliamentary Secretaryship or two, became Minister of Education. Had he lived, I have no doubt he would have reached greater heights. However, I count his contribution to the Irish Republic in the last decades of the twentieth century, and his influence into the twenty-first, as the most important of any single political figure's. In my opinion he was the catalyst for the amazing growth in the educational and economic life of the Irish nation.

'Ah, my young Socialist friend, sit down,' said Charlie from behind his big desk at Haughey & Boland Chartered Accountants. That was his and his colleagues' usual mode of address to me, referring to my membership of the Labour Party. He had left a message at Groome's that he wanted to talk to me, and would I stop by his office? This was before he held a Ministry.

Donogh O'Malley had got into an argument with Geoff Golden, the actor — a rare visitor to the hotel — in Groome's, after hours, one night not long before. It had grown rather nasty. Mrs Groome had asked them to leave, which they had. Outside it had escalated to fisticuffs. In the ensuing fracas Donogh had tackled Geoff and hurt his leg. Geoff was suing him for damages. I had been there that night, though not involved.

This business, Charlie told me, could seriously harm Donogh's political career. 'The Chief', as Éamon de Valera was known to his colleagues, had already warned Donogh that any more unseemly public conduct would not be tolerated — in spite of, or maybe because of, the fact that he was a favourite of de Valera's and the Chief had great hopes for O'Malley's political future. Would I be prepared to talk to Ernest Blythe, Charlie wanted to know, and ask him to use his influence to persuade Geoff to drop the charges?

Well, of course I would. Apart from the fact that I liked and admired Donogh very much, I knew that, if guilt there was, 'there were two of them in it,' as the saying goes.

Blythe spoke to Geoff, who refused to drop the charge. Either there was a small out-of-court settlement, or the case was held without any publicity. Certainly there were no repercussions in political circles. Joe and Patty, and all who regularly sailed into Groome's, were appreciative of my good offices.

Over the next few years Donogh drove me to Galway a few times, on his way home to Limerick, though it was a long way out of his way. He was always a stimulating companion, and we both enjoyed the cut and thrust of our political differences.

One day Phil, Angela and I were to have lunch with him and Brian Lenihan at the Dáil, before being introduced to the Taoiseach, Éamon de Valera. There was a debate in the House, and we were in the public gallery. The Dáil was in session. My image of Donogh, after all these years, is still of a young, powerfully built, dark-haired man in a perfectly tailored navy-blue suit, lolling back in the front bench, making short mocking comments in his nasal Limerick accent, his legs stretched out before him, displaying, above his expensive shoes, socks that were bright, daring red!

I wish I had been there the day his inspired Education Bill was passed in 1966 — almost out of the blue, it seemed to me — not long before his early death. It gave free secondary education to every boy and girl, rich and poor, in the Republic of Ireland. I thought when he died, and I think now, that he must have known he had no time to waste. None of us have.

I met a priest from St Mary's College, my *alma mater*, on the top of a bus, shortly after Donogh died. 'You must be delighted with the new Education Act,' I said.

'Oh, yes,' he said vaguely. 'Though we have not elected to be part of the scheme. The parents of our boys opted to stay out of it. They felt it might attract some of the wrong sort of boys to Mary's.'

I got out at the next stop and waited for another bus. Not that that made any difference!

I could count on my fingers the nights I wasn't in Groome's in those years. I was not in Groome's the night Jim Fitzgerald punched superstar Robert Mitchum into world headlines. Fitz was drinking and being belligerent. I was sleeping off a day at the races in Pat Layde's flat in Clyde Road, Ballsbridge. Groome's Hotel was the social centre of my life for more than a decade. Except on Sunday nights, if I was in Dublin, I was in Groome's; so were most of the people I liked or wanted to be with. Not the night of *L'Affaire Mitchum!*

Jim was a very talented director. He drank himself out of a great career — and, eventually, even out of his entrée to Groome's. Some people thought we looked alike; I wasn't flattered by that. I liked him, though, and admired his work greatly. He was touching the heights in those sexy 60s. His productions of Hugh Leonard's delightful fantasy *Madigan's Lock*, with its ghost narrator, and *Stephen D.*, his brilliant adaptation of Joyce's *Portrait of the Artist*, were memorable and enviable. We lost T.P. McKenna, when Blythe refused to release him to go to London with Stephen D. The Abbey's loss and my own was the Globe Theatre's and Gemini Productions' gain. London's gain, too, in the long run. Mike Butte, the Golden Orient's Irish-Indian proprietor, was heard to say in his lovely sing-song Indian accent, at the first night of *Stephen D.* in London, 'I am proud to be an Irishman tonight!'

Just as the death of some special person is often balanced by the birth of a child in the same family, the *Stephen D.* year brought Liam Lynch's *Do Thrushes Sing in Birmingham?* It was a first for me — a play about the modern world, where young Irish people were forced to work and live in England, in circumstances for which they were wholly unprepared. It was directed by Frank Dermody; I had a challenging leading role opposite a promising new acting and writing talent, Eoin O'Sullivan, son of Maurice O'Sullivan, the Kerry author of *Twenty Years A-Growing.*

Then came one of the great playwrights of the twentieth century: Brian Friel. The Abbey actors in his play *The Enemy Within* knew something very special had happened. Someone very special had arrived. The play was well cast, but we were in no doubt that it could and would have done better if Dermody had directed it instead of Ria Mooney.

The leading character, played by Ray MacAnally, was St Colmcille, and it was set in the sixth-century monastery, on the Isle of Iona, of which he was founder and abbot; and yet this play was as immediate to us as the morning newspaper headlines. It gave me, at thirty-three years of age, the part of a pious, over-sensitive seventeen-year-old English postulant, Oswald, who reveres the irreverent warrior abbot as a saint. It also gave me one of the two most frightening moments I have ever had on the stage.

As the end of Act I is approaching, Oswald is telling Colmcille — who is growing angrier by the second — how much he admires him as a man, a monk and finally, in a kind of ecstasy, as a saint. This goads the abbot into hitting the young postulant a fierce blow across the face. The boy, stunned momentarily, turns and runs out, Colmcille calling after him, 'Oswald, I'm sorry!' It always proved to be a powerful curtain.

Interestingly, though, no one in the audience, after the show, ever expressed any concern that I, Vincent, might be hurt. The reason was that, though Ray hit me full on with a lot of strength, we were using the method T.P. and I had developed with Frank Dermody in *Long Day's Journey.* The assailant, hands very relaxed, hits the assailed full force on the neck, just below the jaw, on the upstage side — the side furthest from the audience. That way there is sound and fury but no muscle. The victim, if totally relaxed and absolutely still, will feel only a sharp sting. That was how Ray and I did it, very effectively, for about two weeks.

Then, one Saturday night, in the last moments of the scene, Ray stumbled over a line; and I knew, as certainly as if he had shouted it, that he was going to compensate with a blow that could knock me into the middle of the next week. As he moved towards me, bringing his arm and hand back to deliver the blow, time stood still. I thought: *Either I turn and run, and spoil the curtain, or I stay, relax every iota of my face, neck and body, and hope for the best!*

I chose to stay. He hit me. I saw one huge flash of bright light. As I staggered out, I heard Ray call, 'Vin — Oswald, I'm sorry!'

My German friend Arnold Hintze, a great photographer and a great theatregoer, who saw the play that night, told me he was snapped out of it completely by the blow. He could only think, *Vincent* — not Oswald — *must be hurt!* Everyone I spoke to in the bar after the play that night had the same reaction!

'Of course,' said Dermody, when I told him. 'It's the difference between the art of acting and life! The *essence* is what we are about, not the piddling reality. *Real* violence? *Real* sex? *Real* tears? In the *theatre*? Jesus!' he spluttered contemptuously.

This was also the year Donal McCann came to prominence in the Abbey. He lit up a mediocre play by his father, *A Jew Called Sammy*; but I don't think any of us, at that time, had any idea of what Donal had in store for Irish theatre, at home and abroad, in his all-too-brief stellar acting career and often unhappy life. Certainly our crowd were extremely cruel to Donal — not intentionally, but our contempt for his father's plays seemed to show in every conversation about our work and life in the National Theatre, which, of course, was the constant topic. I think we hurt him deeply.

A Book of Verses underneath the Bough,
A Jug of Wine, a Loaf of Bread and Thou
Beside me singing in the Wilderness —
Ah, Wilderness were Paradise enow.

Playing Richard in *Ah, Wilderness*, who is an even younger Eugene O'Neill than Edmund in *Long Day's Journey*, really was Paradise. Dermody was at his best. It was successful, too. I remember I treasured what John Jordan said in his critique in *Hibernia*; alas, I didn't keep it. Later we took the production to Belfast, where it went even better.

After the run-through the morning we were opening, Dermody walked with me to my bus stop. There was something in my performance that was niggling him; yet, as was so common with him, he couldn't articulate it. I was getting upset. Here I was, opening the play in a few hours, and he was draining my confidence away with every word he said.

Then, just as my bus was approaching, he burst out suddenly with, 'You're losing the prince.'

'What prince? I'm not playing a prince. I'm playing a young American boy in a brothel, drinking himself sick and idiotic!' I almost shouted at him.

'Yes,' said Frank triumphantly, 'but he is a drunk, idiot prince, in his unhappiness.' And with me on the platform and the bus pulling away, this little mad genius, running behind the bus, oblivious to everything, finished: 'But he is always the prince!'

Of course, he was right. For me, anyway. I have used that thought as an actor, and to help other actors and actresses, a hundred times.

I had my hair dyed gold for *Ah, Wilderness*. I was into the 'first year of my public life' when it opened. I had decided to grow a beard at the beginning of my thirty-third year; but by the time I reached that advanced age, in September, I had cut it off. I woke up, a little slowly, to the fact that my beard and my age were my only similarities to the Saviour. It was just as well. My brown beard wouldn't have gone too well with the yellow hair, which, as the dye grew out, turned a sickening green.

I had a great barber in those days. (He didn't dye hair, though; I had gone to a ladies' hairdresser in Grafton Street for that.) Bernie had a one-room shop over a tobacconist's, next door to the cinema on Collins Avenue. I always went to him for my haircuts. 'I'm playing a teddy boy at the moment, so I have to keep enough to have a quiff and a duck's-back. Starting Monday I'm playing a military fellow, so it's got to look very "jildee" — you know, short! Then I'm playing a young monk at the time of Colmcille....' Bernie would be delighted. He always produced exactly what I needed. I don't believe I ever used a wig in the 60s, except comedy ones in the Irish pantomimes, and even those rarely.

Lord, the 60s were so full. I don't know how I could have done all that I did — acted all the parts on stage, radio, TV and film; involved myself with all the people; gone to all the places; fallen in love with, or at least been attracted to, all the girls; gone to all the meetings of the Players' Council and Actors' Equity; enjoyed myself so often at Groome's and O'Neill's — and started a business with Pat Layde, Ronnie Walsh and an accountant, Tommy O'Connor (Soundtrack Ltd, I named it), in hopes of relieving the constant pressure of making enough money to live in some dignity. Apart from my acting, it was the Players' Council that was most important to me. Its concerns were issues like the overall artistic direction of the theatre; the quality of play directors; a salary scale for actors; the right to choose our stage names; and the extension of artistic policy to include the more frequent use of non-Irish works 'that tend to elevate and educate our audience'. These issues affected us everywhere we were, in and out of the Abbey.

12

Behan – The Laughing Boy is Silenced

Oscar would have loved it!

December 1961 brought the first television broadcast by Radio Telefís Éireann. With the advent of this new medium, there was a lot of speculation among actors on the effects it might have. Ronnie Walsh and Pat Layde, driven by the desire to capture some of the money it would engender, invited Tommy O'Connor and me to join them in forming our own production company. It had great potential – which, the poet Patrick Kavanagh says, is wealth – but Soundtrack was destined never to make any money.

In about four years, we did manage to make one television commercial, for Kennedy's Bread. It had a nifty little jingle and a cartoon figure in a canoe rowing about a lake in the mountains. The music was written, scored and recorded under the direction of the composer Sean O'Riada, under a *nom de plume*. He was the only one in Ireland who made any money out of the project.

At the suggestion of Michael O'Duffy, the tenor, I was asked by an Australian impresario to put together a variety tour of his country and New Zealand. The late great comedian Jimmy O'Dea, the tenor Josef Locke, the classical pianist Charles Lynch, a popular céilí band, a soprano from the RÉ Singers, and the versatile Vernon Hayden made up the stellar company. I devised a show with the artists, rehearsed it and previewed it at the Gaiety Theatre. I planned and made the business and travel arrangements, arranging lucrative terms for all of them. I did see that they were paid, though why I did not go with them I don't know. What I do know is that I didn't get paid myself.

When the company arrived in New Zealand, the presenter there put a 'sobriety' clause in the contracts for Jimmy O'Dea and Josef Locke. Jimmy accepted it. Josef threatened to sue them for defamation of character, or something. They had to pay Joe's fee, or he would have refused to perform; so the New Zealand management withheld my guarantee until Mr Locke agreed in writing there would be no suit. That he would not agree to do. So I was never paid my fee – six hundred pounds. That amounted then to almost a year's Abbey salary. It only hurts when I laugh!

I think Joe Locke probably thought I had plenty of money. Godfather to one of his children, I gave the baby a silver spoon! Joe, who was well-off by then, had been born dirt poor, and he saw the humour in my gift. He gave me the use of a room in his apartment on top of the Corn Exchange because he liked my company. I stayed there much of the time, often with a pretty girl working in the costume department of a nearby theatre, when Brenda and the children were in Mosney with the Danny Cummins Variety Company, and sometimes even when they weren't.

Whenever Joe had a show at the Gaiety, I always had the Royal Box. He'd stop the show and introduce me — 'Abbey Theatre, Christy of *The Kennedys of Castlerosse!*' Great applause; then, his eyes twinkling, he'd hold up his hands: 'That's enough,' in the Derry accent he never lost. He was the showman to beat all showmen and afraid of no one. At London's Palladium, the top of the tree for a variety performer in Britain, he was threatened with being sacked if he did not cut a line from his singing of 'Galway Bay' that was critical of 'the English'. He refused, and even the powerful Val Parnell was afraid to sack him.

As a young man, after a season with Jimmy O'Dea at the Gaiety, Josef learned that he was to travel by train, not in the stars' limo, for an opening in the provinces.

'I'll not be there!' he said, and he wasn't. They had to send a car to Dublin for him.

Delightfully wicked and flamboyant, he took to driving himself to the theatre, be-cloaked and top-hatted, in a coach drawn by two white horses, a beautifully costumed girl at his side. I wouldn't have missed a minute I spent with Josef Locke, not even for six hundred pounds!

Kenneth Besson, Ireland's foremost hotelier, was a man of vision. He entered an unlikely but practical alliance with Michael Mullen, Secretary of the Catering Branch of the Irish Transport and General Workers' Union. They engaged Soundtrack (read Vincent Dowling) to develop a *son et lumière* show for presentation annually at one of Ireland's great castles, as a tourist attraction.

This form of spectacular dramatic/historical recreation employed sophisticated recorded scripts, acted by top-class actors, aided by technically brilliant sound, light, music and effects, and electronically controlled by complex systems. They played at historical, visually interesting buildings and sites, like the Sphinx in Egypt, *Les Invalides* in Paris, the châteaux of the Loire Valley and the Parthenon in Athens.

Ken took a group of us to France for a week, to meet experts who had been very involved in creating these spectacles. The group included cookery author Monica Sheridan, sound engineer Gene Martin, Ronnie Marsh of Phillips Electrical, an architect to examine French hotel design, and me.

The summer tourist season in Paris was just over. Ken had special show-ings for our little party of some of the finest spectacles in France. Because the Paris Motor Show was on at the time, Ken hired a large new Citroën and driver for the week. and lodged us at the Barbizon Inn, near Fontainebleau. 'The Ritz is full and there is no other hotel in Paris I would want us to stay in!' And that was that! In Nice we stayed at the Negresco. There was room there because King Farouk happened to be back in Egypt that week — not yet aware how rare an experience that would soon be for him.

One night, after a dinner in a more plebeian part of Cannes, my thoughts and those of two other young men travelling with me turned to the joys offered by the ladies of the night. We engaged in some lowly bargaining with three young women. I claimed one whom I considered extraordinarily attractive, and we repaired to a room with bed and bidet, in a corridor of rooms apparently identical in appearance, purpose and accoutrements. The young woman pointed to the bidet. I gathered, with some comfort in the thought, that she wished me to wash my nether parts. Apparently, I attended to it too slowly; her voice a little impatiently reminded me that she had only limited time. X marks the spot where romance vanished — well, diminished!

'Mademoiselle,' I stammered in fractured French, '*il est avant passé.*' My comment, as well as being ungrammatical, was unnecessary. She could see for herself. She was embarrassed, I think. Gently, she called me over to her and invited me to lie beside her. I did. I turned to kiss her.

'Non!' she cried, very distressed. 'No affection! Please!'

Again in my bad school French, I told her that, without some affection, I couldn't do it, adding lamely, '*Je suis un artiste.*'

Well, she was sorry, too, but no affection! *Absolument!*

I said something about understanding, that it was OK ... and *oui*, I under-stood she'd have to be paid. I gave her the money, as gracefully as I could. Then, as they say, I adjusted my dress before leaving. She did hers, too, but much more quickly. She stood hesitantly at the door; came back to me, concerned; kissed me on the mouth, quickly, and left.

In the street, the Irish lads were still talking to the other girls. As I walked in their direction, 'mine', without looking my way, moved away from them and disappeared into the shadows. I appreciated her sensitivity. I thought a lot about prostitution after that with a little more depth. I never pursued sex that way again. I've often thought about the girl. Was it just a way of making money? I still wonder. Or had she no choice? She was really very lovely.

Extravagant breakfasts were brought to my enormous, bright room every morning by a squad of waiters carrying white-tablecloth-covered tables. For Monica Sheridan's benefit and the future clients of Irish hotels and restaurants, lunch and dinner every day was not only in a different restaurant, in a different town or village, but was also a totally different experience. By the end of the visit we all dreamed of a pot of Irish-brewed tea, home-made brown bread covered with Irish country butter, and a fresh brown boiled egg, with pepper, salt, and a little butter in an eggcup.

I wasn't earning any money, but I was having a fantastic time.

'Why don't you move your wife and family into one of my pubs for a few months?' said Kenneth Besson. 'Pubs' is how he always referred to his two top-class Dublin hotels: the Hibernian on Dawson Street and the even more exclusive Russell Hotel on St Stephen's Green.

I was having lunch with Ken at the Hibernian, on a January day, and had arrived late because Brenda had fainted in our kitchen that morning. Her doctor thought 'she had been just doing too much'.

'You can have a suite at the Russell till spring. You'll be my guest,' he said off-handedly. He was like that.

'But, Ken, I have three children. The baby is only four months old.'

'All the more reason. We'll have a room for the children, cot, nursemaid. All meals in the dining-room will be included. You must pay for dancing girls, though!'

For two months we lived a fairy tale. Bairbre and Louise in their Dominican Convent Eccles Street uniforms, arriving in the splendid dining-room of the Russell, where a *maître d'* — French accent included — and perfect Dublin waiters in formal attire danced attention on them. Bairbre fell in love with the youngest of them, David. They were Ken Besson's staff; they were Mickey Mullen's 'men'. For years afterwards, in the best restaurants in and around Dublin, I'd meet them. There remained a real bond between us — the ghosts of Ken Besson and Michael Mullen peering at the menu, checking out the food and service.

Over the next two years, via phone calls, letters, interviews, another journey with Ken to Paris, and the Dutch and French experts' visits to Dublin, I learned a lot about *son et lumière* and made a lot of progress toward production. The theme became 'the duality of the Irish'. The site would be Dublin Castle — the story, the dramatic events connected with it from earliest times to 1922. My title for our *son et lumière* was *The Light of Other Days*.

The great theatre artist Micheál mac Liammóir had triumphed in his one-man play *The Importance of Being Oscar*, directed by his partner Hilton Edwards. They raised the money for a commemorative plaque on 21 Westland Row, where Oscar was born. On a cold, wet, windy day, a small group of literary folk gathered to watch the unveiling and to hear Micheál, in a great black poet's hat and cloak, say a few brilliantly chosen words about the great playwright, poet and humorist. The unveiling revealed a modest stone plaque saying, in English and in Irish, 'Oscar Wilde the poet was born here on October 16 1854'.

The group moved to the lounge of Kennedy's public house nearby. Drink and conversation flowed; everyone was feeling good that tribute had at last been paid publicly to Oscar.

Micheál felt a tap on his shoulder; a reporter with pencil and pad. 'Excuse me, Mr mac Liammóir, could you tell me how much you collected for the plaque?'

'Mm ... we collected.... Hilton!' He raised his voice above the chatter. 'How much did we raise for Oscar's plaque?'

'Two hundred and fifty pounds, dear boy. No, two hundred and fifty guineas, I think,' said the famous director.

'Of course,' said Micheál to the reporter, 'guineas! I remember distinctly it was guineas.' He turned back to the company.

'Mr mac Liammóir, how much did the plaque cost?'

'Hilton, how much did the plaque cost?'

'Ten guineas, dear boy, exactly ten guineas,' he stated without hesitation.

'Of course. It cost ten guineas,' said Micheál agreeably, and again turned towards the counter.

'Mr mac Liammóir, what did you do with the rest of the money?' enquired the reporter.

'Hilton and I went to the Riviera,' he said with relish, 'and I bought this hat. Oscar would have loved it!'

Micheál agreed to write the script of our *son et lumière*. He would do it while on tour in England with *The Importance of Being Oscar*.

'I will have nothing else to do all day in those dreary English towns, dear boy, except go to mayors' parlours and sip tea or sherry with little old ladies at endless receptions,' he purred in his rich, perfectly articulated, special brand of Irish brogue.

He found very soon that one can't do anything else and tour a one-man play. From England he wrote me by hand a long letter. Having explained the practical problems of writing, acting, and touring, he wrote, 'I hope, my dear Vincent, you won't treat me like Georgia, who kept a waterfall beside her bed and, when she tired of her lover, pushed him out and drowned him?'

Then I got Walter Macken to the point of almost finishing a very interesting script. But Ken's withdrawal from daily contact with normal life to receive medical treatment for alcohol problems, the refusal of Phillips Electrical (Ireland) to accept a financial penalty clause against failure to deliver the uniquely designed equipment in time, and the absence of a fully completed script, caused Ken's friend and financial angel for the project to withdraw his support. He was Mr Schlesinger of Schlesinger Tennis Racquets and Squire of

Powerscourt Demesne. He rode a bicycle round Dublin — by preference, he said.

Contemporaneously with these high-flying goings-on, as well as working at the Abbey, I hosted one of the first TV shows on RTÉ — black and white television, of course — and had countless 'steam' radio shows to script, produce, create and service. I made some unspectacular one-scene appearances in films like *The Devil's Agent*, with Billie Whitelaw, and *Johnny Nobody*, starring and directed by Nigel Patrick. In the latter I had the role of a waiter on a moving train, which provided a brief 'comeback' for the Bray-Harcourt Street railway line; and I was one of a group of Abbey actors used for a play scene in the film *The Rising of the Moon*, directed by John Ford. Soon after that, Ford was able to fulfil a lifetime ambition to act with the Abbey. He stepped in to act for one night and had one line to say in Irish in Mairéad Ní Ghrada's play *Oíche Mhaith a Mhicí Domhnaill*.

One of the most inhuman actions in Irish labour history was the great lockout of 1913. We can't blame the English for that! The Irish Transport and General Workers' Union asked me and my brother Jack to create a suitable dramatic production for the fiftieth anniversary of the lockout. Since Jack had played a major part in the success of a Military Tattoo and re-enactment of the Battle of Benburb produced by the Irish Army, he was a natural choice to be involved with this initiative.

Working with poet and playwright District Justice Donagh McDonagh (son of Thomas McDonagh, one of the signatories of the 1916 Proclamation of the Irish Republic, who was executed as a leader of the Easter Rising), we worked up a script and presented it at the Olympia Theatre on Dame Street for two weeks. *Let Freedom Ring* was a piece of docudrama with the ambition of an epic; it covered the period from Wolfe Tone to the Dublin employers' pyrrhic victory over the workers, which paved the way for a powerful trade union movement in Ireland, the Easter Rising and the formation of the Irish Free State.

Small in physical stature, District Justice Donagh McDonagh was a substantial poet and an important playwright. He had a gnat-like, stinging sense of humour, a brilliant mind and a liberal outlook, and he made a great friend.

Inspired by black American civil rights struggles, Donagh wove together poetry, song, history, dance, famous speeches and his own talent for pithy dialogue in what he called a 'masque'. From memory alone, some powerful performances from the huge company of actors, singers, and dancers still live for me. Seamus Forde was 'the man of no property', Wolfe Tone. Terry Rigby, afterwards a major player in the Royal Shakespeare Company, in London, Broadway and British film and television, was a towering 'Big Jim' Larkin;

Niall Tóibín was splendid as James Connolly; and, in a tiny but significant anticlimactic climax to the work, a young girl in her first professional role sang a snatch from the patriotic ballad 'All around me hat I wear a tricoloured ribbon-o', the very thought of which still makes my blood tingle. Her name is Fionnuala Flanagan. Some of her stage and screen performances — like *Joyce's Women* and *Waking Ned* — still resonate in Ireland, in America and round the world. The great baton charge in O'Connell Street — against a huge, painted, strobe-lit backcloth, painted by artist John Kelly from the photograph by the early twentieth-century photographer Cashman, with our dancers, actors and musicians choreographed by Desmond Domigan — dominated the experience. That no permanent record of this watershed event in the theatre was made is a loss, even a shame. That's show biz!

I loved every moment of this endeavour and every moment working with Jack, Donagh and the company. We all knew we had been part of something that mattered, and we were paid decently for it to boot. The union members loved it, too, and took great pride in their involvement. The ITGWU leadership were pleased. The real pay-off, for me, was to be their invitation to me to recite the Proclamation of the Irish Republic at the opening of Dublin's first 'skyscraper', the new Liberty Hall.

We were an odd trio. Anew McMaster, in his seventies, tall, well built, handsome, with a noble carriage, a beautiful unaffected voice and a courtly manner; a living legend. Advancing years had driven him off 'the road' in the early 1960s. Sam Thompson, a typical Belfast Protestant worker in the shipyards, with a strong Belfast accent and a no-nonsense manner — typical except that he was a playwright hailed in London, Dublin and Belfast, a Northern voice passionate in his denunciation of intolerance and bigotry. His plays *Over the Bridge* and *The Evangelist* should have been sought and given their Dublin productions at the Abbey, but that glory went to the Gaiety. The third person of that trinity was myself. In my early thirties, I barely looked twenty; slim, well groomed, never a hair astray; incurably middle-class.

I particularly value a few special occasions I spent with one or other or both of them. One Saturday, Sam and I met coming out of the Olympia Theatre. We had seen a matinée of a really satisfying London production of *As You Like It*, starring John Neville and Virginia McKenna. Sam told me, 'That bamstick Blythe, and others, too, keep telling me I must set my plays in one room. I've learned more today from Billy Shakespeare, a man dead three hundred and fifty years. It's like someone took the handcuffs off my writing hand.'

Beppo, a non-singing role in the comic opera *The Maid of the Mountain*, was the last paid role that Mac, as we called him, played — a romantic lead at the age of seventy or more. On the final night, Sam and I went round to his dressing-room to take him for a drink. He was wearing a light-brown toupée, a peasant shirt open to his navel, big pirate earrings, and light tan make-up on his face and body. 'You must be sorry it's over, Mac,' I said.

'I should be, but I'm not. I listen for long stretches while the young singers sing. But when I have speeches, they ask to be allowed go off because *they have nothing to do!* The director allows them! Of course, we know, dear, listening is what acting is all about!'

Mac's actual last performance was in a scene from *The Bells*, Martin Harvey's great melodrama. As a member of Irish Equity's Executive, I directed a series of benefit concerts to raise money for our cash-strapped union. Mac had agreed to top an all-star bill drawn from every area of our profession. Like everyone else, he donated his talent. Fred O'Donovan, then manager of the Gaiety, had given us the theatre free.

Mac was magnificent as the miser. The first concert was a complete success. Mac was happy as a boy on his birthday. We had a packed house, ensuring that the next concerts would be SRO — standing room only!

At the second concert, a week later, Eddie Golden, President of Equity, announced that our beloved Mac had died the previous Wednesday. He is buried in the cemetery at Kill o' the Grange.

On 15 February 1965, Sam died in the office of the North of Ireland Labour Party. His father was a lamplighter. Sam Thompson, also, lit lamps that will stay lit as long as men and women read plays, and as long as those he influenced pass them on.

Over the Bridge (published by Gill and Macmillan Ltd) ends with these lines for all people in all divided communities:

I've wondered what sort of Christians they were who would form a mob and maim a man and murder another in the sacred name of religion. [pause] A man told me yesterday that when that mob went into action he walked away, and so did hundreds of his so-called respectable workmates because they said it was none of their business. None of their business, Rabbie, that's what they said. Then they walked away, and that's what frightens me, [he sobs quietly] they walked away!

My father was the first of my immediate family to die.

Jack and I had been visiting him occasionally. At this time, Jack, back from a sojourn in England, was living in a new house with his wife Betty, son John and daughters Gráinne and Deirdre. He was, round this time, researching and editing *The Shell Guide to the Shannon River*. One of his team was Dominic Roche.

My brother Paul had moved to Southampton with his family after his poster business crashed. There his marriage crashed. Temporarily, he dropped out of our sights. Kitty, Brian and their children were living in Holland. Brian was a captain in KLM. They came home at least once a year, and always saw me at the Abbey, and in Groome's afterwards.

Sam was working as a quantity surveyor, thanks to Carmel's husband Paddy McCarroll. Carmel and Paddy lived in Rathgar then; after their twin girls were born they moved to Monkstown, Co. Dublin. Their first-born was a boy, Joseph. It was probably a mistake to give him the same name as the head of the Holy Family! Joseph, in later years, was an outspoken leader of right-to-lifers, against all rights to birth control, divorce or abortion.

I saw Carmel, Paddy and Mammy constantly, but not together. My sister and mother did not get on. I realise, now, that it had a lot to do with the late Father Donnellan. Carmel told me that he had tried to sexually molest her. I dismissed the idea as some kind of delusion, and I told her so. Mammy, I suppose, refused to believe it, or was afraid to admit it might be true. The McCarrolls came to every show and were very supportive, and we always went together to O'Neill's pub afterwards. Then Carmel had what was called in those days 'a nervous breakdown'. She drew, in pen and ink, very disturbing religious pictures. But, to me, she was still the same loving, lovable sister. I assumed they had a great marriage. I knew so little about mental illness. In our ignorance, we saw it simply as this: there was violent behaviour, for which people were locked away, and there was eccentricity, which was mostly harmless. Everyone in Ireland, practically, belonged to one group or the other. Everyone except me, we all thought!

My eldest sister Marie, her husband Jim and their large family had moved to Limerick. Jim had been promoted to 'Receiver of Wrecks' in the Department of Customs and Excise. He had started on the slow, hard road away from alcoholism. With the help, love and loyalty of Marie, my nephew Redmond and the other children, he painfully and quietly won his way to an alcohol-free life.

Add me, and you have the family 'Daddy' had sired, but can hardly be said to have raised.

'I think Daddy is dying.' Jack called me during rehearsal on the public phone of a hotel. 'Can you come with me to see him?'

I was rehearsing but not playing, so I said I could. I arranged to meet him in a small working-class pub on the North Strand, just round the corner from the modest town-house where my father lodged and would soon die. Like my maternal grandmother, he would die with none of his family at his side.

I had no emotional relationship with my father — present or absent, alive or dead. He had lived almost all of my life separated from us. In the short periods when I had lived or spent time with him, I had realised how lucky I was that he had left us. I didn't dislike him, resent him, blame him for anything. I was sorry for him. I thought it right that I should see him from time to time, and be respectful, as a matter of filial responsibility and good manners. It was always a relief when a visit with him was over.

I am only now beginning to realise that I have inherited from him an ability to separate, completely, various aspects of my life. To come and go from one area or stream of life to another, in blinkers, and at will. It is a good thing for an actor. Maybe not so good for a husband or father.

Oddly enough, at this particular time we were rehearsing in the Grosvenor Hotel, on the corner of Pearse Street and Westland Row — which normally we never did. In this hotel, fifty years earlier, my mother's mother had been 'allowed' to come home from England to say goodbye to her five children. When my mother was five years old, my grandfather had put her out of their home in Trim and sent her back to Bradford in England, never to return to his house. He suspected, probably wrongly, she was having an affair with a man working in Trim. About fifteen years later, my very beautiful grandmother had terminal cancer, and Grandpa paid her way to this hotel so she could see and say goodbye to her children, before sending her back to England to die, practically alone. This is the family that gave my brothers, my sisters and me our mother.

Daddy looked very small in the armchair in front of the modern, tiled fireplace with its turf fire. His face and expression were still proud and hawkish. His mind was crystal-clear. He was being well looked after by his landlady and her husband. He was eighty-five, though. He had seen the priest, a friar from the Franciscan church on the quays that he used to walk to, every day, to hear Mass. He was content, unafraid. He was sipping a glass of Power's whiskey; the little baby Power bottle was empty on the mantelpiece. He'd keep the one we brought him for another night, he said, and laughed a little sardonically as he added, 'If I'm still here.' We didn't stay long. Both Jack and I kissed him, glad, as usual, the visit was over. At least, I was.

The next time we saw him, he was lying dead in his big single bed. He was dressed in a habit of the Third Order of St Francis, rosary beads twined round his cold white fingers. We knelt and said a decade of the rosary. As I kissed his cheek, I noticed again that little depression on his forehead; I wondered, but did not ask Jack if he knew, what caused it.

The landlady told us that the night before, after dinner, had been the only time his mind had wandered. He asked her husband to get him not a baby Power but a pint bottle of Power's whiskey, giving him a half-crown for it — the price of a bottle fifty years earlier!

'"You mean a baby Power," said my husband. "I mean what I said," was Captain Dowling's reply, and he sat back in his chair and closed his eyes.'

When her husband brought back the baby Power, which was all half a crown would buy, she poured it into the glass my father liked. He drank it down, leaned forward to put the glass on the mantel shelf, and fell forward dead.

'It was a sailor's way to go,' I said.

The night Daddy was buried, I was out after the Abbey with a very beautiful girl I was seeing around this time. Her name was Harriet Danger. Exciting! I had met her on a boat on the Shannon. I was particularly glad of her company and understanding the night my father was buried. I was disturbed at not being disturbed by his death, if you follow me.

I was driving Harriet to her home, and we stopped the car on a level lane between Waterloo and Burlington Roads. It was just midnight; a church clock on Pembroke Road had started its chimes leading up to twelve. We were engaging in gentle petting when I felt the car move forward, slowly but steadily.

'Someone is pushing the car,' I said, turning round in the seat and looking through the rear window. There was no one in sight.

It was like a cold hand gripped my stomach. I turned the key in the ignition, pushed down on the clutch, put it in second gear and slowly let out the clutch, just touching the accelerator. *Dear Jesus, let it start*, I thought, and it did. I took off down the lane. At the end I turned and drove back fast, my lights full on. Not a thing, moving or standing, the length of the lane!

I went back next day, in daylight, and parked the car in the self-same place. It didn't move. The night before, there had been no wind. I'm sure of that.

'Vincent takes after my family. He is a Kelly,' Mammy said all my life. 'You wouldn't think he was a Dowling at all' ― until she saw me play the old, unshaven, grey-haired jockey in *The Glorious Uncertainty*. That was one I took over at a day's notice. When I came on stage Mammy didn't recognise me at all; but the moment I moved and spoke, she thought it was Daddy! 'I got the fright of my life, Vincent, I thought it was your father!'

Over the next few years, the same thing happened whenever I played 'character' parts. It was good for me, as an actor. I also found it helped me to understand my father better. I only have to put on a shower-proof coat, wear a hat, carry a stick, and limp, and I feel that I am he. It roots me.

My father had extended his working life with the Dublin Port and Docks Board by ten years after he reached retirement age, by writing his arguments in letter and memorandum form. 'The written word, sonny, is better than a sabre, when it comes to repelling corporate boarders,' he told me. When the Board retired him, on age grounds, as captain of the dredger *The Sandpiper*, he showed them ― in letter and memorandum form ― that they needed an overall Supervisor of Dredging for the whole river mouth, and that he was the only one that could do it. They saw he was right. It was a lesson that saved my bacon over and over. Daddy has been much more help to me since he died than he was in the years he was alive.

Subconsciously, thanks to him and his treatment of my mother, I abhor violence. His violence led to his separation from us. My fear of returning violence for violence led to my leaving my wife and children. That is not an excuse. It is one of the reasons.

Dubliners have a genius for pinning on you exactly the right nickname. Brendan Behan had a buddy in Dublin, Liam Ward. Dark and swarthy, in a trench coat and a snap-brim felt hat, he looked, talked and acted as if he had just stepped out of a John Ford film about the Irish Republican Army. Whether he was, or ever had been, in the IRA, I don't know. He certainly gave the impression that he was. His nickname was 'the Shadow of a Gunman' (the title of the famous O'Casey play). If you met Liam or passed him by, even on the far side of a busy city street, when Brendan was away in America, he'd shout to you, 'I had a letter from himself.'

'From whom?' I'd say, for fun.

'Brendan, of course!' would be Liam's answer. His tone said, *Why do you have to ask?*

Brendan finally got back from Broadway and the Chelsea Hotel, where he had successfully out Dylan-ed Thomas in the liquor department. More and more he was stupidly drunk, endlessly repetitious, surrounded by a small, rowdy coterie of hangers-on drinking his liquor and money. More and more, his literary and theatre friends were avoiding him. I was among those who looked the other way and hoped he wouldn't recognise us. Mostly he didn't. That is what I did the last time I saw him alive.

I was having dinner alone upstairs in Glynn's Restaurant on College Street. Near the end of my meal, I heard Brendan behind me. He was sitting between me and the exit. I saw at a quick glance that he was holding court over a bunch of tough-looking, ill-mannered drunks. I had enough time to pay my bill and make the half-hour call at the theatre, but no more. I rose unobtrusively, turned my head the other way to look out the window and shamefully slunk by him.

I had known Brendan for a long time, known him when he was drinking and when he wasn't. During his play *The Quare Fella*, in which I had played in both productions at the Abbey, he was 'off the drink' for the entire rehearsal period and run, the first time. The second time he was drinking, but not heavily. He was a delight, marvellous company. He was at every rehearsal and every performance, and afterwards he was always in the dress circle bar of the Queen's; funny, supportive, generous, charming the audience, delighting the staff and the actors. 'You know,' he'd say, with that slight hesitation in his deep, throaty Dublin, 'the barmaids in the Queen's were taught by my uncle to get twenty glasses of whiskey from a ten-glass bottle, *before* they took their own cut!'

All Brendan asked was that you'd listen. If he was telling a story, he'd wait till he got everyone in the bar to listen before he'd begin. During all that time, I never heard him backbiting anyone. Oh, he'd lacerate someone's attitudes and beliefs, if he didn't like them — he hated hypocrisy, especially of the religious kind — but he'd exonerate the person, somehow, with good humour. His mother was right: he was the Laughing Boy. We all loved him, laughed with him, drank with him, till he needed us the most; then most of us, the ones I knew, turned the other way.

Like Brendan himself and his plays, his funeral had a strong dash of comedy in it. On the driveway outside the hospital where Brendan died, on 20 March 1964, everyone who was anyone in the world of art, literature or the media, plus a squad of IRA men, was waiting for Brendan's coffin to be brought out. His remains were being taken to the Sacred Heart Church in Donnybrook, for the lying-in and the Requiem Mass next morning. A squad from the outlawed Irish Republican Army had earlier marched in behind the hearse, in disciplined military manner, with the orders given in Irish. They were now standing at ease, ready to slow-march behind the hearse, in front of the limousine, for Brendan's wife Beatrice and his family.

Liam Ward arrived late and moved from person to person of his acquaintance, shaking hands, as if he was the chief mourner. I knew from his demeanour that he had taken everything in, and wondered what he would do.

He kept close, but not too close, to the squad and the hearse. Then, when Beatrice and the family were in the first limousine, the squad leader barked the orders 'Attention!' and 'By the left — slow march!' And Liam, with perfect timing, stepped neatly in behind them. He was now part of the squad, a 'true' rebel, and he marched through the admiring poor people of Dublin who lined the streets to pay their sad farewells to their truly beloved, silent 'Laughing Boy'.

There are two side chapels in the Sacred Heart, Donnybrook, and there were two funerals, one in each chapel. The family were taken behind the altar to meet the priest, and a score of us, Brendan's friends, had started to say the rosary when a woman rushed over to tell us, 'That's not Brendan's coffin!' Some claimed they distinctly heard Behan laughing.

I lived in Santry, on Dublin's north side. Brendan was going to be buried in Glasnevin Cemetery, also on the north side. My mother always said Glasnevin was 'the dead centre' of Dublin! Word had it that the IRA were going to slow-march with Brendan's 'remains', as Dubliners euphemistically term a corpse, from Donnybrook, on the extreme south side, through the centre of Dublin City and over O'Connell Bridge on the River Liffey — a journey of about six miles — at the height of the morning rush hour!

The funeral was due to begin at ten o'clock. Rehearsal that morning at the Abbey Theatre had been set for noon, so that the 'decencies' could be observed by the working actors attending the famous playwright's funeral. The 'decencies' included staying for the interment, the prayers at the graveside, the speeches, the shots fired over the grave by the outlawed IRA men, the bugle sounding 'The Last Post', and at least a pint or two raised and lowered in memory of the great man in Kavanagh's of the Middle Road, a pub where Brendan had done as much or more for many a less famous drinker, on countless occasions.

The phone rang at my home just as I was leaving the house. I had succumbed to pressure and installed a phone. It was Maureen McCormick, Mr Blythe's secretary. 'Are you going to the funeral?'

'Yes, I am.'

'Do you think Harry Brogan will be there?'

'If he's still alive, he will.' Harry, the Abbey's oldest and greatest comic actor, had never been known voluntarily to miss the funeral of friend or enemy. He had just been released from hospital, where he had spent over three months battling consumption. I hoped it was the end of the downward path that I had seen start the morning Blythe had vocally keel-hauled him on the Queen's stage during the rehearsal of *All the King's Horses*.

'Well, if you see him, bring him with you to rehearsal. He has to go on in *Juno and the Paycock* tonight!'

'What part?'

'Joxer. Pat Layde has the flu.'

'Joxer? He hasn't played that for more than two years, and he's only just out of hosp —' I was talking to myself. Maureen had already hung up. What matter? Harry knew every line of every one of O'Casey's great plays. Besides, playing Joxer was the perfect medicine for Harry, then or at any time.

It was a nice spring day, and the company was good. I was not the only one, by a long shot, to go straight to Glasnevin and skip the wear and tear on the car and nerves that the slow-marching funeral would inflict.

Harry was there, too, and accepted the Joxer news philosophically. 'At least I'll be the first actor to be taken out of Glasnevin Cemetery to play on the Abbey stage!' he said. Then, after a beat, his long, pointed nose tilted heavenward, his eyes half-closed against the sunlight, his deeply lined, sculpted face serious, he added, 'Come to think of it, maybe I'm not!'

Ten o'clock came and went. So did 10.30, with quips about the 'late' Brendan Behan and 'being late for his own funeral'.

'If it goes past eleven o'clock we'll have to leave before the end,' I said to Harry.

'Not me,' said Harry, ungrammatically but not uncertainly. 'A man only dies once. His friends should see him put down properly.'

'Well, I'm leaving at a quarter to twelve. I'm on early,' said I. 'How will you get there?'

'There are plenty of buses.... Here they are now!' he cried. And Brendan's flower-laden hearse, followed by the guard of honour, family, friends and colleagues who had braved the six-mile walk, nosed through the cemetery gates. We all waited while the gravediggers transferred the coffin onto a four-wheeled trolley and followed it into the Mortuary Chapel. Inside were a priest in black vestments, two altar boys, and the smell of incense; prayers for the dead and a homily were the cue for our exit through the upstage rear door of the chapel. By this time it was coming up to a quarter to twelve. I brought up the rearguard, determined to stay with them till 11.45, and then cut up one of the pathways to the main gate *for my car parked on the roadside.*

As the crowds, led by Dominic Behan, streamed along the path and over the old graves lining each side of it, I ruminated, in a casual way, about all the people lying underneath us, getting scant respect from this crowd, many of whom were really only there because Brendan was famous. Then I was on my own, walking up a long, empty, well-kept pathway; slowing down to see if I chanced upon any of our Dowling family graves.

As I came in sight of the main gate, I heard behind me the lonely notes of the bugle blowing Brendan to his last rest. I crossed myself as I pictured him being lowered into the grave. Then I saw another hearse enter the gates, and noticed that there was only one man, one mourner, walking behind the coffin. I compared the public show of sorrow for the playwright with the lack of it for this unknown and uncelebrated human being, who must, at one time, have meant everything, or at least something, to his mother, wife, or child. Then I recognised the lone man, old trench coat, straight back, marching proudly, bravely, and unmistakably, carrying a look on his face that said, *'Thanks be to God, I, at least, turned out to bury my friend Brendan.'* It was, of course, the veritable *Shadow of a Gunman* — Liam Ward! He didn't look my way.

I met Liam many years afterwards, on a return visit to Dublin. We walked around old haunts and talked of old friends, bemoaning the passing of 'the good old days'. While we were having a parting glass, I told him my story. He disagreed absolutely with my interpretation of his part in the incident. I stick to it, absolutely. We parted still good friends.

12a

Strike! The Thin End of a Long Wedge

You're a cute hoor, Dowling.

A m I going to say to my children, ten years from now, "Well, there was this man called Blythe running the Abbey, and it's all his fault, everything"?' I do know I said that clearly to myself, that morning, on the way into rehearsal. I said it to the Players' Council later.

I suppose I just suddenly woke up. We had been shilly-shallying with Blythe for more than ten years. Sure, we had made progress. We had our names in the programme in two languages, those of us who wanted an English version. I was born and reared Vincent Dowling; who the hell was this Uinsionn Ó Dubhlainn playing Edmund Tyrone in *Long Day's Journey into Night*?

That particular morning, one of my children had asked me why I had my name in Irish in the programme if I didn't want it. And the more I tried to explain about the actors who had their names in English only, and the ones who had theirs in Irish only, and the ones who had Irish and English on one page but only Irish on the cast list, the more I realised we were just playing into Blythe's hands. He'd give us a concession here, or a concession there — soap and towels in the dressing-rooms; the costume shop open an extra hour; no rehearsals on Holy Thursday for the Annual Catholic Stage Guild Retreat in Mount Anville; a pound a week here, two pounds there — but nothing somewhere else. A production for Dermody every now and then, for Eddie Golden once in a blue moon; but Ria was still the producer, and Blythe still picked the plays, often going so far as to cast them.

What galled the actors, too, was the replacement of experienced actors like T.P., Brian O'Higgins, Michael Dolan, Joe Lynch, Ronnie Walsh, Bríd Lynch, Ita O'Mahony, Rita Foran and Doreen Madden with Irish-speakers who had no professional training; some had real talent, but some had little.

'Though we've got an extra week of rehearsal for some plays, most plays for the past thirty years have been under-rehearsed. Only one play — *Long*

Day's Journey — was given proper rehearsal, because it had only five actors and was "harmless rubbish"! Nothing has changed. What are we going to do but wait for him to die?' I told an initially sceptical Players' Council. 'We must make it a trade union issue. Even if he won't deal with Equity, it's our trade union. Through them we must demand a salary scale at the Abbey, a liveable salary related to length of service.'

'He won't do that. You know damn well he won't. "Some will rise quickly, some won't rise at all." That's his answer now. That will be his answer as long as he's alive,' said Phil, imitating Blythe and, as usual, looking and sounding more like Blythe than Blythe himself.

'Good! If he refuses to accept a fair Equity demand, or refuses to negotiate, we'll bring him to the Labour Court. He can't refuse to go. There's no doubt that when they see the salaries paid here, they'll make a recommendation that he will not be able to pay. He'll have to go to the government to get the money. They won't give it to him until the theatre is completely reorganised,' said I.

'Suppose they say they won't give it anyway? "Let you sink or swim by yourselves. A plague on both your houses! We aren't giving you any more!"' someone asked. In a way, this was what everyone in the company would ask, one way or another, over the following months.

'They'll give it, if we show we have a real alternative to what's going on now. We are the only international cultural card they have. We'll get the support from Foreign Affairs, and the Groome's Fianna Fáil young ministers and sundowners,' Phil said confidently.

'Yes,' I went on, 'if we can show that the whole company and Equity are behind it — *if* — and that we have a better, workable alternative to Blythe, on every front.'

'We'll get Equity, all right; it won't be easy, but we will get Equity!' That was from Eddie, who was President of Equity at the time. 'The problem will be some of the company. Fear of losing their security — our security. The half-a-loaf syndrome. Let's face it, there aren't many lifetime jobs for actors anywhere in the world.'

'They are not going to lose anything except their indignities,' I said. 'I think they'll go along eventually. Every one of them desperately needs the money.' Nobody disagreed with me there.

Eddie suggested we meet with Dermot Doolan, General Secretary of Irish Actors' Equity, and Louis Nolan, legal advisor, before meeting with the players. I offered to take the first shot at writing an outline of a policy for a National Theatre. Eddie gave me a word of advice, at this point, that informed my attitude through the long — nearly two years' — journey into light: 'Avoid being emotive, at all times!'

Though Mr Blythe didn't know it, with that meeting, as Dermody would say, 'The cock flew at him!' For a long time most of the company would echo my mother's spin on it: 'You might as well dream here as in bed.'

The first word we got from Equity wasn't too encouraging. Dermot Doolan pointed out that Blythe didn't recognise Equity's right to act for the Abbey Players, and that we all had salaries above the Equity minimum. 'All Equity can do is set minimums,' he said. 'We can't tell any producer what they have to pay above that.'

'Don't mind what Dermot says,' I said, 'watch what he does!' And I was right. Dermot Doolan and Louis Nolan were there for us at every turn and every barricade. Besides, the Radio Éireann Repertory Company of the national radio station had a salary scale; surely the actors of the National Theatre, subsidised by the government, deserved as much!

Of course, we knew there was a difference — one that Blythe could certainly use against us. The Abbey Theatre's legal name was The National Theatre Society Limited; it was a private company, which received a government subsidy. However, Yeats and Lady Gregory had seen it as a national theatre movement. That was why they called it the National Theatre Society. That was why I offered to write the policy document for our struggle. It would be part of our policy to have the Abbey officially recognised and reconstituted as a national theatre, which many people in and out of government, and outside Ireland too, deemed it to be.

Over the next weeks, I wrote a document, about two pages long, which I headed 'A National Theatre'. The preamble stated that the subsidy to the Abbey was an acknowledgement by the government that theatre was a vital need in its people's pursuit of happiness. It made a case, at Eddie Golden's suggestion, for the idea of 'a company of players, because only when writers are writing for a known company, on a known stage, are there continual periods of excellence in drama'. The document, which had over a dozen clauses, also dealt with governance of the company; separate artistic leadership; a level of remuneration for artists on a par with other professions; and the right of an artist to choose his or her own name.

At a subsequent meeting of the Players' Council, we broached the subject of a salary scale. Blythe's response was, as Phil had forewarned, 'Some will rise quickly, some won't rise at all.' His answer to the issue of our right to choose our own names was to the effect that the policy on names might be changed in the future. When we asked for a timetable, he responded that 'any change would be as gradual as the sands in the sea'.

The following Friday brought a surprise: when we got our little brown pay envelopes, it became clear that he was applying his favourite motto, 'Grasp the talon and the bird is lost'. Each of the members of the Players'

Council, and Eileen Crowe, received an increase of over 50 per cent. Nobody else got anything.

We said 'thank you' and proceeded to press our case with him, while still pushing forward our plans with Equity. Around this time he reiterated his refusal to recognise Equity in any negotiations on behalf of the Abbey Players, stating categorically once again, 'I would rather die fighting than commit suicide!'

The Council accepted my document, with the inclusion of Eddie's clause on 'a company'. Then it was decided that *all* the Abbey Players should be brought to a meeting with the Equity Executive.

That gathering in the Equity meeting-room had all the excitement of an audience on a first night. There was a fear in the Council that some of the Gaelgeoirs — as we called the group who had their names only in Irish — fearing they had no possibility of theatre work outside the Abbey, might not go along with our demands. If the determination to bring about change was not unanimous, Blythe would make mincemeat of us.

Dermot Doolan and Louis Nolan advised us that the proposed actions were part of a normal trade-union process of settling a dispute between workers and management; that there were ample safeguards against any victimisation, which they did not expect to occur anyhow. It was Equity's plan to press for a minimum salary scale based on length of service, which would mean a substantial raise for every actor, but would not interfere with the right of individuals to negotiate above the minimum; the right of actors to choose their own stage names would also be demanded; the Players' Council, which had been made a subcommittee of Equity, would handle the negotiations.

Unions representing the non-acting staff of the Queen's promised us full support. That was crucial. A presentation of our case to the Labour Court was a likely outcome. The vote — after questions, answers, discussion, and heart-cheering endorsement of the action from the oldest members of the company — was unanimous in favour of every demand. The absolute need for confidentiality was impressed strongly on everyone. Amazingly, this was never broken, as far as we could see. As a result of the meeting, I was confident that we, the Players' Council and Equity subcommittee for the Abbey Theatre, had the authority to bring the negotiations to a satisfactory conclusion.

Solidarity stumbled, however, as we approached the presentation to the Labour Court some months later. It was key to our case that we should show the Labour Court the appalling inequities in the treatment of some long-serving and vulnerable — particularly female — company members. For instance, May Craig, the doyenne of the Abbey Players, was earning, if my memory serves me, seven pounds per week after forty-seven years' service! Even after Blythe's recent 'talon' raises, no actor at the Abbey was earning twenty pounds a week. Eileen Crowe had risen to the dizzy heights of nineteen. I had one pound less than she had.

Bríd Lynch refused to write down her salary, years of service and name on a list. It became clear that a number of others felt the same. Of course, it was maddening, but we understood the embarrassment — indeed, for some, the sense of shame — at the indignity of their financial worth to the Abbey. Eventually, I broke the stalemate by getting Frank Ellis, our humorous, elderly property master, to make a wooden box with a slit on top; each of the twenty-three members of the company would write their length of service and weekly salary on one of twenty-three identical, un-numbered papers and insert it in the box, which Frank would safeguard. When he had counted twenty-three visits from company members, he gave the Council the box. We typed the information on Players' Council notepaper, and it became the explosive that blew Blythe's case out of the Labour Court.

The truth, of course, was that we could not help knowing, from the two items of information, to what Player each salary belonged. We did not let ourselves think about that, let alone talk about it. The niceties were observed, and that was important.

The Labour Court hearing itself was not memorable. A number of men in ordinary clothes sat across an ordinary table from us, the Players' Council; on our left was Mr Blythe. We presented our case for a salary scale and the right to choose our own names. Who steals our salaries steals little, but who steals our names damages us in many ways! We presented our information on present salaries, showing the unfairness of them to a number of Players with long service, making a strong point of May Craig's situation. We showed evidence of the disparity in conditions between us and the RÉ Repertory Company, who read their parts and could redo mistakes in performances before exposure to the public.

Blythe presented no written material, and carried none. He read a note he had written for himself on the back of a little book of matches. How he had that, I don't know; he didn't smoke. He dismissed our point about May Craig, saying she was really retired, and bringing her in to work in small parts from time to time was 'charity'. He said he would very much like to pay us more, but he simply did not have the money. The Abbey Players had permanent employment and all were paid more than the Equity minimum. He saw no need to bring Equity into the matter. He met regularly with the Players' representatives. They could and did discuss everything. In a very casual way, he showed that he considered this exercise at the Labour Court irrelevant to the Abbey situation.

We were officially advised in due course that, while the Court accepted the validity of our case, they recommended that we try to work out an agreement acceptable to both the Abbey and the Players. We would have liked the court to make an award, but all in all we had made a giant step forward. The government, the press, and some of the Board of the Abbey — particularly Dr Seamus Wilmot, a recent appointee — recognised that we had legitimate grievances. We were never quite sure whether Gabriel Fallon was for us or 'a Guinness', as we liked to say.

We went back to the table, and on at least one occasion Dermot Doolan was present in Blythe's cubby-hole for a Players' Council meeting. Philip and I intensified our 'lobbying' with our political friends in Groome's Hotel, particularly with Brian Lenihan and Donogh O'Malley, and — less frequently, but to no less support — with Charlie Haughey, Sean Flanagan, and Eoin Ryan, son of the Minister of Finance, Dr Jim Ryan.

The work of the Players' Council took on a new edge and urgency with the laying of the foundation stone of the new Abbey Theatre, by President de Valera, on 3 September 1963. I was there with T.P.'s friend and my companion in Frejus/Bejasus, Michael Coffey. I took photographs of the historic occasion with a 35-millimetre camera with a built-in light meter, the first camera I had ever owned; it was given to me by my friend Arnold Hintze. I left the films in to a chemist on Grafton Street. Nearly two years later, I had both the time and money to get the prints; the shop had dumped them because they had not been claimed within a year! The same happened with Louise's First Communion photos. As my mother used to say, we were always just 'pulling the divil by the tail'.

In 1963 and the first half of '64, the odd bit of filming kept the wolf from the door. John B. Keane's *The Man from Clare* was produced at the Abbey, to our delight. With its Gaelic football background, it was rollicking fun for us and for audiences. Pat Laffan and I played half-witted twins, Petey and Packey; by getting John B. to let me give all the lines to Pat, with me repeating the last few words of each of Pat's speeches, we made quite a comic contribution to the success of the play. More important, I got to know John B. well and spent priceless hours with him, both in Dublin and in his native Listowel. 'You're a cute hoor, Dowling,' he'd say to me again and again. Of course, I took it as a compliment.

The revival of *Long Day's Journey into Night* brought Ria Mooney on stage for the last time. In spite of another nine weeks' rehearsal, and all of us doing extra line rehearsals with her in the theatre and at her home, she was never secure, though often magical. Patrick Laffan had generously agreed to prompt her. He sat tucked into a special seat, unseen by the audience, but clearly within earshot of Ria. Without him she could not have played it at all. Even at that, Phil and I had some truly hair-raising times with her.

One night in Act III, in the scenes after father and son get back from Edmund's visit to the doctor, she went blank again and again. When we improvised and got her to a later part of the scene, she would take us back to areas we had already covered. Phil and I were close to breaking point. Somehow we survived, and miraculously the audience were blissfully unaware. All credit to the depth of Dermody's direction, plus Pat Laffan's concentration and sensitivity on the prompt book.

In the dressing-room, Phil and I both were shaking with aftershock. There was a timid knock on the door, and Ria's voice asking if she might come in.

Phil looked at me. 'Poor thing! She's coming to apologise.' Raising his voice, he called out pleasantly, 'Come in, love.'

A tiny figure entered in an old blue flannel dressing-gown, her costume for her last scene, with a green hair-ribbon in her hand. 'Boys,' she said simply, 'I want to tell you that I'm going to wear this green ribbon for my last entrance tonight, instead of the blue one. It won't throw you, will it?'

Ria developed an imbalance, something to do with her inner ear. Then followed some kind of breakdown, and she resigned as producer. Her place was taken by Frank Dermody. The tragedy, I think — and it was a tragedy — was that this great actress, and teacher of the basics of good acting, had taken on the role of producer in the Abbey, directing up to twelve plays each year, under a man insensitive to artists and opposed to the very idea of the Abbey as a theatre where the art should be practised. He would repeat again and again, as we moved towards a showdown with him, 'The Abbey is not an art theatre but an instrument of national defence!'

Most of us remember where we were when President John F. Kennedy was killed in November 1963. I was in a play set in a TB hospital, written by a big, gentle man, Michael Mulvihill. It was called, all too appropriately, *A Sunset Touch*. During the run the sun set abruptly on our innocence, with the assassination of the young Irish-American President. Strange how it still hurts. In my life in Ireland, I never saw one person capture so completely the love of so many — particularly during his visit in June of that year. I can see the picture still, from the roof of a small hotel on Eyre Square in Galway: the Secret Service men on top of the Great Southern; beside me Phil, Angela, and old Tadhg Folan of Spiddal; the streets on all four sides of the square jammed with happy people, every window opposite filled; and the tall, youthful, charismatic figure of John Kennedy, like a visitor from *Tír na nÓg*, with the small statue of the poet Padraic Ó Conaire behind him and all of us spellbound, listening to the magic of his Boston Rs and the hope in his message.

In 1964, Sean O'Casey lifted the ban on Irish productions of his plays that he had imposed six years earlier. Peter Daubeny of the World Theatre Season at the Aldwych Theatre in London had invited the Abbey to present *The Plough and the Stars* and *Juno and the Paycock*, opening on 20 April, each play running a week, with *Juno* continuing on to the *Théâtre des Nations* in Paris. This was cause for celebration, indeed. Cause, too, for some careful planning on the Players' Council's part. The 'new' Abbey, the foundation stone having been laid, was a reality just down the road. As far as our policy for a National Theatre was concerned, I felt it was now or never! At the same time, getting up these two masterpieces, two of the greatest Abbey plays in our short history, took centre stage. Dermody was to direct both. Ernest Blythe named Tomás Mac Anna, who was working in Iceland, as designer. Blythe would also decide who would play Juno.

He chose Maura O'Donnell, who was his favourite. She was a fine actress in her role, none better, but her role did not include O'Casey's quintessentially Dublin Juno. Dermody was unhappy from the beginning. Alas, however great his talents and artistry, he had not the courage to oppose Blythe in this misguided casting. Everyone with a titter of wit knew it was a mistake. What we did not anticipate was the damage Dermody would allow it to do to himself.

Fortunately *Plough* opened first, in February, to packed houses, and continued to draw and delight audiences through its pre-London run. Phil O'Flynn, no longer on the Players' Council, was Fluther Good; Eric Gorman was Uncle Peter; and I was the Covey, a young Dublin doctrinaire Socialist with more big words than sense or courage. 'Have you ever read, Comrade, Jenersky's thesis on the origin, development, and consolidation of the evolutionary idea of the proletariat?' Try saying that quickly. God, I loved that part! So did every young actor in the company. It was one of Phil's great 'cribs' that he was taken out of the Covey in his early twenties and put into Fluther, because he was losing his hair!

In three of the four acts, I took to the Covey like a duck to water. But in Act III, the great bar scene, Dermody was not happy with me. He couldn't explain why. The nearest he could get was, 'You are coming in lazy.' But if I came in strong or fast or loud, it would be, 'Don't tell me, for Christ's sake! Take me there!'

Then I did what I realise now I was prone to do. The very night I shouldn't, the night before the first dress rehearsal, I drank too much and stayed out too late! My only saving grace was that on these rare but not unheard-of occasions, I knew better than to have 'a hair of the dog that bit me'.

The last time I had had a hangover like this was three years earlier, the morning after the night before the dress for *The Honey Spike*. I had made the mistake of calling in sick and going into town for a soda with a dash of angostura bitters, for the stomach's sake. Then hot towels, shave, hair-wash and haircut. I came out of the barbers, feeling like a two-year-old, and walked straight into the arms of Frank Dermody! He looked at me with loathing. I thought he'd never speak to me again!

This time, I went to our friendly local chemist and confessed all, and she gave me one little tablet — it was purple, shaped like a heart — and it did it! I felt great!

Before the Act III bar scene, after giving us his notes, Dermody came to me. 'What happens to the soles of your feet when you are anticipating something exciting? Come on! Come on! Feel it, boy. Feel it,' he urged me.

'My toes curl?'

'Attaboy,' and he was gone. I never had any trouble with the bar scene after that. Curl my toes, and it's like a shot of adrenaline shoots up me from toe to top. It's worked for a lot of actors I directed in other plays, too.

Juno was not a happy experience. Nobody liked the set, least of all Dermody. That, and not being happy with Maura in the title role, made him edgy, sometimes vicious. I remember one Holy Thursday. We weren't supposed to rehearse that day, the day of the Annual Catholic Stage Guild Retreat. Whatever else I didn't go to, I wouldn't want to miss that; it was always more fun than a wake! But Dermody insisted that we rehearse when it was over, starting at 6.30 that evening. Theatres, cinemas, dance halls, all closed in Ireland on Spy Wednesday, Holy Thursday and Good Friday. We were due to open on Easter Monday.

The rehearsal started on time, in work-lights only, with the curtain down — the stagehands had those three days off, and Blythe would not pay the overtime. Aideen O'Kelly, as Mary Boyle, reading from a newspaper. Pat Laffan, the crippled Johnny, sitting gloomily at the fire. The rest of the cast off stage. Dermody, his long black overcoat open, his little flat felt hat pushed back on his bald head, his face like the Grim Reaper's, swinging out of the parting in the curtain, very drunk.

'On a little by-road out beyant Finglas....' Mary is reading from the paper.

'Jesus, girl! Don't tell me. For Christ's sake, take me there!'

One and a half hours later, Aideen had never been allowed to get any further with the line, though she said it a hundred ways and times. Frank spluttered, spat, weaved, swayed, and pontificated, hanging on that curtain. That he didn't fall off the high stage into the orchestra pit was a miracle! Finally we told him we were leaving, and we did.

The company was due to leave Dublin for London on the Sunday before we opened *The Plough and the Stars* at the Aldwych. The Players' Council had its regular monthly meeting with Blythe on the Friday afternoon, a week and a day before our departure.

The previous few meetings had been mostly taken up with details relating to the upcoming rehearsals and visits. Blythe had been procrastinating, as was his way, in the matter of our two main demands: salary scale and the right to choose our own names. He had agreed to allow Dermot Doolan to be present at the meetings. He didn't often come, though.

After the pleasantries had been observed, I asked Blythe if he had made a decision in the two main matters. He said pleasantly that he had. He was not going to implement them.

I asked if that was final. He said it was, and smiled. I rose without looking at the others, said, even more pleasantly, 'Thank you, Mr Blythe, there is obviously nothing more to be said,' and led our little delegation out. I was quite sure he was pleased at the attitude we appeared to have taken. I guessed he thought our talons had been 'grasped' and the bird 'lost', for the moment anyway, by the lure of London and Paris.

Outside the door, before anyone could say anything, I suggested that we go next door, for afternoon tea or coffee, at the new upstairs café in Goulding's, an airy, pleasant nursery store. It was quiet in the early afternoon, and, as yet, we weren't known to the staff.

The feeling among the others seemed to be disappointment and resignation to the fact that we would wait till after London and Paris, and probably the June vacation month, to take the next step. I disagreed calmly.

The Aldwych, we knew, was sold out. There was a lot of money involved, for both the Abbey and the World Theatre Season. We were required to give one week's notice of intent to strike, which we just had time to do. We would never have such a chance again. The timing was forced on us by Blythe's intransigence and refusal to implement the recommendations of the Labour Court. It was fortuitous, but coincidental, as far as the Players' Council was concerned — the Council as a whole, anyway; I had believed Blythe under-estimated us, and I had let him procrastinate. The nearer the London visit, the better for us!

I said we had no alternative but to advise the Board of Directors that the Abbey Players would withdraw their labour, as of midnight on Saturday 17 April, unless they acceded to our legitimate demands or agreed to binding arbitration by a mutually appointed arbitrator.

As if it was what everyone wanted, but hesitated to say, there was immediate and unanimous agreement. There and then, we agreed upon the wording of the letter, the hand-delivery of copies to each member of the Board of the Abbey, the manner of informing the company what we had done, the decision to advise the ageing Sean O'Casey of our action and confidence in victory; we acted upon all this before that day was done.

We went to Equity Offices in Lower Gardiner Street, wrote, signed and addressed the strike notice to Blythe at the Abbey, Séamus Wilmot, Gabriel

Fallon and Roibeárd Ó Faracháin, and divided the delivery duties among the Council members — Bill Foley, Eddie Golden, Mick Hennessey, and myself. Then I wrote to Sean O'Casey, to the effect that we knew he, as a trade union-ist, would support our stand; that we were confident that we would win and be at the Aldwych in the next two weeks, but that if we weren't, we would win in the long run; and that our real purpose was to bring about a reorgani-sation of the Abbey that would allow it to fulfil its potential to be 'the greatest little theatre in the world'. I can say with certainty that the members of the Players' Council had not lost sight of that ideal at any time during this entire process. It motivated everything we did.

Philip O'Flynn, to my dismay, was outraged that we had served strike notice just as we were going to London. It was Pat Layde who persuaded him he was wrong — not that Phil would have come out against us; I don't think that for a moment.

Dermody went ballistic. He got drunk, came up to the men's dressing-room before the show, railed at us, and wailed at the ruin and shame it would bring on the Abbey; we could hear him through the open window as he staggered, still raging, up Park Lane to Pearse Street. A few were genuinely worried about their livelihood and the survival of the theatre, but the line held, and the great majority were solidly behind us.

Next night, during the third act, I was alone in the dressing-room. As Gerry Devine, I had done my part and was waiting for the curtain call. There was a knock on the door, and Mr Blythe came in.

At moments like that I go cold. Blank. Relaxed. My mind clear as a bell. I who am afraid of mice, of rats, of being alone in a house at night by myself.

Here is this man Blythe, who, if you touch — or he thinks you touch — one of his no-trespass points, goes white as death, dangerous as an adder. I'd seen it happen several times. A man who had ordered the executions of seventy-seven of his former comrades in Ireland's Civil War. A man who believed it was better to kill ten innocent men in war, than let one guilty go free. A man who believed the Abbey Theatre was an instrument of national defence. So was this war? He clearly had waited to come to the dressing-room when I would be there alone.

He came to the end of the long green dressing-table with its line of lighted make-up mirrors.

'Would you agree to Dr Todd Andrews as an arbitrator?' he said simply, normally.

'I would have to ask the Council,' I said after a moment's thought, 'but personally, I would recommend they accept him.'

'Could you do that after the play tonight?'

'Yes,' I said. 'We're all in the play.'

'Thank you. I'll be in my office.' He could have been talking about the weather.

Dr C.S. 'Todd' Andrews was head of CIÉ, the Irish National Passenger Transport System. He was the man who had been chosen for the unpopular job of closing down uneconomical rail lines and stations. As one wit put it, 'Andrews would close the stations of the cross.' A confidant of and fighter for President de Valera, he had previously headed the Electricity Supply Board and the Clondalkin Paper Mills, where he had broken a major strike by workers. He was a tough man, a cultured man, a man who was interested in and supported the arts, a completely honest man, a fair man. I believed we could not have a better arbitrator. If he should find in our favour, his recommendations could not be refused by the government. The Council agreed.

Next day we were on our way to London. I hardly thought about Equity, or the Council, till we got back. I certainly never talked about it to Blythe. To give him his due, he didn't talk about it to me either.

Dr Andrews asked to see representatives of the Players' Council. Two of us went: Eddie Golden, who was President of Equity, and myself, as Secretary of the Council. We had both actually met him before, but could not be said to know him. However, he was a lifelong friend and comrade-in-arms of Sean and Frank Dowling, my favourite Dowling relations. I had spoken to Sean about him, after we had agreed to him as arbitrator. Sean, as I had expected, told me he would be absolutely impartial, though he and Blythe had been on opposite sides in our bloody Civil War. He also said that 'Todd' knew and understood the arts. I was counting on the fact that our case was patently in the interest of not only the Abbey, but the country as a whole. I was quietly and absolutely confident we were going to win.

Dr Andrews received us, very informally, in his large Chairman's office at Kingsbridge Railway Station, now renamed Heuston. He encouraged us to talk about what we thought was wrong in the Abbey. It seems to me that he pretty quickly made the point that, while he heard and understood us, he would need a written plan that showed we knew a better way of doing things than the present directorate. We told him we had one that was supported unanimously by the Abbey Players, and we had brought a copy of it for him.

Hugh Hunt writes in his history of the Abbey that the Labour Court forced Dr Andrews on Blythe as 'a mediator'. I believe Blythe and the Abbey Board, having received our notice of intent to strike and our offer of arbitration, suggested the good doctor for much the same reasons as we accepted him. Certainly that is the impression Blythe gave me. Perhaps the Labour Court offered Blythe the suggestion. The Court did not suggest it to us, the party instigating the proceedings.

The Andrews award was announced, and was a total vindication of the Abbey Players' action. Dr Jim Ryan, the Minister for Finance, called the Abbey Directors and the Players' representatives to a meeting with him and his Department heads. We met in the Department of Finance office in the great neoclassical government buildings on Merrion Street, which looked down on the basement of 67 Merrion Square, where I had started life. Dr Ryan explained to us that it was his government's policy to nationalise businesses and industries that were necessary to the welfare of the nation only if the private sector found them uneconomical. While they looked on the Abbey as the National Theatre, they felt the national and the theatre's interests would be better served by an increase in the annual subsidy and a reorganisation of the National Theatre Society Ltd, the governing body, with two government-appointed directors instead of one, and a body of 'shareholders' (appointed by the government and the existing Board) who would, with the directors, appoint or re-appoint the directors of the Abbey Board. The 'shares' would have no monetary value. It was understood by all parties that the government, like the Abbey Theatre and Players, accepted the other recommendations in the Andrews award.

We were well aware that the key to the implementation of our policy and Dr Andrews's award depended on the person the government appointed as their second director. Blythe held — and the existing directors echoed his conviction, though all of them may not have shared it — that 'the Board members of the Abbey Theatre, in the apostolic line from Yeats, Lady Gregory and Synge, *are* the artistic directors of the Abbey'.

Our friends in Groome's, climbing fast in the hierarchy of Fianna Fáil — then the government party — now proved to be friends indeed. They would soon deliver both the government-appointed directors, if we could find the person with the talent and credibility for the job of running the Abbey and neutralising Blythe. Phil and I spent nights with them in Groome's, hours with them in private meetings in the Dáil and in their offices — more with Brian Lenihan than with anyone else. I was then spending almost all my 'free' time and holidays on the Shannon River, much of it in or about Lough Ree and the Hodson Bay Hotel, with Paddy Lenihan, who owned it. Paddy was Brian's father, a government backbencher, and a wonderful companion. We shared interests in the river, boating, poetry, theatre, good food, and an occasional drink!

The long and the short of all this was that Brian nsisted that we could only achieve our ends if we found *the man*. I held that we must create the structure; with the help of both government appointees, we would attract the right candidates.

'Let's call Tyrone Guthrie and ask if we can go and see him.' It was Phil, calling me at home one Saturday morning. 'We'll tell him we want to talk to him about running the Abbey.' I wasn't rehearsing. Phil was, until one o'clock. Neither of us was playing that night. It had rained for days.

Despite the awful weather, which slowed our journey down, we arrived at Annaghmakerrig that night, a bottle of whiskey in hand. Tyrone had asked us to pick that up at his local pub. Even Philip, who was about six foot two, looked small beside the famous director, giant of English-speaking theatre. His large country house was very much a home. We were aware of out-houses, trees, and fields as we drove up. The Guthries grew berries and marketed jam made there, under their supervision, by the local people. There was a fire blazing in the comfortable, lived-in dining-cum-sitting-room we were brought into. We had a few stiff drinks by the fire, and we talked.

The jam business wasn't doing too well, we learned right away. That wasn't the worst news for us! Tyrone was committed to going back to Minneapolis, to the theatre that he had founded there. It was something he simply had to do. Over a full hot dinner, though it was after midnight, he suggested two possible candidates for the job at the Abbey. First, Jim Fitzgerald — yes, the one who had punched Robert Mitchum. A fine director, without doubt; but to anyone who visited Groome's, including our political friends, Jim would be as acceptable for this job as a nymphomaniac in a convent. Tyrone's second suggestion was a young American director with whom he was very impressed. Phil and I said we were sure he must be very good, but there was no way the government would appoint an American as their nominee.

We fell into beds in our hotel in Newbliss about 4.00 a.m.

Not long out of Newbliss, the next morning, Phil suddenly said, 'There is only one person for this job. He's Irish. He's a famous novelist and successful playwright; he's an Irish-speaker, but not a fanatical one. He knows Blythe, knows how to handle him. Blythe admires him. He'll be acceptable to the government and to the Players. He's a friend of ours. I say let's ask him!'

'You're right,' I said. 'Let's call him as soon as we get home!'

We called him at his home in Oughterard. After a moment's hesitation he said ironically, in his rumbling Galway voice, 'You're nice friends, I must say! I suppose I'll have to say yes.'

And Walter Macken was on his way to becoming artistic advisor and government nominee on the Board of the Abbey Theatre. Little did we dream, any of us, that this decision would contribute to his early death.

Miss Sheridan, the skinny, toothless charwoman who swept out offices and dressing-rooms, and Maureen McCormick, private secretary to Mr Blythe, were probably the only two employees who had any idea of what transpired at Board meetings. Miss Sheridan had gone into Abbey lore by breaking into a Board meeting in session, exclaiming accusingly, 'Mr Blythe! Excuse me, Mr Blythe!'

'What? What?' answered Blythe impatiently.

'Do you know what the actors have?'

Even more impatiently — 'No! What?'

'No soap!'

Well, you can imagine our curiosity the night of Walter Macken's first Board meeting. The meetings were held in a large room off the Upper Circle of the theatre, during performance time. The Council had arranged to meet Wally, as we called him, at O'Neill's pub on Pearse Street, after the play.

When we were tucked into our favourite table with our drinks, Walter gave us a quietly humorous replay of the proceedings. 'I'm not sure, but I think I should tell you this, Vincent. When the subject of the Players' request for the right to nominate some of the shareholders came up from Séamus Wilmot, Mr Blythe broke in: "That comes from Vincent Dowling — a skilled labour agitator. I have come to distrust anything coming from him as the thin end of a very long wedge!"'

It was scary, coming from a man like Blythe; but I had to admit to myself that for once he was right! I had come up with that suggestion; and, thanks to support from Dermot Doolan and Brian Lenihan, it came about. The shareholders nominated by the Players would be David Thornley, a political writer, later elected to the Dáil; Professor Denis Donoghue of University College Dublin; and Charlie McCarthy, a barrister and former member of Radio Éireann Repertory.

In February 1965, as we were in rehearsal for *The Face of Treason* by Eoin Neeson and Colm McNeill, the Articles of Association of the Abbey were altered to accommodate the shareholders. Walter Macken was named and accepted as the second government director. In November, fiercely resisted by Blythe, the creation of the position of Artistic Advisor was voted in and Walter Macken was appointed to the position.

Among the plays produced that year was Sean Dowling's play of the Civil War, *The Best of Motives*. It was not as well received as his first play, *A Bird in the Net*. In November we gave our first Bertolt Brecht production, *The Life of Galileo*, both directed and set excellently by Tomás Mac Anna. Michael Hennessey gave a powerful performance in the title role. Aideen O'Kelly and I gave particularly well-received performances. My daughter Louise appeared in the *commedia dell'arte* scene in the *The Feast of Fools*.

1965 was, on the whole, a pretty satisfactory year for the Abbey Theatre, from many points of view.

14

You Say Condom, I Say Illegal

What's an atheist like you doing in a place like this?

You say condom. I say French letter. Like all 'unnatural' forms of birth control, they were forbidden by the Catholic Church. Selling them, importing them, even advocating in print their use was deemed unlawful by the Irish government. My brainwashing was complete. The very idea of using one was repugnant to my sensibilities. Though I did not condemn it, I thought it was a pretty low-class thing to do, like peeing in a bedroom sink. It was nothing to do with logic. It was prejudice, which usually I abominate.

I was thirty-five years old. It was a Saturday night. I had met Violet, my wonderful English friend and sometime lover. She had asked me to a house-warming in her new flat near Herbert Park. She told me the English playwright John Arden and his wife, Margaretta D'Arcy, would be there.

'I suppose you'd have no use for a French letter?' said one of my friends in the theatre, out of the blue, after the show.

On the spur of the moment I said, 'Yes, I'll take it. How much?'

'On me,' he said. From such insignificant beginnings do momentous events flow.

I arrived at Violet's, like most of the men, shortly after the pubs closed. Her flat was on the third floor of an impressive, red-brick, semi-detached dwelling. There were three other flats on that level, all occupied by young single women. The party was flowing not only from flat to flat, but out into the landing and down the stairs. One large bathroom-cum-toilet served the whole top floor — nothing remarkable in those days. It was a good party, and I talked a lot with John Arden and sparred verbally with his actress wife about the Abbey.

Everyone gone, I helped with the clean-up and retired to Violet's bed. She was happily surprised that I was prepared to break my prohibition on 'protective sheaths', as she put it. 'Waste not want not,' I said.

We made love, happily. 'What am I going to do with this contraption?' I asked, not wanting to risk meeting the other flat-holders on my way to the bathroom with a semen-filled condom in hand.

'Tie a knot in it,' she laughed, 'and let's go to sleep.' I did, and slept soundly till late on Sunday morning.

'May I have a bath?' I asked, while Violet was making the normal Sunday breakfast of bacon, egg, sausage, white and black pudding, toast, marmalade and tea.

She said 'Do,' and gave me the pennies to put in the geyser for the hot water, reminding me not to be all day, as there were at least three others who would be wanting the bathroom. She added that she supposed I was going to Mass.

Of course I was. 'Twelve o'clock at Donnybrook. My old parish church.'

Violet knew well my paradoxical position in the matter of religion. I was a convinced Catholic. I could resist most things except sexual temptation. Giving up my religion would have been a second wrong that wouldn't make anything right. That was my sincere, if somewhat blinkered, pose at that moment.

Now the comedy started. In the locked bathroom, while the geyser was running hot water into my bath, I tried to flush the loaded rubber down the toilet.

It wouldn't flush. I held it down and flushed again. Up it bounced. I tried to undo the knot. It refused to untie.

A knock on the door and a voice asking 'Will you be long?' made me jump into the scalding bath. 'Jesus, Mary and holy Saint Joseph!' I screamed.

'No,' said one of the other flat-dwellers, 'just Mary! As soon as you can, Vincent.' Mary, the girl in the front flat!

'Two shakes of a lamb's tail,' I cried. I put the damnable object into my trouser pocket and turned the cold water on full.

All through breakfast, I could feel the thing burning a hole in my pocket, and could hardly wait to get out and get rid of it. The car was parked on the gravel drive in front of the house. I realised there was no way I could bring myself to throw the evidence of my spent passion somewhere others were going to have to deal with it. Besides, Violet's three neighbours were coming down the front stone steps in their Sunday best, going round the corner — 'to church', they said. Protestants! So I drove out and crossed the bridge. It was much too far to throw it into the Dodder River flowing underneath — not that I could have brought myself to do that anyway. No, there was only one thing to do: try and get a place on the road to park, adjacent to the Chapel, near a rain drain, and surreptitiously slip it down it.

Fat chance. Bumper-to-bumper cars, shoulder-to-shoulder people; everyone I ever knew, it seemed, was at twelve o'clock Mass in Donnybrook that day. After three or four failed attempts, I gave up.

I went to the door of the north chapel. It used to be always good for a seat. A notice greeted me: 'Offering at this door, one shilling.' It used to be one penny. Class distinction in the house of God! Blessed are the poor, for they shall sit in the back row, or stand!

Well, it's hard to break habits. I stood, knelt, sat, put my head down for the Consecration, with everyone else. I realised, though, that I was going through the motions.

What the hell am I doing here? I was thinking. *It doesn't make any sense. Do I really believe that I'm obliged under pain of mortal sin to be here? That what I did last night with Violet is anything to do with pope, priest, or God? My God! If he was God, he would never allow those ghastly plaster images of himself and his mother to disgrace his house!*

It wasn't escapism and it wasn't guilt; on the contrary, I was enjoying myself immensely — laughing at myself. The incongruity! The stupidity — my stupidity! For more than twenty years I had used whatever wit I had to defend this Catholic Church, never for a moment questioning it, doubting it. Now, suddenly, from nowhere, as if a stray bullet had shattered a mirror in front of me, my clear image of life and religion had splintered. Nothing left; nothing but relief. *If it's ritual I want, the theatre is the place! For holy pictures and statues, I'd be better off in the National Gallery!*

Here in the church I was seeing for the first time a social control mechanism, emotional blackmail. *'If you disobey me you'll be damned!'* Is that love? Is that justice?

A floodgate had opened! *Of course, Jean Louis Barrault is right: theatre is the art of justice. And I'm right: it's the art of charity. Good and evil are in me, in everyone. It is up to us ourselves to nurture the good, control the greed, the selfishness, the damage we do to ourselves, others, the world. Imagination, intelligence, and free will — the right to choose: that's what makes mankind unique. The Church tries to control those elements in me! It's as bad as Blythe!*

I noticed the priest was at the last Gospel, the Gospel according to Saint John. I've always liked it. 'In the beginning was the Word....' It still is the word: in poetry, like the Bible; in prose, like Dickens; in drama, like Shakespeare, Synge, O'Casey, O'Neill. The word is God! I was having an epiphany, an existentialist epiphany, albeit an eccentric existentialist epiphany! But an epiphany!

I didn't get thrown down, levitate, shout or sing. I just shuffled out after the others, keeping my head down, hoping I'd see no one I knew — not until I got rid of that yoke in my pocket. Like a good Irishman, I decided to take my problem to a pub.

As with most problems, and most Irishmen, nothing was solved for me in the pub. I ordered a glass of stout in Lalor's, between Herbert Park and the bridge. I went into the tiny water closet and locked the door, determined to drown the little 'divil', which was taking on a life of its own. Again I failed to untie the knot. Again I failed, though I had rolled it in wads of toilet paper, to sink the buoyant little bugger; but I did start to laugh at it bouncing about in the swirling water. I laughed and laughed, the tears of laughter rolling down my cheeks. *I better get out of here*, I thought, *before they come to lock me away*.

Five minutes later, in the Sunday quiet that falls on Dublin between last Mass and the afternoon football games, opposite the American Embassy, I got out of the car and dropped the offending device down a drain. It lay across two bars of the iron grating, making its last effort to thwart me. I turned it lengthways with the toe of my shoe and poked it into Stygian darkness.

I thought about what that French philosopher Jack gave me to read — what was his name? Gabriel Marcel — talked about: the leaps over logic the mind sometimes makes to an illumination. Nonchalantly, I went back to my old car and drove to Violet's for Sunday lunch, freer than I had felt for years.

Bill Thompson of the *Evening Herald*, who had become one of my close friends, met me at the airport the night I returned from the London and Paris festivals. He, Fidelma Murphy and I went to supper at the flat of a lady friend of Bill's on the North Circular Road.

I was feeling no pain when they woke me up, in the back seat of Bill's car, in the early hours of the morning. 'You're home, Vinny,' I heard Bill say — he was the only one who called me that.

'I can see I am,' I said, 'but why is the house upside down?' They thought I was joking. I wasn't. It had been a long day's journey and a half, with even more liquor than Eugene O'Neill, his brother Jamie, and his father could have consumed together. I felt great, though, and in very good humour.

Brenda was awake, and to my amazement really glad to see me. She wanted to hear about London, Paris and the plays. My edited version of the trip made her laugh a lot, and we made love, I remember, which we hadn't in a long time.

Brenda didn't come with me to the Shannon River, where I was spending most of my holidays. Oddly, for a girl with such physical energy, she didn't share my interest in country activities like boating, fishing, hiking and scenic drives. The inevitable pub nightlife was anathema to her.

Swiftly, alas, our relationship slipped back to fairly peaceful accommodation. Players' Council matters, learning lines, seeing films, and lunch at least once a week in Lucan or the Strawberry Beds out along the River Liffey, with some of our crowd, occupied the afternoons. Ninety-nine per cent of the talk was about theatre! I always had an hour's sleep before dinner at home, listened to the BBC Radio Newsreel, then did the show.

That summer and fall, rehearsals for a series of new plays, most of which I was in, took care of the mornings; nights were spent performing, followed by a drink in the theatre bar and/or O'Neill's, thence to Groome's. Every night someone would join me after the show: my mother; Carmel and her husband Paddy, Kitty and Marie with their husbands and children, when they were in Dublin; my brother Sam; or some friends or relations. Brenda would come once to see each show — on the first night, if she wasn't working. Reluctantly, she came to O'Neill's, less often to Groome's.

I saw my eldest brother, Jack, more than any of the family, when either of us could make time — at his house with Betty and their children, or walking, fishing, a few times camping, in Co. Meath, where Mammy was born and Daddy's ancestors came from. Everywhere, always, we were talking: the philosophy of art, poetry, drama, television, and religion. He was my university education. He constantly stretched, and made me stretch, my mind, imagination and vision. I enjoyed and loved every minute of it. Once he arranged for me to give a lecture on my art to the Benedictine student monks at Dunamon Castle. I worked on it for weeks, Jack constantly challenging my writing and content, never telling me what I should say. What Dermody did for me as an actor, Jack did for me as a person.

I thought I was in love with Fidelma, then. I think she probably felt much the same. As with all of the girls I fell in love with, I never even thought about the future of the relationship. I was married. I had three daughters I loved. There was no divorce in Ireland. I was never going to leave the Abbey. Financially, we were getting by quite nicely, but we had no money in the bank. Having a second home with someone was not realistic. That was that! Besides, we were artists, we believed in free love. This was the way artists lived! *Mea culpa, mea culpa, mea maxima culpa.*

I had a rude awakening from that siesta. Brenda told me she was three months pregnant. She had missed two periods; her periods often played that game with her, but the doctor's test said she was a third of the way along the road to Galway. The baby was due to arrive in February.

I told Fidelma I would not be going out with her again. It was very painful for her, and for me to do it to her. I believe I had no choice.

Rachael, healthy and beautiful, was born in February 1965, just before Walter Macken was appointed to the Board. I was in a new world, and it needed new thinking. On all fronts!

As soon as Brenda was on her feet again and had a handle on the new routine, I asked her to do as the wives of most of the other Abbey actors did: join us after the show every night at the theatre, go for a drink with us, perhaps go to Groome's one night a week, and go home together. I knew, and Brenda knew, that after the show was my danger time. Wound up, on a high after the day and the play, I could no more do without a woman who understood my feelings than I could go without a cup of hot tea in the morning. I knew it was no excuse for my philandering, falling in love, or infidelity, but it was a reason.

Brenda couldn't bring herself to do it. Partly because it would have been difficult, with a twelve-year-old, a seven-year-old, a five-year-old and a new baby. Besides, it would have cost money. On the other hand, if she had work in the theatre, that would have been true, too. The main reason — which I understood, but did not agree with — was embarrassment. Brenda felt that people, most of whom knew our marital history, would think she had become a clinging vine. Anyway, why would I not just come home?

Well, I did for a while. Then I met a young girl, Sinéad Cusack. She was working in the Irish pantomime of 1965 — *Emer agus an Laoch (Emer and the Swan)*. She was seventeen. I was thirty-five. I really fell in love, for the first time in my life. For several years, sometimes wildly happy, other times shatteringly miserable, I believed I had found the perfect partner, the one who was made for me and I for her. Like Chekhov's young poet in *The Cherry Orchard*, I believed, and still believe, 'there is happiness!'

My fellow Dubliner Oscar Wilde, often most profound when he is funniest, told us that life always imitates art. To commemorate the fiftieth anniversary of the1916 Easter Rising and the Proclamation of the Irish Republic, the Abbey presented three one-act plays, by Lady Gregory, Roibeárd Ó Faracháin, and Patrick Pearse. Pearse, teacher, poet, playwright and visionary, led the Irish Volunteer Army in this idealists' rebellion, signed and publicly read the Proclamation, and was executed by a British firing squad with the other leaders and signatories. His play is called *The Singer*. It was written a year before the Rising, for which it is a blueprint. The singer of the play, whom I played, is a teacher who preaches the idea of a 'blood sacrifice' to his people as the only hope of raising the nation to revolt against the tyrant. Like Pearse, the singer goes out to fight knowing he is going out to die. Pearse and his heroic comrades played out this plot, knowingly, to the death.

'You never know who is out front. So if there is only one person in the audience, give it everything you've got,' Brendan Smith had taught me. Though *The Singer* did only fairly well, this little play would lead to the most far-reaching changes in my life, and influence tens of thousands of other lives, because of who was in the audience one Easter night. His name was Eugene P. Foley. With US Senator Eugene McCarthy, he had brought a small group of American political leaders as an unofficial delegation to the 1916 celebrations. Gene Foley was Assistant Secretary of Commerce, and first Director of the Small Business Administration, in the Johnson administration. He was born in Minnesota, into a large Irish-American family that had been captivated by the 1930s Abbey Theatre American tours. The performances planted a seed in Gene Foley and his siblings that would grow into a love for theatre in general, ours in particular. I found in them a family of friends. Without Gene's help and friendship, I would never have moved to America to live and work.

Gene and his group came backstage to see us. Aideen O'Kelly, who played opposite me in *The Singer*, and I joined them later in Groome's. Our conversation, arguments and vision for the Abbey's role in our lives, Ireland and the world — not to mention Aideen's beauty — captivated Gene. (Though Aideen and I were, by this time, really good friends and colleagues, I had at one time fallen heavily in love with this beautiful person and actress.) Gene's group sat on the government viewing-stand for the official Easter Rising march-past and were wined and dined with the powerful, but Gene told me again and again, over the years, that the performance and the talks with us in Groome's were the highlight of the visit. He cancelled a speech he was to have made in England to see us and *The Singer* twice more.

Walter Macken, after a dress rehearsal for *The Singer*, told me that he liked what I was doing, but that I needed 'more fire in my belly'. He must have thought I found it. Shortly afterwards, he told me that, in the first play to be produced at the new Abbey, I would be cast as Fluther Good, the great male character role, in *The Plough and the Stars*. I told him I would prefer to stay in the Covey, that I had another five years in that part and would grow further in it. Equally important, Phil O'Flynn and Angela would be shattered. 'Phil is Fluther and can have twenty more years in it,' I told Wally.

Wally said, 'Vincent, if we are ever going to change the Abbey, we have to begin breaking the old ways of doing our famous plays. You'll play Fluther, Phil will play Uncle Peter, and Angela won't play Rosie, she'll play Mrs Gogan.'

Phil and Angela were shattered. They thought we should refuse. They were pretty pissed off that I wouldn't agree. I hated giving up the Covey, but I was dead against opposing Wally's first decision as Artistic Advisor, which I disagreed with in particular, but applauded in principle. 'There is no good in feeding a dog and barking yourself,' I told Phil and Angela. They didn't think it was funny!

I can't leave the Queen's Theatre without paying tribute to a few more of the scores of people who added to my work and slow growth. I have only good memories of Mary Kimberley, a dancer in the earlier pantomimes who had talent, personality, and letter-writing skills. There was Joe Ellis, who succeeded Sean Mooney as stage manager of the Abbey. He gave me support at every turn — though he didn't return Father Luke's chair, which I had lent him for the Abbey! I forgive him for that because it spawned a great story. Then there was an American girl who brought Pat Laffan and me to our first Thanksgiving dinner, in a house near the banks of the Royal Canal. She wrote me a poem in memory of the time she seduced me.

There is one other girl. She shall be nameless. What I failed to do with her, for her, troubles me still. She was married. She knew about my marriage, and my reputation. She had liked me from the start, but had grown to respect me. She wanted me to give her a child. She loved her husband very much, only him. They couldn't have a baby — he couldn't. He did not know that. She had taken every test that money could buy at the time, and she could have a baby. Well, would I? I talked to her for a long time. I couldn't, I couldn't in cold blood. The phrase still plays in my head. I was flattered, honoured, I told her; but I couldn't. She cried very little. I never saw her again. I don't know if they ever had children. The irony is that I couldn't because she told me. She couldn't without telling me.

Finally, in my Queen's Follies, Mr Ernest Blythe. When the Andrews salary scale was made known, my new salary showed very little improvement over my old one. My salary had been very much ahead of my years of service at the Abbey. It had taken into account my professional experience before joining the company, a unique situation at the Abbey for many years. I asked for a meeting, on a personal matter, with my boss. The meeting was short and sweet. I made my case for a higher salary. My salary would reflect my experience and the new salary scale, he said. 'I never considered it being otherwise,' he added.

'What's an atheist like you doing in a place like this?' asked Paddy Long, when I asked him to help Sinéad Cusack with stage management for the one and only performance of *Ross* at Maynooth College. Here, young Catholic males were prepared for the priesthood. I was the latest in a line of Abbey actors invited to direct the annual production there; I had directed Terence Rattigan's drama about Lawrence of Arabia.

The performance was in the mid-afternoon. The three of us drove down in my green Peugeot. Joe Ellis, the Abbey stage manager, had lent me the props, including a .45 revolver. It was illegal for us to possess or transport this weapon, even for stage purposes and with no ammunition, so I had it concealed under the driver's seat.

The play went beautifully. On the way back to Dublin, we stopped for dinner at a pub/restaurant in Lucan that our crowd frequented when we had the money — and sometimes when we hadn't: Bob, who owned the place, was very understanding! By the time dinner was over, I was extremely tired. I asked Paddy to drive home; he liked to, I knew. I sat in the back with Sinéad and promptly fell asleep.

I woke to Paddy slamming on the brakes and hissing urgently, 'Vincent, wake up! Have you your tax and insurance? We've been stopped by a motorcycle cop. Give me your driving licence, mine's out of date!'

I had just time to say, 'Tell him you're me, and you'll bring it to the police station, and the tax and insurance are in the post!' and flop back in the seat, pretending to be asleep. What was really worrying me was that the policeman might search the car and find the gun. Not only would I be in trouble; Joe Ellis would lose his licence to keep guns, which were irreplaceable props in many of our plays. He could even lose his job for lending me one.

Paddy wound down the window, and the huge policeman leaned on the roof of the car. 'Your car tax is overdue,' he said in his rich country accent.

'It's in the post,' replied Paddy in his high-pitched Dublin.

'Have you your insurance?'

'I sent it in with the tax things.'

'Show me your driving licence.'

'It's at home, Officer,' said Paddy, very politely. 'I'll bring it to the station tomorrow morning.'

'What's your name?' asked the policeman.

'Vincent Dowling,' said Paddy casually.

'Where do you live?'

'24 Shanowen Road,' said Paddy, as if he had lived there all his life. I felt really proud of him.

'What station will you show your licence in?' asked the policeman.

'... Drumcondra — Griffith Avenue,' said Paddy quickly, after a tiny hesitation.

'Drive carefully, now!' said the policeman. He swung his leg over his motorbike, kicked it into life and roared off!

'Jesus, Mary and Joseph,' gasped Paddy, 'that was a near one! I wasn't sure if Santry or Griffith Avenue was nearest you!'

In those days you had about ten days, I think, to show your licence, insurance and tax receipt. But the next morning I was leaving to adjudicate Kilmuckridge Drama Festival — and, of course, I forgot all about it.

A few weeks later I was summoned to the District Court for failure to show driving licence and tax and insurance certificates. The hearing was on a dress rehearsal morning, so I asked Tommy O'Connor, a Groome's and Fianna Fáil lawyer (not to be confused with my Soundtrack partner of the same name), if he would act for me, and gave him my documents.

The night the hearing had taken place, I was in Groome's. 'You owe me a pound,' said Tommy. 'You were lucky Donagh MacDonagh was the judge.' Not only was Donagh a regular at Groome's; he had worked with Jack and me on *Let Freedom Ring*. That's Ireland for you!

'When he came to your case, Donagh asked, "Is that Vincent Dowling the Abbey actor?" Which,' said Tommy, 'gave me the cue to explain why you weren't in court and why you had failed to bring the documents to the station. Donagh said that, while he understood the pressures you were under, he was sure that Mr Dowling would be happy to contribute a pound to people less fortunate than he, by way of the court poor-box!'

As I was thanking Tommy he interrupted me, dismissing any need for thanks or payment. 'An extraordinary thing happened than. As I left the court, the policeman who had brought the charge came up to me. He said he was sorry to bother me, and he understood the case was over, but there was something strange going on; the accused Vincent Dowling wasn't the Abbey actor! I told him that of course you were. "He can't be," the policeman insisted. "I know Vincent Dowling the Abbey actor. If it had been that Vincent Dowling, I'd never have brought him to court in the first place!"'

Well, I explained the mystery to Tommy, which only increased his enjoyment of the whole event. A few days later I went into Store Street Police Station — to which, I had discovered, the cop belonged — and made a full confession to him.

'Thanks be to God, Vincent,' he said with feeling. 'I was really beginning to wonder was I losing my mind!'

I was able to repay Joe Ellis for lending me the gun, too, in a way that he loved. At the Kilmuckridge Drama Festival, I had been knocked sideways by a wonderful production of *The Playboy of the Western World*, which swept the board in practically every category. It was directed by a young priest, Father O'Regan, from a Co. Wexford hamlet called Monaseed. Everything in that production, down to the draught stout drunk by the actors in the little shebeen, was as authentic as the country actors and actresses.

'You must have used real stout,' I said to the young priest. 'That's one thing you can't fake; we use Coke, but it looks like Coke. But drinking real liquor on stage is a bad idea. I don't approve of it, artistically.'

'But it *was* Coke! We tried everything. It was driving me nuts. Eventually I tracked down a girl who works as a chemist in a brewery, and I told her what I wanted. She made up some stuff; you just pour the Coke on top of it, and it looks exactly like the real thing!' said Father O'Regan, with justifiable but ungodly pride.

I got Joe Ellis the formula. As usual, he promised to get Father Luke's chair to Mammy.

'It's really coming this time,' I told Mammy, who had been anxiously enquiring about it, for the twentieth time.

'So is Christmas,' she said. 'Again!'

The last night at the Queen's was really a non-event. In our imaginations we were looking across Butt Bridge, over the River Liffey and up Abbey Street, to 18 July and the opening of the new Abbey, almost on the anniversary of the burning of the old Abbey fifteen years earlier. Someone had set fire to a few small pieces of wood of some sort from the Queen's building. A metaphor, I suppose. It was smouldering on the footpath opposite the dress circle steps.

Sinéad Cusack, who was with me, said suddenly, 'I'm going to miss the Queen's. This is where I've spent my whole life as an actress.' Her whole life as an actress was a little over six months, but I sympathised. Though I was happy to be going to the new Abbey, my life as an Abbey actor, nearly thirteen years, had been spent working in the Queen's. I wouldn't have exchanged the experience 'for all the tea in China'. Still, it was time to move on.

In that June of 1966, even before we opened the new Abbey, Wally gave Phil and me warning that he was not the man to run the Abbey, and that he would soon have to make it public. He promised us he would continue to act as Artistic Advisor and stay on the Board until a new government director was found.

'Ring-a-ring-a-rosy, a pocket full of posies, asha! asha! we all fall down!' That was our chant as children as we held hands in the sea, dancing round in a circle, splashing down in the cold water on the last word. But there was no time for games. First there was a Grand Opening — in fact, a week of grandish openings. Rather than a play, Wally had chosen to present a dramatisation of the Abbey's history and work. He called it *Recall the Years*. This would be followed by Frank Dermody's new production of Sean O'Casey's masterpiece *The Plough and the Stars*, with Vincent Dowling as Fluther Good.

These two historic happenings notwithstanding, we had to mobilise our political forces, and without delay.

15

The New Abbey

I'm savng my money for to go to Shakespeare

In the presence of President de Valera and a distinguished gathering, Seaghan Barlow, stage carpenter, now eighty-six years old, stood onstage audience left with a great drumstick in hand and struck the Abbey gong thrice. The curtain rose on *Recall the Years* by Walter Macken, a series of vignettes dramatising highlights of the Abbey's history, the people and plays who made it — the first public performance in the new Abbey Theatre. It was 18 July 1966.

Some might say my prayers had been answered, others that 'the devil's children have their father's luck'; either way, after fifteen years in the company, my multiple roles in *Recall the Years* included one scene as Christy Mahon in *The Playboy of the Western World*. Another of my parts was one of the devils/merchants in Yeats's *The Countess Cathleen*. Not sixty years earlier, nationalists and Catholic Churchmen had condemned these plays as immoral, degenerate, an insult to a Catholic Irish nation. That night they were there to honour the vision, courage and talent of the men who had written them and the actors who played them. I found it hopeful.

The new theatre was small, but not intimate. It took us a while to realise this fully. We were delighted with the comfortable blue seats, the wide passages and aisles between them; the spacious, winged, deep stage; the motorised elevators that, at a touch of a button, gave us a thrust stage, an orchestra pit, different levels from towering heights to sunken troughs of varying sizes. We had the latest in light and sound, follow spots and recording spaces; a large control room with perfect views of the stage; and easy access to the lighting instruments by catwalks. The whole ceiling of the auditorium had baffled acoustic sections that could be raised or lowered electrically. The proscenium opening could be widened and narrowed at will.

For the actors, there was the Green Room and new dressing-rooms, with proper mirrors and coloured lights, dressing-tables with drawers that locked, clean showers, basins and toilets. Yes, Miss Sheridan (who had died, alone), the actors no longer had 'no soap'! In every dressing-room there were racks to hang costumes, speakers that relayed the calls and the performance, and telephones linking one room to another. Of course, each actor's name was in the programme in the language of his or her choice! Joe Ellis had his office under the stage, complete with Father Donnellan's chair, which would be returned to my mother as soon as he had a truck going 'that way'; she really wanted it back!

To top it all, there was a large rehearsal room with glass on two sides, opening out to a roof garden on one side and overlooking Marlborough Street on the other. We even had a table-tennis table, with equipment supplied by the management. What more could any actors ask?

How about a theatre that worked better for the plays, for those doing them and those watching them — a theatre with adequate office, workshop and storage space? In fairness to Michael Scott, he wasn't given much land to work with, and he did build in a second experimental theatre, the Peacock, a gem.

It was bad enough that I had to refuse a good role in Joseph Strick's film of *Ulysses* to do Fluther Good in the first play at the new Abbey, without Angela Newman trying to shaft me in *The Plough and the Stars*. In the opening scene between Fluther and Mrs Gogan, Angela, subtle but savage, stayed upstage of me, constantly moving, doing distracting stage business, all of it in character but at exactly the wrong time for me. I quickly became aware of it on the first night. I did nothing except redouble the intensity of my concentration on the door lock that I actually repaired in the course of the scene. Fortunately, knowing that I have two left hands, neither of them used to useful manual work, I had researched and practised the carpentry until it was second nature. I refused to let her, as Fluther says to the Covey, 'flutter a feather of Fluther's'.

I didn't feel angry with Angela. She was doing it out of loyalty to Philip, in protest at Wally Macken's casting me as Fluther, and doing it with artistry. All in all, I had a totally invigorating experience with the role.

In the next play I played God. Typecasting, Brenda called it. It was a modern version of the Everyman morality play. Written by the North of Ireland poet Louis MacNeice, it is set in a television studio; God is the director, up in a control room. It is a play with music, a lot of very clever and moving parodies of famous folk songs. I have always wanted to do it again and never have, though Louis MacNeice's widow Hedley gave me permission. She also, later, allowed me to use some of his poems in a show that Brendan Kennelly and I titled *Irishmen Make Lousy Lovers?* Sinéad Cusack, who was a student at UCD at the time, introduced me to MacNeice's poetry. I was really sorry that MacNeice — who had felt that Dublin rejected him — had not lived to see his play done with such love in Dublin.

It was Pat Layde, brilliant in the MacNeice play, who suggested that we approach Mícheál Ó hAodha (Michael Hayes) to replace Walter Macken as government appointee on the Abbey Board. He was Director of Productions at Radio Éireann. Third from the top of the administrative aerial, he was a director, writer, and administrator who spoke and wrote in Irish and English. Pat said he was very well versed in theatre and really loved it.

I had reservations — not because I didn't like or respect him, but because I was concerned that he might have a civil service mentality, a problem common in Radio Éireann and not unknown at the Abbey. He was after all, a civil servant, as was his boss, Roibeárd Ó Faracháin, which would give us two senior civil servants from the same department, the Department of Post and Telegraphs. Dr Séamus Wilmot, the other government appointee on the Abbey Board, was also a kind of civil servant, being Secretary of the National University, though our crowd at the Abbey liked Séamus and felt he was the most sympathetic to the Players. Gabriel Fallon, a former part-time Abbey actor, was also an ex-civil servant. Blythe, an ex-Minister of Finance, had helped create the Irish Civil Service mentality. We felt we needed at least one Board member from a more freebooting background.

I couldn't immediately name someone better, so I went to see Mícheál Ó hAodha and realised at once that he was no pushover. There was no implied promise that he would be our man if we could get him appointed. He would, I felt, be a fair, unafraid, if unadventurous advocate for what he thought was right. He wouldn't be looking for the job of Artistic Advisor, which we had not given up hope would one day soon change to Artistic Director. We were confident that, with the Andrews award and the composition of the new shareholders group, we, the Players, would have influence on that appointment. We still had a lot to learn about Blythe.

When Walter Macken had announced his intention to resign as soon as a new government director was appointed, it quickly became clear that Blythe's man for the job of Artistic Advisor would be Tomás Mac Anna. I, just as quickly, emerged as the Players' candidate. I had the confidence of a majority of the actors, maybe all. Nobody openly opposed me. We mobilised our shareholders, Groome's and government friends, Abbey staff and Players to lobby the Abbey Board. I know that Brian Lenihan and some of his contemporaries in government lobbied for me. I bearded the lion in his den and made my case for the job to Mr Blythe, expounding a well-thought-out, practical policy for English- and Irish-language theatre. I wooed each Board member, and told Gabriel Fallon that if he didn't vote with his actor's conscience and oppose Blythe he was damned!

Tomás Mac Anna, of course, had been a key figure in the Abbey for the previous seventeen years. He was not only a producer, writer, adapter of plays into Irish, set designer and director of many Irish Christmas pantos; he had also been chiefly responsible for directing most of the plays in Irish since entering the Abbey in 1947. He had also written and presented the pageant at Croke Park commemorating the 1916 Easter Rising. The Players felt he was Blythe's man and not an actor's director.

Philip O'Flynn warned me that being seen so often and so openly with Sinéad could sink my chances. I refused even to entertain the thought of giving her up, and continued to lobby up to the hour before the decisive Board meeting. Before the night was out, I knew I had lost.

Other factors that mitigated against me were my lack of Irish and of any directing experience in the Abbey. The directors didn't know, though the actors did, that Dermody and Mac Anna had encouraged me — even depended on me — to involve myself in directing the other actors in their productions. But what really beat me was Blythe. He still ruled his Board, and he had shuttered out the shareholders from the appointment process. He was to lose both these powers in the future, as a result of the Players' Council's influence on the shareholders.

Tomás Mac Anna was appointed Artistic Director as from December 1966. Of course, I was disappointed at not getting the job, but not for long. I had no hard feelings for Tomás, nor he for me. On the contrary, he always cast me well, and he would offer me my first Abbey directing job.

If the Queen's Theatre was a movie in black and white, the New Abbey was in glorious technicolor! That year saw the last Irish pantomime on the Abbey main stage, *Ferdinand agus an Rionn Óg*. It was televised by RTÉ. I played a Chinese character named Sin Sin — a bilingual joke. I sang the pop song 'Bang Bang' in Irish, with a Chinese accent. Somebody said I was playing a 'rice Paddy'!

One day Jack said to me, apropos of nothing, as he was wont to do, 'We all have hundreds of masks, one for each person we know. Subconsciously, we slip on the appropriate mask every time we meet a particular person. It doesn't matter if we haven't seen them for fifty years.'

I knew it was true. I began to realise that I could be in a group of, say, ten people, three of them women with whom I had some intimate relationship, and present to each of them the 'mask' or 'message' that he or she expected. The years playing Ignatius Kelly in John McCann's plays hadn't been entirely wasted for me, on or off stage! We try to reveal our real selves on stage; off stage, we try to hide our real selves, pass off acceptable versions to others.

Off stage, in the ordinary world, I was acting all the time, playing leading roles in far too many situations and settings. My *real* life was lived on the stages of the new Abbey Theatre and the Peacock. I was beginning to realise, with the help of Dermody and my brother Jack, that I only really felt whole during the creative process and practice of acting.

24 Shanowen Road, Santry, was where I lived a home life that was part of my 'ordinary' life. I played the chief provider and concerned, loving father of four beautiful young daughters. Though I lived there (sometimes arriving back in the early morning), I was not cohabiting with my wife. On Sundays I breakfasted with the family and went driving with my daughters, and even sometimes with their maternal grandfather. During Brenda's infrequent theatrical engagements, I played a much larger role in the domestic life and, in general, enjoyed it and did it well.

After Groome's Hotel, the centre of my social life was P.J. Molloy and Co., which was situated on a corner of Talbot Street, one block up from Amiens Street Railway Station. The premises consisted of a fine old working-men's public bar, with a long mahogany counter and a private snug for female customers, and a modern, comfortable lounge with its own small bar, entrance and round smoked-glass window. Not only did the charming, intelligent landlord, P.J. Carroll, keep and serve only the finest drinks and bar food, but his lounge housed a superb collection of recent paintings by Ireland's best painters. P.J.'s was the best pub in Dublin — nay, the world — for me! Only Groome's at its best drew as select a clientele — painters, actors, writers, journalists, broadcasters, and interesting 'respectable' people.

P.J.'s had an early-morning licence, which allowed it to open legally to thirsty workers from the markets. P.J. gave himself a licence to serve and drink with his friends after closing time at night, if he was in the mood. He mostly was. However, he had given me a rash promise that whenever I tapped on the circular glass window over the lounge bar and recited in clear tones 'Some boyo whistled '98 on Friday night in College Green', by Arnold Bax, the door would be opened to me and a reasonable number of my companions! In the very rare instance of an after-hours police raid, the customers retired to P.J.'s living quarters above. Women in the WC at such times were told to stay where they were and to refrain from flushing the toilet. My mother, on one occasion, walked out of the ladies' room into the arms of a startled young policeman; P.J. saved the situation by introducing her as his mother. Needless to say, P.J. kept his promise to me, and the Bax poem did its 'Open sesame' until Molloy's changed hands.

My love life, like Hemingway's Paris, was a moveable feast. It mostly took the form of heavy necking in my green Peugeot motor car, which had a CIP number-plate (Paddy Long said it should be pronounced 'kip') and a sliding roof to provide romantic moonlight effects. Otherwise, it was love *al fresco* in fields, in woods and by riversides, when weather permitted. It didn't often. A small hotel or B&B was an attractive alternative, when finances permitted, which was even less often. Some very good friends in better material circumstances, like Wesley and Helena Burrowes, were generous with their hospitality. But they lived in Avoca, too far away for any but rare visits.

My work life — that is, gainful employment, other than at the Abbey — was usually in or about Dublin. The exceptions were amateur drama festival adjudications. These could only be done when I was not performing in a play. The festivals, mostly in distant provincial venues, lasted one to two weeks, paid good fees for that time, and usually included comfortable board and lodgings. They also provided escape from Dublin. I, a thirteenth-generation Dubliner, loved my native city less and the countryside more; so it was, and would be, world without end.

Though I didn't realise it then, I was constantly walking, running, dancing, driving, weaving through all my lives, often on a thin tightrope, continually changing masks, and insulating, as well as I was able, one life from the other. Exhausting stuff!

Danny Cummins had got married some time earlier. Brenda hadn't done much, if any, work since Rachael was born. She had not, I think, taken up with anyone else. I guess she was pretty frustrated with life. Anyway, she began to get very edgy with me, sarcastic about Sinéad, goading me. I refused to be goaded, and my very coolness, as always, made Brenda angrier.

Then, one morning, she physically attacked me. I had to hold her down on the bed. She bit my arm quite savagely, badly breaking the skin. It was really painful, and I was frightened by this escalation of violence. I have always had a real horror of violence between a man and a woman — a direct result of my father's violent behaviour towards my mother. Brenda knew this. Many years before, after provocation, I had returned her a slap across the face. I was so shocked at doing this that I told her if she ever hit me again I would just leave. It was clear that I meant it.

This time I knew the children were outside our bedroom door. I reminded her that they could hear, and I told her that if she even laid a hand on me again, ever, I was going for good.

Next morning, she attacked me again. I took my clothes, washed and dressed in the bathroom, and packed a bag. I brought the children down to the front room and told them that I would have to go away, but that I loved them and would see them and take care of them.

It was raining heavily as I drove down Shanowen Road. The windscreen wipers, pushing the pouring rain across the windscreen, somehow opened my usually dry tear ducts, and — rare indeed for me — I cried.

I never went back to live at Shanowen Road.

Though I saw the children in those first years and took them out once a week, I made a terrible mistake. I acted on the totally false premise that, as I had lived, and lived better, without my father, brought up by my mother and sisters, the same would be true for my children — they would be better off with their mother. When I legally separated from Brenda, within the year, I gave her the Shanowen house, unconditionally, and complete custody of the children, except for very minor visiting rights. Only once, several years later, did Brenda very reluctantly allow Rachael and Valerie to stay with me for one weekend. I was then living with Olwen.

A new setting became the centre of my extraordinary 'ordinary' life. It was a one-room studio on the third floor of a large town-house, over looking Pembroke Lane. There, most nights, two long back gardens away, the seductive shadows of slim female forms moved behind drawn blinds like fairy dancers. They provided art objects in my humble, often lonely abode. I shared a bathroom and toilet with a severe-looking, private, middle-aged lady. We were mannerly, non-intrusive neighbours. We both lived alone, and both had occasional quiet visitors, mine somewhat more numerous and frequent. I don't think we ever met on the steps to or from the bathroom. She did use the clothes-horse there for airing, discreetly, articles of old-fashioned feminine clothing.

Good Abbey Theatre work would occupy me during 1967. In the first half of the year, we took a new Dermody production of *Long Day's Journey into Night* on the first Abbey tour of Ireland since before the war, so I had little time to brood on my triple loss of children, home and the top job at the Abbey. Later I played in Frank O'Connor and Hugh Hunt's play *The Invincibles*, and I was assistant director to Tomás Mac Anna on *Borstal Boy*, adapted by Frank McMahon from Brendan Behan's juvenile prison journal. In this play I played a seventeen-year-old Cockney homosexual sailor, which would earn me a part in a English prison film, made by an independent television company, playing a Londoner.

It is strange that Hugh Hunt's history of the Abbey Theatre does not even mention the *Long Day's Journey* tour of Ireland, North and South. It was completely successful, artistically and financially; and it pointed the way, as we on the Council intended it should, to the vital place that rural and provincial Ireland ought to hold in the real life of the National Theatre, the Abbey. My own experience of touring the fit-ups (unique in the Abbey at that time), and the few Abbey run-outs we had made, left me with no doubt that the Abbey needed to nourish and be nourished by its roots. The rural population's love and understanding of drama in general, and their theatre, the Abbey, in particular, was a resource for both. I believed that touring would increase and strengthen government support for our theatre.

At thirty-eight years of age, I had thought I would be moved from Edmund, the young consumptive, to the older brother Jamie. Phil was of course again playing the father, James Tyrone, and Angela was cast as his drug-addicted wife, Mary. Dermody suddenly decided that I would stay as Edmund, and Patrick Laffan, ten years my junior, would play the older Jamie. Deirdre Purcell, relatively new to the Abbey, was chosen to play the maid.

It was also decided to 'shave' the script. We were going to be playing mostly in halls, with the audiences on hard wooden seats; four and a quarter hours might prove a strain on audience attention and anatomies! All the cast were against the cuts in the script. We felt the repetition was a necessary ingredient in the greatness of the play. 'A spiral staircase going downward and inward,' an American critic had accurately called it. Dermody, always surprising, counted the words, lines, sentences and pages in the script, and came up with a tiny average number of words that needed to be shaved from each paragraph to bring the running time to just below four hours. Phil and I, who had already rehearsed for a total of twenty-two weeks for the earlier productions, did most of the cutting, though everyone had the right to offer cuts in their own parts. It worked perfectly. No one but the ghost of Eugene O'Neill would have missed what we left out.

I asked Joe Groome, Chairman of the Fianna Fáil party and close friend of the President, what he thought of asking Mr de Valera to give the cast and crew an official send-off from the presidential mansion in Phoenix Park. Joe thought it was very appropriate and told me to leave it to him. A few weeks later, the company and Board spent an afternoon with this friendly, interested, very humorous statesman, having afternoon tea in his great reception room, followed by photographs on the balcony, interspersed with intimate stories of his own early life teaching girls in a convent (there was always a nun present, until the morning after he got married!) He also gently poked fun at his former enemy Ernest Blythe. The newspaper and television reports that followed helped raise our theatrical venture into a triumphal tour.

Mayoral receptions, after-theatre parties, lunches, scenic tours, packed houses, newspaper headlines — old and new friends met us everywhere. Above and beyond anything we had experienced in Dublin or Paris was the quiet, intense emotional involvement all audiences had with the play. Again and again, the quality of the audience involvement took us, and them with us, below, above and beyond O'Neill's family, their own families, ourselves and our families, into life itself — suffering, laughter, love and forgiveness.

In Galway the Chief of Police, in his exuberance at seeing the play, wanted to give us a motorcycle escort out of town. On second thoughts, we realised it might be misinterpreted! The old Connemara faces of Tadhg Folan, Tommy Hughes, Jim Faherty, Festy Conlan and others were unforgettable as they tried to connect, and separate, the 'us' they knew so well and the spirits from another, yet a familiar world, that had lived in us for that eternity of four hours on the stage, and in their vivid, lonesome western imaginations. We knew, talking to them after the performances, that they had been part of the magic that Frank Dermody and Eugene O'Neill had created with us.

In Sligo, there was Paddy Dooney and his stories of travelling actors of his boyhood — the farm labourer who wouldn't go to the melodrama when the play-actors were in town, because 'I'm saving my money for to go to Shakespeare!' There was our arrival in the town to meet the mayor at the Town Hall at 3.00 p.m. The door was locked, no one there. Then a man on a bicycle, in dungarees and peaked cap, rode up and dismounted at the stone steps; took his bicycle clips off his ankles; nodded to us; produced a large key; opened the door and went in. 'Excuse me,' said Philip, 'we're here to meet the Mayor of Sligo.' 'I know,' he said. 'I'm the Mayor. Come in. You're welcome!' From the hotel below Knocknarea to the pub on the lake-shore where the waters lap from Innisfree, we were welcomed. Nor did Alan Barlow's 'melodeon' setting, designed to expand or retract depending on the size of the stage, lose anything of the play or the playing in the small Sligo Town Hall.

Athlone, the centre of Ireland: a young American Catholic priest, Father Jack Trahey from Chicago, doing his dissertation on Molière in Paris, came to see us. He was stunned by what he saw. I was invited to Loyola University as a Visiting Theatre Scholar for three months in 1969! Deirdre Purcell and Sinéad Cusack, who was visiting me, were later offered scholarships to study there. On my beloved Shannon River, I took the company to see the ancient ecclesiastic city of Clonmacnoise and its Dowling chapel.

We played Limerick and stayed at Todd Andrews's son's Eglington Hotel. Listowel — John B. Keane, Bryan MacMahon, and Maurice Walsh home country — was on our itinerary. Was there ever a small town with so many great writers? We met Roger, 'Lord Listowel', as John B. humorously introduced this town character. Roger, long coat and flat peaked cap, marched up and down like a sentry on guard duty, all the time he talked. He was the only soldier in the history of the Irish Army, he claimed, who was pensioned from the Army because he was shot and wounded in the chest by a sausage!

Though he was anxious to see our play, and we gave him a free ticket, Roger couldn't break the cautious old country habit of waiting till after 'half-time' to hear if the play is any good. Though the interval was at the end of Act II, it was in the beginning of Act III that there was a banging on the door of the hall, and I knew deep down it was Roger. It was!

After the show, in John B. Keane's bar, we heard the story of Roger's wounding by a sausage. He was an army cook, bare-chested under his white jacket, preparing and serving breakfast for a long line of hungry soldiers. He stabbed at a sizzling hot sausage with his long fork; the greasy thing shot up and stuck to his chest, burning him. The wound turned septic, there were complications. He was discharged with a pension on medical grounds — wounded in the chest by a sausage!

At the Cork Opera House, Sean O'Riada came to visit us in the dressing-room before the show. He didn't come to see the play. He told us a long joke about a monkey in a Sputnik. He was smoking a small European cigar, his face as white as ever. He was living and writing his music in West Cork. I always thought he had left Dublin at least partly because of Angela. Maybe not! He told us he was writing a Mass. I never saw him alive again. I doubt he was yet forty.

Fidelma Murphy's mother saw the performance. She thought Angela should move 'more Ibsen-like'! I thought Angela *was* Mary Tyrone. The play was better than I had seen it for her performance. Pat Laffan — though very different, of course, from T.P. — was also absolutely Jamie Tyrone. Deirdre Purcell, as the maid, was as real as good home-made brown bread. What I wouldn't give to have tapes of either production!

The most memorable place — and truly, they were all, without exception, terrific — was the tiny village of Carrickmore. The name means 'big rock'. It looked more like a hill rising up out of the surrounding flat fields. It is situated about an hour from the town of Omagh, in County Tyrone, where we stayed, because it had a hotel. Carrickmore didn't. It had a hall, though, which was used for dances, functions and performances. The hall was quite new; it had a very good stage, wings, dressing-rooms and decent chairs. The local Catholic curate, with his congregation, had raised the money to build and equip it. It could seat 1,200 people!

Over three nights, in that village of a little over three hundred people, 3,600 patrons sat transfixed on those wooden seats for four hours. They appreciated, applauded, and became part of this production of *Long Day's Journey into Night*. Every night one of us made a short speech of thanks. Angela didn't want to make one. Mine was always about Anew McMaster, who had kept alive the habit and love of great drama in Ireland with his Shakespearean company, playing in towns and villages like this. Some Irish university should award him an honorary doctorate — posthumously!

When the play was over, sipping whiskies, we watched the lights of long lines of motor cars disappearing in every direction, as far as the eye could see. They came from all over the North, we were told; some had come from Britain, wanting to see the Abbey Theatre in their home village.

In Omagh, I met Rita Dorman in the chemist's shop she and her husband owned. They had come to see the play, I was told. We talked a little about Portstewart and Coalisland. I liked Omagh. A friend, Ben Kiely of the *Irish Press*, a great admirer and reciter of Yeats's poems, is from there; I felt I had been there before, in his novels and stories about the place. He was in

Dublin. He probably liked it better than I did. I probably liked Omagh better than he did.

When we played the Theatre Royal in Waterford, I saw my sister Marie, her husband Jim and all my O'Hanlon nephews and nieces. I brought Sinéad Cusack over to see them one Sunday in Tramore, when she visited me on tour. They were very taken with her. My niece Judy, long afterwards, called her daughter Sinéad. The company stayed in a hotel in Dunmore East; the trees around it had the loudest blackbirds I have ever heard. They started at the crack of dawn. I used to fantasise about having a shotgun and waking them up when they were asleep!

On the first night, we had a party in the big hotel opposite the Theatre Royal. Father Phil O'Regan, who had won first prize from me for his direction of *Playboy*, was invited. He was quietly, you might say, impressed.

'How much would it cost to bring it to Monaseed?' he asked me. Monaseed is a hamlet outside Gorey in County Wexford.

'Bring what?' I said.

'Tonight's play!'

'Where would you put it on? The stairs wouldn't fit in the door of your little hall, don't talk about the whole set.'

'We'll build you a set that will. Exactly the same, but smaller. You know we can do it.'

'You'd better talk to Phil Kelly, our manager,' said I, and brought him over to Phil. Father O'Regan said he would charge one pound per seat — unheard-of at the Abbey in those days — and meet the figure Phil Kelly had quoted to cover salaries and royalties, which I would guess to be two hundred pounds.

For a half-mile round the little hall outside the hamlet of Monaseed, the fields were manned by locals who parked the legions of cars. The hall was full, but, as usual, we had requested that there should be no smoking.

The silence. The laughter. The gasps. The sobs. The link between each of us in the play, around the play, watching the play, Dermody who directed the play, Eugene O'Neill who wrote it, and the play itself, was steel. There was never anything like it in my life. This was where theatre began, belongs and lives, and where our national theatres need to keep coming back to, with plays and performances of this breadth and depth.

Gus Smith of Dublin's *Sunday Independent* attended the opening of the tour in Galway. In a long, thoughtful article and critique, he wrote:

'The newcomers to the cast were a revelation. I don't think I have ever seen Angela Newman scale such heights.... In the case of Patrick Laffan I have never seen this talented young actor performing so heroically as in this production.... Philip O'Flynn and Vincent Dowling reflect the sweeping power and poetry of their parts in impressive style.... There is a captivating cameo of the maid Kathleen, played by Deirdre Purcell.... This is Dermody's finest moment.... A memorable occasion, then, for Galway playgoers. They truly exploded the myth that serious drama is not the theatrical menu for the provinces. When the Abbey Company intimated some time ago that it planned a provincial tour with *Long Day's Journey into Night*, there were those who scoffed at the idea, claiming that the Abbey tour would be more success- ful if the company presented a comedy or peasant drama. I feel the way is now open for more such tours of Irish centres. How ironical it is that provin- cial Ireland is seeing one of the world's greatest dramas while in Dublin itself there is not a play of any magnitude being presented in the theatre.'

Not until the 1970s, when the Irish Theatre Company was formed, were there significant quality professional theatre tours to the provinces of the Irish Republic. I believe the Abbey paid dearly for its failure to engage in continual long tours into rural Ireland.

16

America, Here I Come

The upperosity of him!

'Vincent Dowling,' said Tomás Mac Anna with that clipped precision of his, 'if you will be my assistant director with special responsibility for the acting on my next production, in addition to casting you as Charlie, a Cockney sailor, one of the best parts, I will arrange that you will direct your first production for the Abbey Theatre in the New Year!'

I shudder to think how near I came to saying no. The production he referred to was an adaptation of Brendan Behan's juvenile prison memoir, *Borstal Boy*. Not only was it a joy to do, being a watershed in the history of what was and wasn't permissible on the Irish stage; it would earn me an ITV film role and directing opportunities at the Abbey, the Gate, the Gaiety, the Pergola in Florence and the Odeon in Paris, and it would change my life gloriously and permanently.

Tomás knew that he was going to need me, and didn't pretend otherwise. Still, not many directors, anywhere, would have been so open to a rival in such a recent fight for the artistic leadership of the theatre. I made one mistake: I should have said, 'Only if I am named as co-director,' which is what I was. I didn't, and that cost me in the short run — not in the long run, I think.

Besides, I would not have wanted to miss being a mate of any of those fifteen (was it?) teenage boys in short blue trousers, long socks and grey shirts. How many actors get a chance like that at thirty-eight years of age? Well, Paddy Long did, and he was over forty. Most of the male actors who would dominate the Irish — and to some extent the English — theatre, cinema, radio and television for decades were Borstal Boys, part of that wild, woolly, talented, disciplined team of young artists.

I was released, during the phenomenally successful run of this play, to go to London to play a Cockney prisoner in a TV movie starring Liam Redmond. If I had not been paid a penny, it would have been worth it to work with this great former Abbey actor. A week into rehearsals, I asked Liam if he was not going to use a British accent. His role, the prison warden, was described by another character as having been born in India and brought up in London. Liam had a deep, midland-Irish, educated drawl off stage.

'If they want me, this is the accent they get,' he told me. 'I've played generals, colonels, politicians, policemen, businessmen, bishops, lords and commoners. I've never used any but this accent you hear now, and never will.' Then he launched into:

Goodbye, Knockanure,
So cold and so poor,
Your church without a steeple,
And bitches and whores
Looking over half-doors
Making fun of respectable people.

The Abbey actors always credited Liam with writing that Sinéad had moved to London a few months earlier, leaving my ordinary life hollow and empty as a church at night when everyone is gone. Nobody would have known it, to see me at the theatre or at P.J.'s afterwards. P.J. knew, though. I realise, now, I was lovesick! So going to London was more about seeing her than about making a movie; but, as always, each life was full and separate.

In London I stayed with Pat Neville, a journalist friend, and his lady. He developed a very bad backache while I was there; I learned afterwards that he pulled a muscle trying to make love quietly — there was only a light partition between them and my makeshift bed. There's friendship!

I saw a lot of Sinéad; I even saw her a few times at her father's house in Islington. Sometimes Cyril was very understanding of my feelings for her: 'You and I have to help each other, Vincent,' he'd say. Other times he was very angry. Once, as I was saying good night to her at the top of the steps leading down to his basement flat, he came up, ordered her to go down, and produced a carving knife — 'I'll kill you, you bastard, if you don't leave my daughter alone!'

I knew how he felt. I didn't often let myself think about it: the gap in our ages; my marriage and children; an Abbey salary and financial responsibilities; her being over in London, me in Ireland; how much I missed her; how much I wanted her to have a career, but hated her being away ... the litany was endless! Physically, I am not a brave or rash person, but I said to Cyril, and meant it, 'You'd be doing me a favour.'

He looked at me for a moment. Deep down I felt he hadn't meant it. Both of us were in much the same boat. We muttered good-nights, and I turned and went back to Pat's place.

I had met Sinéad's mother, Maureen, who was also an actress in London. We talked about Sinéad and me. Of course, we came to no conclusion. I liked her. She listened as I stumbled on about how I was now legally separated. There was no divorce in Ireland, but maybe it would be possible and realistic for me to get a bigger flat or a cottage in the country. Sinéad wanted to act, and would undoubtedly do well. I was ready to make a commitment to her, and maybe we could make a life together.

Maureen phoned me before I left for Dublin. She told me frankly that, before we met, she had not thought too well of me or of the effect I was having on her daughter. After seeing me and talking to me, she realised that I cared deeply about Sinéad, saw how unhappy I was about it all. She asked me — begged me — to give her daughter a chance to make her own life, her career, and in time have a marriage and children. I knew she was right and that she was saying these things for the right reasons. Before we hung up, I had promised to try. Which I did, for a while. For a long, long while.

We certainly didn't move in together and start a new life. I didn't even leave my little flat on Herbert Place. Sinéad got more and more film and television work in England and in Ireland. Tomás Mac Anna was as good as his word, and in the New Year I started working on a production of Sean O'Casey's *The Shadow of a Gunman*.

On New Year's Eve, I had a few friends around for a meal. Sinéad was one of them. I had made up my mind that I was going to give up drink. I had lit a fire in my little recessed fireplace. At midnight we — I think there were four of us, Paddy Long one of them — drank a toast. The party broke up. I left some whiskey in my glass on the mantelpiece and drove Sinéad to Dalkey. When I got back, about an hour later, I did one very stupid and one very lucky thing. The stupid one: I had given up drink for the New Year, so I took my glass off the mantelpiece and flicked the whiskey in the fire. *Whoosh* — the flame flew up from the fire to my hand. Just in time, I flung the glass into the red ashes. I was scared silly. I decided I wasn't giving up drink!

That wasn't the lucky thing. The room was getting cold. Of course there was no central heating of any sort in the house, so I moved my little bed from the wall over beside the fire. For the rest of the winter that was where it stood, and it kept me warm — well, warmer.

One morning, I was struggling to find my way out of the traditional setting, moves, sounds of lines that I had lived with since coming to the Abbey, in every production of *Shadow* I had been in or seen. I was also struggling with getting my breakfast dishes into the kitchen, from my warm position on my bed beside the fire. Rather than move the bed, I found myself stepping onto and over it, dishes in both hands.

Of course! I realised. *This is the sort of thing O'Casey's characters lived with all the time!* As Jack always said: 'In O'Casey, look at the Dublin outside.' I did. I saw in my memory and imagination the stone wall and steps outside the window of the bitterly cold basement in Merrion Square into which I had been born. I heard the poor Dublin children chanting and playing their street games, and saw the fire, the beds as near as possible, the doors, walls and rat-holes.

The cold- and poverty-driven moves and actions of tenement life in Georgian Dublin circa 1920 — the blocking — came naturally as life. I knew I had hit gold. So did Tomás Mac Anna. He designed me exactly the basement I asked for. I had already cast the play with the actors I wanted. The actors, I knew, would follow me down Dermody-like daft avenues, in search of the twin pressures of what the play had said to O'Casey and what it would say to us today.

At the first rehearsal we made a rough recording of the play, for the Italian simultaneous translation that would be used in the Pergola Theatre in Florence, Italy. Yes! My first Abbey production was destined for the Florence International Festival of National Theatres. We would later record a more advanced rehearsal.

I had also made a decision that rocked the Abbey management and also the Dublin critical establishment: I would not expose this production — probably the first new look at the play since the original, forty-odd years earlier — to the Dublin critics until *after* it had played in Florence. 'The upperosity of him!' said Paddy Long. What I would do was open *Shadow* in Loughrea, Co. Galway, the first place in Ireland, outside Dublin, that the early Abbey had taken a play to. I knew Loughrea, the hall, the audience, and I loved the story of the visit that the Fay Brothers had led more than fifty years earlier.

This is how I heard the story:

Early in the century, after the Abbey's success in London, they brought a comedy to Loughrea. The full house sat silent, very silent, without a single laugh, through the play. At the end, the local priest who had organised the performance came on stage and thanked the actors on behalf of the people of Loughrea who had so enjoyed the work of this great company.

Frank Fay replied that he was sorry to contradict the priest, but the people had not enjoyed it. This was a comedy and they had not laughed once!

'That was out of respect,' the priest protested. 'They didn't think they should laugh at such famous actors.'

'Very well,' said Fay, 'we'll do it again, and they can laugh at us as much as they like!' There and then the Abbey Players did the play again, and everyone enjoyed it to the hilt!

We spent the day of the dress rehearsal with Lesley Scott lighting the set literally as our stage-management staff built it. We had a dress rehearsal at eight o'clock that night. It was attended by three Board members: Séamus Wilmot, Roibeárd Ó Faracháin and Gabriel Fallon, an O'Casey expert, a friend and a part-time player in the playwright's young days. I had agreed that John

Finnegan of Dublin's *Evening Herald* could attend, if he didn't write a critique, only a report. I knew he could be trusted.

The opening performance sang. The audience was enthralled. John Finnegan's report the following night made no secret of the fact that something wonderful had gone on in Loughrea. Florence, here we come!

But — whoa! not so fast! — the real drama took place after the dress rehearsal, the night before the opening, at the hotel in Ballinasloe. Phil and Angela waited up to have a drink with me and tell me what had happened. When they had arrived in for supper, the three directors had been in very solemn enclave. They had been weighing what they saw, and they were sadly determined to call the Abbey in the morning and advise Blythe they wanted the production cancelled. Briefly, what they had seen was not *The Shadow of a Gunman* as they knew it and as Sean O'Casey wrote it!

I have little doubt that, if the directors had spoken with any other two actors in the Abbey at that time, the production would have been cancelled. But Phil and Angela were more highly respected, as people and as players, than any other two in the company. They knew, and others agreed, that the play was being realised truthfully and more fully than they had ever seen or played it before. They were confident enough, and strong enough, to persuade the directors to 'wait and see'.

Our Aer Lingus flight from Dublin to Rome landed in Switzerland for just long enough to have a photograph of the company taken and to smoke a cigarette. Then we had a day and a night in Rome and a private audience with Pope Paul VI— private, that is, with about two hundred others. We presented him with a special copy of *The Playboy of the Western World*. There was no intentional irony in the choice of a play by the communist O'Casey! We went to St Peter's. The Sistine chapel was closed, at the time, to visitors. There was a reception at the home of the Irish Embassy's First Secretary, to which we were escorted by siren-wailing Italian police. We liked Rome and it liked us!

And we loved Florence. The Pergola Theatre was in a quiet street, around a corner from the Duomo; it was like a large, beautifully made, Italian Renaissance toy house. The wooden stage machines under the stage, in working order, were works of practical primitive art in themselves. The stage was just like good working stages the world over, but open the curtains and you looked out on an exquisite theatrical dream house. The rich seating on the sloped stalls; the mezzanine, an off-white, delicate, elongated horseshoe of small curtained boxes the whole way round. The third one from the stage on the actors' right was for me, the *regista* — the director.

Traditionally, the Abbey gave a paying audience not less than three acts for their money. *The Shadow of a Gunman* is a two-act, so it was decided that we should do John Synge's one-act *In the Shadow of the Glen* as a curtain-raiser. It was directed by Frank Dermody. We always talked of the two plays together as 'the two *Shadows*'.

My Lady Luck, who seemed to have watched over me from Day One of this production, saved me again. The day we arrived, as I was going over the schedule with the stage manager and staff, I mentioned something about the curtain-raiser — would we rehearse them in order of showing?

'Oh, yes,' he told me, 'your play first!'

'No,' I explained; 'my play, the longer one, always goes on last.'

He was appalled. 'No. Absolutely *no*! The audience in Italy would be outraged. The big play must be first!'

I got Phil Kelly, the manager. He agreed that when in Rome, or Florence, we must do ... et cetera! So *Gunman* went first. It went perfectly. The simultaneous translation by two brilliant, pretty girls must have been perfect. We never even lost a laugh! During *The Shadow of the Glen*, however, at what would have been our second act, the translation system broke down!

The souvenir programme records the superb cast and production team. Besides *regia* — directing — I am credited with playing '*secondo ausiliario*'. I didn't. Our manager Phil Kelly played it, to allow me to watch my first production from out front.

The production was truly a smash hit with everyone in the audience, on stage and backstage. Well, out of thirty reviews nationwide, twenty-nine were raves, one mildly critical. One reviewer said, 'The direction was like salt in soup. You can taste it but you can't see it!'

The night before the opening, a party was given for the company. In a castle atop a hill, outside the city, lived an Italian prince who had married a beautiful Irish girl. The girl, our hostess, had been one of a very successful group of models in a Dublin agency where my daughter Bairbre did a lot of work as a child. These girls were all wonderful to Bairbre, and very nice to me — I usually brought her to and from shows.

I arrived at the party very tired from the rehearsal and from working with the translators. At the first opportunity, I found a quiet sitting-room, sat down in an armchair, and — as I could always do — went fast asleep for a few minutes and woke up refreshed.

I woke to the sound of a lovely, very English female voice. I opened my eyes. Instantly awake, I saw elegant boots, a dark-purple skirt swinging gently about them. I looked up along a cloak into a classically beautiful Nordic face, slightly tanned and surrounded by glistening natural-blonde hair. She was another guest at the party, and her name was Kristin Jameson. Part Irish, part Norwegian, she looked every inch the part — Irish enough to be attracted to trouble, Norwegian enough to control it! I fell instantly in love with her. She was studying painting in Florence. She became friend and guide to Pat Laffan and me during the remainder of our stay, and drove us to Rome — she had her own small car. There she put us in the hands of two delicate, exquisite aunts, on her Norwegian side, at the Villa Norden. They had turned their villa into the most elegant guest-house I have seen in the world! Pat Laffan and I looked out from our princely apartment over the Basilica of St Peter. Kristin, alas, left the next day for Florence.

Pat and I seemed to exude some kind of glow. Wherever we went, the next few days, people were drawn to our light. Our glasses flowed with bubbling red champagne. The world of man, which I almost always hugely enjoy, never seemed more full of promise and light. Truly, I felt I was astride the moon.

In Catalonian Spain, if we didn't fall off the moon, we barely hung on — principally because we hit on Paddy's Bar in Sitges. We arrived there the day it opened for the season. We spent too much time there, like many of the other Irish visiting Spain for sun, song, señoritas, cheap liquor and cigarettes. We, who usually had to watch our money like Scrooges in a credit squeeze, were buying drinks 'for the house'. Ten shillings a round! We couldn't afford not to drink! Fortunately we were well fed and cheaply housed in a good hotel run by a Catalonian, Sobre by name, but not in politics. He was an ardent nationalist, not a comfortable thing to be in Franco's Spain.

As a treat for us, Sobre drove us forty kilometres into the mountains for 'a very special dinner'. The only entrée on offer was rabbit — the only thing I won't eat! Halfway home, at midnight, we were stopped by a Fascist soldier at gunpoint. Sobre was offered two choices: drive to Sitges and back immediately to get some identity document (he had three with him); or go to jail on the spot! We went to Sitges and back, and to Sitges again, before we slept.

We saw a bullfight in Barcelona. Interest in the opening rituals turned to disgust. Sorry, Mr Hemingway! We got so drunk in Paddy's Bar, one night, that the next morning we returned, still drunk, and warned the people to make for the high ground — God was going to send another flood! That is the nearest I got, ever, to the DTs. I'm lucky. That experience scared me off!

Having spent my last pesos on presents, I had no money to buy a drink on the planes from Barcelona to London, London to Dublin. When I met Sinéad, she told me she was going out with a young actor in the Abbey, Donal McCann. Home is the hero!

So Sinéad was dating a young single actor, much more 'suitable' than I. Why couldn't I leave it at that? Was it that I couldn't bear to lose? Partly, though even in retrospect only a tiny part. The biggest part was that I had built my own prison — a premise: I had found the perfect match, the perfect person in the world for me, the person I was made for. It was only a matter of waiting. In the meantime she was getting nearer her majority. Not much nearer, but time flies. Her career was taking shape; my directing future was doing likewise. We would soon be financially able to set up house together. That was a reasonable hope, I thought! The driving force was, of course, feeling. I felt certain that I was in love, that I loved her, and that she loved me. Feeling doesn't necessarily make it so! Once again I was living on false premises, and Sinéad and I returned to our old ways together.

This was the beginning of more than two years of moving in circles emotionally, though career-wise in straight lines, and somehow managing to do both at the same time. She, Sinéad, was with me only a fraction of the time. Other times she was at her parents' home in Dalkey; in London; on location; working with other young and famous actors. My suspicions, jealousies, loneliness, tortured me. 'Iago touching her,' I wrote in a poem of the time. Behind my mild blue eyes, my green-eyed monster ate my insides. Then there would be a few hours or days of hope and happiness, a meeting, a letter, a phone call — and the circle began again.

Yet in the days, and the evening hours before midnight, I lived my real life — acting in the theatre, in television, in radio, even in film. My Florence *Shadow of a Gunman* was named Production of the Year! 'No *Gunman* will ever be done again that does not owe something to this one,' John Finnegan said — or words to that effect — in the *Evening Herald*. Of course that would not prove true, but it felt so good! I made some money and had some fun, in the midst of my emotional misery, making a Walt Disney movie on location at Sixmilebridge in Limerick. It starred the very young Kurt Russell and one of our Borstal Boys, Paddy Dawson. I played what they termed 'a heavy' — all 130 pounds of me. There were evenings in Dublin with Kurt's father, Bing; heartbreak in Galway, where Sinéad was on location. *It's all over for ever —* again ... and again!

When Tom Murphy's masterpiece *Famine* moved from the Peacock to the Abbey main stage, I took over from Eamonn Morrissey the twisted mind and body of the hunchback Micilín — a great part in a great play. During the run, there was the madness of a Sunday with Frank Grimes at the Merriman Festival; Siobhán McKenna reading *The Midnight Court*; meeting the sanity of Jack, Lelia Doolan, and Sean Mac Reammóin; pint after pint of black porter and, against Frank's much better judgement, driving dangerously to drop in on Sinéad on location! We find her horseback-riding in a meadow with a man, a film actor. I spend a nightmarish night in Gort. A hotel, empty courtyards, climbing walls, talking, singing, shouting at the moon. Then driving drunkenly back along country lanes to pick up Frank. Fall asleep on a fairy mound in the woods nearby.

Next night, back in Dublin, exploring my pain and anger in Micilín's twisted body and his anger. This Gort misadventure I didn't get over so quickly. Frank Grimes proved a loyal friend. My Brendan Smith Academy lessons saved my health, my career: Never drink before the show! Always eat enough good food to keep body and soul together, no more, no less! My weight dropped to 97 pounds in the next two months. Night after night, mostly alone, deep in self-pity, even after Groome's and P.J.'s I went to the market pubs, arrived home at daylight, slept all day most days. The play was the thing that kept me sane.

The cast list went up for *The Playboy of the Western World*. 'Christy Mahon — Vincent Dowling.' I took off again for the moon! It was to play at the Lyceum Theatre, the best venue at the Edinburgh Festival. I'll play the *Playboy* for the Abbey! 'All things come to those who wait,' the man said. The younger actors, Des Cave, Donal McCann, John Kavanagh, went round singing, to the air of the popular song:

> *Where have all the good parts gone?*
> *Gone to Dowling every one.*
> *When will they ever learn?*
> *When will they ever learn?*

At the first reading of the play — Tomás Mac Anna, dear old Tomás, directing — we reached the last line, which is 'I've lost him, surely. I've lost the only Playboy of the Western World.' As Aideen O'Kelly, playing Pegeen Mike, read, 'lost him, surely,' I chipped in with: 'You've lost the *oldest* Playboy of the Western World!'

The young actors organised a knockout table-tennis competition. They were streets ahead of me at the game. Somehow I reached the final — I had the easier passage there — and met young Donal McCann. He played like a Japanese champion, fast and hard; I play a gentle, childlike pitty-pat. They were flabbergasted: I won! There's life in the old dog still!

At Edinburgh we broke the box-office record at the Lyceum. The thrill of a lifetime: one of my idols came back to see me after the matinee — Miss Wendy Hiller, who played Eliza Doolittle in the movie of *Pygmalion* with Leslie Howard. Said the *Sunday Independent* of our production: 'It was a critical success and the cosmopolitan festival audience were singing the praises of Harry Brogan, Vincent Dowling, Aideen O'Kelly, and Eamon Kelly. [I add Maura O'Donnell as the Widow Quin.] The Abbey can henceforth cast a play acceptable to international audiences from its own company.'

In his summing-up for the year, Gus Smith said that Cyril Cusack in *The Shaughraun* was the best actor, mine was the best performance. Fair do's!

What Playboy had done in Edinburgh, *The Shaughraun* did for the Abbey in London, though both I and Cyril were decades older than the title roles we respectively played. What was it Blythe had said? 'Like Cyril, you'll be able to play juveniles at forty.'

I had one more first in '68. I directed my first production at the Gate Theatre, Tom Murphy's extraordinarily gripping and fascinating look deep into the minds of two *Orphans*. This was Phyllis Ryan's company offering for Brendan Smith's International Theatre Festival. At the Abbey, Madame Knebel from the Soviet Union directed *The Cherry Orchard* so economically in terms of sets, furniture and props, so truly in terms of actors, that I saw it and was changed. Cyril Cusack, John Kavanagh and cast were superb. Only Siobhán McKenna, for me, was out of place and time.

In 1969 Alan Simpson, founder of the Pike Theatre, chose *She Stoops to Conquer* for his first production as Artistic Advisor to the Abbey. Written by Irish-born Oliver Goldsmith, the play is traditionally set in England. Alan brought it home to the Irish midlands, in brilliant designs by Alan Barlow. It took on a new, immediate Irish life with Donal McCann at the Three Jolly Pigeons Inn. Patrick Layde as the Irish aquire, and Angela Newman as his outrageously funny and vulgar wife, brilliantly breathed Irish country air into Goldsmith's great comedy. Patrick Laffan, Aideen O'Kelly — who stooped to conquer him — Máire O'Neill and myself, were the two pairs of seriously funny lovers. My character's name was Hastings. In the late 60s, letters from England carried the message 'Hastings — beloved by tourists since 1066'. I adopted it as my own.

Little did I know, but a young woman from America, who saw the play and came back to our dressing-room with her parents, would marry me, and we would live, mostly, happily ever after! Her parents were Dan and Elsie O'Herlihy. I suppose I was introduced to their children, but I have no recollection of them.

John Bull's Other Island, Shaw's play about Ireland, is visionary, funny, painfully accurate theatre. It is difficult, too, but it provides dazzling parts for actors. Especially good are Broadbent, the Englishman infatuated with Ireland, and Larry Doyle, a disenchanted Irishman. I played Doyle; a charming English actor, Richard Gale, was a delightful Broadbent. He did, however, make alarming sounds as he did his vocal warm-ups before each performance! I never learned to master his routine, but I learned from Richard never to go on without doing vocal warm-ups. Sean Cotter directed. We had a ball and a success. John Finnegan — who worshipped at the shrine of Micheál Mac Liammóir, who had played Larry Doyle some years before me — was particularly impressed by my Larry.

Deirdre Purcell had accepted a scholarship to Loyola University in Chicago and was over there. Sinéad, on a short visit from London, was having dinner with me at the Roundwood Inn in the Wicklow Mountains. She had also been offered a scholarship to Loyola, but she told me she was not going to go. Her film career was developing and her agent had some things 'in the works'. It was a disappointment, no doubt about that, but not wholly unexpected. I was going at the end of May. I had arranged 'leave without pay' from July to September — which, unlike in the song, proved not to be a long, long time! June was an Abbey actor's great perk — a month's holiday with pay.

Borstal Boy had gone to Broadway! Michael Macaloney, the producer, found it was not viable to bring the whole Abbey Company. It was agreed that it would be 'the Abbey Theatre Production' and that Tomás Mac Anna would direct; from the cast, only the Older and Younger Behans and Charlie would go. Other roles would be cast in New York. Niall Tóibín as the older Behan, Frank Grimes, and I as the gentle homosexual Cockney, were to go. No, said American Equity; the two Behans are okay, but we can cast Cockney sailors from our own union members — and anyway, we already have a Vincent Dowling in our union!

I wanted to go as assistant director. But assistant directors are like vice-presidents: necessary on the ticket to get elected, an embarrassment at the White House. I cursed the fact that I had not insisted on being co-director. But don't weep over spilled theatre whiskey; there's plenty of water in it already!

What you lose on the swings, you gain on the roundabouts. I got to direct *Borstal Boy* myself, in Paris, with *She Stoops to Conquer*, to re-open the Odeon Theatre; it had had to be closed when Jean Louis Barrault was director, a year earlier, during the student riots. The Paris authorities, fearing more riots on a reopening, hoped that 'a rebel theatre with a play by a rebel author' might not rouse the rioters. Hence, the Abbey and Behan to the rescue! It did add a spice to the opening reception in this magnificent theatre, and to the opening performance! Happily, all the drama was on the stage, and we were the only actors.

Before leaving for America, I directed a new play by an interesting, promising playwright, who kept his promise — Tom Kilroy. It was on a fascinating subject: the Great O'Neill, an Irish prince raised in the court of Elizabeth I. He turned against her, nearly brought her down, and caused Essex to lose his head — literally! My interest in the Great O'Neill, whetted by Sean O'Faolain's book of that name and fostered by working with Tom Kilroy, a professor at Galway University, has only grown with the years.

It was to be my first directing job at the Peacock Theatre, an exciting challenge in itself. I set about getting a terrific Abbey cast and a famous Irish stage and screen actor, Joseph O'Connor, for the title role. Although I had worked with many of the actors, I had a number that were new to me, and I had a 'star'. Joseph had recently finished a prestigious series for BBC Television, *The Forsythe Saga*, and in film a major role in *Oliver*.

Kilroy's play was not in the Abbey's kitchen-or-thatched-cottage tradition. It was more like a Shakespearean history play. Acting had been my life, and still is; but I was finding that working with actors, helping them to realise other levels in themselves and let them come out truthfully, was even more fulfilling. Drawing the audience in, instead of 'going out to them'. Passing on what Frank Dermody had taught me. Joseph O'Connor said in an interview, among other things, that I allowed him and other actors the freedom to make fools of themselves in the search for their performances. I liked that. I practised, too, what I had learned from the fit-ups: the first part of the experience, for audiences, is buying the ticket. Your box office and ushers are the prologue to the play!

I had recorded as many *Kennedys of Castlerosse* scripts as I could get the writer, Lee Dunne, to write ahead. Lee was great. He would do anything possible to see that any one of us didn't lose money. We were actors; he had no money either. The money from that series, still the most popular piece on radio five days a week — TV couldn't knock it off its roost — was vital to my economic lifeline. Even with the Andrews award, we were still grossly underpaid.

I had bought, next door to P.J.'s, a large suitcase that would carry all I was bringing for my three-and-a-half-month stay in America. P.J. gave me a black leather briefcase. 'You can't walk into a university lecture with your papers in your fist!' he said. I carried that briefcase till it fell apart, and then replaced it with a replica — twice.

I was packed, I had done my medical exam, and I was awaiting my X-ray photo for a visa. Two days before departure, I got a call from the American Embassy to go and see the doctor again because of an unexplained spot on one lung. No visa unless it was explained! The Americans had, in those days, an X-ray wall in place against Irish TB.

My stomach in knots, I saw the doctor. Had I ever had TB? 'No!' There is nothing on your medical history form to account for it. 'I had pleurisy when I was ten, could that be it?' Yes, you nincompoop! Here's your X-ray. Go and get your visa. Good luck.

I didn't kiss him, but I could have!

Earlier I had gone to London, seen Sinéad, gone to a show and said goodbye. Odd: that part is hazy, but I clearly remember that I bought a light-blue zipped jacket and a pair of grey slacks with a knife-edge crease in Cecil Gee's, and a pair of shoes made of corduroy in Oxford Street. I thought they would look pretty sharp on me!

On 31 May 1969, I took off in the early afternoon on an Aer Lingus plane from Dublin for New York. I looked down on Shanowen Road, too high to see a soul, let alone my own little souls. The hostess brought me the *Evening Herald* early edition. Robert Briscoe, TD and several times Lord Mayor of Dublin, had died that morning. I had met him a couple of times; his son, Ben, I knew very well. But now I was looking forward to being met by my friend Eugene P. Foley, with whom I would stay in fashionable Larchmont, New York.

Then I'd go with him to Washington for the wedding of his niece, and renew my acquaintance with her sister Mary Pat, whom I had met at the Abbey and liked very much. Thence to Chicago — gangsterland, in my mind, and even more frightening than New York and D.C. Newspapers and magazines in Dublin, never mind my movie images, had me apprehensive about the violence in these cities. I wasn't telling anyone of these fears, and I wasn't showing it. I was an Abbey actor. I was going to open a new theatre with my production of *Orphans*. For my other production, I had selected *The Gingerman* by J.P. Donleavy. Oddly, though I felt the characters and plot would interest college students, it was the poetry of his dialogue that made me do it. Then I would do several public lecture programmes and teach a course in Shakespeare to a class of teachers at a university — I who had left school at sixteen years of age, two years before graduation! That tickled me.

It was night when Gene picked me up and drove to his home. There would be a supper party in progress, a small group of successful Irish-American neighbours to welcome me. Gene was a senior vice president, by this time, of Dreyfuss Inc., one of the biggest financial companies in America. He also had been Campaign Manager for Hubert Humphrey's presidential bid in New York State — one of the few states where he had won! All this and more Gene told me as we drove. 'If we had two Gene Foleys, Humphrey would be president!' Larry O'Brien, National Democratic Chairman, had said to me in the Abbey, when he visited us with Bing Crosby's widow.

It was a great party for a while, until Gene and I ran out of poems, and stories after supper, and continuous alcohol intake. Would I do something from an Abbey play? To Gene, and all the Foleys, being an Abbey actor was next in importance only to being the elected occupant of the White House.

I demurred — I didn't like to act, even at a party, with drink taken; but then I thought of an appropriate passage from *John Bull's Other Island* about drink, religion, Ireland and the Irish climate. Mr Shaw at his best!

Enough to say that, five minutes after I had finished Shaw to an almost-stony silence, Gene and I were alone at the party. His wife Fanny had been spared the embarrassment. She had gone to bed after supper was served, pleading the early start she had with the children going to school.

The next night, me in my dinner jacket, we went to the Waldorf Astoria Hotel for a thousand-dollar-a-plate dinner, a benefit to pay off Humphrey's debt for his failed attempt at the presidency. As we were going up the several floors to the Ballroom in the lift — which, in time, I learned to call the 'elevator' — Gene made an announcement to the elegant fat cats who could pay a thousand dollars for dinner without noticing it. 'Ladies and gentlemen, I would like you to know that you are riding in the same elevator with Mr Vincent Dowling of the world-famous Abbey Theatre!'

A tall, handsome, faultlessly groomed man, in the silence that followed the earth-shattering announcement, leaned towards me. 'Act!' he said, and exited as the lift door opened.

'Apart from that, Mrs Lincoln,' as the saying goes, 'how did you like the play?'

Actually, it was an amazing evening for everyone, let alone a Dublin jackeen a little over twenty-four hours in America. I met, shook hands and had one-on-one conversations with Edward Kennedy — brief; Edmund Muskie — substantial; and Hubert Humphrey — insincere, like a tired old actor in makeup, signing autographs at the stage door. I was and am an admirer of him as a politician; I just felt disappointed in the persona.

Senator Muskie I spent much of the evening with. I felt I would cast him as Lincoln, and, if I had a vote, give it to him for President of the United States. I also met the father of the young man in the elevator. His name was Dowling — Robert Dowling, a Broadway producer and owner of the Hotel Pierre. He asked me if I was the Dowling who had directed *The Shadow of a Gunman* in Dublin. I told him I was. 'The best production of an O'Casey play I have seen,' he said. I heard afterward he even said it behind my back!

This was June 1969, a year after Bobby had been assassinated. Teddy, last of the three, spoke from the stage of the Waldorf Astoria's plaster-moulded Ballroom. I, at Gene's table, was front and centre. Muskie and Humphrey both spoke well. There was an air of excitement even among this savvy, politically sophisticated gathering.

The excitement increased as the young, handsome Edward Kennedy, the hope of millions for a Democratic president to oust Nixon next time, came out and stood behind the podium set on the narrow apron of the stage, a few feet in front of me. The waiters, I noticed, for the first time stood quite still. You could hear the proverbial pin drop. His familiar Boston-Irish voice, for me, instantly conjured the young John F. Kennedy I had seen in Galway. I was drawn in completely, thrilling to every line.

Suddenly there was a sharp *crack*! Time stood still. The implications were heart-stopping. The 'waiters', all at once, had guns in hand. Above and around us, figures appeared from behind the heavily curtained areas, guns in every hand.

Then I saw a piece of plaster on the floor in front of the podium. Probably at the same moment, others saw it too. 'Jiminy Moses!' said Ted Kennedy, and he went on with his speech. A large lump of plaster moulding had chosen that moment to fall off the ornate ceiling of the Waldorf Astoria Ballroom on the last of the Kennedy sons.

I was still somewhat the worse for wear on the shuttle plane to Washington D.C. Maybe that's why I see it in my mind's eye as a movie montage. The Foleys, Mary Pat, and the Fearons, parents of the bride, make me one of the family.... Georgetown at night; Father Hartkie, the theatre priest; summer theatre in Olney, with Jim Waring the director.... A drink in an Irish bar with Gene; a man runs through followed by armed police, like something from the Marx Brothers. No one, save me, seems to notice.... My first American radio interview: a herd of performers to be interviewed; the lady host sweeps in ten seconds before the start. As the red light comes on, 'We have an Irish actor with us. Mr Vincent Dowling. Tell us the funniest Irish story that you know!' Live in Washington! I discard twenty dirty ones in no time flat. Brendan Behan joining in the rosary in hospital floats into my mind and saves my reputation. Charlie Parker, I think, was the next victim.... I see the X-rated movie *I Am Curious Yellow*; when a man on screen starts talking serious politics to a woman giving him oral sex, in spite of the money spent, I say 'Let's go, Mary Pat!' ... I see the last performance of Brian Friel's *Lovers*, with Art Carney and Dublin actors Anna Manahan, Fionnuala Flanagan and Eamonn Morrissey, at the National Theatre. A cast party afterwards at the Irish Embassy; the Ambassador, Gerard Fay, a son of one of the Abbey's Fay brothers, is the host. We chat for hours, arrange to meet in Dublin in the autumn. 'Vincent Dowling, this is Vincent Dowling' — I meet the American understudy for *Lovers*, the actor who kept me out of *Borstal Boy* on Broadway. At least he's older than I am!

I never liked the idea of tipping. I found it demeaning. Washington taught me it wasn't always so. There was a restaurant very near the National Theatre, with tables on the sidewalk; I'd been introduced to a pretty girl, and I invited her there for dinner. A couple of cocktails, wine with dinner, dessert, coming up to coffee — with almost no warning, she got sick. She just had time to turn to a potted evergreen beside the table! Our young black waiter took care of everything as though it had never happened. No one even noticed. 'Can you sit down and have a drink with us?' I asked him gratefully. 'No, sir,' he answered evenly, 'but you can tip me well!'

Gene brought me to the Shoreham Hotel. 'There's a political satirist here. I want you to hear him,' he said. 'Mark Russell, one of America's very best.'

He was standing at a piano, playing a little, expertly, and commenting on the events of the time — brilliant and effortlessly funny. Gene had told him about me, and he referred to the Irish actor in the audience. It reminded him that on his recent trip to Europe he had heard a speech by the Reverend Ian Paisley — a kind of leprechaun Hitler! He played on, wickedly funny about Republican President Nixon and about Gene Foley's Democrat friends. *Mark Russell*, I thought, *is a national treasure*. I met Mark, and talked, and was invited out by some of the forty or so people at the performance. I loved everyone, everyone loved me — or so I thought!

Gene and his wife Franny were standing a few yards from me in the elegant lobby, talking to three men so tall that Gene, a fine cut of a man, looked like Jack looking up at the beanstalk. I realised that there were unfriendly words passing between them.

I'll calm this, I thought. As I walked towards them, I heard the tallest of these 'dudes' — all carrying enormous ten-gallon hats, dressed in light, elegant American-cut suits of grey and grey-blue — say with a lazy, danger-ous Texan drawl: 'Ah don't cayah what yore friend is. Ah don't lahk his accent. Ah don't lahk his beard. Ah don't lahk his long hayah. And, most of all, Ah don't lahk the way he's laughin' at America!'

Before I had time to speak, Gene told me quietly and emphatically to wait for him outside. For once I had the sense not to argue, and did what I was told.

Outside, I ran out of sense. A limousine as long as Lent swept up to the entrance where I was kicking my heels. I saw it was full of black faces. What a relief, after those three bigoted beanstalks! I — this well-dressed white man — stepped forward and, without a by-your-leave, swung open the rear door and said with panache, 'Allow me, gentlemen. Welcome to Washington!'

As I introduced myself and explained my intrusion, they gave me their cards. They were presidents and vice-presidents of local trade unions in Chicago. They told me courteously and gently that they appreciated my welcome, but begged me, for my own safety, never again to approach a car full of strangers, white or black, at night! 'You could find yourself seriously dead,' one of them suggested. On hearing my story, Gene and Franny heartily agreed with the advice!

The taxi driver who took me to the airport for my plane to Chicago was Italian. He was a singer, he told me. I told him I was an actor and director.

Would I like to hear him sing a little opera aria?

Certainly, I would.

Would I mind hearing him on a record? It was safer, driving in Washington, for him to concentrate on the traffic.

That was fine, I said.

He uncovered a small record player on the seat beside him, put on a 45-rpm disc, started it and manually put the needle on the groove. While I lis-tened, he gave me a newspaper cutting over his shoulder; it was headed

'Washington's singing taxi driver'. When we arrived at the airport, he asked me if I might have any part for him in one of my productions; in case his bald patch made him look too old, he had a toupee! There and then he put it on and, kneeling up on the front seat, turned to let me admire it. I explained that I didn't work in D.C., but I told him that, if I ever did, I had his newspaper cutting. America, I was finding out, isn't Ireland!

Next stop Chicago!

17

Past Love – True Love?

When the Chinese water their horses in Lough Neagh

My life for the next three months would revolve principally round the Mullady Theater at Loyola University, 1500 North Sheridan, with Lake Michigan in its sights, and Bruno's, a small neighbourhood bar on the west side of Sheridan, directly opposite the university.

I had two casts of college students; one student was a Jesuit priest, and one was about to be. Father Jack Trahey SJ, who had brought me there, was Head of the Department and the new theatre, which my productions would open. I had a summer directing class of about eight, almost all teachers, which included two nuns, the priest and clerical student, two Jewish rabbinical students, and a black teacher from Marion, Indiana, more than a score of miles away. All the religious wore lay street clothes. I was using *Julius Caesar* to do scenes.

On three Sundays spread over my stay, I did public lecture programmes, accompanied by P.J.'s black briefcase, in the theatre auditorium. I talked about theatre in general, the Abbey and Dermody in particular; I told stories of plays, players, playwrights and critics, all laced with poems and passages of prose and drama. Interestingly for me, of all the poems of various kinds I recited, Yeats's short love poem 'Never give all the Heart' was the one most requested.

We rehearsed at Loyola five nights a week, and Saturday mornings. Directing classes were in the afternoons, two or three times a week. I went to various other classes whenever asked, which was often. There were lunches at conservative, business, art and Playboy clubs (white bunny tails in your face are not conducive to good digestion, but the food, drink and company were good) and receptions at Loyola and at other arts, educational, service and business organisations, continually. I was on every radio talk show, the best being Studs Turkel's, and I still have my Kupp Show cup to prove I was on the best television show too. Tony Bennett got his cup the same night. That show was a big deal. City and suburban newspapers interviewed me constantly. I loved it all. Everything — plays, programmes, classes, publicity, picnics and other community interaction — was fun, frequent and valuable for Loyola. I don't remember a bad day, or night, in the three months.

Deirdre Purcell (who was playing a heartbreaking Miss Frost in *The Gingerman* and assisting in the production of *Orphans*) and Rob Weckler, later her husband, were my constant guides, helpers, friends. She and the girls she shared a house with were like a family for me — sewed on buttons, mended tears and comforted lonely hearts. I had it bad, as we say, for one of them. Many's the night I walked the mile home alone from a party at their place, wondering why I was ever afraid of living in Chicago.

The night the American astronauts landed on the moon, I was at the Court Theatre, the University of Chicago's open-air stage, seeing an excellent *Richard III*. We went backstage to see the actors, and on television we saw the moon landing. Jack Trahey and I both felt there was something very right about being with Shakespeare that night.

'The bums at Bruno's' is how a small group of older local men always described themselves. 'Hey, Professor, why do you waste your time with bums like us?' they'd say.

'Because you are not bums, and because you are the best company in Chicago,' I'd answer, and mean it.

For me, it was like dropping in on a miniature Harry Hope's and the dreamers of *The Iceman Cometh*. In the afternoons, after classes, I would stop by Bruno's and have a beer, before going home for my afternoon nap, TV dinner and bath and heading out to rehearsal.

There was Harry, clearly the strongest personality: about fifty-five, looked and acted tough like Broderick Crawford, a heart as soft as a Frisbee landing. He talked about money that was going to be left to him, and how then he'd follow the sun.

The others, retired loners, lived in Harry's 'rooming house'. Bernie was a small, gentle, well-spoken, highly intelligent, interesting widower. I think he had been a clerk in the US Postal Service. The oldest of them, Anthony, was in his eighties. In Ireland we would call him a '*duine le Dia*' — a person with God; part of him lived in another world. Once a month he drew his Social Security, and no matter what Harry and Bernie did — going with him, watching the exits — he would escape them. Much later that night he would arrive at Bruno's, penniless for another month! They believed he spent it on 'whores'!

Bruno, a young, married, red-haired Italian, ran the bar and take-away liquor business. There I purchased my party drink, beer and Cutty Sark. I brought everyone who visited or met with me to Bruno's. Many of the audience followed me there after a performance.

What I really hated, and hate, about TV is that in spite of myself my eye is always drawn to it. So, in Bruno's, I took to sitting on a stool where I couldn't see it. Then, one night in August, Bruno said to me when I came in, 'You'll want to see the news, Vincent. There is a spot of trouble in your country.' It was the 'Bloody Sunday' carnage in Derry. I had watched Burntollet and the civil rights marches and protests, and supported them. My brother Sam, who then lived in Newry, north of the Border, was deeply involved in civil rights.

'How can the British be so stupid?' I said to my friends in Bruno's. 'Why are they always so stupid when it comes to Ireland? It isn't religion. That's only the tool used by people on both sides to keep the poor poor — fighting each other for crumbs, instead of uniting and fighting for their fair share through their trade unions and the ballot box. When will they learn?'

'When the Chinese water their horses in Lough Neagh,' my mother would say, 'which they will. It was prophesied by Saint Colmcille,' she'd say emphatically.

Mike Richardson standing, his right arm held up, his great black fist clenched; in his booming bass he preached, 'In the order of creation there is God — Mohammed — Buddha — John Wayne — myself — and all you other bums!' That was the only party piece I could ever get my good friend at Loyola to do. A big, black teacher/student with a classical handsome face, he was carrying too much weight, which I told him was a shame for such a handsome man. Mike laughed: 'Every morning I look in the mirror, I say, "Hi, beautiful, where are we going today?"'

Almost every night I had an Irish-style party in my apartment. American parties didn't, I found, follow the same pattern: drink, food, then everyone doing a party piece — song, poem, story, even dance or conjuring trick. Everyone in the cast, the directing class, the Loyola faculty, Deirdre's house-mates, occasional visitors like Gene Foley, and 'the bums from Bruno's' all played 'party' my way. Mike did so only rarely. Although he always referred to himself as 'the token black', I didn't realise how deeply he felt it until one day in class I had him play Julius Caesar and had his white classmates kneel at his feet. Though he laughed like a child, broke character and said, 'Hey! I like the feeling of being Julius Caesar! Slave, kneel when you talk to Caesar,' I knew it was a mixed moment for him. Days the classes went particularly well for him, he was more likely, that night, to do his 'Order of Creation'.

Often Mike would stay at my apartment, if someone else had not already reserved the spare bed. He loved to tell of my first appearance in class: 'We had heard so much from Trahey about this famous actor from the Abb-ey The-a-tre! Excitement was high, man! At last the moment had come! Enter Cool Vince — blue eyes, wavy hair, trim little beard, charming smile, cool blue linen windbreaker, fawn slacks creased like a knife-blade — and *fairy shoes*! Corduroy, man!'

After my first lecture, a young man with an Irish face, figure and accent walked unannounced into my dressing-room. He wanted to know if I had a part for him in my plays. I said, 'Only for students at Loyola.' He wasn't one. He was an electrician and carpenter. I told him he could make a strong Georgian door, which I wanted for one scene of *Orphans*. He made a perfect one. We became friends. He had a young family, and lived nearby. They gave some real Irish parties for us. I noticed as I got to know him well that, though very bright and forward, he had a tiny hesitation in his speech. When I knew him well enough, I asked him about it. This was his story as he told it to me.

'I was doing a wiring job on the building of a skyscraper downtown. The whistle went for lunch. I was using an electric drill, and I decided I'd finish drilling this hole into the wall. I was alone up there when I hit a live wire. The shock and the current stuck me to the wall and my hands to the drill. I couldn't let go, or cry out for help. I knew everyone was gone to their lunch. I thought about my children. If I died, what were they going to do? I made up my mind I wasn't going to die. I don't know how long I was there. I kept saying, "Don't give up!" Eventually, someone turned off the power. I woke up in hospital. They couldn't understand how I survived. I knew I wouldn't let myself die. But something in my brain is gone, a part of it that has to do with speaking. That's what that impediment is.'

He was second-generation Irish, but he spoke, behaved and looked as if he had never left Kiltimagh!

The day before I left Chicago, Bruno, on behalf of Bernie, Harry, Anthony and himself, gave me a silver bracelet, engraved on the top with 'Vincent' and inside with 'From the drunks at Bruno's — Chicago'.

Having said all our goodbyes, Mike Richardson and I set out for New York in his convertible, to stay with Gene Foley in Greenwich Village. An odd couple we must have seemed in those days, but I was blissfully unaware of colour. After a day or two, we left New York at midnight and drove to Rehoboth Beach in Delaware, to join Franny and Gene's children at their vacation home. Mike's car developed trouble. We had it fixed, but Mike felt he had better get back to Marion; the new school year was fast approaching.

Though I wrote, and in later years in the Windy City made many attempts to contact him, I never saw him again. I hope his life went well. I got no real sense, that summer, of how hard it is to be black in America. I had followed the struggle from Ireland; with the coming of civil rights laws, I thought discrimination had simply ended. That's like thinking that after the death of Christ everyone would love their neighbour!

'Who do you think was staying with the Foleys?' is how my mother would have phrased my coincidental meeting with old friends at Gene's. It was Gerry Parks and his wife Maureen, who had emigrated to Canada since the Brendan Smith Academy and fit-up days. With them they had their most important production, a lovely daughter, Susan. In the world of acting, Maureen and Gerry had done extremely well. They were splendid actors. Gerry was having his vacation from the Broadway production of *The Representative*. Being on the beach with the Foleys and the Parkses, with the little sandpipers skipping in and out of the tide, was the perfect wind-down to my virgin visit to America.

I didn't like going home in those days. I had always dreaded the end of 'the holidays away'. I had enjoyed every moment in America, but I was keen to get back to see how were things in my love life – did I have one? How were things with my children? How were things at the Abbey?

I didn't seem to have a love life – at least, not with Sinéad Cusack. We met at the flat she was staying in, on the morning I arrived in London. She had been touched by and thanked me for some flowers I had sent from America for one of those special private anniversaries that people in love keep. She told me about the film she had finished opposite Peter Sellers. I remember the morning light; the atmosphere between us sweet; two very close friends, who loved each other, meeting after a long absence. I also knew that I was getting 'the bullet' – that *it* was over. It was not said, but I felt I had lost out to the Stellar Sellers. Strangely, I have no sense that I was devastated. Knowing me, I probably pulled down the blinds on it.

The Saturday of the week I got back to Dublin, I took Bairbre, Louise, Valerie, and Rachael, who was only four and a half, to ROSC, an international art exhibition at the RDS in Ballsbridge. I still have an image of the catalogue, and a big yellow painting with rows of white iron nails in it. The first few paintings we came to, the girls wanted to know what they meant, why they were done that way, and all that. I said, 'I think we should just look at them. When we've looked enough, move on to the next one. When we've seen them all, we'll go into the cafeteria and have lemonade and biscuits, and each of you tell us which three you liked best. Ray can have the catalogue. When we're looking at a picture, Rachael, you can find it in the book and show it to me.' The four of them – sixteen, eleven, nine, and four – went quietly from picture to picture for nearly two and a half hours, completely engrossed. We went to the cafeteria then, and each one ordered her favourite biscuit and drink; then, starting with the youngest, each told us what she had liked best.

No hesitation, no uncertainty; they were bursting to share their opinions. That night at the Abbey, I told Pat Layde their choices. They were the choices of the top critics! I had confirmed for myself what I was coming to believe, with P.J.'s help: that the enemy of appreciating artwork of any kind is to feel you must say something clever. If the image stays with you, and continues to please you, it is good! As Louis MacNeice said in 'Meeting Point':

> God or whatever means the Good
> Be praised that time can stop like this,
> That what the heart has understood
> Can verify in the body's peace
> God or whatever means the Good.

That same month, another group of children gave me as important a lesson in acting as my own had given me in visual art. Both little groups contributed to my three Honorary Doctorates in Fine Art as much as Frank Dermody and my brother Jack. That's not hyperbole!

The International Actors' Equity Association Conference was held in Dublin that autumn. With Dermot Doolan, Gerry Alexander and Bill Foley, I was a delegate. One afternoon I took a group of actors, American, English, French and Balkan, to the Strawberry Halls — my favourite daytime pub, owned by Vera and Des Cummings — and thence to the Wren's Nest, one of the oldest pubs in Dublin. There we found ourselves watching a group of poor children, from about three to ten years old, playing 'house' under a big tree. The older ones were making imaginary tea and food in improvised cookers made of boxes, serving it to the younger ones, who were sitting on upturned anythings at a table made of two planks on bricks. Cans for cups, pieces of cardboard for plates. The concentration, the quiet joy and the belief of the children in what they were doing was complete, as they recreated their parents and themselves in their own spontaneous dialogue. We were enthralled.

One of the children saw us, then the others. Some of them started to show off, others to giggle, clown, hide their faces, turn away, or stare back at us. The magic vanished. Beauty and delight was changed to coy attention-getting. The loss was palpable. 'Now this overdone, or come tardy off, though it make the unskilful laugh, cannot but make the judicious grieve,' said Lord Hamlet. 'The will doing the work of the imagination,' said Mr Yeats. There is a lesson for critics, as well as actors, in those children's stories.

'Too many chiefs and not enough Indians!' Barry Keegan, my Captain Boyle in *Juno*, would complain, one side of his mouth pulled down in disgust.

'They're all cowboys,' was another of his grumbles, against anyone who didn't measure up to his critical standard. That was most people, most of the time.

He was serious about all this, but then again, he wasn't; you were never sure. I'm not sure he knew himself. It had become second nature for Barry to criticise, while his golden quiff fell over his eyes and constantly needed the attention of his long fingers to get it back in place. He could be the most disagreeable and the most likeable fellow you ever met, both at the same time — until you got to know him, and him you. Then you loved him, or couldn't stand him. I loved him. All of the cast of my *Juno* did.

I'm not claiming *Juno and the Paycock*; that was all Sean O'Casey, his *magnum opus*. This particular *Juno* was mine only in that I directed it. As Jack had taught me, I began with the city of Dublin — the kind of place where the people in the play lived, with the sound of seagulls 'hooverin'' over the Liffey, as Phil O'Flynn once heard a Dublin man say.

The Paycock had to be Philip — but he was away doing a film. Why the hell, I thought, are we doing *Juno* with Phil away?

Then I remembered Barry Keegan, as Dublin as Molly Malone's father's ghost, and very much alive-alive-o! Here was a Paycock — a Captain Boyle — who would come to the part with none of the baggage about 'famous lines' and 'famous scenes' that throttled creativity so often at the Abbey. He wasn't even an Abbey actor, though he should have been. I had no doubt I wanted Angela Newman as Juno Boyle; I knew she would trust me to help her find her Juno. Barry's mate, a former Abbey man, had made a big name for himself in London in television and on stage: little Dermot Kelly. He was Joxer — on and off stage, you might say. So I cast the play. Every actor and actress was the one I wanted.

I didn't want the set designed as much as painted. I wanted a front-cloth that would capture Dublin. I wanted an artist to bring his or her artistry to bear on the tenement home of the Boyles, and the staircase that brought the flotsam and jetsam of poverty and civil war into their house and into their room. I didn't get an artist — I got three: three close friends, inseparable, when they were not actually doing their own work; the finest painters in Ireland at that time. I knew them and their work from P.J.'s. There was George Campbell, whose wife played big sister to the other two — Arthur Armstrong and Gerard Dillon.

This cast of actors and this trio of designers not only made my working days full, rich and creative; they made the time between and after rehearsals and performances a continuation of the process. It was all so exciting; all so important; but all so much *fun*! Only in our sleep were we apart. In bed, at this time, I was very much alone, and at peace with it.

Comparisons are odorous, some wit once said. I agree, especially where theatrical criticism is concerned. So I'll just say the poet John Jordan was a fine critic, as opposed to simply a reviewer — I think one of the finest in Dublin in my time. I treasure some of his critiques. I remember in writing about Micheál mac Liammóir he observed, 'The great actor is always the same and always different.' I especially cherish John's piece on my *Juno* in Hibernia, describing the work of those who gave me such joy and pride in this production.

If there was a journalist in Dublin who truly loved the theatre and all who worked for it, in those years, it was JJF — John Finnegan of the *Evening Herald*. Because he was kind, in Dublin — where the 'bitter word', as O'Casey calls it, is often preferred — his knowledge and sensitivity were not fully appreciated.

He praised strongly the 'new look' of this *Juno*. 'It has become re-invigorated.... The sets are also unique by A.D.C. Arthur Armstrong, Gerard Dillon and George Campbell — the old house's windows just before the curtain rises, the tenement setting and the stairs and landing, all adding new dimensions to the play. It is an Abbey production that should rank with the greatest of its predecessors.'

A.D.C. also stands for *aide-de-camp* — camp assistant, assistant to a general. I'm not sure anyone got our little joke!

We took the production to the Cork Opera House, where we played to fantastic audiences, houses and reviews. Having a drink after the last performance with the actors in our hotel, the Arbutus Lodge in Montenotte, Barry, delighted with the whole experience, hating it being over, growled to the group at large and me in particular, 'This cowboy Dowling — no, this sheriff — comes round to me after the performance tonight — the last performance, mark you — and I not even a member of the famous Abbey Company, from tomorrow morning unemployed, and he gives me, excuse the expression, Angela, fucking *notes* on my performance tonight. Where and when am I going to play Captain Boyle again? Who else would be idiot enough to cast me in it?' And he grabbed me and hugged me in a massive bear hug!

The favourite cant with the theatre people in Dublin, then, was 'forty, fat and a failure'. I became forty on 7 September 1969. I'd moved up in the world, but not for long. After I got back from Chicago, I got a hall door flat on Upper Fitzwilliam Street. I got an ulcer, too. That was earned over a long period, and it would remain more faithful to me than I to my women friends, and some of them to me. Hiding my feelings too often behind a smile was the cause of the ulcer, a doctor told me. I weighed about ten stone, 140lb. Getting fat wasn't a worry. The failure, I didn't believe in. Of course, I had a permanent — and now, thanks to the Players' Council and the Andrews award, pensionable — job at the Abbey. Ah, but, as Robbie Burns knew, 'there's many a slip 'twixt cup and lip!'

I stayed in touch with Sinéad by letter, and less frequently by phone. It would take me a decade or more to make a long-distance phone call for anything but an emergency, a job, or an anniversary forgotten! One night Sinéad arrived unexpectedly to see me. Wounded. She wasn't able to stay long. Her work was in London, mostly. Thus another cycle began. It would be the one the cobbler hit his wife with — the last!

I am like W.B. Yeats in this, at least: 'my glory was, I had such friends'. Two of these were, and are thirty years on, the Burroweses, Wesley and his truly beautiful wife Helena. Helena, whose artistry turns woollen scarves, blankets, and other homespuns into wearable art; and Wesley, whose talents with words, Northern humour, and music have made him one of Ireland's best and most successful television and theatre dramatists.

Wesley's play *The Becauseway* won the first Irish Life Assurance Drama Award, and I directed it. I had a dream cast: Niall Tóibín, Dermot Kelly, Aideen O'Kelly and Desmond Cave, supported by a half-dozen or so shop-window mannequins in place of a crowd. Their performances were stiff, but they never argued with my direction.

The play was Wesley Burrowes incarnate: funny, satirical, stylish, imaginative, original, and entertainingly surreal to mask an acute, serious sensitivity. The play was also successful. I was invited to direct at the Gateway Theatre in Chester, in England, with Dermot Kelly and Sinéad Cusack, both of whom had name recognition in England. I accepted.

The evening before we were due to leave, Dermot Kelly, who was subject to strong mood swings, suddenly told me in the crowded Plough — then the Abbey actors' watering hole — that he wasn't going to Chester unless I advanced him a week's salary. I think that was around twenty pounds! It was an outrageous thing to do. I wasn't management; I would be waiting for my own first payment till the end of the first week in Chester. At this time, my Abbey salary was all going to Brenda — not that 'all' was much; I survived thanks to what I earned outside the Abbey. So when Dermot Kelly, who could be difficult, demanded a week's salary in advance, I borrowed the money at the Abbey. I paid it back the next week.

So we went to Chester on the mail boat. Dermot, in spite of promises, didn't repay me in his lifetime! Eccentric to the last, he left it to me in his will.

Sinéad had got herself a really nice place out in the country, on a large farm, for the rehearsals and run of the play in Chester. Her landlady had no room for me!

The director of the theatre brought his agents to the show. One of them, Ron Lacey, was also a successful actor. They signed me on, though they weren't interested in the play for London.

My acting would take me to weird and wonderful places in 1970. The first was in an adaptation of Flann O'Brien's bizarre comic novel *At Swim-Two-Birds*, in which the characters from a book within the book rebel against the author. Included in the cast were Eugene Lambert, Ireland's foremost ventriloquist/puppeteer, and Eamon Keane, a fine but introverted actor from the Radio Éireann Rep., who played the Author and several other parts splendidly. In one scene Eamon was 'born' on stage, at the age of twenty-three years. A door opening revealed this event, and Eamon entered, with a look of beatific innocence. Some of the audience got the joke. In rehearsal, with director Alan Simpson's permission, I added the long sentimental sound Dublin women make when they see a new baby: 'Ahhhh!' It got a much bigger laugh.

Then I got another idea, but too late to rehearse it. *They'll like it*, I thought. As I said 'Ahhh,' I patted the 'baby', very gently, on the top of the head, as old gentlemen do. The whole house got it — a huge laugh! Pleased, I turned upstage, my usual move. *Wham!* A sickening punch to my kidneys from the 'angelic' author. He didn't like to be touched, it seemed. Unequivocally, I should not have done the 'business' without rehearsal. I reported him, but asked he be given nothing more than a warning, this time. Thereafter that particular scene was not so much fun.

However, there was no shortage of fun. Lambert produced voices from everything in and around us; and there was the polite tea-party scene, with Joan O'Hara, Pat Laffan, Des Cave and myself — excruciatingly funny and painful, Flann O'Brien at his side-splitting best. Our quartet of working-class Dubliners, trying to be middle-class over afternoon tea, with put-on 'posh' accents politely discuss the merits and demerits of boils, blackheads and pimples. The audience would start to laugh and laugh, and when we'd try to resume they'd go into convulsions of more laughter. Nightly it got to the point where none of us on stage could finish one word without going into convulsions, too. In desperation, I would break from character and say with absolute authority, to actors and audiences, 'Now, stop. No more. Let's concentrate. All right! Here we go!'

There'd be a moment's silence; then a tiny laugh would start in the audience, roll through the auditorium, and we'd all be in convulsions again! We tried every trick in the book, but to no avail. It never happened to me before or since, in any other play. It was a nightmare — pure torture, every night!

At this time, I thought everyone liked me. That's pretty naïve, but I thought, *I like everybody, so why shouldn't they like me?* I had a rude awakening.

One afternoon, in the Plough, I had hurried in to have a quick coffee and sandwich. As I passed an erstwhile friend, with some pleasantry, he turned on me and spat real hatred and anger at me. Though it was obvious he had drink taken, in some ways it was more shocking than the kidney-punch on stage. So everyone didn't love me! Surprise! Surprise!

There is so much rejection in the actor's life, it is a miracle that such happenings are so rare. I'm lucky: I don't hold grudges. Hates, yes — one or two!

My next acting project was a homosexual film director, a patient in an asylum for the insane, who spoke with an American southern accent at the rate of a speed typist working on an electric typewriter. It was in Syd Cheatle's startlingly original one-act play *The Director*. It gave me one of the most interesting roles that ever came my way. Syd and I became good friends in the process, and I would have more fun and some success with his plays.

Peter O'Toole arrived at the Peacock to see Marie Kean during an early rehearsal of *The Lover* by Harold Pinter. At the break, Sean Cotter, who was directing, and I chatted with them in the Flowing Tide, the other Abbey watering hole.

'You are playing Richard in *The Lover*, are you, dear fellow?' asked O'Toole. 'It's a cricket match, you see. Harold is both bowling and batting — the husband and the lover! It's his revenge on a lady, you know. He heard she was having it off with someone else while he was acting here in Ireland with McMaster. A game of cricket, old boy. That's all you have to remember.' It was very helpful.

Of course, there is a lot more to this little play than that. We found it, too — Sean Cotter, Máire O'Neill, who was splendid as the wife, and I. I love playing English parts, working-class or upper-crust. Pinter gave me both, and in one body, in his sizzling sex story.

Ron Moody came to see it. He told me after the performance, 'If you had given this performance in London, mate, they would never have let you play anything else, and you would have been made for life!' In Dublin, as Philip O'Flynn had so often complained, you are proving yourself anew every time. If you let yourself think about it, it could get discouraging. So I didn't. If thoughts like that crept up on me, I went to bed and slept. I called it my 'ostrich complex'!

Hatchet was a violent play set in Dublin gangland. It was by a mild, working-class, bespectacled Dublin man, 'Henno' McGee. He looked like a Dublin Mr Moto, one of my favourite movie characters. I arranged a rehearsed reading of Hatchet at the Peacock, with a splendid cast led by Anna Manahan, John Kavanagh, Donal McCann and Brendan Ó Dúil. It was a fully rehearsed reading with moves, costumes, sound, light and an audience. Henno's was a Dublin I didn't know; so for months I did my drinking with him at his local pubs, around the Liffey, down near Collins Barracks. I also moved into a new flat, near the Five Lamps on the North Circular Road, close to the docks. Both gave me the feel of the play. I had given up my posh Fitzwilliam abode. Couldn't afford it.

That summer I bought my first painting, for sixteen guineas. It shows the bare back of a blonde young woman on a bed.

John Kelly, one of my favourite people and artists, had asked me to open his exhibition at the Project Gallery, opposite the Abbey stage door. John — a small dark man, with a straggly black beard and curly longish hair — had painted the huge 'Last Supper' backcloth for *The Successor* at the Queen's, and designed and painted the sets for *Let Freedom Ring*. To help me with my opening speech I asked him to tell me what motivated his work. He said, in his unaffected Dublin way, 'I get an idea, and I paint a line around it, and that's my idea and my painting!' They may not be his exact words, but they are as near as dammit!

Then I went alone to a preview of the exhibition during my lunch break. I zoned in right away on the bare-back picture, and put a deposit on it. The Project was an artist's co-operative. I gave the young woman looking after the Gallery five pounds, and undertook to pay ten shillings a week until it was paid off. I must have been pretty preoccupied. I failed to notice that the young woman was beautiful and American.

Tragically, Pat Layde's wife, our beloved friend Kay, had died, at barely forty years old. They had two very young children, a boy and a girl. Pat fell apart, understandably. I got a message, one lunch-time, to meet him at the Plough. Few short meetings have left me with such a disturbing memory. He was sitting at the end of the bar counter, his back to the wall. He was dazed, a black-ringed Guinness stain round his mouth. He wanted to know if he could move in with me for a while — the sooner the better, it seemed — till he got things sorted out.

I said, 'Yes, of course.' As I had rehearsal that afternoon, I ran down the list of things he had to do about his children, who were being taken care of by relatives; showing his house, which was for sale; and making arrangements for what he needed to bring to my flat in the way of bedclothes and so on. He stopped me with a low, animal, anguished wail: 'Please! Stop! Stop! Stop! I can't think as fast as you do!'

Hatchet was a sensation at its Sunday-night performance. It got full productions in the Peacock, in the Abbey and on RTÉ television over the next few years.

Pat Layde later met and married Joyce, the lovely young widow of a marvellous actor friend of ours, James Neylin. My other Abbey friend Patrick Laffan and his wife Eileen offered me their fine apartment on Waterloo Road, for an indefinite period, which I gladly accepted. The depressing house on the North Circular had served its purpose, but I was glad to leave it.

When I read the fifth bad notice from the five Dublin papers for my performance as Trigorin in Chekhov's *The Seagull*, I laughed. I knew they were right! Still, I had to play it in the Abbey for two more weeks.

Hilton Edwards — who had directed it, and me, in his only Abbey production — was at the stage door, all the newspapers under his arm. 'I'm sorry, dear boy,' he said in his plummy English. 'I take full responsibility!' Though I had argued with him, and we had discussed the role very thoroughly, he had insisted that Trigorin must be played 'not effeminate, but effete'. What he really wanted me to do was recreate what Micheál mac Liammóir had done with the part.

Susan Hallinan, a beautiful girl and actress whom Hilton had asked to have brought into the Abbey for the play, fared better. Not as well as she was capable of, though, she and I both felt. It was a disappointing experience for Hilton, too. I was really sorry about that. Perhaps we had, like Ezra Pound in his sad little poem, over-prepared the event?

The Becauseway was televised on RTÉ, directed by one of their staff directors. Sinéad came back from London to appear in it. Jimmy Bartley, one of our Borstal Boys, was in it too. Sinéad and I had not seen much of each other in the months leading up to this. Letters and occasional visits were short and not always sweet. I still believed that somehow everything would work out right — whatever 'right' meant! Certainly the moving finger was writing, though I didn't know it.

There was a party to celebrate the televising of Wesley's play. Dan O'Herlihy, the Irish film actor, nominated for an Oscar for his performance as Robinson Crusoe, was there with his daughter. I had been asked by Tomás Mac Anna and Joe Dowling, who were running the Peacock, to direct a rehearsed reading of a famous American play with a large cast — *In the Matter of J. Robert Oppenheimer*. They had also said I could put 'a star' on an Abbey salary for the rehearsal period. Hence I had my eye on Dan. I talked with him; he was interested in the part, especially as it was a reading and for the Abbey Theatre. We clinched the deal on the phone, which his daughter had answered.

The last act of Sinéad and Vincent's sweet, often sad saga has four scenes. Scene One takes place in or about the *Late Late Show*.

Sinéad is being interviewed about her career in connection with the TV showing of *The Becauseway*. Another guest is a soccer player. He engages in some 'kidding' with her. Vincent is watching it on a home television screen; his green-eyed monster jumps on his shoulder and starts whispering sweet jealousies in his ear. Later Sinéad agrees not to keep a date made with the footballer, but only if Vincent telephones and telsl him she won't be there! He does. The two men exchange rude words. Compliments fly when the quality meets!

Scene Two takes place, some time later, in the studio of Radio Éireann on a Sunday morning, where a large group of well-known actors and actresses are recording instalments of *The Kennedys of Castlerosse*. A copy of an English Sunday newspaper with a large circulation in Ireland is lying on a chair. Having finished a scene as Christy, Vincent sits on the chair beside the paper, glances at the headline, looks away, does a double-take. He picks up the paper and reads that there has been a mini-riot by young women gathered outside Sinéad Cusack's apartment in Islington, demanding the appearance of one George Best, the well-known soccer player, who is sheltering within. Vincent realises that he is one of the only ones in the studio who has not already read this news. He coolly resumes recording at the microphone. At the tea break, he calls London on the public phone in the hallway. He gets through to Sinéad. Yes, she had gone to dinner with George Best. It was all a kind of silly joke. It didn't mean anything. He is reassured, goes back to the studio and tells Phil and Angela the glad tidings.

Scene Three: Outside the Abbey next afternoon, Vincent gets an early edition of the *Evening Herald*. The headline tells a continuation of the story of Sinéad and the soccer star in London. There is a reference to a boyfriend in Dublin. (They might at least have given me a credit!) Vincent goes back to the flat in Waterloo Road and does his famous ostrich trick.

He awakes about an hour later. Sits up smiling, symbolically spits her out of his system; declares out loud to himself, pleasantly, completely without rancour, 'It's gone. I'm free. I've been an idiot. It's over. It's been over a long time. I'm going to have fun. Call off the search for the perfect partner!' He gets up, lights the geyser, turns on a bath, starts setting his dinner table, takes the makings of a mixed grill from the fridge, checks the bath now and then — singing the whole time, Mel Blanc-like, his laughing version of 'Somebody Stole my Gal'!

Scene Four will take place in London in March 1971, a few pages on!

We had a powerful cast for *Oppenheimer*. The whole process was a joy. Dan O'Herlihy and I hit it off from the start. Of course, I had worked with his brother Michael at the Abbey and I had seen a lot of him socially; indeed, I had put up posters, with him and my brother Jack, all over Dublin one night for the Globe's first production, and I had sat up with him, the night before Michael sailed across the Atlantic, in the *Ituna*, his small sailing-boat.

In the Peacock lobby, before the performance, I was very nervous because I was acting as well as directing *Oppenheimer*. I had met Dan with his wife Elsie, her sister Yvette and her husband Frank, both of whom I had known and liked for years. Frank had been Phil's, Angela's and my dentist since I joined the Abbey, and he came to most of our shows, sometimes coming to Groome's. They introduced me to what I took to be a rich, mink-coated New York divorcée. I missed her name, but she seemed cold and thoroughly uninterested in me. As it was a Sunday, the Peacock bar would not be open; I was going to P.J.'s after the play and didn't press them to join me there, as they seemed anxious to get home.

I was also rehearsing a part in *The Plebeians Rehearse the Uprising*, and I invited Dan to come and see it the following week. He settled on the Saturday night performance. Later in the week he phoned me to confirm our date and asked if they could have four tickets. The play was fascinating — Joe Dowling gave an excellent performance as Bertolt Brecht — but it wasn't packing the house, so I said yes to the tickets. I had only one scene, but it was quite a strong dramatic one: I burst into the auditorium and ran down the stepped aisle through the audience and up on to the stage.

In the bar after the play, on that Saturday night, I joined Dan, Elsie, Yvette — Frank wasn't able to come — and a young, blonde American woman. Nobody introduced me.

While I was waiting for my drink to be served, she asked me, 'Were you not afraid of tripping? Running down the steps, in the dark?'

'No. I wasn't,' I replied, 'but I will be from now on!' And I walked over to her — she was lovely — and asked her, 'Why has nobody introduced us?'

Surprised, she told me we had met at *Oppenheimer*. I couldn't believe it. This couldn't be the cold, rich New Yorker? It was and it wasn't. Not cold, rich or a New Yorker, she was Dan and Elsie's daughter Olwen!

Well, as I was going on to the annual agency party at Richard and Susan Hallinan's, I asked them all to come. Olwen and I danced at the party, I drove her home to her parents' house, and the die was cast and I was heading for the moon.

Little Big Man — my favourite kind of film, a Western, starring Dustin Hoffman — was our first date. I had free tickets to the New Electric Cinema opposite P.J.'s. We had a drink there beforehand with an usher, a friend of mine. Afterwards we had oysters, sold by a kind of male Molly Malone! He sold them with all the trimmings from a large basket, which he carried daily from Dundalk, by train. His name was Hughie. He was a welcome regular at several good pubs. His oysters were fresh and inexpensive. Oysters are said to be an aphrodisiac. Olwen had never tasted oysters before, and I wooed her with them.

Some nights Olwen volunteered at Deirdre O'Connell's semi-professional Focus Theatre. I would pick her up, go to a play or film, then a pub, and drive her home by midnight. We laughed a lot, we liked to listen to each other, our kissing was affectionate rather than passionate, and although she 'didn't smoke' she always managed to smoke my last cigarette!

Occasionally Dan and Elsie, her parents, joined us at some theatre event. I was made very welcome by them, but I found it strange that, when they left us in their house, they didn't say goodbye. In the Dowling family, nobody ever went out before they said goodbye to everyone staying behind. I thought, at first, it was a sign of disapproval.

To me, Olwen — divorced in her early twenties, living with her parents, with a two-year-old son, Cian — was very American. I teased her about her ASC. 'What's that?' she asked eventually. 'American subculture,' I told her. It is still a code word between us, to describe something peculiarly American.

Our relationship remained platonic, though Olwen visited me in Avoca for the weekend after Christmas and stayed at the hotel with Cian. I was with Wesley and Helena in their house above the Avoca River, in that Vale that Thomas Moore immortalised in his melody 'The Meeting of the Waters'.

Olwen had told me she was interested in the arts and theatre production, and was looking for a job. She had some experience working at the Focus Theatre and in the Project Gallery. I brought her to the party for the announcement of the second Irish Life Playwriting Award. Wesley again had a play in the running: *A Loud Bang on June First.*

The 'loud bang' is the sound of the young hero bursting from overfeeding. Again Wesley had served us an extraordinarily imaginative, surreal satire. Des Cave played an actor brought into a palace to impersonate the king. It was prophetic, in a way: within a decade, America and Rome would have former actors as President and Pope! The whole middle act of the play was a brilliant, stylised. musical dance game between the visible King (Philip O'Flynn) and Queen (Angela Newman), to original music, with visible objects moving 'magically' by themselves in otherwise total darkness! The lighting was ultraviolet, the costumes and objects painted with ultraviolet paint. In the darkness, dressed all in black, Olwen moved the actors and objects 'magically', precisely, and to the music. That was her first professional theatre job. She did it perfectly.

In spite of superb performances — especially from Angela, Des and Phil — a superb set dominated by a twelve-foot-high throne (designed by the artist Barry Cooke), and dazzling dialogue and lighting effects, many of the critics tore the play and Wesley to pieces. It was cruel, unusual and undeserved punishment. It looked for a long time as if he would never write another play. He did, but irreparable damage was done to his relationship with the stage.

Our loss was television's gain. His succession of realistic rural serials raised that form of television drama to new high levels, made stars of numerous Irish actors and provided experience and income to countless Irish artists and production people.

I remember my brother Jack's point of view — he loved the play, the new areas it had attempted and often reached: 'They're always asking for change; when they get it they complain it's not like the good old way!'

Finally I got Father Donnellan's chair from Joe Ellis! Not back to Mammy, though; to the Players-Wills Theatre in Dublin.

On a visit to London after the Chester production of *The Becauseway*, my agents gave me a play by a young client of theirs, John Peacock. *Children of the Wolf* is a terrifying piece on revenge, terror, and murder, in which a twin brother and sister plan to murder the mother who unsuccessfully tried to abort them. I offered it to Wendy Hiller. She didn't like it. I thought it a powerful play, but not exactly Abbey material! Brendan Smith accepted it for the International Theatre Festival that was taking place in March 1971.

So did Yvonne Mitchell, an award-winning English theatre and film 'star' actress, who wanted a comeback from a five-year retirement in the South of France. She was perfect for the mother. Sheelagh Cullen, an Irish actress working in England, and Shane Bryant were also ideal casting. Adam Durley, the son of my fit-up and Academy colleague Ruth Durley, was our stage manager, Olwen the assistant stage manager. The fourth character in the play was a murdered, mutilated corpse! The play had one set, an empty, shuttered upstairs room, bare except for a heavy, iron-based mahogany swivel chair, on which the revengeful twins tie their mother — Father Donnellan's chair!

'What goes "Ha, ha, ha, bonk"?' asked Yvonne Mitchell, this exquisite, distinguished lady of the British theatre, as we were nervously waiting to be photographed on the little theatre's stage, minutes after we brought her from the airport. 'I get so self-conscious being photographed, I must keep talking. Do you know what goes "Ha, ha, ha, bonk"?' We shook our heads as the photographer clicked merrily away. 'A man laughing his head off,' said Yvonne, laughing with us. From then until we said goodbye, months later, it was unparalleled joy for all of us in and about *Children of the Wolf*.

'I love you, but I am not *in* love with you,' I told Olwen one night in the flat in Waterloo Road. She has never let me forget that! What I meant by it I'm not sure, especially as that night we made love for the first time.

Shortly after that I shaved off my beard. I think it was somehow symbolic — a kind of ritual end to the previous relationship, a clean start, and the realisation that I owed it to Olwen and myself to look before I leaped fully into her and Cian's lives. I knew this was for real, and slower would be better.

'This is John Barber, theatre critic of the *Daily Telegraph*,' a very English voice told me on the phone in the flat. I knew of him as a very well-thought-of critic in one of Britain's prestige newspapers. We were having our first full dress/technical rehearsal that Saturday afternoon. He had just learned that Yvonne Mitchell, whom he greatly respected, was playing in the second week of the Festival. He was committed to reviewing a play that night and had to return to London on the morrow; he knew it was a most unusual request, but he would appreciate it if I would permit him to attend the dress rehearsal. He would make every allowance in his review for dress-rehearsal shortcomings, and that sort of thing. I said I would have to have Yvonne's and the author's agreement, but I would strongly recommend that we accommodate him. Everyone was agreeable. The dress rehearsal went as well as we could have hoped. On the Monday there was a splendid review in the *Telegraph*, as well as in every Dublin paper.

On the Monday night, Mr Richard Mills, General Manager of the London-based Lord Delfont Theatrical Organisation, invited us to bring *Children of the Wolf*, directly we closed in Dublin, to the Apollo Theatre on Shaftesbury Avenue, in the heart of London's West End. Delfont would supply us with a larger, stronger, but in every other way similar setting; a lighting designer; understudies; and an actor to replace the dummy we used for the murdered man. We would bring the same cast, stage management, and swivel chair! Everyone was happy — except my mother, but she didn't refuse. So Father Donnellan's chair travelled in Adam Durley's van with other props and costumes, to appear in the West End!

Olwen and I stayed at the Boston Arms, an inn round the corner from Barry Keegan and Madame Tussaud's Waxwork Museum. We were happy and very comfortable there, and made good friends with the landlord and his wife. They gave an after-show party for the cast, crew, and old London and London-Irish friends.

The area of Soho which surrounds the Apollo was my stomping ground as a young actor, in my unemployed and *My Wife's Lodger* years. To see my name in lights as a director, beside Yvonne Mitchell's, on the Apollo marquee on Shaftesbury Avenue was very sweet. The extracts from the reviews and posters surrounding the theatre entrance were more than a dream come true. They were beyond the wildest dreams of the Irish boy I still was.

Scores of old friends from every walk of my life came to see us. Sinéad wrote that she would like to see me and asked me to call her, which I did. I agreed to spend the day with her on my day off.

I told Olwen it was something I wanted to do for old times' and friendship's sake. There was nothing more to it than that. I no longer loved Sinéad. It was over. It was true, too. I knew calmly and quietly that I loved Olwen and hoped to spend my life with her.

She seemed to understand, to believe me. It was only later I found out how hurt and frightened she was. It was years before Olwen believed that I had not come to her on the rebound.

The day was not any happier for Sinéad. I had been there for her for so long that it was hard for her to believe it was no longer so. Other than one phone call to my office at the Abbey, a few accidental meetings in Dublin streets and theatre, and seeing her on stage or film, our paths have not crossed again.

Late in the afternoon of the first night of *Children of the Wolf*, Clem — who represented the Delfont Organisation on our production, and looked after me, and all connected with us, so wonderfully — told me it would be a dress affair. I had a dinner jacket with me, but no dress shirt. I asked Olwen to get me one while I was doing the last touches with the designer on the lights. She came back with a beautiful linen evening shirt from Harrods, for what I thought was an outrageous price — enough to buy a suit, never mind a shirt, I said. Quietly, simply, and without any affectation, she said, 'Harrods is the only shop I know in London.'

The 'yellow' press hated the play — saw it as an attack on women's right to abortion. The quality press saw value in it, but not enough to keep it running. The day before we closed, Harold Hobson, the 'grand old man' of London newspaper, wrote a review in *The Sunday Times* that, had it come earlier, could have kept us running. As well never as late! The Irish papers, when we opened in Dublin, had given one rave review after the other to play, performances and director. If we had let it run in Dublin, as we like to say, 'it would be running still.' But I'm glad we went. I wouldn't have missed the Shaftesbury Avenue feeling for the world. Clem and Richard Mills, for the Delfont Organisation, gave us not only every support and encouragement, but so many personal kindnesses. We remained friends for years.

A couple of days before our run ended, there was a phone call at the stage door. It was Hugh Hunt, Artistic Director at the Abbey, asking if I would accept the position of Deputy Artistic Director for the remainder of his term, six months. He felt, and the Board agreed, that I was 'the only one who had the confidence of the Abbey Company'! I was flying in higher altitudes!

I liked the challenge. I returned to Dublin, to meet with Hugh Hunt at his rented house, beside Joyce's Tower and the Forty-Foot, in Sandycove — not far from the Christian Brothers in Dun Laoghaire, where I went to school.

Adam Durley was given responsibility and expenses for bringing the props back to Dublin in his van. Whether Adam or the van returned to Dublin, I do not know. What I do know is that Father Donnellan's chair has not again felt the damp touch of Irish airs. How do I know? That answer must wait its cue. Surely the longest pause in theatre history!

18

The Director's Job at Last

I've got a pal in Kalamazoo!

Hugh Hunt, Artistic Director of the Abbey, was also a professor of theatre at Manchester University. The Abbey was taking up too much of his time. As he had his season chosen to the end of his contract, he felt that if I took over the wheel, he could safely return to England. We would, of course, keep in communication. I said I thought it would only work if I had authority to make decisions, and if everyone in the Abbey understood that. There is one crisis per day even in the best managed theatres — that's if you're lucky.

On a Saturday night, towards the end of a performance at the Peacock, one of our best mature actresses, from the auditorium, loudly and repeatedly heckled the actors on the stage. It was distressing for the artists, disturbing for the audience and an embarrassment for the Abbey. I was at the theatre that night. It was clear she was very drunk. Everyone in the management and company knew she had a serious drinking problem.

She was playing one of the leads in an O'Casey revival on the following Monday. I went to my office and wrote a letter telling her she was laid off from the company and would not be reinstated until she produced a letter from a medical doctor stating she had received treatment for her illness — alcoholism — and was carrying out the doctor's instructions. She would receive no salary until then, but it would be kept for her and paid in full when we heard from the doctor. I called another Abbey actress, Kathleen Barrington, who was free at the time, and told her my decision.

She agreed to play the part on Monday. On the Sunday, I worked with her and some of the actors who were in her scenes. On Monday we had a full dress, and that night she went on without script and gave a splendid performance.

I got pleas to give the ill actress another chance, threats when it was clear that I wouldn't, and curses when I persisted. I gave them all the same answer: that while her behaviour could not be tolerated, equally important was the fact that this option could save her career, perhaps her life. Over the weekend I had called a psychiatrist friend and he assured me I had done the right thing.

About a month later, she came in to see me and thanked me for what I had done. For the rest of my time as Deputy Artistic Director, she remained her old sweet, beautiful, sober self. I heard, I'm sad to say, that within a very few years after I left the job, she became gradually dependent on alcohol again and a beautiful actress was lost to the Abbey stage. Her beauty as a woman she certainly had not lost when I saw her years later.

During my Deputy tenure, I persuaded the Abbey Board to introduce a bursary for playwrights — something that would allow a young writer to give a year to writing without worrying about earning a living. I thought the only condition ought to be that he or she offered the work first to the Abbey. Olwen and I spent a wonderful long weekend with Brian Friel, in his cottage at the tip of Donegal, talking about the idea. He told me there should be no conditions attached to the bursary. This took me a while to swallow.

The first winner was a young man — Gallagher, I think his name was. I know he wrote a one-act which we put on as a showcase in the Peacock. Bizarre and funny, it ended with a man winding out paper bus tickets from one of those bus conductor's little gadgets, down between the open, artificial legs of a woman lying on a beach. The actress I cast in the role of the woman has not forgiven me to this day! I lost a friend. 'There's a sacrifice in every work of art,' the young monks at Dunamon had taught me when I lectured there.

In the Plough, one morning over coffee, a visiting American student, hearing one of our number being 'ribbed' about his weight, observed, 'Remember, inside every fat man, there is a thin man trying to get out.'

'Yes,' remarked the wittiest of us there, 'and outside every thin woman there is a fat man trying to get in!'

This was the inspiration for me to approach the poet Brendan Kennelly about writing a show for me about 'love and the Irish', drawing from his own works and from famous songs, stories, and poems by other writers.

With one of our best actresses, Aideen O'Kelly; a talented, attractive folk-singer and guitarist named Heather Hodgins; and myself, we premièred Brendan's *Irishmen Make Lousy Lovers?* early in June of 1971, at the first Listowel Writers Week, in that hometown of Brendan Kennelly, John B. Keane, Maurice Walsh, Bryan MacMahon, and George Fitzmaurice.

There are ballads, great lyrical poetry, and wholesome bawdiness in Brendan's *Irishmen Make Lousy Lovers?* The show is laced with outrageously funny poems about Kennelly's Listowel Renaissance man, Moloney. The first of these deals with an Irish farmer going to Lourdes to pray for a cure for his small 'dicky' — penis. This poem comes quite early in the show. To my dismay I saw, when the stage lights came up, that the whole front row of the packed hall was filled with *nuns*! I considered dropping the poem and skipping to the next cue. *But there is nothing wrong with this poem, I thought; I owe it to author, actors and audience to show that!*

Well, there were little laughs, some big laughs, and small applause when it was finished. There was a beat of silence. Then a little titter started at the very back of the hall and rolled forward, growing as it passed each row, and arrived with a roar behind the nuns, who started to laugh, slap their knees, and slap one another's backs. Two or three actually fell off their chairs laughing. From there on, we were all together astride the moon!

In the *Evening Herald*, JJF called it 'an Irish *Oh! Calcutta.*' John B. Keane had the last word again, as he did the first time we met: 'You're a cute hoor, Dowling!' With responses like that, we moved it to Dublin in the autumn, to the Busáras Theatre, where it packed out every night till Aideen had to leave, after several one-week extensions, to keep another engagement.

Ah, but … I was punished for my sins. Between long days at the Abbey and nights at Busáras, I got nodules on my throat. They were removed, tested and found to be 'maybe' cancerous. Cobalt treatment was ordered at St Luke's Hospital in Rathgar — something I would have to deal with later.

When one of my students came back from her time in Chicago and Loyola, I asked her about my carpenter friend from Kiltimagh, who had made the door for *Orphans*. She told me that he was dead: he had had some disease, had been taken to hospital and given extreme unction, and had died there.

Some months later, I was in my office on my own at lunchtime. Everyone else had gone. Paddy, the front-of-house man, rang me and said, 'There's a man here to see you — from America.' He mentioned his name but I was up to my eyes, and I just said absently, 'Send him up.' It was only after I hung up that I realised, *But he's dead!*

And then the door opened, and it was him. I said, 'You'll have to give me a minute. I'm in shock. I thought you were dead!'

So he told me the story. He had indeed been in hospital, in a coma. Members of his family had taken it in turns to stay by his bedside; and one day, through his coma, he heard one of them saying that one of his young daughters had spilled a pot of boiling water over herself and been badly scalded. And, somewhere inside his coma, he thought: I can't die. I have to get well and look after her.

And he did. For the second time in his life, he had come back from the middle of the River Styx!

You don't go out to Inishbofin, the Island of the White Cow; you come into it. You go out to the mainland on the mail boat, a large fishing trawler. The mainland here is Cleggan Harbour on Connemara's battered shore, some seven miles of open Atlantic to the east-northeast.

I think it was Tiffin Maguire, Olwen's employer and our friend, who suggested Inishbofin to us. Certainly, we met with her there. Alan, Justine, Jeremy and Andrew Rynhart, Cian, Olwen and I shared a house in the East Village for the month of June: a wheel of Stilton cheese; a case of vintage port; fresh crab legs; lobsters; good walks; swims; boats, fishing; rabbiting; partying, drinks and darts in the Day family's hotel. We made friends, special ones: Malachi — the Pirate, I called him; his brother, sister and mother; Margaret and Paddy Day; and Pat Concannon, a survivor of the Cleggan Disaster, the storm that had decimated the fishing families of the west coast decades before. Pat told me that the night of the disaster he held on to his fish-filled nets all through the night, while his fishermen friends let their currachs run with the wind to be smashed to pieces on the Cleggan rocks. When I say he held on, he had the nets looped over his wrists. The cords cut his flesh through to the bones of his two arms.

There were poets, local and imported, on the island that June. One was Tom MacIntyre, a playwright. I introduced his work to the Abbey and together we owned a currach. Debbie Tall, an American poet, shared his heart, hearth, and home. There was Sydney Smith and, for a few days, Joseph Brodsky, newly arrived from bondage in the Soviet Union.

Inishbofin is Ireland in miniature — about three miles long and a half-mile wide. Mountains, valleys, streams, ponds and a lake where the 'White Cow' appears, sand hills, beaches, a soapstone quarry, a harbour, high cliffs where seals respond to your whistle. A Cromwellian ruined fort, miles of dirt roads — boreens — with almost no cars, no police, hedges with fields and bogs beyond them, horses, donkeys, cattle, sheep, dogs, cats, hens, geese, and on every side that ever-changing sea, overhead the sailing clouds. Inishbofin is different from Ireland only in that the rabbit disease, myxomatosis, couldn't swim the salt sea from the mainland. The thousands of rabbit burrows, I always feared, would yet sink this brave island.

As the end of Hugh Hunt's absentee Artistic Directorship of the Abbey and my term as Deputy approached, I re-directed *The Shadow of a Gunman*, with Lady Gregory's *Gaol Gate* as a curtain-raiser. The Abbey board still insisted, against my advice, on giving the audience three full acts for the cheapest tickets in the English-speaking capitals of the western world.

I learned four valuable lessons from Professor Hunt:

1) Great plays have pressures of time — the times in which they were written, are set, and are being performed — that must be deeply considered in directing.

2) Actors' talent and creativity are as delicate as flowers and must be nurtured and protected if they are to blossom.

3) In the move from rehearsal room to stage, trust your actors to adapt. The work done will show itself after they adjust.

4) Be very cautious of people whom you graciously put yourself out to help; they are likely to try to put you down so they needn't feel grateful.

Though the players wanted me to, and Tomás Mac Anna generously encouraged me, and my standing with the Board and shareholders was high, I did not apply for the position of Artistic Director. I think now I was wrong. It was partly fear of being rejected, but largely the realisation that I would have to sack some colleagues who should never have been made members of the Abbey Company. Equally difficult, I would have been obliged to require drastic changes in attitude to the work day, to the matter of rehearsal hours and to the question of playing one part while rehearsing another at the same time, all of which would hurt those closest to me. Anyway, I owed it to myself to concentrate on my own acting and direction.

Brendan Smith offered me the direction of a Brian Friel première for production at the Olympia Theatre. The play, *The Gentle Island*, was inspired by the evacuation of a small island off the coast of Brian's home county, Donegal. The excitement of doing a new Brian Friel, with the actors and designer I would work with, was further enhanced by a plot that tackled leaving home and 'the love that dare not speak its name'. Bosco Hogan and Sheelagh Cullen were the young marrieds, and Liam Redmond was a kind of Pat Concannon of *The Gentle Island*; they were the trio that have refused to leave their island home. Shane Connaughton and Edward Byrne were two homosexual strangers from the mainland. The design was by David Wilson. This combination of talents provided me with the kind of project I dreamed about.

My voice, which had been damaged during *Irishmen Make Lousy Lovers?*, was getting worse. I had had the nodules on my vocal chords removed at the Eye and Ear Hospital, but a few days later Dr Curtain, the Abbey throat specialist, phoned to say that I should make an appointment at St Luke's Cancer Hospital. There, cobalt treatment was prescribed as necessary and urgent.

Would it affect my voice, I wanted to know?

I might lose one or two notes, but it would hardly be noticeable.

But would I be able to use my voice during the next weeks of rehearsal, particularly on the dress and technical rehearsal days? I gave them the dates. They calculated and said that, if I waited till the next Monday for the cobalt, it wouldn't affect me till after the dates I had named.

The following Monday at 6.00 p.m., I presented myself at St Luke's. The specialist's assistant apologised: his superior was ill and their calculations had, on second checking, proved incorrect. We would have to postpone the cobalt treatment for a further week.

As I walked out in the dark evening onto Highfield Road I met Lelia Doolin. She lived round the corner. A mutual friend, Finn O'Shannon, an actress, was there, and they were expecting my brother Jack. When they heard my tale, they begged me not to have the treatment. Finn knew a brilliant voice doctor in London, Sir Norman Punt, whose clients included the Covent Garden Opera Company. I thanked them but said I would trust the Irish doctors every bit as much, and I left shortly before Jack arrived.

Next morning Jack called the Olympia Theatre and tried to persuade me that I must go to London. He told me he had been talking to Brian Friel, who agreed with him. At the end of rehearsal, Brian walked with me to the Abbey and not only lent his voice to Jack's and the others, but told me, 'I have a thousand pounds I don't need. I want you to take it and go, please — for all our sakes, as well as yours!'

For once in my life, I had some spare money of my own; but I was moved and impressed that all of these people were confident that, in this area of medicine, at the time, there were greater skills available in Britain and Europe. So I went.

Norman Punt was waiting for me in a formal morning suit, though it was after six o'clock in the evening. I had brought the slides with the offending particles of nodules. He examined them carefully and said, 'I will be sending these to the best man in the world in these matters. I wouldn't say this if I was not relatively sure, but you have not got cancer on your vocal cords. Enjoy yourself for the next day and a half. Call me first thing on Thursday morning and I will give you the good news officially.'

It was only when I called at about 8.30 a.m. that Thursday morning, and he confirmed his opinion, that I realised how tense I had been. I hadn't even shown it to myself. I put down the phone and danced and pranced about my small hotel room, whooping like a child playing an Indian brave. I knew it was a silly thing to do, but I couldn't stop. Then I called Olwen with my good news. And I gave up smoking then and there.

'I spend a lot of time writing and rewriting my plays,' Brian Friel told me, 'and I'm sure some people can improve them. But, you see, I want to see *my play* done, however imperfect it is, not someone else's version of it.' That is not to say he didn't listen to suggestions. He always listened to them, considered them, and mostly rejected them.

I loved working with Brian. There are playwrights who see a script as a collaboration, and those who see the script as sacrosanct. Generally, the latter are better playwrights. As a director, I loved that Brian had an opening scene in the play where we met several emigrating islanders, beautifully captured in a few lines, as they left home for the last time. We had top-class actors like Maureen Toal and Eamon Morrissey to play them. But as a producer, I know that the cost of several more actors lessens the chances of *The Gentle Island* being produced, and that's a pity.

I don't always love my productions in retrospect, but this play is as satisfying and true to me today as it was all those years ago. Vivid, if brief, images of each actor in Brian Friel's play on David Wilson's island are extraordinary. They are themselves, not themselves — Brian's characters, not his characters — five unique beings complete with souls, more real than the person next door and more alive than the birds at my bird-feeder. I count myself 'most prosperous' that I know them in their ordinary and imaginative lives.

In December 1971, Lelia Doolin was appointed Artistic Director of our National Theatre. She had the vitality, the vision, the artistic and educational experience. She had the character to harness these gifts to move the Abbey Theatre to a higher level of theatrical excellence and purpose. She had the will and the way to do it. But she did not have the support in the Abbey or the obliqueness to build it. Curious coalitions brought her down. Fear of change, like misfortune, makes strange bedfellows.

The White House was the name of a play by Tom Murphy, and of the pub it's set in. The pub owner is inspired by the presidency of John F. Kennedy, 'the darlin' of Ireland'. Part I takes place nine years after the president's death. It draws largely on an earlier work of Tom's, *Conversations on a Homecoming*. Part II deals with the Camelot-like development of the White House pub and all who live, love and drink there. Threatened by old prejudice and narrow minds, the Kennedy-like publican is finally brought down, on the day an assassin's bullet brings down the young Irish president in Dallas.

The first half gave me perhaps the most perfect writing and acting I have been associated with, excepting only the Moscow Arts production of *The Seagull* that I brought to the Abbey twenty years later. In the second half, though much of the writing and acting was first-class, the Kennedy parallel inhibited the play and players.

The *Herald Tribune* found Dan O'Herlihy's portrait of the Kennedyesque publican entirely convincing. The London *Times* called the play 'a resonant work by a writer of passion'. These two British papers and the *Telegraph*'s John Barber praised the acting of Nuala Hayes, Maura O'Donnell, John Kavanagh, Bosco Hogan, and Dan O'Herlihy. Lewis Logan's sets and Leslie Scott's lighting got honourable mention. My direction and casting were praised in terms that pleased me. The designers and I achieved a rare intimacy in the Abbey auditorium by lowering the acoustic ceiling and closing in the proscenium.

In later years, Tom Murphy, a poet and playwright of the highest order, reshaped his story and won universal praise. He concentrated on the *Conversations on a Homecoming* theme, with much smaller importance given to the Kennedy-influenced publican. Tom and his plays provide artists and audiences with glorious challenges, and all of us in Irish theatre are the better for it! I am, for sure.

'Vincent,' said Tom to me at the *White House* rehearsals, 'that move you gave where he looks back over his shoulder — I've seen you give that move before.' He was right, and I changed it. At the end of the run of the play he told a group of us, 'For six months after a play of mine is put on, anything that is wrong with the play is someone else's fault. After six months I begin to see,' he said with his infectious grin, 'some of them may be mine.'

'Olwen, if you are really serious about Vincent, you had better move in with him. That fellow would be happy to date you for the rest of his life,' said my friend and fellow actor, Dan O'Herlihy, to his eldest daughter, mother of his first grandson.

Whether that was true or not, I loved Olwen as I had never loved anyone before; and before you could say Daniel O'Herlihy, we were ensconced in Crosthwaite Park, in the middle-floor flat of the summer home of John Millington Synge. Below us were a marvellous actor friend and his beautiful model wife, Emmet and Sarah Bergin. Overhead was another handsome, talented actor, Brian McGrath, and his wife Caroline. The garden flat housed the caretakers and their young red-haired Stacey family. We all lived together in the house, which an American actor, Philip O'Brien, owned, and for which he charged his colleagues too much rent — especially one who had two families to keep! We all looked out our front windows onto a quiet, grassy, tree-lined park, a half-mile above Dun Laoghaire harbour.

Olwen furnished our flat with fifty pounds that I borrowed from the Abbey. Her parents contributed a few pieces of furniture. Olwen, who thought nothing of rearranging furniture and paintings in a motel room where we were staying only one night, was a miracle home-maker. She also got herself a job with Tiffin Maguire's local fashion shop. Cian went to a kindergarten, and we were very happy there — till the rent went up some two years later, which made me so angry with Philip O'Brien that I used to dream of setting his house on fire! Fortunately, that dream didn't come true!

The last play I acted in at the Abbey Theatre was in 1972. Sean Cotter and I worked together like Scotch and soda. He was directing Eugene O'Neill's *The Iceman Cometh*, and he asked me to play Hickey. I was almost forty-three years old, but I still looked ridiculously young for my age on stage; so I wore a white, tight wig that made me look like Mark Twain. Our designer was Polish, Voytek by name; and a terrific American black actor, George Webb, who worked mostly in Europe, further internationalised our production.

I think Eugene O'Neill would have loved to have seen the Abbey Company in his great play. He had always spoken of how the Abbey, on its first visit to America in 1911, had inspired him to go on writing the kind of plays he wanted to write. Harry Brogan as Harry Hope, Philip O'Flynn as Larry, Raymond Hardie, Des Cave, Bosco Hogan, and Bill Foley were amongst the most notable in the enormous cast. Said the British drama critic, Robin Hornber, 'The Abbey Company not only breathe a warm vitality into these dramatic parts and enrich the two pivotal roles of Hickey and Larry but they give an impetus that carries us deep into their desperate worlds.' The production opened in May and played until we closed for the annual June holidays, which Olwen and I spent on Inishbofin.

Iceman reopened in July. I had done a lot of thinking about my role on the island. I felt that I mastered this mountain of a role and caught a few more 'rays of the unrisen sun', as GBS says. I abandoned the wig and nobody missed it!

Tomás Mac Anna sent word that he would like to see me as soon as possible, in the Peacock, where he was watching a rehearsal for lunch-time performances of short plays by European writers, mostly. These were extending the range of the company and building new audiences.

'Vincent Dowling, how would you like to direct *Borstal Boy* in America this summer?' said Tomás, turning his long frame round in his seat and leaning over the back of the seat next to him, as I came into the row behind. 'I have spoken to Lelia Doolin and the Board, and they are prepared to release you.'

He explained that he had been asked to go to the Missouri Repertory Theater (MRT) to direct the Behan play, and direct another Irish play with the University of Missouri, Kansas City (UMKC), in addition to giving a number of public performances over three months. However, because he had just been appointed to the Abbey Board of Directors, Mr Blythe felt he should not absent himself from felicity so soon and for such a long while. 'I told MRT,' he went on, 'that no one in the world knows more about *Borstal Boy* than Vincent Dowling.'

On the public phone in the Plough at lunchtime, I called the number Tomás had given me and asked for a Pat McIlrath. A lady's voice answered. For some reason I took her to be the Artistic Director's secretary. She was expecting my call. She told me that the fee was ten thousand dollars, but that I would be responsible for my fare, board, and lodgings. They would help me to find a suitable place. I would be the holder of the Cockefair Chair of Continuing Studies at the University of Missouri Kansas City, and Visiting Director at the professional Equity MRT. The other recipients of this annual honour had been

John Houseman, Adrian Hall, and Alan Schneider, three of the most eminent men of American theatre. What really impressed me was the money! Even though it was dollars, not pounds, it was nearly two years' salary at the Abbey.

Whither thou goest, I will go; thy people shall be my people.... Ruth had nothing on Olwen. 'If you are going to America for three months, we are going with you!' she said bluntly.

'What do you mean, *we?*' I demanded.

'Cian and I.' We had agreed that we were never going to let work separate us, she reminded me firmly. That was true. We had. We both knew that few relationships in our profession could withstand long separation. There was no divorce in Ireland, and therefore no legal marriage for us.

We sublet our flat in Crosthwaite Park to Alan Barlow, the new designer/director at the Abbey Theatre. Sean Cotter graciously agreed to replace me in *The Iceman* with Clive Geraghty, though there was some rumbling and grumbling amongst the players. I flew off into the sunset and to the heartland of America. Olwen followed with Cian a week or so later, having sold my second-hand Standard Herald to pay their air fares!

The Bellerive Hotel, where we would stay, could have been the setting for a Tennessee Williams memory play. Unfairly nicknamed 'Cockroach Kingdom' by visiting actors, it had a good bar and a large swimming pool, where Olwen became the lifeguard and Cian learnt to swim. Our apartment had a large, high ceiling, two bedrooms with big windows, and spacious dining, living and kitchen areas. The white-tiled and marbled bathroom, too, belonged to an older, more elegant era.

The magic of the rising, glowing fireflies; the music of the cicadas; the moon on the land, lawns and trees; the smell of barbecued ribs and hamburgers; the colours of the girls' dresses, the men's shorts; the laughter and friendly voices; the cowboy songs at Colonel Graham's farm, south of Kansas City ... these set the scene for the beginning of my love affair with this Missouri city, its people, and its theatre. This love affair would in time embrace all these extraordinary United States, the land and its lore.

Pat McIlrath was, of course, not the Artistic Director's secretary. She was the founder of MRT and Chair of the theatre department of UMKC; she was an enlightened teacher, producer and director. I think of her as the Lady Gregory of American theatre.

I would need (and love) to have the Great Wall of China to record in stone the names of every actor, designer, director, student, administrator, teacher, technician, typist, theatregoer, patron, friend, journalist, man, woman, and child in the street, shop, bar, restaurant, or private home who welcomed, entertained, protected, and assimilated us into the life, community, culture, and heart of this wonderful city, which is itself the heart of America.

Gene Foley came to see us, stayed and introduced me to his democratic friends the Corcorans in Topeka, Kansas. He also brought me to Immigration in Kansas City and made me apply for an alien residency — the invaluable Green Card. Don Quinn acted in *Borstal Boy* and lent us a stick-shift car for our entire stay; he and his wife, Vicky, opened their house and Mexican restaurant to us, gave Olwen a job in their law office, acted for me in my divorce proceedings. They introduced us to our banker, John Sullivan, our accountant, Joe Starkey, and their own close friends, who became ours — like Judge George Berry and his wife, Dee — and they made Cian one of their beautiful family. It was Don who, when my application for a Green Card was questioned, swept aside the opposition and set me on the five-year road to full citizenship. I have only scratched the surface of the riches of love, friendship, loyalty, and support that Don and Victoria and their family heaped and continued to heap on us.

Robert 'Bob' Elliott played the younger Behan in *Borstal Boy* and quickly became my friend and favourite actor. Steve Ryan, who played the sympathetic warden at the boys' prison, also had the title role in *The Director*, by Syd Cheatle, with the brilliant Kathy Grodie and Bob Scogin. It was a phenomenal success as a lunchtime performance. Sally and Michael Mertz (who played my role as the sailor boy), Holmes Osborne (Cragg, one of the Borstal boys, and later an amazing Seumas Shields in *The Shadow of a Gunman*) — these actors I looked for whenever I was directing anywhere in America.

The standards of costume, lighting, and set design at MRT were awesome. I worked with Vincent Scassellati (costumer), Joe Appelt (lighting), and John Ezell (set) wherever and whenever I could get them. John Ezell was 'my designer' all through the years to 1984.

'Do you mind that I always refer to you as "my designer"?' I once asked him.

'No,' he smiled. 'I always call you "my director".'

Dinner in a posh restaurant in the Country Club Plaza with my hostess, Ophelia Demare, and another guest, Cecile Burton. We were introduced to the Senator for the State of Kansas. One of his hands was damaged, I noticed. His name was Robert Dole. Cecile, a retired teacher, was at every worthwhile cultural event that took place in or around KCMO. She had metal pins in her hips, but she did not let her crutches interfere with her love of the performing arts, or the parties given to support them. I met her first at the University Women's Club, where she invited me to speak. 'Love and the Irish', in poem and play, was my subject; it was the first of scores of lectures I gave to groups in each and every walk of life, as well as on radio and television.

The Mayor of Kansas City, Missouri (to distinguish it from Kansas City, Kansas, across the state line), invited me to address the City Council in City

Hall and presented me with the key to the city. I accepted, gave a talk on theatre and recited 'Meeting Point' by Louis MacNeice. Mayor Charles Wheeler and I became good friends, and, like so many of our friendships from KCMO, this one has lasted through the years.

The biggest challenge I accepted was from Michael Mardikes of Continuing Education, who asked me if I would help the people of the college and city to see 'the Troubles' in the North of Ireland from an Irish artist's perspective. Michael undertook to fill an eight-hundred-seat auditorium with the interested, intelligent, and influential, by ticket only — a black-tie affair covered by the top media people in the city. Part of the promotion was a photo essay. Michael himself shot photos of me in various locations throughout the city.

The night of my lecture arrived — 11 October 1972. As I was putting the final touches to my script, dressed in my tuxedo, the house phone rang to say that my limo had arrived. I decided I had better go for a pee, for safety's sake — I had timed my lecture at well over one hour. As I zipped my fly, my mind on my lecture, I caught, pinched and trapped my penis in the metal teeth of the infernal contraption! I screamed in agony; then, half-laughing and half-crying, I implored Olwen to be careful and gentle. She was, and — hey presto! I was free and in one piece.

I had done nearly two months' research in the city and university libraries, and written countless letters to informed friends in Ireland. I had formulated my presentation as a three-act play for a reader's theatre: Act I — What is it all about? Act II — How did it come about? Act III — What to do about it now? I squeezed in a thousand years of Irish/English history, the exploitation of religious differences for political and economic gain, and advocated a Republic of Northern Ireland solution and proportional representation. I was introduced by Homer Wadsworth, head of the Kansas City Trusts and Foundation, and my hour-and-a-half presentation was later published in the magazine *Perspectives* by the William Jewel University.

This appearance and presentation, and Homer's and his colleague Patricia Doyle's association with it, were the end of a long wedge that would open the door to the ten most productive years of my life, in another state and city, under the spell of William Shakespeare.

My production assistant on *Borstal Boy* was Liz Gordon. She and her husband Dick, a doctor, shared many a drink, meal, and word with me over that summer and autumn.

Olwen — who had been working part-time at Don Quinn's downtown office, acting as lifeguard at the Bellerive to keep the pool open, and minding Cian and me, not to speak of doing the continuous theatre and social round

— collapsed one afternoon at our apartment. We called Dick, and he arranged her admission to the hospital where he worked. This was my first awakening to the wonders of American health insurance. Having delivered Olwen into the care of the emergency person, I parked the car and then arrived at the emergency office to find that she was being held up until I gave details of my health coverage. Surprisingly, they accepted my Irish Voluntary Health Plan, on which, with rare foresight, I had included Olwen and Cian. She was well looked after and her immediate problem solved, but they warned us that there was serious work to be done on her ovaries when we got home.

By the time we left Kansas City — loaded with gifts, a large linocut print by Robert D. McGraham that Olwen had bought me, and several reviews from the *Kansas City Star*'s Giles Fowler — I was as well known as a begging ass, as my mother used to say.

Perhaps the reason I live in America and not in Ireland is that Olwen and I decided to drive Route 66 to California when my work at the university was done, towards the end of October. We had arranged to deliver/drive a big Ford saloon from Kansas City to San Francisco via Topeka.

Cian, dressed as a cowboy, was put in the hands of an air hostess to be flown to Los Angeles, where he would be picked up by Olwen's sister Patricia. I can still see this little nervous four-year-old, bravely stepping out beside the stewardess in his cowboy outfit, worried that they might impound his toy pistol, but even more worried that he was leaving his mother behind. I wanted to have this adventure alone with Olwen. It was wrong of me.

One morning, early on in our drive west, Olwen said to me that I would have to share the driving — that she couldn't drive six hundred miles a day, every day, which we would have to do to deliver this car on time.

'I'd love to drive if it was a stick shift. No way I'm going to drive one of these automatic yokes. I'd rather walk,' I said emphatically. 'You know the trouble I went to in Kansas City to get a stick shift.'

'I know the trouble the Quinns went to, giving us their stick shift,' was her truthful comeback. 'But there's nothing to it. You just tuck your left foot under the seat and only use your right foot on the gas and the brake.'

'Why didn't you tell me this all summer?' I cried when I found how simple it was.

'You didn't ask me,' Olwen said. I said nothing. I know when I'm licked!

The drive was a journey through every great Western film I had seen. The excitement of the Texas panhandle, Dodge City, New Mexico with its Painted Desert and Canyon de Chelly, Santa Fé, the Grand Canyon Caves, the Saguaro National Forest, and the barren hills and desert into California sealed my commitment to this vast and varied land from sea to shining sea. Kansas City had given me a grasp on a town; this drive made me long to grasp every facet of this amazing continent.

High up on Kings Road in Hollywood, we were welcomed warmly to the feudal domain of Michael O'Herlihy (main director of the television series *Hawaii 5-0*) by Michael, Olwen's beloved aunt and my old friend Elizabeth, their son Conal and their daughters Niamh and Emer. We stayed and we partied — at least, Olwen did. Next morning I departed, alone — well, alone with my hangover — to the City of the Golden Gates.

I got a ticket in San Francisco to ACT (the American Conservatory Theater) and was impressed by Bill Ball's direction of *Cyrano de Bergerac*. This resident professional not-for-profit theatre, like scores of others across the US, had production values at least as good as the best I had seen in Ireland or Britain. Later I met Desmond Grogan, of Brendan Smith Academy days, and later still Judy Dolan, one of Missouri Rep's brilliant costume designers. She was working on a Yeats project at Stanford University in Palo Alto. I was so impressed with her and her group that I put her in touch with the Abbey, where she became a costume designer for some years. She stole one of our actors — Raymond Hardie, whom I had brought into the Abbey Company — married him and spirited him away to California.

During one of the O'Herlihys' parties, Gene Foley called me from New York. He wanted me to rescue a benefit for an Irish arts group, which, with its director's sudden exit, looked as though it could not be put together again.

'Get me a first-class Equity stage manager,' I said, 'and I'll do it.' They got me Les Robinson, and we put Humpty Dumpty together again.

'Do you know who they only had in it?' as they might say in Dublin. A group of brilliant Irish traditional musicians in their American debut, friends and colleagues from Sean O'Riada's Abbey Theatre pit orchestra and Ceoltóirí Culainn — later reformed by Paddy Maloney as the Chieftains; actress Geraldine Fitzgerald; the poet Tom Kinsella, with his epic poem *Táin*; and the actor Dermot MacNamara. All these in the Abbey Theater on 13th Street in New York (no relation to the Dublin Abbey).

I stayed with Gene Foley in Hastings-on-Hudson, outside New York. With him I visited Alan Schneider, the well-known Samuel Beckett director, a small dark man bursting with eager interest and energy. Appropriately, his chosen means of transport was a spluttering motorbike. He wanted to meet me, as he was next to sit on the Cockefair Chair at UMKC. I reassured him he had nothing to worry about in the matter of the quality of actors and designers — far from it!

I went with Gene to the Chelsea Theatre to see David Storey's *The Contractor*. 'Bobs' Fitzgerald, an old Irish actor, was in it. He wanted to see me to give me a photo taken on Easter Monday 1916, the day of the Irish Easter

Rising. It was taken in Wexford on a picnic outing for the local opera company, which included the Hantons, Dan O'Herlihy's mother's family.

When I got back to California, Olwen and I spent time at Ojai with the McIsaacs on their ranch before flying the North Pole route to Ireland on Aer Lingus. I carried with me images and memories of people, places, and possibilities in America; images of actors, trained and talented, committed to their regional resident professional companies — so open and eager to give themselves fully to the play, instead of to the next television, film, Broadway, or London West End production.

Between 1973 and May 1974 I did two of my best productions for the Abbey Company, as well as the two most cruelly murdered by the critics. Back home after Kansas City, I took over as Director of the Peacock, determined to test some of the borders that surrounded our work. At the suggestion of a taxi driver, who was one of a group of new playwrights in a weekly workshop, I made my first choice.

'Do you want to do the best play ever written?' he said, in his flat Dublin accent.

'I do,' I said, without hesitation. 'What is it?'

'*Exiles* by James Joyce.'

'I'll read it, and if I agree with you, I'll do it.'

So I read Act I. I said to Olwen, 'If Act II is as good as Act I, I may have found my first production for the season in the Peacock.' Act II was so good, I was afraid to start Act III in case I'd be disappointed. I took a deep breath, crossed my fingers and read on. It was exactly as it should be.

I sought out the taxi driver the next day and gave him the news. 'I'm delyred,' he said, as only a Dubliner can say 'delighted', and shook my hand.

I got precisely the players I wanted. If the ghost of James Joyce had come back and waved a magic wand over the script, these would have been the actors he conjured. Bosco Hogan, cold as fury outside, a volcano below the skin. Nuala Hayes, the vision in moonlight that Joyce describes in the play, yet with the character's working-girl hands. Kevin McHugh, the 'other man' in the rectangle, made for the part. And Máire O'Neill, as sensitive as a thoroughbred, as private as a priestess. Even for the smaller parts of the housekeeper and the boy-child, May Cluskey and Donald Reynolds acted as if they belonged in this household.

But wait a minute! What's experimental about *Exiles*? The fact that the play was virtually a Joycean autobiography, and the darkly sexual implications in the plot, make it interesting but not experimental. The fact that it had not worked when done in Dublin by a first-class cast for one night, years before, only made it dangerous, ripe for a ripping apart by reviewers and scholars.

But supposing this *once* the critics joined the creative team in the pre-production planning and stayed with it through the rehearsals, opening, and run of the play, imparting their educated, experienced responses, through the director, to the actors every day? If this experiment helped artistically or creatively, further study would follow. If it didn't, there was a good possibility that the critics' critiques of this approach would be valuable to artists, critics and their readers alike. Each newspaper, magazine, radio and television outlet would be encouraged to send reviewers to write a review of the production in the usual way, while each 'participating' critic could publish a personal evaluation of the experience at the end of the run.

I presented this proposal at a press conference in the Peacock. There was a lively exchange of points of view; no one took up the challenge except Sean Page, one of the best critical minds to engage in theatre that I know. As Deputy Artistic Director, I had invited Sean to read new plays for the Abbey. He had said no; he was haunted that he would have rejected *Waiting for Godot* if he had read it before he saw it. 'So would I!' I replied. I persuaded him to change his mind. As he worked with us every day on *Exiles*, Sean's presence, insights, suggestions and objections made his contribution to the astonishing success of the production equal to that of any of the cast.

The reviews ranged from very good to excellent. Still, the question lingers: if the pursuit of perfection in drama is important to the pursuit of happiness in life, was Sean Page's contribution to this production of *Exiles*, to everyone in it, and to everyone who saw it, greater or less than that of the reviews in *The Irish Times*, the *Irish Press* and the *Irish Independent*?

Other works I did, many because they were new or by women writers, included *Rites* by Maureen Duffy and an old Abbey one-act by T.C. Murray, *The Briary Gap*, with material written by Mary Maher of *The Irish Times* interspersed, pinpointing facts and statistics relating to Irish girls' adoptions and legal abortions in Britain. With *The Doll in the Gap* we used non-commercial 'commercials' on our intolerance towards tinkers. I co-directed some of these plays with young, up-and-coming directors like Jim Sheridan and Bryan Murray. There was also a new play about a very old historical figure, *King Herod Advises*, by Conor Cruise O'Brien. Marie Kean, directed by Jim Sheridan, provided a memorable *Happy Days* by Samuel Beckett, and Lelia Doolin and Colm O'Brien co-directed an Irish-language rock musical called *Johnny Orfeo*, based on *Orpheus in the Underworld*.

One afternoon, a woebegone Valerie and a sad, bedraggled little Rachael, followed by a covey of their school pals, streeled into the Peacock during rehearsal. Hugs and kisses on tearstained faces comforted my unhappy little ones.

It all came out. They had been caught stealing a book in Eason's on O'Connell Street. It wasn't the first time they had done it. The second? Maybe the third; and 'they' had been watching for the little book-snatchers. 'They' wanted to speak to Brenda or me. I was the one Valerie chose to tell first.

Of course, I realised this shoplifting was everything to do with me and my not being with them. I promised them I'd look after it, there would be no more said about it, but there was no way this could be allowed to happen again. I saw 'them' at Eason's, paid what was owed and explained the family situation. They could not have been more understanding and helpful. It never did happen again.

The Shame of It was a tale of two brothers, their parents, and two towns, Dublin and somewhere in Wexford. The idea that I should do it was a tale of two cities, too. John Berry, director, actor, and the self-appointed conscience of Irish theatre, told me in New York that I must do it. Ronnie Walsh, shortly after I was appointed Director of the Peacock by Lelia Doolin, pitched it to me. The play, by the poet Anthony Cronin, had been published in the *Dublin Magazine*. John and Ronnie both pressed copies of it on me. I read one but still have both.

I loved it. The shame children have for one or both parents — I had always felt it, never dared think about it. I loved my mother. She loved me. How could I be ashamed of her? But I often was. I particularly hated to see her sit on an armchair or sofa, her knees apart, showing her old-fashioned pink knickers! I find it difficult even to write that.

The play is pure poetry, long, wonderful sentences and speeches Shakespeare would not be ashamed to claim. Funny, painful, honest. It could be called *The Pat Layde Story*, I thought, when I read it. It needed careful cutting — a lot of cutting.

Ronnie would play the Tony Cronin part; Des Nealon — a lovely, true actor and friend — was the slightly shifty, not quite criminal but certainly damaged brother. I was to direct.

With something like a week's rehearsal still to go, it became clear that Ronnie could not learn the huge amount of dialogue — dialogue that had to be spoken accurately: to improvise it would be like messing around with Beckett, Tom Murphy, Brian Friel or Shakespeare. So I took over. Ronnie sat in the director's seat, but he let my direction stand.

Olwen had gone to see a specialist; it was a recurrence of her Kansas City medical problem. An immediate and serious operation to remove one of her ovaries was undertaken at Holles Street Hospital. It was a success, though she had to — and could, in those days — recuperate in hospital. I used to stop by every day after rehearsal and lie on the bed beside her, and she would hear my lines. She loved the language, the story, the poetical, comical, tragical, familial, revealing piece it was — to us.

The play wasn't cut to pieces by the critics. It was shredded, mashed, burned to ashes. By the end of the first week — and it was clear there could be no second week — Tony and I called everyone we knew. We invited them *free* to the Saturday night — the last night. You *never* get complimentaries on a Saturday! Next to none of our friends or families could come, wanted to come or came; but Mr Charles Haughey TD brought a small entourage of henchmen and their better halves, plus a case of excellent champagne. Together, cast, crew, author, House Manager Lily Shanley, and Charlie laid this murdered corpse of Anthony Cronin's perfectly named play *The Shame of It* to rest with a wake that Finnegan would have been proud to call his own.

Later that summer, I returned to Kansas City, Missouri, to direct Syd Cheatle's *Straight Up* with much success and a wonderful cast headed by Harriet Levitt, Steve Ryan, Michael Mertz, Priscilla Lindsay and Kathy Grodie. Being in Kansas City felt like I really had come home. In the autumn I went back to do a series of higher education lectures and workshops in Kansas and Missouri. While I was there, I edited my 'Irish Agony: An Artist's Perspective' for William Jewell College in Missouri. My editor was a young female faculty member; I stayed with her and her husband.

A greater shame than *The Shame of It* — my shame, though I was in the US, and the Abbey Company's: Frank Dermody's last productions ever, the John Synge one-act *In the Shadow of the Glen* and *Coats* by Lady Gregory, opened with no fanfare, closed with no moaning at the Plough, the Flowing Tide or any other bar.

Some months later, I met him one night after closing time, as I was getting into my car on the quays round the corner from the Abbey. I told him about my latest American trip — how in everything I did over there, every actor I worked with, I was using what he had taught me. How I gave him credit to them. They all knew him, almost as well as I did.

'Yes.' He listened quietly. 'I am told you always give me credit. I appreciate it, Vincent.'

Then for an hour or more I asked him, begged him, to settle for just 'first-class' with actors in rehearsal. 'Let them get it right and build on that. For the good ones, and most of them are good, that will be the launching pad into the "glory" you're looking for — the perfection that will make "God stand still when they move"!'

I knew at the end, though he was listening, he didn't hear me. He couldn't settle any more for anything but 'glory' from the very beginning.

I'm afraid there was an element of old-fashioned jealousy about Radio Éireann's decision to axe perhaps the most popular radio programme ever — *The Kennedys of Castlerosse*. We were suddenly told that we were to go to the Henry Street studios and record *the last episode*.

There was great talk from cast, writers, even some of the public, about this disgraceful Radio Éireann decision. 'The people will never allow this to happen,' they said. I said, 'I'm taking it to Actors' Equity.'

Dermot Doolan, too, was outraged, but he said RÉ had the right to do it. I held we had a right to financial compensation in place of due notice being given. RÉ did not accept that premise. Equity were not prepared to go to battle for it. I proposed that the cast of the series mount an unofficial strike and put a picket line at the entrance of the studio on Henry Street. (The entrance is actually a side door to the General Post Office, which was seized by the Citizens' Army and the Irish Volunteers in the 1916 Rising.) We should refuse to record the last episode, I said, and keep a picket there till the series was restored or adequate compensation in lieu of notice was paid. There was no question in my mind that we had been shamefully underpaid for nigh on eighteen years.

The *Kennedys* cast — bar one: 'meself' — decided to record the episode. It would be a historical episode; they wanted to be part of it.

That last Sunday was a cold day, I remember. Well wrapped up and carrying a home-made wooden shoulder picket sign, made by Olwen, proclaiming 'STRIKE', I stood outside the studio entrance. The other cast members sheepishly slunk past me, as did RÉ staff. Only one actor refused to cross my picket line — or should I say my picket dot?

That was Des Nealon. We went across to the Pillar Café and had a coffee, and I persuaded him — and it took me some time to do so — to go in. I knew I was going to spend a lot of time in America in the future; also, I was permanent and pensionable at the Abbey. Des was a freelance actor and shouldn't antagonise RÉ. I withdrew my picket, and he reluctantly entered in. The series director read my part of Christy Kennedy. As long as there is a Des Nealon, Romantic Ireland isn't quite dead, not altogether gone!

Olwen and I found a tiny restored cottage in Kilpedder, County Wicklow. My American voyages had earned me enough to cover a deposit. Another of my dreams had come true: Olwen and I would live in the country in a tiny village under the Wicklow Mountains, a mile from the sea, with a pub next door, no phone, and no TV.

As we were leaving Crosthwaite Park I said to Olwen, 'Did you see a box of letters? All my letters from Sinéad Cusack. Someday I intend to make a play from them, a kind of *Dear Liar*....' I was rambling on and I realised she was purposely ignoring me. 'Olwen, did you hear what I said?'

'Yes, I heard you,' she said defensively, and I felt she was somehow very upset. I couldn't understand why. I had told her about the letters, made no secret of them.

'Well?' I asked.

'I burned them!' And she had.

I was flabbergasted — not annoyed, not angry, just flabbergasted. At the same time it was dawning on me that she had burned them because she loved me; she was jealous of a past that had taken place before we even knew each other! I was still flabbergasted, though. The letters were gone! No more! Forever! But I loved Olwen even more, if it was possible, because of why she did it. Was I actually beginning to grow up at last?

Tomás Mac Anna, who had taken over as Artistic Director of the Abbey when Lelia Doolin resigned, made Joe Dowling his right-hand person. (Though Joe Dowling is much younger then I am, when people asked me if we were related I always said with a straight face, 'Yes, he is my father!') That Lelia had not been supported by the Company or the Board was not to their credit. That they chose Tomás to replace her, however, ensured that the Abbey tradition would be safe for a time — guarded. Still, I was saddened that so much of Blythe's debris still cluttered the Abbey.

Tomás and Joe offered me *The Glass Menagerie* to direct at the Peacock. I had seen the play years before at the Gaiety, presented by Illsley-McCabe Productions. They were known in Dublin as 'Fish and Chaps': Stanley Illsley was very English, and Leo McCabe's money came from a high-class fish shop.

I read and read again Tennessee Williams's exquisite play and decided I very much wanted to do it. The budget I was given was negligible and I had to cast within the Company. I was offered — or did my daughter Bairbre suggest him? — Lester Livingstone as designer. He was, I remember, when I met him in his flat in Monkstown, not enamoured with the idea of doing a play at the Peacock. When I told him my idea of doing it as a black-and-white film, which was literally how I saw it when I read it, he became wholeheartedly my partner in the project. He took the idea and pursued it through sets, costumes, props, furniture, and somehow lights. We couldn't afford a scrim, a gauze curtain, so he created a wall made of taut strings that could be painted and looked solid when lit from the front; lit from behind it disappeared, just like a scrim.

Maura O'Donnell was my Amanda, Terri Donnelly was Laura, Bosco Hogan was Tom, and young Bryan Murray was the gentleman caller. Terri, I knew, was a good actress and had the delicate frame and features for Laura. She wasn't conventionally pretty, though, and her concern about this was affecting her performance in rehearsal. I knew I had to make a breakthrough with her or replace her, or she might replace herself. We went downstairs in the Flowing Tide one day and talked. Somehow, in the talk I got her to smile. When I saw that smile I knew it could be our salvation. When she smiled she didn't become pretty, she became beautiful. Terri's performance, in every way, was beautiful. She glowed from within. She was as beautiful as, or more beautiful than, any Laura I had seen.

We opened the play in Cork. Bryan Murray was not making it as the gentleman caller. I think it was inexperience and self-denigration. I was able to do for young Bryan what Dermody had done for me: help him find his centre. Bryan went on to make a name for himself all over the English-speaking world as Florrie, the Irish charmer and co-star in *The Irish RM* on television. Maura O'Donnell had moved into Amanda right away, and Amanda took over Maura O'Donnell. This was Maura fulfilling her potential.

Bosco Hogan was himself, he was Tom, he was Tennessee Williams. That is the way great acting should be. We have a secret, Bosco and I, which even now I don't tell. This much I will say: there was something magic that I felt could happen in Tom's final speech, if Bosco could accept a thought I whispered in his ear at the last dress rehearsal in Dublin. I promised him I would tell no one, ever, what it was. Well, thereafter, God dared not move whenever Tom told us his memory of his sister, Laura. If ever I had proof that the subconscious of an actor could talk to the subconscious of the audience, this was it.

There are plays that can hit the critic hard, below the belt, causing a gut rejection of the play or the performance. There is no doubt that Anthony Cronin had touched many raw nerves in other writers with his play *The Shame of It*. Anthony, of course, had done pretty nifty carving of others in his career as a literary critic. That is not an excuse for what they did to his play, but it is a reason.

Now, Wilson John Hare had carved nobody, but in *The Bloom of the Diamond Stone* he provoked those gut reactions — and how! Wilson John was the son of a Belfast mixed marriage. Though raised a Catholic, thanks to the Catholic Church's rules for these marriages, he had worked in the Belfast shipyards. He told me he continually allowed his Protestant workmates to assume he was a Protestant. This had caused a heavy strain on his psyche and a lot of deep heart-searching. As a result, his play seethed with 'a plague on both your houses'.

Wilson John Hare's uncompromising distaste for violence from anyone aggravated many nationalist nerves. *The Irish Times* critic, several months after he had made one of his frequent 'pilgrimages to Knock' the Abbey (as Paddy Long called Abbey first nights) and had participated in the next day's ritual carving of the play and my production, again attacked the mutilated remains of *The Diamond Stone*. He accused me of dishonesty because a part of the film that I had made, from TV coverage of the North of Ireland, and used to link the scenes in this Belfast drama, was taken from an incident that had taken place *after* the period in which the play was set! 'The light of lights sees the motive, not the deed. The shadow of shadows sees the deed alone,' wrote W.B. Yeats in *The Countess Cathleen*.

I planned to take the cast, those who were not involved in another production at the time, to Belfast for a weekend. I wanted them to get the feeling of life in the working classes during these Troubles. I think only three came with me: a stage manager, a young boy in the play, and Veronica Duffy, the young actress who played the lead so truthfully and so well.

The most interesting thing for me was that Father Desmond Wilson — with whom we stayed in Ballymurphy, one of the Catholic concrete bunkers of Belfast — and a large group of his parishioners, many of them practising Catholics, some of them maybe practising gunmen, all of them nationalists, came as a party to the play in Dublin. They were very moved by it, and many of them told me, 'There's a lot of truth in it all the same.'

'I've got a pal in Kalamazoo!' That was my refrain from the time Bob Smith played the Catholic priest in the MRT production of *Straight Up* in Kansas City. Bob arranged for me to direct *The Playboy of the Western World* in Kalamazoo at Western Michigan University. More than that, he linked me up with George Gunkle, Chair of the theatre department at California State University at Northridge, California. I now had my alien resident's card; I also had an offer from Dr McIlrath at MRT to direct and act in a whole season in the summer of 1974 and a short winter season and spring tour in 1975, followed by a directing gig to open the 1975 summer programme. So I asked the Abbey for a year off, without pay, from 1 July 1974, to 1 July 1975. I was actually able to go in early June because of the annual Abbey holidays. I was confident I would be able to fill the gaps in my year when I got to America.

Before going back to the US, I accepted an invitation to direct one of my earliest theatrical loves — Anton Chekhov's *The Cherry Orchard* — at the Lyric Theatre, Belfast, from the founder, the visionary, Mary O'Malley. Madame Ranevskaya would be played by Blánaid Irvine, who had starred in my *Orphans* production at the Gate, and for whom I had, many years before, harboured romantic longings — which, like several others, I'm glad to remind myself, grew into an affectionate friendship.

This was the year of the car bombs in Belfast. Crossing the car-lined streets, I found myself continually playing the game of choosing at which car to cross the street, to what car on the other side. I used the make of the car, the colour, the age, whether it was mud-splashed or newly washed, to make my choices. It wasn't funny, and it was literally ulcer-making. However, I'm here to tell the tale, and so I must have been doing something right. My old friends at the Agnews' Club Bar on University Road had been bombed, and all pubs and the theatre demanded examination of any package or case carried in. P.J.'s black briefcase was opened and closed as often as eyelids.

There was a real sense of company at the Lyric, and very good actors. We worked hard, and a few of us frequented the Belfast Arts Club most nights. I saw a lot of Eugene and Maureen Black, who had returned from Bahrain and bought a little off-licence liquor shop just down from the theatre. They acted, unwillingly, as bankers for the IRA and Protestant militia groups: both sides withdrew money from them, at gunpoint, at regular intervals. Well, Eugene had survived a short career on the stage and a longer one in the Middle East working for an oil company. He would in time look back on Belfast, too, and laugh.

Maureen asked me to give a talk at the convent where her daughters went to school. It was on the Falls Road, in the Catholic ghetto. I did. It went well, and the convent proved to be the only school in my long experience where the glass of water I asked for was three-quarters gin and one-quarter tonic. They weren't called the Mercy nuns for nothing! 'It's all right,' my mother used to say, 'to drink with a nun, as long as you don't get into the habit!'

Two fellows at the Belfast Arts Club asked me, that same evening, to a prize-giving dinner for volunteers in a boys' club in a suburb on the north side of Belfast. Our car ride would take us through Sandy Row, a Protestant section of the city. It was late on a Saturday afternoon. We were due at the dinner at 6.30 p.m. I told my companions that I would like to stop and have a drink in Sandy Row.

One of the fellows, Alan, was English. The other, Bill, was a Northern Irish radio producer, if I remember correctly. 'Not on your life,' was their unequivocal response.

I argued a bit, said I was disappointed, I wanted to get a feel of the Protestant side of things. Sure, I was from the South and sounded like it, but I was an actor, an atheist, and anti-violence in any form.

No, they said. It was dangerous, not worth the risk, and there would be drink at the dinner we were going to.

'Wait a minute,' said Alan suddenly, a few minutes later. 'There's a pretty decent hotel, with a restaurant and bar, just down here in its own grounds, and it's definitely on the Protestant side. We could have one there.'

As we walked down the hall towards the lounge bar, I took a quick look at the dining-room. 'Look at that! That's encouraging.' There was a show card for my production of *The Cherry Orchard* hanging on the bent wood hatstand.

The tables in the lounge were all taken, and the three of us made our way to the crowded bar. I ordered drinks from the barmaid and paid for them, making good-humoured small talk with her. When I had given the lads their drinks and got my change and my own drink, I turned to say 'Cheers' to my friends.

They were looking at me warningly. I saw a tiny line of sweat standing out on Bill's upper lip. With a distinct but almost imperceptible movement of his eyebrows, he drew my attention to a quartet sitting at the table directly behind him, saying very quietly and casually at the same time, 'We're going to be late; we really ought to hurry our drinks. We're due at the prize-giving at half past six and it's after six o'clock now.'

'Oh, a bird never flew on one wing!' I said loudly in my actor's voice and Southern accent, laughing and knocking back a mouthful of gin and tonic. I was keenly aware of one man sitting at the table of four. Black leather jacket, thick black oily hair brushed back from a white boxer's nose and face.... I heard my inner voice say to me, *He's not listening to us with his ears any more, he's listening through his pores. He can't figure out why we are here.*

I started talking about acting and the need for theatre, saying something like, 'The response of those schoolgirls I was talking to this morning ...' I was conscious of the dread in John's and Alan's eyes that I might be going to mention the convent on the Falls Road, which I had no intention of doing. At the same time I was coldly and clearly aware that, unless I could disarm the big black-haired man's suspicions, we were in danger of not leaving the grounds of this hotel of our own volition or even alive. I knew, too, that the only way I wouldn't sound as if I was acting was to talk about theatre sincerely, as the most important thing in my life, which it is.

Then, instinctively, at exactly the right moment I finished my drink and made one more attempt to get my two friends to have another; when they wouldn't, I turned, put my glass on the counter, thanked the barmaid, made good-natured fun of my *English* friend's fear of driving with a second drink on him, and, leading the way out, resumed my talk about the schoolgirls' responses to the school matinée of *The Cherry Orchard* which they had seen at the Lyric Theatre.

Would the man follow us, I wondered? Walking backwards for a moment as I talked to my friends, I saw that no one was following.

As we drove out of the hotel drive, Bill sank back in his seat. 'It's only when I became conscious of those four boyos at the table, listening to you ordering drinks in your Dublin brogue, that I remembered that a Catholic was found dead six weeks ago, a bullet in his head, in the boot of a car in that drive leading up to the hotel!'

Well, it was a pretty hair-raising experience, and we were damn glad to be out of it and alive. I was damn glad, too, that we had gone there — the memory, the image of someone listening through his pores! I've seen my dog do it, and I've used it in acting and directing a lot of times since.

'You have a massive ulcer,' the doctor told me after my barium meal test at Sir Patrick Dun's Hospital in Dublin. 'You need surgery.'

'I'm going to America for a year. I've been released from the Abbey without pay and I have two families to support,' quoth I.

'Well, six weeks in bed and a rigorous diet ...' conceded the medico.

'What would you say to the six days on the SS *France*?' I said in a voice that clearly left no option but to accept my offer.

'Beef tea and crackers, a deck-chair, and a warm rug around you!' was the doctor's face-saver.

'Done, Doctor! Patrick Dun!' I punned, trying to end on a funny note.

He also gave me a stomach relaxant, telling me that my trouble was that I was a stomach worrier. I knew he was right. I don't hear things through my ears. I have a huge, highly sensitive ear in my stomach. Any noise, any tension, tweaks that ear violently and painfully.

It was the last scheduled voyage of the SS *France*. I chose to sit in the dining-room at a table for one; I spent the mornings and afternoons wrapped in a rug on the upper deck, where I was served beef tea and crackers. I saw a school of whales, enjoyed the food and rough Algerian wine, amused myself at the dining-table spotting doubles of friends, enemies, and family I had known on land. I particularly cherished the picture of a little wild-haired waiter who looked, walked and sounded exactly like a French Paddy Long. I arrived in New York with a less active ulcer than I had been used to for a long time.

Gene Foley and I saw Tom Clancy, of the Clancy Brothers, play Phil Hogan with Colleen Dewhurst and Jason Robards in *A Moon for the Misbegotten* on Broadway. Unlike the rest of the world, though I love O'Neill, I was not totally enamoured of the production. Gene introduced me to Harvey Lichtenstein, a great man of the theatre, at the Brooklyn Academy. He asked me if the Abbey would send my production of *Exiles* to his theatre. I wrote to Dublin with the news, suggesting November/December 1974, which would fill an empty space for me after Kalamazoo.

I was awful as the stage-Irish Sir Lucius O'Trigger in Sheridan's *The Rivals*, the first play in MRT's 1974 season. The most exciting thing in the production took place at a dress rehearsal — fortunately! In a sword-fight, Steve Ryan's sword flew into the audience with such force that it impaled a wooden seat in the front row and remained there, vibrating like Excalibur!

I had to join American Equity to act in *The Rivals*. My resident-alien status made that possible, but I created a dual personality in the process. Equity insisted I change my name, as they already had a Vincent Dowling. I toyed with a few exotic stage names — including 'Vincent Gerard' and 'Gerard Vincent' — but when it came to the crunch I couldn't bring myself to give up 'Dowling'. So as an actor I became V.G. Dowling; as a director, in the same programme, I was Vincent Dowling. Who steals my purse steals trash, but who steals my good name ...!

We had a sweet, critical box-office smash with my production of *Peg o' My Heart* by Hartley Manners. Jeannine Weeks as Peg, and Steve Ryan as the man she loves, were heavenly. A beautiful Kansas City girl who had become a very good friend of Olwen's and mine, Mary Linda Rapalye, brought elegance, beauty, and class to Ethel. The greatest joy for me was having my favourite comic actor, John Q. Bruce, as Alaric. A grand old man of theatre, Art Ellison, well into his eighties, also enriched my life and honoured my production. Peg's mongrel dog disgraced us and brought the house down on the first night by peeing on the statue of Cupid on Peg's first entrance.

The costumes at MRT were always everything costumes should be. Year after year, Vincent Scassellati — or one of his protégés, like Judy Dolan — gave MRT productions costumes that were lovely to look at, delightful to wear, thrilling to touch, helpful to actors and audiences. The most creative partnership of my career as a producer/director began in *Peg*. John Ezell is an artist to his fingertips, every inch a gentleman, a designer for all seasons, for every kind of play. His philosophy of art is the philosophy of an Aquinas: 'The undeviating determination of the work to be done.'

The primary purpose of design in the theatre — be it the design of scenery, costumes, lights, sound, or the movements of the actors — is to maximise the concentration of actors and audience on necessary questions of the play. While designers, willy-nilly, will reveal themselves in their choices and visual execution of them, I insist they must do so within the boundaries of that primary purpose. While I have worked with a dozen other designers over the years who have created beauty and truth in my productions, no one did it more often, more brilliantly than John Ezell, Vincent Scassellati and their protégés.

Giles Fowler, the dramatic critic at the *Kansas City Star*, wrote, 'Mr Dowling was a force, a presence. He gathered friends everywhere and in some indefinable way, he charged the City's atmosphere.' If what Giles wrote is true — and I like to think it is — Kansas City, Missouri, and those 'friends everywhere' charged my soul with a love for America and the resident theatre movement that has energised me, personally and creatively, ever since.

19

A Not-So-Puritan Pilgrim

If you don't go to the theatre with love, you will most assuredly leave with it.

Adrian Hall was the founder and artistic director of Trinity Square Theatre, Rhode Island — the most exciting theatre company in America, in my experience, in the 70s. He had adapted Ibsen's masterpiece *Peer Gynt* as a play with music composed by his partner Didi Cummings. He originally wanted me to play the older Peer Gynt, but when I proved to him that I really could not sing, he cast me as the preacher the young Peer Gynt hears 'preaching over his own grave'. I played it in a Suth'n accent. That was a pretty risky thing to do with a Texan director, and in Missouri; but I never had any doubt it was something I had to do, if I wasn't to play only Irish parts in America. It always gave me a kick when people meeting me after the show were surprised to find I was Irish.

I am often asked how I have kept my Irish accent after thirty years in America. I think it is because right from the start I avoided Americanisms. An American's automobile may run on gas; my car goes on petrol. I've had to capitulate on 'ride' in place of 'lift', when I have no car and want to be driven someplace; back in Ireland, I have to be careful not to ask a woman if she wants a ride home with me!

Tomás Mac Anna wrote that the Abbey would not send over my *Exiles* to the Brooklyn Academy, because this would be the first Abbey visit to New York for many years and he and the Board wanted to send one of the Abbey's famous plays. The star-laden *Plough and the Stars* they sent did the Abbey's reputation little good. It also left a gap in my schedule and a hole in my pocket. Angela Newman as Mrs Gogan was the only winner, in my opinion.

So we called Nancy McIsaac in Sun Valley, Idaho. Nancy is Olwen's best friend Cathy McIsaac's sister. She told us that, if we could do something at the Arts Centre in Sun Valley, she could get us our expenses and a nice big house from early December to the day before Christmas Eve — 'You can move in with me for Christmas, as the big house is rented for the holidays to Barbara

Streisand.' This was typical of the hospitality and generosity, personal as well as material, that was lavished on us.

One morning in October, our little white VW bug — named 'Little Vico' after a road in Dublin — packed with everything we had with us, the back seat arranged so Cian could sit, see and sleep, and our farewells said, we set out for Kalamazoo in Michigan.

This was not an inconsiderable journey, but for me there was, and is, no better feeling. A sunny morning; the open roads; farmland; wide horizons; rivers; lakes; hills; snow-capped mountains; villages; towns; as few cities as possible; *The Playboy of the Western World* to be done; in love and loved; and miles to go before we'd sleep in Kansas City again, over thirty thousand miles by car before we'd leave America for Ireland!

At Kalamazoo, gout reared its ugly red head on the joint of my big toe. I spent a day on the phone trying to get a doctor to see 'the broken bone in my foot', as I thought it was. I failed. The pain was excruciating. I said, and I still hold it is true, that it was like having a baby through your toenail. I think what brought on the attack — my first that I know of — was wearing the new, beautiful cowboy boots given me by my cast at Missouri Rep. They were beautiful but too narrow! A Professor of English, Edward Callan by name, wrote a poem in praise of my gout — the glory being that it was in my big toe and not in another protrusion!

Apart from giving classes and addressing assemblies in Western Michigan State University and at Kalamazoo College, where Nelda Balch ran a splendid theatre department, I did my *Irishmen Make Lousy Lovers?* as a thank-you to both schools who had co-sponsored me with the support of the Upjohn heiress. Miss Upjohn, Olwen and I became frequent companions during our weeks there. She and Charles Brown, a professor of philosophy, loved my show; they thought the bawdy, humorous, poetic way Kennelly and I dealt with sex was very healthy.

Almost everyone liked *Playboy of the Western World*, which was hailed as 'the best student production ever at Kalamazoo, and perhaps any college theatre anywhere'. A number of the faculty at WMU, however, forbade their students from being in my production, telling them, 'He [me, that is] is too advanced for you'! I tackled these teachers, from my wheelchair, about the matter. They maintained that they had the greatest respect for me but insisted their students weren't ready for me! Outside that coterie, I didn't meet anyone who believed them.

What play I would do at California State University Northridge (CSUN), a few months later, was still unsettled. In the end, the only thing they could agree on was Aristophanes' *Lysistrata*. Why not? It was the most logical thing in the world to do: bring an Irish actor/director over from the Irish National Theatre and have him do a Greek play which he knew nothing about! This would make it more difficult for him to appear 'too advanced for their students'! Hoping there would be no more interfacultine war waiting for me at CSUN, I started reading *Lysistrata* — which concerns the withholding of sex by the women until the men stop making wars.

As we drove west, I loved the open road, the emptiness as far as the eye could see; the recreation inside me of the feelings the men, women, and children from Ireland and Europe must have had when they saw such vast valleys, plains and horizons for the first time. Again and again, I heard myself repeating out loud one of my mother's favourite lines: 'The valley lay smiling before me!' The fact that the saying had nothing to do with America didn't make it any less satisfying.

The Hemingway girls, Joan (they called her 'Muffet') and Margaux (named for a French wine), came back to see me after my poetry and story programme at the Grand Ballroom of Sun Valley Lodge.

'Daddy is giving a party for you tonight. You and Olwen can follow us!'

'Was he here tonight?' I asked, hoping he had been.

'No, he couldn't come, but he wants to meet you!'

Jack Hemingway was a big teddy-bear of a man, bushier-bearded than his father, Ernest. He welcomed me warmly with a hearty handshake and a big hug. Another, much younger Hemingway sister was scooting about the place as if she were on wheels. Her name was Mariel; she later became a movie star.

'Come into my study. I have a good drop of Scotch and a story I want to tell you before the others get here,' said Jack, as Mary Hemingway, Ernest's widow, and Mariel took Olwen to see the house.

We sat in comfortable leather armchairs on either side of a wood fire, cut-glass tumblers of good Scotch in our hands, as Jack told me his story:

'About a year after my father's death, I was demobilised from the Navy. Coming through New York on my way back here, I was feeling very lonely for him. *I'll go to the Algonquin Hotel*, I thought. My father used to take me to the bar there at the Happy Hour — two drinks for the price of one, and little rolls of bacon on toothpicks free — to meet his writer friends. I was hoping some of them might be there.

'Well, they still had the bacon rolls and the two drinks for the price of one. But the place was empty, except for two men at a table in a corner. I sat at the bar, more lonely than before.

'Then I heard a thumping sound and saw a red-faced, white-haired man beating his fist on the table and saying passionately, "The greatest storyteller of them all was Ernest Hemingway." That was my cue. I ambled over.

'"Excuse me, gentlemen," I said, "I was earwigging." The two of them turned towards me, practically snarling. "I hope you'll forgive me," I said quickly, "but I'm Jack, Ernest Hemingway's eldest son, and I'm here on a kind of sentimental journey. I'm sure you gentlemen will be interested to know that he often talked to me about that very question: Who is the greatest storyteller of them all? He was very certain who it was. He is a writer you gentlemen may not have even heard of! The greatest storyteller of them all, my father used to say, was an Irish writer called Maurice Walsh."

'"Oh, my Christ!" said the white-haired man. "I'm Maurice Walsh."'

I directed *Burning Bright* by John Steinbeck at the Lodge, with a local cast which included John Benson, who became a good friend. *Burning Bright* deals with an older man, his young wife's pregnancy and their hired hand's part in it. The play made me feel better about having refused to father a child for that young woman in Ireland! The performance led to them asking me to come back in the summer, to run a series of acting workshops and do a mini-season at their lovely old Opera House for the Arts Centre. They promised they would make the improvements I suggested to the stage and lighting.

While Barbara Streisand slept in our bed, we moved to Nancy McIsaac's cosy cottage. We moved in with Santa Claus, on Christmas Eve. On Christmas morning I read *A Child's Christmas in Wales* on the Valley radio station.

In January 1975 we moved into a town-house in Ketchum. It came with a hot outdoor swimming pool and a sauna beside it. To dash out of our house under the high mountain, run through the snow, plunge into the warm water, swim around for as long as we liked, then make another dash through the cold to the sauna, never failed to send waves of exhilaration and wonder through Olwen, Cian and me. The sports, cross-country skiing, skating picnics, parties, workshops, and scenic drives to nearby towns, villages, television and radio stations, continued unabated. We were wined, dined, and danced everywhere and by everyone we met.

My divorce from Brenda came through. It was made absolute. There had been a long hold-up, as Brenda's lawyer had accused me of not supporting my family in Ireland; fortunately, Olwen had kept meticulous tax and bank records, and we were able to provide proof that the accusation was without foundation.

Olwen and I felt that we owed it to her parents, who had been very supportive of our irregular liaison, to make it legal. Olwen's mother used to introduce me to her friends as 'Olwen's ... mmmm ...'! The morning we went to apply for a marriage licence at the Town Hall, we ran into Margaux Hemingway and her fiancé. They were going to be married in Paris in the spring. That's where Jack had been born, as those who have read the book

A Moveable Feast know. A line from that haunts me, from the chapter where he has sold a story at last; Hemingway then tells us, 'We forgot to knock on wood.' I never do!

John Benson is a sweet man with an open innocence about him. He promised to be our best man when we came back in the summer. Olwen, inspired by John's camper, vowed she would only go on the winter Vanguard tour of Missouri if we rented a *large* mobile home! I thought she was crazy — three months of winter living in a motor vehicle! I was wrong — again!

I played George Bernard Shaw in *Dear Liar*. I loved playing Shaw; it was like being a wicked Father Donnellan. Pat McIlrath, who directed it, was my kind of director. We rehearsed it and ran it for a couple of weeks in the campus theatre, before taking it on the road with *Peg o' My Heart*. I played the butler, and directed; Olwen was the maid.

The Vanguard tour was the Irish fit-ups all over again, a little more comfortable, a lot better paid! This was what I had left Ireland and the Abbey to seek in the small towns, colleges, and cities of Missouri. Instead of the theatrical digs, east winds, rain, and damp village halls of our little island, we had snow, freezing rain, school auditoriums, sometimes gymnasiums, college theatres, and life in a luxurious Winnebago Chieftain Recreational Vehicle (RV).

Our RV was our transport, hotel, bedrooms *en suite*, restaurant, wine cellar and bar. We also had television. Working days, Monday through Friday, we plugged into the power and water outlets nearest the stage we were playing. Friday night, after the performance, the company returned to KCMO in the company cars, meeting us at the next 'date' on the Monday. We moved our RV to a State Park convenient to our next stop, usually bringing one of the company with us for the weekend.

I loved the names of the towns. My favourite was Tightwad, the gunstock capital of the world. There was also a hamlet called Elsinor. I was thrilled at the idea that some pioneer lover of Shakespeare had struggled through storm, flood and 'hostiles', his *Complete Works* in his pocket, built himself a cabin and named the spot Elsinor. The real story, as I was told it, was that some illiterate with two daughters named Elsie and Nora put them together and got Elsi-nor!

These months repaid a hundredfold our investment of time and energy. The meetings of the minds, the shared experiences with the students, teachers, theatregoers, local people we met and above all the actors and technicians we were working with, all added more than I had ever hoped to the meaning of who I am, what I do, and what I needed to do.

'Do you think you could write your own version of *The Cherry Orchard*?' Pat McIlrath asked me. It was going to open the 1975 summer season at MRT.

I would direct it. It would save them quite a lot of money in royalties, which would be very helpful.

Well, it was one of my favourite plays. I had done it at Brendan Smith's Academy and the Lyric in Belfast and had seen the Abbey production in 1968, directed so sparely by the Russian director Madame Knebel, which had influenced and delighted me. I'd give it a go!

Over the next two months I lived in Chekhov's mind and with his beautiful people. I read version after version. Slowly, I began to feel and see why one translator would say one thing, while another said something quite different in meaning, in certain key moments; this led me to meanings that satisfied their differences.

An abiding memory: in the moody second act Bob Elliott, playing Trofimov, lost his lines. He sat there, as did all the actors, lost in the thoughts and feelings of the moment. The silence went on and on — but there was no discomfort in the audience, in the actors, in me. Bob rose from the ground where he was sitting and wandered round behind the family sitting on the long bench in the sunset. He sat a moment. Then, quietly, he spoke his next line. In his review in the *Kansas City Star*, Giles Fowler wrote, 'I recall a long, long, hush, midway through Act II, the characters posed in a silent tableau of summer costumes and raised parasols. It is a fine touch.'

Dear Liar at the Opera House in Sun Valley delighted the fans and the Jansses who owned the resort. The play was even better than it had been on the Vanguard tour. The intimate space, the promised improvements made, the added experience from the tour that I brought to it, were among the reasons; but the biggest gain was that I had persuaded Sally Mertz to play Mrs Pat Campbell. I had wooed her out of giving up theatre, out of a steady job in Washington D.C., by promising her any part she wished to play, in a small-cast play, if she would do Mrs Campbell. I had seen her work in MRT.

'All right,' she had offered. '*Happy Days* by Samuel Beckett.'

'Done!' I conceded. Not your everyday summer fare!

I arrived at the Opera House an hour before opening on the first night of *Happy Days*. I knew we had a wonderful show, but I wasn't expecting too much in the way of box office — but there was a line stretching from the box office all the way around the long pond in front of the theatre. More people of all ages were arriving by the minute! *There is a God*, I thought! *It must be word of mouth from* Dear Liar.

The buzz of excited and muted chatter from the absolutely packed house — I had even given up my two director's seats — was thrilling, as it always is. About fifteen minutes into the play, there were little whisperings in the audience, mostly from men; shushings from their womenfolk, bless them.

There would be no theatre in America without them — women and Jewish people!

A man stood up quietly and left his seat without disturbing too many others. Another man here, another man there, several men everywhere, left, not quite so quietly as the first, some banging their seats. By intermission most of the men were gone.

A devout coward, I was first out as the curtain fell at intermission. I was dying inside for the actors, for myself, for the Arts Center. I went backstage and told the actors they were great — 'Just keep doing what you're doing. It is right. It is true' — then made my way to the control room. 'Does anyone know what's going on?'

Yes: people are going home.

'Why? Why in such numbers?'

They were waiting, then getting anxious, then realising he wasn't going to appear.

'Who? Godot?'

No — the Fonz! Henry Winkler! They thought they were going to see the TV show *Happy Days* live!

The sixty or so who knew what they were coming to came back after intermission. They loved it and told their friends, and it did well — not quite as well as *Dear Liar*, but that's show business!

Jack Hemingway had a sequel to the Maurice Walsh Algonquin story. We stood on the veranda of his Western-style wooden home, looking out on the mountains, sipping Scotch.

'You remember my story about my father and the Irish writer?'

'I've dined out on it a score of times,' I replied.

'Well, as you know, Margaux was married in Paris. After the newlyweds had left, the womenfolk retired early for the night. That same loneliness for my father hit me. I decided to go around some of his Paris haunts, maybe even find someone who knew him, remembered him. I didn't find anyone who had heard of him.

'Feeling very low, making my way back to the hotel, I was just beside the Sacré Coeur when, passing a café, I heard singing — in English. I'll have a nightcap here, I decided. I sat at the bar sipping a cognac and listening. A young man started to recite a poem about "the trout".

'As you know, I'm a sports writer; fly fishing is my speciality. *This is my cue*, I thought. I waited till he finished, and applauded with his friends at his table. As I ambled casually over, I thought about you, Vincent, and telling you my Algonquin tale — a sort of *déjà vu*. I congratulated the young man, apologised for intruding, and said something like "You don't know me, but I'm —"

'"Yes I do; you're Jack Hemingway and you live in Ketchum in Idaho," said the young man. "Will you sit down and join us?"

'I asked him how he knew where I lived. "Have you ever met an Irish actor and director who has been working up there in Sun Valley?" was his answer.

'I told him that not only had I met Vincent Dowling, I had been thinking of him as I walked over to the table.

'"That's my Uncle Vincent," he said. "He's my mother's brother. My name is Redmond O'Hanlon."'

A couple of days a week, I gave an acting workshop. One day I gave each of my pupils a task: identify a particular emotional moment in his or her life. Just identify it, do no more. We would talk about it at the next class. I assigned a different emotion to each one — 'happiest', 'saddest', 'most embarrassing', and so on. The point I wanted to make was that the image evokes the emotion. To Ann, a middle-aged mother, I gave, quite randomly, 'most prejudiced moment'.

Ann came to me at the end of the class. She told me that her life's work was, and had been for a long time, involved completely with fighting prejudice. She thought the idea of the task was great, and she wanted to participate, but she literally had no prejudices.

So I gave her another emotion, and as an afterthought threw in, 'Do the prejudice one as well.'

'Sure,' she said happily.

All the moments, as the students told them, evoked emotion in them and in all of us listening. A few of them moved the teller and listeners quite powerfully.

Ann stood in front of the class and started, very quietly and simply, 'The emotion given me was "prejudice". I really believed I had no prejudices. In the spring, I finished a long, often nasty campaign to give minorities certain voting rights in our area. I live in Santa Monica. We won! I was exhausted. I went with some of my women friends and our children to a private beach near where we live. I fell asleep sunbathing; when I woke up, I saw a little black girl playing at the water's edge near my children. *How did she get in here?* I thought, alarmed. *They're not allowed in here!*'

As Anne said that, the tears streamed, poured, down her face. It was a healing moment, for her, for all of us. It was the first time I remember associating healing and theatre.

'I suppose, coming from the Abbey Theatre, you know all about Ezra Pound,' had been the opening gambit of a very attractive Idaho radio and television personality, Rosemary Hailey, when she interviewed me the first time I was at Sun Valley. She told me that Ezra Pound had been born down the Wood River Valley in Hailey, and that nothing marked the spot.

I sidestepped her question, but speedily made it my business to find out as much about Pound as I could. A collection of his poems that I found in a second-hand bookshop revealed a poem with the sub-title 'Old friends the most — W.B.Y.'; another was called 'Lake Isle'; a third, 'Epitaphs', has for its last stanza

> *Li Po also died drunk*
> *He tried to embrace*
> *The moon in the Yellow River.*

W.B.Y. was William Butler Yeats, whom Pound captures accurately in a few lines; 'Lake Isle' is a lampoon of Yeats's 'Lake Isle of Innisfree'; *The Moon in the Yellow River* is the title of a famous Abbey Theatre play by Denis Johnston. I knew Yeats had flirted seriously for a time with the Blueshirts, an Irish Fascist group, and Pound had broadcast in support of Mussolini and Hitler from Italy during the war. I learned that the daughter of Olivia Shakespeare, with whom Yeats had a love affair, married Pound.

Well, I liked Pound's poetry; appreciated the tremendous help he gave to other writers, like James Joyce; hated his politics and abhorred his anti-Semitism. Should I involve myself, and the Sun Valley Arts Center, with recognising Pound's link with this region?

After discussions with a number of local friends — especially Jim Belson, the Executive Director of the Center, himself an artist and Jewish — we decided to raise money to put a simple plaque on the house in Hailey, recording the poet Ezra Pound's birth there on 30 October 1885. The white frame house, at 314 Second Avenue South, belonged to a lovely, motherly lady named Roberta McKercher.

An evening of readings from the works of James Joyce, W.B. Yeats, T.S. Eliot and Ernest Hemingway launched the fund. This, with the proceeds from a performance of *Blanco Posnet* in Hailey near the end of our 1975 summer season, paid for the plaque. The Governor of Idaho, Cecil Andrus, visited the Pound house with me and wrote a statement which I read at the unveiling, on 24 August. One line of Pound's poetry is inscribed on the plaque: 'I have beaten out my exile.' I wonder now, has he? will he ever?

'If your parents aren't coming for the wedding, it's off,' I said to Olwen at the beginning of August. 'We're only doing it for them. We are married. We married ourselves three years ago. Saying "I do" before a judge isn't going to make it any more real to me.'

Actually, I was really afraid that a wedding ceremony would somehow spoil what we had, which was working beautifully. I would have welcomed an excuse to cancel the wedding — to just let our friends come, have a great party, publicly announce our love and commitment to each other for ever, and get on with what we were doing. But when Olwen passed on my message, Dan and Elsie immediately booked their flight!

Our wedding, on 23 August 1975, was held in our A-frame in East Fork, which we loved. I had caught, and frozen in cardboard milk cartons, enough trout to feed the multitude; but Olwen had other ideas about food. So I gave a fish-and-chip cast party a few days before we were married, and Olwen ordered a wedding cake and prepared the wedding feast herself. She also had her hair done in a salon in Ketchum, with some new stuff that was intended to make her hair tips more blonde, but turned her whole head — well, the hair on it — *green*.

The wedding guests came by small plane from distant places, by automobile, bicycle, and foot from closer by. The judge looked like a hippie altar boy. He insisted on us all sitting on the floor for the ceremony, which consisted of his reading *The Prophet*, which Olwen hates, and then my saying 'Meeting Point' — which she loved, but which I spoiled by telling a story about an Irish farmer who was married three times over thirty years and refused to pay the priest the last time any more than half a crown because 'That's what I'm accustomed to paying, Father!' The only photograph we have of the whole day was taken on a Polaroid and is so dark that nobody's face can be seen properly. John Benson signed the marriage certificate 'Sir John Benson'; I've always claimed it invalidated our marriage! All in all, it was a pretty good day.

The day after the wedding, we had the Pound unveiling. A couple of days after that, we went on our honeymoon, which, as a honeymoon, was an unmitigated disaster. My uncertainty about a legal wedding and its possible effect on our relationship caused a complete sexual barrier to be erected between us. It was never breached in the eight days and nights of our floating trip on the 'River of No Return', as the Native Americans call the middle branch of the Salmon River. The celibacy of those eight nights was reinforced by the singleness of the size of our sleeping-bags!

As a wilderness experience, the trip was unparalleled for both of us in terms of adventure, majesty, grandeur, friendship, campfire meals, wine and entertainment. I recorded it on audio tape and broadcast it on radio in Ireland and America. The guides were fantastic, the rapids and falls were breathtaking, the natural hot mineral waters were healing, the wild animals, birds, sheer cliffs, primitive cave paintings, sand bars and always-rushing water were endlessly exciting, and the whole thing was unforgettable. We made a lasting friendship with the Alan Pesky family. His young daughter washing her long black hair in the river, thousands of tiny water bubbles catching the sunlight as she tosses it back over her head, is one of my enduring images of that trip. Another is a tall male figure all in black, black-moustached beneath a flat black wide-brimmed hat, alone in the gathering dusk, gliding to the bank below the Impassable Canyon. His name was Mr Muskrat!

I've always wanted to go back and do it all again with Olwen — maybe shoot with a movie camera the story of one Jimmy Parrot, who walked by himself across America, made his way up the river, and lived alone on the riverbank of that canyon, panning gold, for the rest of his life.

Back in Ketchum, Olwen and I quickly found that marriage had done nothing to harm our love for each other, and that our river journey had, in spite of the sexual moratorium, added to our shared experiences.

One morning, a few weeks later, I overheard Cian, aged seven, talking to a neighbour with such pride about 'my dad', and I knew he meant me. I realised how much it meant to him to feel and say I was his father. Throughout his childhood and youth, whatever else I did, I always referred to him and thought of him as my son, not my stepson.

I rewrote, in my own voice, *Lysistrata*, Aristophanes's comedy of war between the sexes to end war between men. In every one of the versions I had read over and over, I found a scene or scenelet that was in no other version. I particularly liked a scene of political corruption, relevant to the modern world, in what I call the Picasso version. His paintings of the erect penises greatly influenced my visual ideas.

I decided to base the hatred between the warring males on difference in hair colour, rather than on their belonging to Athens and Sparta. It would be blondes versus brunettes, which was as ridiculous as black skin versus white skin or one religion versus another. I plotted out a prologue in which blond couples and brunette couples were saying their goodbyes as the men left for famous real and fictional wars.

'Peace' was a beautiful strawberry-blonde girl, rear view naked — a map where the land for peace was delineated! She was delightfully performed by Stacey Pickren. Not only did the audience fall for her; the actor rehearsing Hamlet, next on the programme at CSUN, did also. His name was Jon Voigt. To Jon I passed on my car parking pass at Northridge — an item almost impossible to come by, I discovered when I arrived.

'Well, what are you going to do with the penises?' asked John Forman, the costume designer. 'Are we going to see them?'

'You betcha! They have to be at least a foot long, about two inches in diameter, covered in some kind of material sheath.'

John made them with a thick, tight-fitting sequinned material, each one a different bright colour — truly funny! They were worn as if they were extensions of the warriors' weaponry, like their swords, covered by their military cloaks when they were on duty. I made one other rule: no phallus must touch or be touched by another player, ever. In the great comic scene between Myrrhine and her husband Cinesias, deliciously played by Joan Trossman and Mike Newell, she tantalised him to within an inch of his wife, and, when he wouldn't swear off war, at the last moment evaded his grasp and exited. The lights faded as Cinesias, sexually tortured, started banging his phallus on the bed like a carpet-beater. It was outrageously comic, as was the whole production, and never titillating or kinky.

It was a few nights before the opening of *Lysistrata*. The phone downstairs in the McIsaacs', where we were staying, rang. I stumbled down to get it, figuring someone in Ireland had forgotten the eight- or nine-hour time difference.

It was Lelia Doolin's no-nonsense, concerned voice. She said something like, 'Vincent, it's Lelia here. I'm sorry to call you at this time, but I was afraid no one had told you. Jack is dead. The funeral is tomorrow. I thought you would want to be here. Can you make it?'

I don't know what I said. I know I was thinking back to Kalamazoo, where Sean Kielty and his wife had visited us from Detroit. He had dropped the bombshell, thinking I knew: Jack was dying from cancer. I would have been told if that was true, I had said, and called Dublin. I spoke to Betty, Jack's wife and Sean's sister. No, she told me, it wasn't so; Jack had been ill but was more or less over it. Tell me, I remembered saying; I will go home right after Kalamazoo. She assured me there was no need.

I said something about this to Lelia. She said Betty had been protecting Jack. I could see why.

No, I decided there and then, I would not go home. He was dead. Though I was devastated, my going would do him no good, and I owed it to the production at Northridge to stay there.

I heard his funeral was a great outpouring of love and appreciation, as it deserved to be. He had done the State some service, and a lot of people knew it and loved him for it.

There is so much I wanted to tell him. So much I wanted to ask him. So much more I wanted to know about him. All I knew for certain, at that time and for a long time to come, was that I loved him more than any other man I had known, and would always miss him, and always reflect him. 'Vin,' he would say with a sigh, 'your sinful life shows in my face, my good life shows in yours.' Many a true word is spoken in jest!

'The Action Takes Place!' was the only information on time and place in the programme for our *Lysistrata*. Jack would have liked it. This was a big production, some sixty characters. Over a hundred people — not least Bruce Halverson, with whom I forged a lasting friendship — had given everything they had, for nearly two months, to Aristophanes, *Lysistrata* and me.

On the first night, a few mature patrons rose from their seats and made pointed exits. *Uh-oh*, I thought, *we're going to be in trouble*. But in the eight-night run of *Lysistrata*, to great houses, we never lost another patron. The *Los Angeles Times* said my version was funnier than Aristophanes, and he is pretty funny!

We sold our car, 'Little Vico', following a call from Ed Stern, at the Indiana Repertory Company in Indianapolis, inviting me to direct Shaw's *Arms and the Man*. We wouldn't have time to drive there; rehearsals were due to start very soon after *Lysistrata* opened.

Earlier, I had written to Homer Wadsworth to see if Kansas City funding sources would give me any money to do more research and write a play about Tom Pendergast, the former Irish city 'boss' and Harry Truman's mentor, and his city manager's daughter, Mary McElroy, who had been kidnapped and later committed suicide. I had already done quite a bit of research. I had met Pendergast's son and Mary McElroy's brother, and had won both their confidence, which wasn't easy. I had had a letter from Pat Doyle saying that Homer was now heading up the Cleveland Foundation, she was working with him, and I should come up and see them; there were interesting things happening in Cleveland. Homer was sure there would be no money in Kansas City for a Pendergast play; after all these years, Pendergast was still too close for comfort! I looked at the map, saw how close Indianapolis is to Cleveland, and determined to phone Pat Doyle when I got to Indiana.

'My God! What are they doing to me?' I imploded, when I met the actress they had chosen to play the ingenue, Raina, in *Arms and the Man*. Her hair was cut almost to the scalp, by a knife and fork, I thought. She sat with her feet turned inward, and it seemed to me her eyes had the same inclination.

At least I said nothing. I should have thought nothing, too. Like so many of the best actresses I have known — like Angela Newman, Terri Donnelly, my daughter Bairbre — when she read, when she started to act, little Linda Atkinson shone with an inner light, and she was truly beautiful. Linda Atkinson was my Raina.

The reviews for play, players, and the whole production were as good as if we had written them ourselves. The radio review said of Linda, 'She is at once young, fresh, charming, witty, romantic, delightful and captivating.'

'The mad Irishman from Dublin,' as the radio critic called me, 'says you must approach your art with love. If you cannot, you must stop practising it until you can. He has created a production that Shaw would certainly have applauded, and if you don't go the theatre with love, you will most assuredly leave with it!' *Arms and the Man* broke all records at the box office at IRT, and held that record for some considerable time.

I met Bernard Kates, a great actor, at IRT and saw him, ironically, in Chekhov's *The Harmfulness of Tobacco* — ironically because he was still smoking much too much. Barney became, for over ten years, the leading character actor in my 'cry of players'. Ed Stern would direct some of the finest of my productions in that same company. As they say, there are only ten people in the American theatre!

'Come up and see us some time, and we'll pay your way, hotel and expenses'; that was the offer I couldn't refuse from Homer Wadsworth and Pat Doyle at the Cleveland Foundation. We met with some Great Lakes Shakespeare Festival (GLSF) board and management people. They were 'between artistic directors'. I saw *Bingo*, a play about Shakespeare, at the Cleveland Playhouse; met with their Artistic Director, Richard Oberlin, and discussed the possibility of directing an Irish classic for him.

The next morning, a Sunday, Pat Doyle took me around Cleveland. We talked about my applying for the job of Artistic Director at GLSF. I was quite certain that I wanted to direct at both theatres, but I had no interest in artistic directing for anyone! I had decided that in Dublin, after my stint as Deputy Artistic Director at the Abbey.

It was a wonderful weekend. Being with Homer and Pat was a minute-to-minute joy, and they made it clear they wanted to see me in Cleveland.

One of the first things I did when I got back to Indiana was write to Pat saying that I had realised, on my flight back, that my reasons for not wanting the job at the Abbey had had to do with my personal relations with some actors there whom I would have had to offend mortally or sack; they had had nothing to do with the idea of artistic directing in itself. So, I told her, yes, enter me in the race for Artistic Director in the Cleveland Shakespeare Sweepstake!

We left Indianapolis in a second-hand Jeep Cherokee we had bought there — a step up in the world from Little Vico! Our destination was Providence, Rhode Island, and the Trinity Square Repertory Theatre. Adrian Hall had suggested we should come and see him and talk about doing something for them.

Adrian and I agreed that I would direct a new play for Trinity Square's bicentennial production. The play, by Richard Marks, is about Benjamin Franklin's illegitimate offspring; it is called simply *Bastard Son*.

We drove to New York, then into the welcoming arms and home of Sean and Barbara Carberry. During our few days there, we met with Tom Kennedy and his wife Val. Tom offered me the featured male role in some Aer Lingus commercials to be shot in Ireland over Christmas. I gladly accepted the one-thousand-pound fee!

Sean drove us to Kennedy Airport, and the ground staff hustled us into the comfort and complimentary drinks of the Shamrock Lounge. We gave the Carberrys and their (soon my) good friend Terry Moran the use of our Jeep for the Christmas and New Year vacation. For Olwen, Cian and myself, my year's leave without pay had been extended to eighteen months.

And it was home at last to our Wicklow Mountains! We named our house Ojai Cottage, after the little Californian town where the McIsaacs had their ranch. The Kilpedder people never called it anything but 'O.J. Cottage'!

'No, Vincent. You have been away eighteen months; you must stay, or leave the Abbey Company for good!'

That was Tomás Mac Anna's precisely articulated answer to my suggestion. I wished to work six months a year at the Abbey, and the other six months off Abbey salary in America, commencing in January. I would do as much in my six months in Dublin as I had previously done in twelve. I had worked much harder than that in America; the quality of the work had been at least as good, and I had preferred the extra challenge.

Tomás held to his opinion, and he was now Artistic Director. He pointed out that 'If we allowed you to do that, everyone would want to do it!' However, he wanted me to know that he and Joe Dowling wished me to direct a new production of Brian Friel's *Philadelphia, Here I Come!* and I would go back on salary immediately — adding that, as I knew, after an extended leave without pay the Abbey was permitted to wait a month before returning me to the payroll. Indeed, I knew; I had been one of the Council members who negotiated the terms of the contract with the Abbey management.

I thanked Tomás and Joe and said that I would like to discuss the situation with my wife Olwen, and that I would appeal to the Board of Directors to reconsider my suggestion — which would save the Abbey money: half my salary.

I had *Bastard Son* to direct in the New Year for Trinity Square; I had a thousand pounds to come from Aer Lingus; I had a summer season at Sun Valley; and I had a good possibility that Pat McIlrath would have a production for me, and maybe acting roles, at Kansas City. Balanced against that I had twenty pounds a week in child support to pay to Brenda, and the major responsibility for Olwen and Cian's upkeep. My Abbey salary at this time was just thirty pounds a week, for fifty-two weeks a year. It was one of the few theatre jobs in the Western world that was permanent and pensionable. I was forty-six years of age and had no savings.

The Abbey Board sided with Tomás and Joe, as I had expected. Olwen sided with me; and, crazy as it may seem in our circumstances, we decided to take our chances in America! I had fallen in love with the sheer beauty of America outside the cities, and the vision and acting community of the resident theatre movement. I needed them; the latter, I felt, could use me well.

I walked down the corridor of the nursing home in Cabinteely, County Dublin, towards the room where I had been told I would find my youngest sister, Carmel. Carmel, who had won second or third prize in the Dawn Beauty Contest thirty years earlier, was now fifty-two years old. She had cancer, I was told. I hadn't seen her, or any of the family, for eighteen months.

I knocked gently on the door; I thought I heard a tiny voice say, 'Come in', but I wasn't sure. I opened the door and saw the figure of an old, bent woman with her head twisted toward me over her shoulder. It was a shape I had often seen in church and chapel among the poorer country people. 'I'm sorry,' I muttered very quietly, as I started to back out.

Fortunately, I stopped before I had moved an inch. Carmel's unmistakable voice said, 'Vincent! Come in.' I adeptly changed my movement to make it look as if I was intending to come in and close the door.

I kissed her. She got back into bed. We talked about her operation and the progress she was making. She told me how her estranged husband, Paddy, was coming to see her and sit with her every evening. We talked about her children and mine, my marriage to Olwen, and my experiences in America. After that, I saw her every day I could.

Much of December I was away in Killarney, Bunratty Castle, and other beauty spots in the south-west, driving around in a sidecar and sitting in an aeroplane, shooting the Aer Lingus commercial. I still have the brown sports coat and navy-blue blazer they bought me for the shoot.

I saw Carmel on Christmas Day. They would not allow her to leave the nursing home. I said goodbye to her before I left. I never saw her again. She died a few days later.

Poor Carmel. She was star-crossed; she carried almost all the pain of my father's leaving. She was clinically depressed, I think now. She had been one of my mothers, the youngest one. She loved me and I loved her.

I must have said goodbye to my children, my family. I have no memory of it. Probably this — this knack of making things simply disappear from my mind — was, and is, part of my survival kit. Leaving Olwen and Cian to follow, I set sail (albeit by plane, then Jeep) for Providence, Rhode Island, on 1 January 1976, the first day of America's bicentennial. I felt that was significant. I was a pilgrim — a pioneer. I was starting a new life.

Carryover

'I have never had a hangover in my life, Vincent,' said Paddy Lenihan, owner of the Hodson Bay Hotel on the shores of the Shannon River's Lough Reagh. This was in the mid-1960s — my boating years on the River Shannon. I had just woken up in a single bed across from its twin, which he was occupying. Why not? It was his hotel. We had had a late night the night before around Athlone, followed by a few nightcaps on his own premises. Worried about me making my way on board my little cruiser — a little the worse for wear, as we say — and not wanting to arouse his lady wife himself, he had appropriated an empty room.

'How do you manage that? I have a mother and father of a hangover this minute,' I said, by way of response to his claim. Paddy and I were what I would call good Irish drinkers of that time: we didn't drink before or during work, we always had a few afterwards, and when in particularly good company we might drink too much! We found each other particularly good company. Poetry, drama, politics and songs filled the air around us together.

'Well,' Paddy said, taking a bottle of Redbreast Whiskey from under his bed and pouring two fingers of the golden-brown liquid into a cut-glass tumbler, 'when I've had a little more than a little at night, I always make sure I have a carryover — just one, no more — first thing when I wake up. Do you want one?'

I said, 'No, thank you, I'll suffer. I deserve to.'

I always think an epilogue is a kind of hangover. When my publisher asked me to write one I said, 'No, but I'll write a carryover!'

I am now nearly seventy-one years old. It is five o'clock on Sunday, 27 August 2000. I am in the basement of the tiny New England Town Hall of the village of Chester, Massachusetts, seated in my temporary improvised dressing-room on a rough kitchen chair at a folding table, covered with a towel, surrounded by theatrical make-up, brushes, and the fuller's earth that dirties my hands, arms, face, farming shoes and old clothes. There is a mirror in front of me, held upright by the basement wall. A single light-bulb in a tin container is clipped to a water pipe. I'm holding a small jar of cocoa butter; I rub it on my unshaven, makeup-covered face and start to wipe away the face of Phil Hogan in Eugene O'Neill's tragic comedy *A Moon for the Misbegotten*. It is the last performance of my annual founder's production in Chester for this eleventh summer season of the Miniature Theatre of Chester.

As my own face and skin appears, my mind starts to wander back through those eleven years since I came here; and beyond that, to a space of another three years back at the Abbey. I hear Olwen's voice saying, 'I saw so many Abbey actors in your Phil Hogan.' In the dressing-room next to me I can hear David Birney, a star of television, Broadway and national tours, singing 'Roddy McCorley'. He sings it well. David, our James Tyrone, is relieved, as we all are, that the play has gone so well again, and to another packed house. We are glad, too, that we have a week off before we move to another venue. The play is a hell of a journey each night for both of us and for Jennifer Rohn, the New York actress who plays Josie.

'The reviews in the newspapers and on National Public Radio for Western Massachusetts have been a hundred per cent positive — raves!' someone says, but I hardly register it. I don't want to be pulled out of my backward journey.

Since I left the Abbey, a job for life and a pension, and came permanently to live in America in 1976, my life, I see now, has been like a crazy 'house that Jack built'. Here's the Abbey that gave me the key to open the door of the Great Lakes Shakespeare Festival. Chekhov is the key that opened, in Sacramento, the door to where the boy Tom Hanks was at college. Here is the Tom I discovered, brought to Shakespeare, taught what fun acting is, and made a professional actor; he rocketed to stardom, but remained with his feet on the ground, a grin on his face, and his heart in the right place. Shakespeare's is the festival that opened the door for me to perform for President Reagan in the White House — not once, not twice, but thrice, two of these performances on State occasions! At the first, my dinner partner was Olivia Newton-John. At the second, there was only the President, myself and the Republican and Democratic leaders of the U. Senate and Congress; the Speaker, Tip O'Neill, beating out the rhythm of a song on my shoulder, nearly made me a fixture in the White House floor. At the third, for the Irish Prime Minister, I was mistaken for the jacks attendant at the White House an Irishman designed!

Worse things were tried on me when I left Shakespeare for Santa Maria, the broccoli capital of California, and Solvang — a Scandanavian residential theme park. An academic year as Distinguished Visiting Professor at the College of Wooster, set in Amish country, was miles better. I loved it. All I missed was that I never had the years on a college campus. The work is hard, though — like walking leisurely up a slight grassy knoll at an autumn picnic!

I must have been distracted, at Wooster, by the peace, the friendliness, the appreciation and the feeling of worth I had about the students, the faculty, the people around. I agreed to go back to the Abbey as Artistic Director for three years — provided that I had complete artistic control, and that neither the party of the first part nor the party of the second part could terminate the contract. I knew I was walking into a minefield.

The contract was agreed by all parties. It held, too, as long as Gus Martin was chairman. Then he was voted out of the chair, and we had a well-known theatrical juggler occupying the chair and he took my salaried job as Artistic Director. The *coup disgrace* had been delivered when I was in Chicago playing King Lear. I didn't think that was kosher! I didn't go gently into any goodbye.

Happily for me, having remembered my father's advice about getting things down in writing, and having sold our Vico Road home, I was able to go home to America on my own terms. There I raised money for the Abbey — a little from a *My Left Foot* benefit in Los Angeles, and a great deal from Coca-Cola, with Jim Flannery's help and through the good offices of their President Donald Keough. He is a charming man, and devoted to things Irish. During this last year as the Abbey's Producing Director in the US, I developed support groups in a number of cities to help support national tours of the US and Canada. My production of *The Playboy of the Western World* would be the first. Eventually it was — in spite of 'help' from certain quarters! — and it was very successful at the Kennedy Center and in Boston, Toronto and around the country. All the profits — over a hundred thousand dollars for the three months — went to the Abbey. No producers, no investors, taking the cream; just the contractually agreed fees, salaries and expenses.

That was my swan song for the Abbey. In November 1989 I said farewell to the cast as they left for Dublin. All in all, I wouldn't have missed my time back at the Abbey, especially the tours in Ireland and abroad in places like Moscow — where, in John Costigan, I found a friend and man of the theatre for any season.

Six months later I founded this little theatre in Chester, a tiny village of fewer than four hundred souls, where the train no longer stops and the industries, all but one, have left. I came here, to the wooded mountains watered by pristine rivers, to retire; but the little stage of the Town Hall seduced me. The enthusiasm and energy of an extraordinary man, Newman Marsh — who, like me, had come from outside to spend his life here — encouraged me, and I conceived a professional theatre. The Selectmen of the Village of Chester — led by two Junoes, Marie Morrissey and Fay Piergiovanni — with wisdom and vision, gave and continue to give this theatre its lovely little home in the Chester Town Hall.

Miniature Theatre is the fit-ups of Ireland resident in New England, a miniature Abbey in America, and the theatre of William Shakespeare in that it would 'hold the mirror up to nature; show virtue her own features, scorn her own image, and the very age and time its form and pressure.' It is a theatre of actors, audiences, and plays old and new that address necessary questions in language truly poetic. The bonnie child is young, eleven years old, but is growing.

Everything I have done and learned about life, theatre and the other arts has gone into the making of 'this little miracle', as Jeffrey Borak of the *Berkshire Eagle* called us. Far more than half our plays have been world or American premières. We gave Sebastian Barry his first full American professional production with *Boss Grady's Boys* (I had already produced its première at the Peacock). We've had stars like Kim Hunter, Dan O'Herlihy, and David Birney; great Irish names like David Kelly and Maurice Good; American actors like Peter James and Robert Elliott; and wonderful actresses like my daughter Bairbre, Bonnie Black and Madylon Branstetter, from the great theatres I have worked at in Cleveland, Kansas City, and Rhode Island. They come here for the quality of the work, the quality of our audience, and the beauty of the place, and they come for miniature salaries, too! Our audience is made up of the sophisticated residents and cultural tourists drawn from the Berkshires, west of us, and the academics and educated theatregoers in the populated urban business and industrial centres east of us, and a small loyal coterie in our hills. When we have a 'name performer' like David Birney with us, we get theatregoers from as far as Washington DC, Boston, Los Angeles and New York. Bernadette Ó hUiginn, the artist wife of the Irish Ambassador, was among scores that came specially to see the O'Neill play.

The Theatre has a perilous existence, and that is important, too. We have no rich benefactor, private or public. Fewer than two hundred loyal members, friends, small community groups, businesses and local and State agencies give us about fifty thousand dollars a year between them. We started with nothing. At the beginning of each year we have nothing. At the end of each year we are lucky if we have broken even.

How can you start a professional Equity theatre on nothing? Pay salaries, benefits, payroll taxes, insurance, and put on productions? For the first five years Newman Marsh gave us, through the Chester Foundation, a six-thousand-dollar guarantee against loss. We always returned it. Olwen and I gave our combined administrative and artistic directing experience of sixty years in the theatre, those first years, free for eight to nine of the twelve months each year. When I played in a play I got Equity minimum. Directing a play, I did it for five hundred dollars, about a tenth of a normal regional theatre fee. Visiting professionals received the same. It is little different today. What made it possible was my credibility with theatre professionals and media, thanks to the Abbey Theatre background; my ability to articulate a policy with passion in understandable terms, on paper and in speech; my ability to engage journalists with stories of substance and humour in a context appealing to their needs; my performing skills and the ability to use them in radio, television, platforms, stages, boardrooms, classrooms, offices, clubs, picnics and gatherings of every kind. I have a saying or a story, mostly true, for every occasion. Repartee is only repertoire, I learned many years ago, and I never leave home without mine.

Bob Lehan, who plays Harder and shares my improvised dressing-room, puts his head round my screen. 'See you at Westfield, next week.' He's gone before I can answer.

It isn't that I love Ireland less — I would do anything for her, truly, except live there — but I love North Chester more. I'm aware, though, that everything I am, in both my ordinary and real lives, has its source in Ireland, and I wouldn't want it otherwise. I look forward to going back into that past, there and here, again and again, as long as I live in person or in this new form of dramatic art for me, autobiography and memoir. As the Dublin man in the Theatre Royal shouted to the tenor, after calling 'encore' over and over: 'If you do it enough, you might get it right!'

James Dillon: A Biography

Maurice Manning

'Manning is to be congratulated on an impressive piece of work.
This biography must be strongly recommended.'
The Irish Times

'This is an enthralling book about a fascinating man. [Manning]
has written an outstanding biography.'
Sunday Tribune

James Dillon — A Biography fills a significant gap in the recent
political history of Ireland. It adds considerably to our understanding
of how the State's institutions and political system became defined
after independence. It examines, from a hitherto unexplored perspective, how the processes of parliamentary opposition operated in the
new democracy which was the Irish Free State and, later, the Republic
of Ireland.

Maurice Manning's book is a valuable and original chronicle, from
a unique perspective, of Ireland in formative, difficult and challenging
times. It is an Ireland that is scarcely recognisable today. This is the
story of a public man in the best and most complete sense of the word
— a man without whose commitment to public service, Irish democracy might not be the robust and secure organism which it now is.
Anyone lacking a knowledge of the life and work of James Dillon will
have at best a greatly incomplete understanding of the making of
Modern Ireland. *James Dillon — A Biography* is essential reading.

Hardback (ISBN 0-86327-747-0) £25
Paperback (ISBN 0-86327-823-X) £15.99

AVAILABLE FROM:
WOLFHOUND PRESS
68 MOUNTJOY SQUARE
DUBLIN 1

The Irish Aboard Titanic

Senan Molony

The unspeakable tragedy of the *Titanic* disaster can be fully appreciated only through the tales of the people who were actually there on 14–15 April 1912.

The Irish Aboard Titanic is a comprehensive testament in which these people are at last allowed to recount what happened on that fateful night. This encyclopaedic account features letters, interviews, newspaper reports, family memories, White Star Line records and extracts from the various official sources.

In her wake the mighty *Titanic* cast a long shadow over the thousands forced to endure the terrible wait to hear the fate of loved ones; over the families whose lives would always be filled with grief for those who had perished; and over the survivors who had to start anew, putting behind them their nightmarish brush with death.

Not only a portrait of those on the 'unsinkabe' liner, *The Irish Aboard Titanic* comprises a social history, entering the world of the 1912 traveller through touchstones such as religion, kindred, politics and that very Irish phenomenon — emigration. It also contains an unrivalled photographic archive.

Paperback (ISBN 0-86327-805-1) £16.99

AVAILABLE FROM:
WOLFHOUND PRESS
68 MOUNTJOY SQUARE
DUBLIN 1